THE LAST TITANS:
CHURCHILL AND DE GAULLE

THE LAST TITANS:

Churchill and de Gaulle

Richard Vinen

BLOOMSBURY
LONDON · OXFORD · NEW YORK · NEW DELHI · SYDNEY

BLOOMSBURY PUBLISHING
Bloomsbury Publishing Plc
50 Bedford Square, London, WC1B 3DP, UK
Bloomsbury Publishing Ireland Limited,
29 Earlsfort Terrace, Dublin 2, D02 AY28, Ireland

BLOOMSBURY, BLOOMSBURY PUBLISHING and the Diana logo are
trademarks of Bloomsbury Publishing Plc

First published in Great Britain 2025

A catalogue record for this book is available from the British Library

ISBN: HB: 978-1-5266-6893-6; eBook: 978-1-5266-6894-3; ePDF: 978-1-5266-6896-7

2 4 6 8 10 9 7 5 3 1

Typeset by Siliconchips Services Ltd UK
Printed and bound in Great Britain by CPI Group (UK) Ltd, Croydon CR0 4YY

MIX
Paper from
responsible sources
FSC® C020471

To find out more about our authors and books visit www.bloomsbury.com and sign up for
our newsletters
For product-safety-related questions contact productsafety@bloomsbury.com

For Alison Henwood

CONTENTS

Introduction: Artists of History

The great artist of a great history
De Gaulle on Churchill

I saw General de Gaulle standing stolid and
expressionless at a doorway [at a desperate meeting during
the French debacle of 1940]. Greeting him, I said in a low tone,
in French: 'l'homme du destin.' He remained impassive.[1]
Churchill on de Gaulle

'A rtist of history', a phrase de Gaulle might have applied to himself at least as much as to Churchill, is a more interesting one than 'man of destiny'. Both men understood that in politics words are deeds and that some deeds are primarily important as symbols or statements. The understanding was particularly acute on the part of Charles de Gaulle. His memoirs begin: 'Toute ma vie, je me suis fait une certaine idée de la France' ('All of my life I have had a certain idea of France'). It must be the most famous opening sentence of any memoir in history. It is curious, though, that few quote the following lines, in which de Gaulle says that his idea of France is 'like the princess in the tale.' De Gaulle understood, and expected his readers to understand, that his idea of France was a fairy tale.

I

I have sought to provide an account of the lives of Churchill and de Gaulle that stands on its own and would make sense to a reader with almost no previous knowledge of these two men. This book, however, is not intended to rival the existing biographies of Churchill by, for example, Martin Gilbert, Roy Jenkins and Andrew Roberts, or those of de Gaulle by Paul-Marie de La Gorce, Jean Lacouture, Éric Roussel, Julian Jackson and Jean-Luc Barré. Nor is it intended to replace François Kersaudy's classic book on the wartime relation between Churchill and de Gaulle.[2] My aim in putting two such important figures together was to write a *shorter* rather than a longer book, one in which key themes might be drawn out. It is easier to make sense of Churchill's complicated life when he is seen alongside de Gaulle, who had such a capacity for reducing every problem to its essentials.

Beginning biographical works with the statement 'This is not a conventional biography' has itself become something of a convention; a defining feature of the professionalisation of historical study in the twentieth century was the turn against biography. Lewis Namier's *The Structure of Politics at the Accession of George III* (1929) and Fernand Braudel's *The Mediterranean and the Mediterranean World in the Age of Philip II* (written in the comparative calm of a German Oflag during the Second World War and published in 1949) emphasised, in their different ways that history should be understood as a matter of structures rather than the actions of great men.

Churchill recognised that his own writing, like so many things about him, belonged to the late Victorian age, when politicians were commemorated in long hagiographic biographies, such as the one that Churchill's friend John Morley wrote of Gladstone or that Churchill himself wrote of his father, Lord Randolph. The authorised biography of Winston Churchill begun by his own son (also called Randolph) and continued by Martin Gilbert is the last example of this genre.

Churchill published only one explicit work of autobiography, but all his writing is implicitly autobiographical – Arthur Balfour remarked: 'Winston has written a big book about himself and called it *The World Crisis.*' Indeed, Churchill lived his whole life with an awareness of how he would eventually write about it.[3] When he used a sonorous phrase — 'the mortal gravity of the hour' — during the Battle of France in May 1940, an official remarked in exasperation: 'He is still thinking of his books.'[4]

De Gaulle's relation to biography was more complicated. This may sound odd since half the books he published (all of them after 1938) were volumes of memoirs. For de Gaulle, though, the memoir was different from biography. He took remarkably little interest in personality — perhaps especially his own. His memoirs were even more impersonal than the books on strategy and military history he had written as a young officer. The most important character in his memoirs is not de Gaulle but France. Historians of the Annales school (who had once seemed so resolutely set against the study of individuals) began to let biography in by the back door from the 1960s onwards. Did responding to de Gaulle make them understand that writing about, say, Louis XIV might be a way of writing about France? Recently some historians influenced by the Annales school, such as Pierre Nora and Maurice Agulhon, have turned their attention to de Gaulle himself, or at least to his legend.[5]

Churchill and de Gaulle both began their adult lives as army officers and both spent an important part of their later life as writers. Both remained men of the nineteenth century into which they had been born. Comparable lives, however, are not the same as symmetrical lives. It is largely because of their *differences* that the two men's lives are worth studying alongside each other. Churchill's career began with a bang — he was famous, as a journalist and adventurer, even before he entered the House of Commons at the age of twenty-six.* It finished with a

*He was elected at the age of twenty-five but undertook a lecture tour of North America before taking his seat.

long whimper: his colleagues spent the four years after he became prime minister for the last time in 1951 waiting with increasing impatience for him to resign. The whole world spent the ten years after he did resign in 1955 waiting for him to die. De Gaulle's career began less dramatically. He was less well known as a 48-year-old colonel in 1939 than Churchill had been as a 24-year-old lieutenant in 1899. If, however, the beginning of de Gaulle's life moved at a slower pace, his end came quicker. He resigned unexpectedly as president in 1969. Not much more than a year later, lucid until his last moments, he died. Alfred Fabre Luce – one of the many former Pétainists who would have preferred to see de Gaulle die on the scaffold – likened his death to the ritual suicide of the Japanese poet Mishima.[6]

There was something of the Samurai about much of de Gaulle's life. It had an almost stylised simplicity. One could sum up the broad lines in a few sentences – anyone attemping the same exercise for Churchill would do well to reach 1914. Consider the two men's different relations with the instruments of democratic politics. De Gaulle despised parties and had nothing to do with them until he was in his late fifties. He was never a member of parliament and seldom set foot in the National Assembly. He disliked elections and the mere prospect that he, or a cause he supported, might be defeated was enough to make him contemplate resignation. He was under-secretary of state for war for a little less than a fortnight in 1940. He was prime minister from the summer of 1944 until January 1946 and then again, even more briefly, during the months after he returned to power in June 1958 – on the second of these occasions, he was also minister of defence and of Algerian affairs. From January 1959 until 1969, that is for the greater part of his time as an active politician, de Gaulle held just one office: president of France. He stood for election by universal suffrage only once in his life – in 1965, when his presidential mandate was renewed.

Churchill first joined a political organisation (the Primrose League) at the age of thirteen. He was a Conservative and then a Liberal and then a Conservative again – having worked his way back through several ephemeral party tickets in the early 1920s. He held twelve ministerial offices at various times: two of them twice and two of them in conjunction with other offices.* He was a member of parliament almost continuously for over sixty years, representing five different constituencies. He stood for parliament twenty-one times, five times in by-elections. He was defeated five times – twice losing constituencies that he had previously held. In the late 1930s, he had to work hard to avoid being evicted by the Conservative association in his own constituency. He led his party into three general elections and lost two of them. He wrote:

> Whatever one may think about democratic government, it is just as well to have practical experience of its rough and slatternly foundations. No part of the education of a politician is more indispensable than the fighting of elections...[7]

Churchill, always a parliamentarian, was not always a democrat, or at least not always a believer in equal adult suffrage. There were times before 1914 when he opposed giving women the vote, and in the 1930s he toyed with an electoral system that would have given special weight to the votes of householders and 'heads of families'. De Gaulle was never a parliamentarian but he was, at least after 1945, a democrat. It was his government in 1944 that gave women the vote.

Churchill and de Gaulle were both public men, but they defined this status in different ways. The public persona of the former was

---

*Under-secretary of state for the Colonies, president of the Board of Trade, home secretary, First Lord of the Admiralty, Chancellor of the Duchy of Lancaster, minister of munitions, minister of war, secretary of state for the Colonies, Chancellor of the Exchequer, prime minister. He was minister of defence at the same time as being prime minister and minister of aviation at the same time as secretary of state for war.

a highly coloured version of his private personality. Churchill and Lloyd George were the first British cabinet ministers to refer habitually to each other by their Christian names. But what was most striking about Churchill was that much of the country felt that they were on first name terms with him. The Labour politician Denis *Winston* Healey was born in 1917, as Churchill licked his wounds after the failure of the Dardanelles expedition. John *Winston* Lennon was born, during the Liverpool Blitz in October 1940.

Pompidou, who served de Gaulle for two decades before succeeding him as president, was indignant at the suggestion that de Gaulle might ever have addressed him as Georges.* De Gaulle seemed not to be on first-name terms even with himself; in his memoirs he frequently referred to himself in the third person. Sometimes he talked as though de Gaulle the public figure was a regrettable but necessary creation who imposed some inconvenience on de Gaulle the private man. He wrote to the British foreign secretary in March 1941, drawing attention to 'exceptional elements' on which the Free French were founded: 'The first – I must apologise for having to write this – the personal and symbolic role played by General de Gaulle.'[8]

Churchill was rarely alone and there seemed no part of his life that was not open to other people. Robert Boothby, who served as his parliamentary private secretary when Churchill was Chancellor of the Exchequer in the 1920s, recalled:

> Solitary reflection was alien to his nature ... In the drawing-room, the bed-room, the bath-room, the dining-room, the car, an aeroplane, a sleeping berth on a train or in his room at the House of Commons, the flow of his *private* oratory never ceased. I remember on several occasions being commanded to attend him when he was having a bath and to make suitable notes of what he said. At intervals he turned a

---

*Pompidou also recalled, though, that de Gaulle first appointed him to a post on 23 April 1948 – St George's Day.

somersault, exactly like a porpoise; and when his head reappeared at
the other end of the bath, he continued precisely where he had laid off.[9]

Churchill was famous for receiving male visitors while he was in the
bath.* He dictated letters from this position – a habit that dated to his
time at boarding school. In 1942, Eddie Marsh, Churchill's one-time
private secretary, visited Downing Street, where the prime minister
received him 'in vest and drawers on his way to his bath.'[10]

Churchill cared deeply about his reputation but could be indifferent to his dignity. Once, when walking in the country, he fell into
a stream. Instead of extracting himself, he remarked, with a logic
that would have done credit to William the Outlaw, that, since he
was wet, he might as well enjoy himself. He then spent half an hour
splashing around and building dams.[11] One can imagine the nanny
shouting 'Master Winston look at the state of your clothes', but
there was no nanny present because at the time of this incident
Churchill was His Majesty's secretary of state for home affairs.
People often commented that Churchill's spontaneity, even when he
was in his late seventies, made him seem like a child.

No one imagined De Gaulle as a little boy. He almost never
emerged from the bedroom (a private place) without a jacket and
tie.[12] The notion of conducting business from bed, as Churchill
frequently did, would have horrified de Gaulle. A chambermaid
at the Élysée Palace was sacked for taking a photograph of his
bed.[13] De Gaulle's public persona was like a late-medieval suit of
armour – uncomfortable and largely designed for ceremonial use.
Gaston Palewski claimed that he had known 'de Gaulle before de
Gaulle' (by which he meant de Gaulle before 1940) and added that
the general had once written to him: 'you know the affection that I
have for you *under the carapace*'.[14]

---

*When Nancy Astor became the first woman MP, Churchill said, in a phrase that would
surely interest psychologists, that she made him feel as though she had entered his
bathroom and 'I have only my sponge with which to defend myself.'

Those around Churchill were conscious of the continuous performance, in which he was always either putting on a show or rehearsing some part of what he was about to say in public – visitors on 13 May 1940 were greeted with a brief preview of the 'Blood, Toil, Tears and Sweat' speech that he would deliver later that day.[15] Sometimes the self-consciousness was too visible. Harold Nicolson watched Churchill in parliament on 11 April 1940 'giving an imitation of himself making a speech'.[16] But often those who were summoned to Churchill's presence treated it as a kind of panto-mime – all the more enjoyable because they knew the script so well. On 12 March 1940, the American under secretary of state, sent by Roosevelt on a mission to Europe, called on Churchill:

> As soon as the preliminary courtesies had been concluded, Mr. Churchill commenced ... a cascade of oratory, brilliant and always effective, interlarded with considerable wit. It would have impressed me more had I not already read his book *Step by Step* (of which inci-dentally, he gave me an autographed copy before I left) and of which his address to me constituted a rehash.[17]

The public statements of de Gaulle, by contrast, were the prod-uct of private meditation. He did his thinking alone and presented his conclusions only when he was ready. He hated to admit that, during the war, the British authorities had seen, and sometimes changed, speeches he broadcast to occupied France. His associates were subjected to long monologues, but this did not mean they could follow his thought. Indeed, those who listened to de Gaulle's private statements sometimes became more mystified as they did so. When he became president, his ministers often had little idea what he was about to say. He learned his texts by heart so that they would not appear to be prepared and sought to impart an almost magical quality to his declarations.

Underneath the charm and the clowning, Churchill was a vain man. He knew himself to be exceptional and took it for granted that he would be the centre of attention. Extraordinary though this may sound, Charles de Gaulle's defining quality was modesty. He stood on his dignity when he represented France but made no great claims about himself as an individual. Churchill said he felt that he was 'walking with destiny' when he became prime minister in 1940. Compare this to de Gaulle's description of his return to power in 1958:

> So be it! In spite of the difficulties that I faced in myself: my age – sixty seven – the lacunae in my knowledge and the limits of my capacities ... I would, to serve her [France], personify this great national ambition.[18]

Whereas Churchill (the son of a well-known politician) had been born into public life, de Gaulle had laid out an abstract conception of how a leader or *chef* ought to behave long before he himself attained a position of any significance. He emphasised reserve, mystery and solitude. In 1925, de Gaulle's notes for a course he gave at the French staff college contained the following lines on the qualities of leadership: 'distance – control of oneself, coldness ... sudden and rare interventions (religious miracle)'.[19] De Gaulle was one of the greatest speakers of the twentieth century, but his most impressive quality was one that almost all twentieth-century politicians (Churchill especially) lacked: the capacity to remain silent.

These two different ways of behaving in public reflected two different characters. Churchill was short,* plump, hedonistic and charming. He was fond of money and not too scrupulous about how he got

*When he was a cadet at Sandhurst, Churchill's height was 5 ft 6.7 in; de Gaulle's height at St Cyr was recorded as being 187 centimetres, which is a little over 6ft 1 in. This is obviously too short. Most observers thought he was around 6 ft 5 in.

9

it. One might suggest that Churchill's vices and virtues were ones the British associate with the French* or at least with politicians of the Third Republic. He was above all a parliamentarian and it is easy to imagine him fitting in with the convivial world of what Robert de Jouvenel called *La République des Camarades*.

As for de Gaulle, his vices and virtues were sometimes those the English claim for themselves. He was tall, physically awkward and painfully formal. In financial matters he was incorruptible. When his grandchildren came to tea at the Élysée Palace, he told the footmen to bring him a bill for the cakes they had consumed. De Gaulle's country house (chosen largely because it was modest enough to be sustained on an officer's pay) did not have hot water for the first few years that the family occupied it. Churchill's country house had a heated swimming pool.

Both Churchill and de Gaulle were deeply rooted in their own countries. Churchill belonged to a collegiate ruling class. Even at his moments of greatest success, he could not entirely escape from the fact that a British prime minister is merely 'first among equals' and even at his moments of greatest eccentricity or perversity he was never entirely cast out. He was knitted together with his colleagues by shared experiences of school, by membership of London clubs (for men of his generation, the House of Commons was the most distinguished of such clubs) and by family ties. If Churchill sometimes seemed 'unEnglish', it was because he belonged to a bohemian section of the aristocracy that defined itself against the chilly bourgeois virtues of men – such as Baldwin and Chamberlain – who came to claim that they represented England. De Gaulle's isolation was also rooted in a certain kind of French culture. Not that of the *République*

---

*Churchill himself rejected stereotypes of the French. He wrote in June 1937: 'Many countries, not excluding our own, are apt to regard the French as a vain, volatile, fanciful, hysterical nation. As a matter of fact, they are one of the most grim, sober, unsentimental, calculating and tenacious races in the world.'

des Camarades but that of Catholic royalists who were distant from the republic but obsessively loyal to what they conceived to be the nation.

Churchill lived in an *ancien régime* – incarnated in the houses of parliament, monarchy and established Church. The sprawling complexity of his long career partly reflected the fact that he operated within the baroque convolutions of an English political system in which layers of innovations were built on the past without entirely displacing it. The austere simplicity of de Gaulle's politics sprang partly from the fact that he lived outside any political system other than the one that he constructed himself; his nostalgia for elements of the *ancien régime* did not mean that he made any serious attempt to restore it.

Of course, public personae, perhaps especially those that seem most spontaneous, are artificial creations. Churchill's real character bore a close resemblance to his public image, but this did not mean that he was entirely natural. His informality was calculated. He knew that it was in his country's interest that he should propose rumbustious toasts to Stalin and that he should cultivate friendship with Roosevelt. The moment when Churchill emerged naked from a bathroom at the White House and said: 'the Prime Minister of England has no secrets from the President of the United States' was as full of deliberate significance as the moment when de Gaulle took the salute at a military parade.

The associates of Churchill and de Gaulle recognised that 'myth' or 'legend' were important aspects of their political identity.[20] Sometimes it is hard to trace where the myths that surrounded both men came from. There were even myths about myths. Philippe Barrès claimed in 1941 that inhabitants of France's African empire believed that de Gaulle was a corporal who had been killed in action but was so enraged by the advent of Corporal Hitler that he had risen from the grave to lead the fight against Nazi Germany.[21] Even de Gaulle's name seemed to spring from French legend. At first, many assumed that it was a *nom de guerre*, intended to evoke the race that had once fought against the Roman invaders, and somehow the association persisted even after the war – perhaps reinforced in the minds of French children by the fact that the Asterix cartoon series was launched in the same year de Gaulle became president.[22]

People came to believe things about Churchill and de Gaulle that were obviously untrue – though such beliefs sometimes reflected an underlying core of reality. In 1960, a conservative journalist thought that Churchill gave his name to the tellers in the lobby of the House of Commons because he did not expect to be recognised.[23] No one outside a trappist monastery would not have recognised Churchill in 1960. However, he did often make an ostentatious show of respect for the House of Commons. Similarly, it is unlikely that, as some 'witnesses' claimed, de Gaulle told his Russian hosts, when survey-ing the site of the Battle of Stalingrad, that he admired the Germans for having got so far.[24] But it is true that he respected German mili-tary prowess.

A few writers mythologised themselves at the same time as they mythologised their hero. Maurice Ashley's account of his time as Churchill's research assistant in the 1930s captures Churchill's kindness and sympathy for the young.[25] But readers moved by Ashley's description of his own plebeian origins and left-wing views might be surprised to know that his father, a civil servant, had known Churchill for years.[26] One of the most celebrated evocations of de Gaulle's world view – André Malraux's *Fallen Oaks* – was supposedly based on a single conversation after de Gaulle's retirement in 1969. Jean-Noël Jeanneney, whose father, Jean-Marcel, had been one of de Gaulle's ministers, was himself invited to lunch with de Gaulle shortly after Malraux's visit. He got the impression that de Gaulle and Malraux had talked largely about cats, of whom de Gaulle was fond 'because they are not afraid of me'.[27]

Myths about Churchill and de Gaulle extended even to their appear-ance. A Conservative, describing Churchill's funeral, wrote 'he never smiled';[28] a working-class man in 1940 said that Churchill 'never shed a tear since the day he was born'.[29] In fact, Churchill frequently smiled and cried in public. The image of his features locked in cold determination (that might, depending on one's point of view, go with moral seriousness or ruthlessness) owed much to the wartime photograph by Yousuf Karsh, who achieved the desired expression by snatching the cigar from Churchill's mouth.

De Gaulle's reputation in France first grew among people who knew him only as a voice on the radio and often had little idea what he looked like – some believed that he was short and fat because that was how Vichy caricature portrayed him.[30] After the war, he was often shown in uniform (in both the hostile caricatures of 1968 and the statues erected in his honour), though he usually wore a suit on public occasions after the war. Immediately after his death, his wife and servants laid him out on the dining-room table and dressed him in his uniform. His civilian clothes were burnt.[31]

It is easier for the historian to get to the 'real' Churchill than to the 'real' de Gaulle. Though Churchill's accounts of his own life were often contrived or misleading, he wrote and spoke more than de Gaulle and he did not cultivate the same air of deliberate mystery. Consider a simple question: did Churchill and de Gaulle speak each other's language? We know that Churchill spoke 'execrable but expressive French'.[32] De Gaulle took English lessons when in London during the war but we do not know whether the rare occasions when he spoke the language in public were spontaneous outbursts of emotion or the calculated product of careful preparation.[33] When he published his memoirs, Anthony Eden had known de Gaulle for almost twenty years, but he still had to write to the French ambassador to ask whether he should send the president the English version or wait for the French translation: 'I do not know if the general reads English fairly easily.'[34]

What of the two men's religious beliefs? We know everything about Churchill's. He was not a Christian. That he revealed this fact with such candour was all the more remarkable because Christianity was so central to English public life and because his father had campaigned to prevent an avowed atheist from being allowed to take his parliamentary seat. Winston Churchill had an Anglican upbringing and imbibed the low-church piety of his beloved nanny Mrs Everest, but he lost his faith in his early twenties. Later, he accepted that Christian belief had generally benign effects. Writing a version of the Bible stories updated to modern times was one of the many money-spinning projects with which he toyed, and he often used Christian images in his speeches during the Second World War.

In ecclesiastical terms, Churchill was a reformer. He did not believe that the Anglican Church should enjoy special privileges in education or that it should collect Church rates. In liturgical terms, he was a reactionary who hated the new prayer book (by which he meant the one introduced in 1928) and particularly its rendition of the marriage service.* However, his ecclesiastical reformism prevented him from putting his liturgical conservatism into effect – because, unlike many MPs, he did not think that parliament should exercise its right to govern the Church of England and throw the 1928 prayerbook out. Churchill's overall position on religion could be summed up with his remark on the day of German surrender in 1945 that he would tell the House of Commons and then proceed to St Margaret's church (attached to Westminster Abbey) to give the good news to the Almighty, or with one of his most famous witticisms: 'I am like a flying buttress that supports the Church from the outside.'

At first glance de Gaulle looks simpler. He was born into the Catholic Church and christened Charles André *Joseph Marie* de Gaulle. He went to religious schools. At his funeral, his wife's last

---

*The marriage service in the pre-1928 prayer book stipulates that men should 'not satisfy their carnal lusts' like 'brute beasts'.

gesture was to trace the sign of the cross on his coffin; she ended her own life in a convent. When asked to sum up his beliefs during the war, his laconic response included the words 'I believe in God'. But the apparent simplicity raises questions. His aides noticed that he was bored when he attended a mass he had asked them to organise.[35] He was tolerant, even admiring, of those who killed themselves rather than endure dishonour[36] – though suicide was a mortal sin in the eyes of the Church.

Like many intelligent men, the Catholic novelist François Mauriac found it hard to be rational when he came up against de Gaulle. His writings on de Gaulle in the 1960s are marked by such gushing enthusiasm that an uninformed reader would not guess they were written by the man who had published *The Knot of Vipers* in 1932. But, after a chilling description of de Gaulle's willingness to countenance dealing with Stalin, Mauriac's tone becomes less confident. At the end of the passage, he admits:

> I do not know de Gaulle. On the pew in his parish in Colombey-les-Deux-Églises or perhaps in the evening at the foot of his outsize bed, what does he say to the infinite being, if he talks to him? And in what tone does he talk to him? What is de Gaulle's prayer? And does he pray? That, we will never know.[37]

What is true of private belief is, *a fortiori*, true of more banal political matters. Churchill's every action left a written trail. This was partly because he was keen to leave a record of his work for history and because his experience in the First World War had taught him how documents could be used to justify controversial decisions. Sometimes he found it easier to tell people disagreeable things in writing than face to face. Even when they were living in the same house, he and his wife sometimes communicated by letter. During the Second World War, he needed to issue clear, written instructions. He once claimed that his 'telegrams, decisions and instructions', when set up in type by the government printer, matched the length of two issues of *The Spectator* magazine for every month of the war.[38] He dictated letters but also sometimes wrote on documents in his own hand. As far as the archives are concerned, many politicians disappear when they attain power. Most of the documents issued in their name have actually been drafted by civil servants. Even Margaret Thatcher's opinions can often be discerned only from squiggles at the side of the page – though she did once sign a letter that had been drafted by her officials and then write in her own hand underneath that she disagreed with the opinion that had been expressed in her name. But Churchill is so tangibly present in the archives that one almost hears the growl as one opens a file. I recall the first time I came across a document he had drafted. I was reading records of debates about the future of conscription in the 1950s. Most were written in the bland patois of Whitehall, but a brief note from the prime minister himself demanded that officials 'give me a cold-blooded view'.[39]

De Gaulle is more elusive. He too was a skilful writer, but his writing was briefer, less specific and usually couched in more abstract terms than that of Churchill. He often cultivated ambiguity about his real intentions. Partly this was a matter of character but it was also a product of the two men's circumstances. In, say, 1942, Churchill needed to make sure that things happened; this was not true of de Gaulle. For most of the Second World War, there was not much point in expressing his wishes in explicit terms because he stood so little chance of implementing them – his power, such as it was, depended largely on bluff and deliberate mystification. Later, when he returned as president of France, the reverse was true. He was now so powerful that ministers would act on what they took to be his wishes, even if those wishes had not been clearly expressed. He remarked that 'every word and gesture' might have an influence even if they were 'wrongly attributed to him'.[40] Indeed, there were circumstances in which it suited him not to have expressed his wishes so that he might be able to blame others if he changed his mind or if things went wrong. Sometimes, the very phrases most associated with de Gaulle – 'l'Europe des Patries', in particular – were ones that he denied ever having used.

Perhaps de Gaulle is particularly elusive because there was always an element of calculation in his cultivation of his own mystique. More than Churchill, he was conscious of the artificiality of the myths with which they both surrounded themselves. Both understood that some stories might be important for a country's sense of itself without being literally true – hence Churchill's impatience with a pedantic research assistant who suggested that he remove the story of King Alfred burning the cakes from his *History of the English-Speaking Peoples*. There was, though, a difference between Churchill and de Gaulle, which may reflect a wider difference between the British and the French. Churchill was sometimes so caught up in the drama of his own account that cold realities – such as the decline of British power – seemed to disappear. Even, perhaps especially, in his moments of most theatrical eloquence, de Gaulle never lost sight of reality. Unlike Churchill, he took a particularly clear-eyed view of myths about himself. Asked in the 1960s about Churchill's claim to have addressed him at their first meeting as 'the man of destiny', de Gaulle denied that the exchange had ever taken place. He added, in words that say much about both men: 'Churchill was a romantic.'[41]

Comparing Churchill and de Gaulle throws light on two extraordinary characters. It also reveals much about their two countries. There is, however, a broader significance to the careers of these two men. When Churchill was born, in 1874, Britain was the richest and most powerful nation the world had ever seen. France was not as great when de Gaulle was born in 1890, but it still ruled the second largest empire in the world. In economic terms, Britain had already been displaced as the world's greatest power by the time that Churchill first set foot in the United States in November 1895. However, both Britain and France remained great military and imperial powers and their power reached its zenith immediately after the First World War when their rivals in Europe were humbled.

We think of Churchill and de Gaulle as the victors of 1945 but the defining experience of their lives was defeat. The Wehrmacht defeated the French army – the largest in Europe – in six weeks. The defeat of France was also a defeat for British forces, but it was followed by an even more crushing reverse that came when Singapore surrendered to the Japanese on 15 February 1942.

Most of all, Britain and France were displaced by an ally rather than by their enemies. The USA, already the dominant economic power in the world before 1941, was the dominant military power by 1945. The great geopolitical drama of the second half of the twentieth century was the replacement of Britain and France as world powers by the United States. On the face of it the transition was easier for Churchill and for Britain than for de Gaulle and France. Churchill had an American mother, admired the United States and was, at least ostensibly, admired by many American politicians. De Gaulle was less sentimental about the United States. He seems, though, to have understood more clearly than Churchill the implications of American power and the need for France to carve itself a new role in the 1960s. It is notable that two of the most far-sighted American strategists – George Kennan[42] and Henry Kissinger – admired de Gaulle. The latter saw him as the heir to the nineteenth century master of realpolitik: Bismarck.

De Gaulle and Churchill achieved much – perhaps as much as any politician in a democratic country can hope to – but democratic politicians are sooner or later measured by how they deal with failure. Equally, all great powers eventually face decline. The question of how leaders adjust to this decline – the question that Churchill and de Gaulle once faced – will one day face the leaders of today's great powers.

I

Early Lives, 1874–1930

How an under-esteemed boy of genius of noble character and daring
spirit seized and created a hundred opportunities to rise in the world and
add glory by his own merit and audacity to a name already famous.
Randolph Churchill on the youth of his father, Winston Churchill[1]

L'enfance! Surtout pas!
De Gaulle's aides on conversational topics for de Gaulle[2]

Youth mattered to Churchill. He liked to surround himself with
the young and often behaved as though he was a boy himself,
even in old age. He was famous for writing vivid descriptions of his
adventures before he was famous for anything else and published
an extraordinary account called *My Early Life* in 1930. Perhaps
Churchill's early life came to matter because it served as a counter to
the popular image of him as an old man. The first volume of his official biography, written by his son, was devoted to the first twenty-five
years of his life. In the early 1970s, a book by his grandson and a film
were devoted to 'The Young Winston'. But de Gaulle saw nothing
special about being young. Shortly before the student upheavals of
May 1968, he remarked that youth was just a stage that everyone
went through. In his published works he referred frequently to the
history of France but almost never to his own early life.

Churchill was born in a palace. It belonged to his grandfather
the seventh Duke of Marlborough. Winston was briefly heir to the

title – a dangerous moment in a political system where real power lay with the House of Commons.* His father, Lord Randolph Churchill, the Icarus of nineteenth-century politics, had held and lost a great office of state before Winston was twelve, which meant that the boy was an object of fascination. His mother, Jennie, was the daughter of a New York financier, Leonard Jerome.

Churchill had the manners of an aristocrat. He took servants for granted. There seems to have been no occasion in his life, not even in the presence of the monarch, when he felt socially ill at ease. He accepted hospitality from people who were richer than himself but never felt in anyone's debt. His recreations were expensive ones. He hunted on horseback for wild boar in Normandy with the Duke of Westminster. And he gambled. In 1922, he lost £500 in two weeks at Monte Carlo[3] – this was a tenth of the annual salary that he would receive a couple of years later as Chancellor of the Exchequer.

In 1941, one of Churchill's advisers suggested that an ancestor of de Gaulle's had been one of the knights who served with Joan of Arc and that 'this would explain much.'[4] Though de Gaulle was interested in genealogy, he made no claims for the distinction of his own family. He came from minor provincial nobility – whose austere virtues he contrasted with the decadence of the grand aristocracy.[5] The encounter with Churchill, when de Gaulle took refuge in London after the defeat of France in 1940, was also de Gaulle's first real encounter with a great aristocrat. Different notions of aristocracy accounted for some of the misunderstandings between them. De Gaulle felt that his isolation in wartime London owed much to his exclusion from circles where 'a few hundred lords and businessmen and bankers have power'.[6] But the power of British aristocrats derived from pragmatism rather than exclusivity. They married, did business and formed political alliances with people from

*Dukes sat in the House of Lords and were not allowed to sit in the House of Commons. Lord Randolph Churchill sat in the Commons because his title (as the younger son of a duke) was a courtesy one that did not entitle him to sit in the Lords.

outside their own caste. In October 1940, Churchill told the Labour minister Herbert Morrison that the French nobility were 'separated from the people by a gulf of blood; here they are sinking noiselessly and unresisting into the background'.[7]

De Gaulle's father earned a living as a history teacher. De Gaulle was also, like Napoleon, a second son – he would have had to make his own way in the world even if there had been money to inherit. Englishmen who sought to understand de Gaulle's behaviour in later life sometimes assumed that he must have had a difficult youth. In 1944, Harold Macmillan wrote of de Gaulle:

> His childhood was lonely, and oppressed by the grim character of a severe and bigoted father. He was brought up in an atmosphere of morbid religiosity lacking all the characteristic buoyancy and jollity of the Bellocian type of Catholicism. His was a dour and hard training, with a spiritual point of view that almost lapsed into the harsh heresies of Calvinism.[8]

This was nonsense. Charles de Gaulle's father, like Charles himself, seems to have been a firm but affectionate parent. De Gaulle had a happy childhood and was throughout his life happiest in the company of his own family. His mother was a devout woman who was said to have regretted that God had not devised a more 'elegant' way for humans to reproduce.[9] But, since she and her husband had five children, one assumes that they submitted to their distasteful duties with good grace in this regard.

De Gaulle's family were marked by an almost obsessive patriotism, but were also curiously ill at ease with the modern incarnation of the country they professed to love. They never accepted the separation of Church and State in 1905 or the institutionalised anti-clericalism of the Third Republic, the regime established in 1870. In fact, the family did not accept the republic *tout court*. They were monarchists who regretted the French Revolution of 1789. This meant that they distinguished the French nation, which they revered, from the

French republic, of which they were suspicious and lived in a kind of internal exile. De Gaulle spent a few of his early years in real exile because he was sent to a boarding school in Belgium to get him away from the secularised schools of France.

Monarchists had a strange relation with the French political system. There had been a brief moment after the deposition of Napoleon III in 1870 when it seemed possible that the monarchy – the Bourbon monarchy displaced by the revolution of 1789 – might be restored. The project had failed partly because the pretender to the throne insisted on the use of the white flag associated with the Bourbons rather than the tricolour flag that had been used by the republic. After this, many who professed to be monarchists understood that they were expounding an ideal or a style of thought rather than propounding a realistic proposal. French monarchists were like some English members of the Anglican Church, who care about the language of the liturgy and the authorised version of the bible even after they have ceased to believe in God. Furthermore, monarchists were intensely patriotic, especially in time of war. They fought for France and did not fight with any less ardour because they disapproved of its political regime. They usually came to accept the tricolour flag and the 'Marseillaise' as symbols of France – especially after these symbols had become associated with victory in the First World War.

De Gaulle traced French history back 2,000 years to Vercingetorix (the king of the Gauls) or 1,500 years to Clovis (the first Christian king), but his fascination with a distant past was rooted in relatively recent events. France's defeat at the hands of Prussia in 1871 – 'an immense disaster, a peace treaty of despair, griefs that nothing can assuage'[10] – was the most obvious of these. De Gaulle grew up in a milieu that dwelt on the prospect of military revenge but also on the belief that a fraction of their own countrymen did not share their patriotic and anti-German sentiments. The most violent manifestation of such sentiments was seen in 1894 when Alfred Dreyfus – an army officer from a Jewish family who had left Alsace to escape the German occupation – was accused of spying for Germany. The case against him was feeble. Nonetheless he was convicted and exiled to Devil's Island, convicted again 'with extenuating circumstances' at a retrial and only rehabilitated in 1906.

Dreyfus divided much of the officer corps from parts of civilian society, Catholics from anti-clericals and royalists from republicans. Writers, politicians and intellectuals lined up on either side. For Dreyfus, or at least against the conviction of Dreyfus, were the novelist Emile Zola (1840–1902), who had to flee France after publishing his open letter 'J'accuse', and the politician Georges Clemenceau (1841–1929), who edited the newspaper that published Zola's letter. Ranged against Dreyfus were Maurice Barrès (1862–1923) and Charles Maurras (1868–1952), who became editor of the newspaper *Action Française* and leader of the political party associated with the paper. Maurras blended anti-Semitism, anti-Germanism and anti-parliamentarianism with support for a restoration of the monarchy (though he did not have good relations with the pretender to the French throne) and the power of the Catholic Church (though Maurras was not himself a religious believer).

De Gaulle appears to have known Dreyfus to be innocent, but this did not make him a Dreyfusard. His brief public remarks about the affair alluded to the damage that it did to the French army rather than to the injustice that might have been done to an individual. De Gaulle admired some officers who had been anti-Dreyfusard – though he also came to admire Clemenceau and eventually worked with the socialist politician Léon Blum, a noted Dreyfusard. The British, unconcerned by the complicated divisions of French politics, had a simpler view of the Dreyfus affair. Churchill praised the stance of 'brave Zola'.[11]

Whatever his view of Dreyfus, de Gaulle was influenced by the thinking of Barrès.[12] He also admired Maurras and sent him copies of his books with personal dedications. Until June 1940, *Action Française** discussed his work sympathetically. Asking whether de

---

*_Action Française_ was the name of the party's newspaper as well as of the party itself.

Gaulle was a Maurrassian is probably a meaningless question. All sorts of bourgeois Catholics read *Action Française* and admired Maurras. But Action Française was an odd kind of party. It contested elections only for a brief period after the First World War and it was never clear that Maurras, whose unworldly manner was exacerbated by deafness, wanted to exercise political power. Lucien Rebatet, a member of Action Française in his youth before moving to more radical forms of politics, entitled a chapter in his memoirs 'At the heart of *inaction* française'.[13] For all Maurras's relentless emphasis on logic and the coherence of his positions, his influence derived largely from the fact that it was diffuse. People drew different things from it: authoritarianism, anti-Semitism, anti-German nationalism. After the defeat of 1940, there were Maurrassians everywhere – in London and at Vichy, among collaborators and *résistants*.

De Gaulle never made a serious attempt to restore the French monarchy. For him, Maurrassianism meant a vigorous nationalism that emphasised the interests of France over any international body. Georges Pompidou, de Gaulle's prime minister for much of the 1960s, came from an emphatically republican tradition but nonetheless recognised that the foreign policy he inherited from de Gaulle was in some ways Maurrassian.[14] For de Gaulle, Maurrassianism also meant distaste for the parliamentarianism of the Third Republic. De Gaulle's royalism was a matter of language more than anything, and language was something that he cared about deeply. Republicans talked of 'liberty' as a single and indivisible thing. Maurrassians referred to 'liberties', which implied a more complicated set of rights associated with the *ancien régime*. In May 1958, de Gaulle said that he had restored 'the liberties' of the French people. Astute observers recognised this as the vocabulary of Maurras.[15]

Churchill's early life was extraordinary, at first for its lack of distinction. His father wrote him a heartbreaking letter expressing the fear that he would become 'a public-school failure'. Churchill's public school – Harrow – was itself a sign of failure. It was an illustrious school that educated two other important politicians – Stanley Baldwin and Leo Amery. All the same, Churchill felt that Harrow was inferior to Eton, which his father had attended and about which Winston was to write with feeling in biographical sketches of Lords Curzon and Rosebery. He would later send his own son to Eton.

Churchill was poor at the subject that mattered most to the British ruling class of his time – classical languages. There were, though, some ways in which academic failure worked to Churchill's advantage. He was free of the inhibitions that might have been instilled by more formal education. He thought things through from first principles – sometimes being put out to find that, say, Aristotle might have reached the same conclusions as himself. He was ruthless in drawing on other people's expertise and unintimidated by academic distinction. He knew the economist John Maynard Keynes and was happy to have him help the government during the Second World War but never paid much attention when Keynes, whom he described as 'a man of clairvoyant intelligence and no undue patriotic bias',[16] attacked his own policies. Churchill knew he had a unique gift for expressing ideas in terms that might seem comprehensible to ordinary people. In 1926, he took a few hours off from his duties as Chancellor of the Exchequer to write a paper that purported to explain recent developments in atomic physics.[17]

Churchill talked of the years he had spent 'in the inhospitable regions of examinations'. But this served to underline how many of his contemporaries had never really left these regions because their youthful displays of scholarly prowess overshadowed their adult achievements. The most exciting passage in the autobiography of Sir John Simon comes when he describes how he and his friend Leo Amery were elected on the same day as fellows of All Souls College Oxford.[18] By 1940, Simon and Amery were both cabinet ministers, as was another fellow of All Souls, Lord Halifax. The three men must have been uncomfortably aware that Churchill was riding in the British army's last great cavalry charge at the age when they wrote their fellowship essays. Churchill's friend, the barrister and Conservative politician F. E. Smith, talked of the glittering prizes for 'those with stout hearts and sharp swords', but he was addressing an undergraduate audience and the prizes of which he talked were won in debating societies. Churchill had seen the sparks fly in the African dawn as the Lancers sharpened their swords for battle – though he was realistic enough to draw a Mauser pistol as he closed on the enemy.

Churchill began life as a soldier because he was not considered able enough to attend university and make a career at the Bar – the profession his father would have preferred for him. His marks in the admission examination to the Sandhurst military academy were not high enough for him to gain a commission in the infantry regiment (the 60th Rifles) that his father hoped for, and he was destined instead for a cavalry regiment (the 4th Hussars). Since the cavalry imposed particular expenses on its officers (another subject of resentment on the part of Churchill *père*), commissions in it were easier to obtain for those who had private means.

Before Winston Churchill entered the army, his father died at the age of forty-five. Winston would later describe this as the great tragedy of his life, but it was also a kind of liberation. Lord Randolph – bitter at his own failures – had been a crushing presence in the life of his son. He was more useful as romantic image than he had been as a living father. A commission in the 60th Rifles had opened up just before Lord Randolph's death but Winston was now drawn by the allure of the cavalry and, as soon as his father was dead, decided that he would stick with the Hussars. He also now enjoyed several years of a close relation with his beautiful young mother – a distant figure during his childhood.

Churchill's regiment was posted to Bangalore in India but soldiering in itself was not what made Churchill famous. As he ruefully noted, in the last years of the nineteenth century there seemed little chance that the British army would do any serious fighting, particularly that it would ever again fight 'white troops'. He compared the fate of his contemporaries to that of their predecessors who had been commissioned a hundred years earlier, with years of fighting Napoleon ahead of them. He must have been conscious too of the comparison with the military careers of men a generation younger than himself. Churchill was a lieutenant at twenty-four when he resigned his commission in 1899. Anthony Eden, his successor as prime minister in 1955, was a major (with the Military Cross) at the age of twenty-one in 1918.

Churchill sought excitement on the polo field and also in a succession of irregular postings to sites of real fighting. This meant first an expedition to Cuba, where he was allowed to join Spanish troops putting down a rebellion, then a posting to the north-west frontier of India, where he fought with a Sikh regiment against Muslim tribesmen, then attachment as a journalist to forces led by Lord Kitchener in the Sudan who were seeking to reconquer Khartoum. It was in the Sudan at Omdurman that he rode in a cavalry charge, of which he left a vivid description. Finally, he went to South Africa to report on the Boer War. Churchill obtained journalistic commissions partly through intervention by his well connected mother, and he blurred the distinction between journalist and soldier. He was in South Africa as a journalist and might have been executed when he took part in the defence of a train that was attacked by the Boers. Instead, he was made a prisoner, escaped in dramatic fashion and then returned to the war as a more or less regular soldier.

Churchill's accounts of his early adventures were published in three books in the space of three years. The early Churchill was a literary creation – both in the sense that he made his reputation as a writer and in that his writing generated an image of Churchill that was to influence the rest of his life. This is not to say that his account of his life was fictional, though he did publish a novel in which the hero resembled himself. Occasionally, he was cavalier about detail. He claimed to have heard shots fired in anger for the first time on his twenty-first birthday; it was actually the following day. He said something about the brutality of war (especially in the Sudan) but did not reveal in his published writings – as he did in a letter to his mother – that the Sikhs under his command on the north-west frontier had put a captive into an incinerator.[19]

The late nineteenth century was a good time for a certain kind of writer. Mass education created new readers, and new ways of printing (especially of reproducing pictures) created a new kind of medium. George Newnes founded *The Strand Magazine* in 1891. It was most famous for the Sherlock Holmes stories but also published Churchill's writings. Its readers (like most of the heroes in the Holmes's stories) belonged to the newly literate class of city clerks and the like. Lord Salisbury sniffed that the *Daily Mail* – founded in 1896 and also a regular outlet for Churchill – was written 'by office boys for office boys'. Churchill was hardly an office boy in terms of social station, but he had something in common with such people. He was intelligent, ambitious and desperate for adventure. He compensated for his lack of formal education by having wide general knowledge – of the kind that might be acquired by flicking through *Pears' Cyclopaedia*.*

The adventure story was the staple diet of the new reading public and Churchill crafted his own life as such a story. The journalist Alfred Gardiner wrote in 1914 of Churchill's career: 'It suggests the clatter of hoofs in the moonlight, the clash of swords on the turnpike road. It is the breath of romance stirring the prosaic air of politics.'[20] The subtitle of *My Early Life* was *A Roving Commission* and these words echoed the title of a novel of 1900 by G. A. Henty (1832–1902), though Churchill's writing also had much in common with that of John Buchan (1875–1940), Arthur Conan Doyle (1859–1930) or P. C. Wren (1875–1941).

All of these men wrote stories that took place at least in part on the wild frontiers of the empire. Narrators wrote in terms of jocular modesty about their own courage. Adventures often involved

---

*A popular encyclopaedia originally published to help sell Pears soap.

'gentlemen' – public school boys in particular – who were cast out of their class by some disaster but then demonstrated their valour and enterprise as, say, Foreign Legionnaires. Churchill's account of his early life had a touch of this. It began with the hero's failure at school and his father's disappointment; it finished with a triumphant return. He had left Britain as Billy Bunter and came back as Richard Hannay, the bronzed, self-made veteran of the Veldt. Being self-made was an important element of Churchill's image. He claimed that his father's debts and legacy had been exactly equal and that he, Winston Churchill, had thereafter made his living by his pen. This was not true. Churchill inherited money from his father, though this money (and the even greater sum he inherited from a distant relative in 1921) was not enough to support him in the style he considered appropriate. Only in the Second World War, when Hollywood studios began to buy up the film rights to his publications, were Churchill's finances consistently in the black.[21]

Churchill's account of his early life can be read in a less benign light than that of boys' adventure stories. This light is provided by the First World War. Churchill wrote his autobiography in 1930, when 'war books' by Robert Graves, Siegfried Sassoon or Guy Chapman were pouring from the press. The war was awkward for Churchill. It had created a sharp generational divide. War memoirs were written by men who had been junior officers and were often marked by hostility to politicians and senior officers. Churchill, who had been First Lord of the Admiralty in 1914 and who was responsible for the disastrous operation in the Dardanelles (of which more below) conspicuously belonged to the older generation who had sent men to fight rather than the younger generation who had fought. Writing about his youth was a way of claiming contact with the young (*My Early Life* was dedicated 'to the coming generation') and writing about war implied contact with the men of the trenches. Churchill claimed that the majority of his own Sandhurst contemporaries had died either in the Boer War or between 1914 and 1918.

It is also interesting to put Churchill's *My Early Life* alongside a novel that was published in 1953, during Churchill's second government. L. P. Hartley's *The Go-Between* begins with an evocative line: 'The past is a foreign country: they do things differently there.' We see the world of the English upper classes in 1900 through the eyes of a twelve-year-old boy. He goes to stay at a grand country house where he is fascinated by the lifestyle, by the beauty and kindness of the daughter of the house, Marian Maudsley, and by the self-effacing courage of her fiancé, Lord Trimingham, who has just returned from the Boer War.

It all turns out to be false. The family cannot sustain their grand house and are seeking to restore their fortunes by marrying their daughter to Trimingham. Marian is having an affair with a tenant farmer by whom she falls pregnant – though Trimingham insists that female honour must never be questioned. The cricket games and bathing parties are seen through a dark lens when we realise that almost all the young male characters are destined to be killed in action by 1918.

Churchill's account of his early life was overshadowed by the approach of war, but also by the scandals that swirled around his own family. Like the writers of adventure stories, Churchill presented women in almost fairy-tale terms. A favourite expression of approbation was 'chaste'.[22] His mother 'shone like the evening star'. He finished his account of his youth: 'I married and lived happily ever afterwards.'

No one reading these words would guess that Winston Churchill's father was believed to have syphilis. Nor would they guess that Randolph Churchill had been cast out of polite society for a time after attempting to blackmail the Prince of Wales with indiscreet letters the Prince had written to a married woman. The episode was so scandalous that Tory notables talked about it long after the event. One of them believed that Lord Randolph had been summoned before an improvised *jury d'honneur* at the Turf Club and that there the Marquess of Hartington had seized the compromising letters from him and thrown them into the fire.[23] He also believed that, when Winston Churchill hurried to meet his mother in Paris in 1910, he was seeking to head off some royal scandal.[24]

Churchill grew up in a world of marital infidelity. His wife, Clementine, and his colleague Anthony Eden were widely believed not to be the children of the men who featured on their birth certificates. Some believed the same of Churchill's younger brother Jack. Winston was born seven and a half months after his parents' marriage. A woman who slept with her fiancé before marriage was more shocking for the late Victorian aristocracy than one who slept with almost anyone else after it. No one doubts that Jennie Churchill slept with many men after her marriage. She had numerous lovers and two further husbands – one of whom was almost exactly the same age as her oldest son. She reminds one of Marian Maudsley: at first glance she looks like a twelve-year-old boy's ideal of perfect womanhood; at second glance she is a spirited woman chafing against the conventions of her time; at third glance she is ruthlessly manipulative. Her efforts to advance her son's career, which also helped sustain her own finances, often involved ensuring that he was posted to places of maximum danger.

De Gaulle's early life was less dramatic. At the age when Churchill had seen four wars on three continents, de Gaulle's longest trip abroad was a *séjour linguistique* in Germany. De Gaulle, like Churchill, joined the army but it was a different kind of army. French officers were required to spend a year in the ranks before attending the St Cyr military academy, which meant that de Gaulle lived for a short time on more or less equal terms with members of the working class. Churchill spent his early military career regretting that he would never fight another European army; de Gaulle knew that the *raison d'être* of the French army in the early twentieth century was to fight Germany. De Gaulle joined the infantry on the grounds that it was 'more military' (by which he seems to have meant more professional) than the cavalry.*

Like Churchill, the young de Gaulle was, like Churchill, prone to romanticism. He enjoyed adventure stories and wrote some as a young man under the pseudonym Charles de Lugale. The conventions of French and British stories were different. The French version rarely presented chastity as a virtue. To an extent that was striking in one brought up in a milieu of Catholic austerity, de Gaulle's stories revolved around seduction (frequently with the frisson of racial difference) and suicide. De Gaulle wrote the last of his stories in 1914 as he recovered from his wounds after his first experience of battle. The hero has just undergone a similar initiation and gives up his mistress out of respect for her husband who has been killed in action.

De Gaulle renounced a romantic presentation of his own life in much the way that the hero of his last story renounced a mistress. Thereafter, de Gaulle refused to see his own life as an adventure story. Whereas Churchill looked back on his youth as a contrast to the horrors of the First World War, de Gaulle's early life was defined by that war. He went into action almost as soon as hostilities began. He was wounded three times. On the last of these occasions, in March 1916, he was close enough to the enemy to be cut by a bayonet and captured. He was to spend the remaining years of the war in German prison camps. This may have saved his life, but he felt his enforced removal from combat as a humiliation; he compared being a prisoner to being a cuckold[25] and he made five unsuccessful attempts to escape.

Unlike Churchill, de Gaulle made little of his youthful experiences of war. He hardly referred to his battles, wounds and escape attempts. In prison camps he met Georges Catroux, who would rally to the Free French in 1940, and Mikhail Tukhachevsky, who

*De Gaulle's son suggested a less admirable reason for his father's choice: horses had to be drilled in the morning and Charles de Gaulle disliked getting up early.

would rise to be a general in the Soviet army before being shot in the Stalinist purge of 1937. For a time he was also in the same camp as Alfred Evans, who wrote *The Escaping Club*, which described camp life in terms that would be familiar to readers of English boys' fiction. De Gaulle almost never talked about his time in prison camp. Other men valued the intimate relations they fostered with fellow prisoners or the excitement of attempts to outwit their captors. These things meant nothing to de Gaulle and the main effect of captivity seems to have been to increase his sense of isolation from his comrades and perhaps from everyone. When he wrote about wars, it was to draw general lessons rather than to describe his own experience. *La Discorde Chez l'Ennemi* (1924), the book de Gaulle wrote on the First World War, based on lectures given in prison camp, concerned the German high command rather than French junior officers. De Gaulle did not share Churchill's enjoyment of films and would later tell his son: 'in the cinema, love is always more beautiful than in reality and war is always less horrible'.[26]

The war reinforced a melancholy in de Gaulle's temperament. He had suffered no permanent physical injury and lost no close relative. His family made a pilgrimage to Lourdes in 1927 because de Gaulle's mother had vowed in her wartime prayers that she would do this if her sons were spared. All the same, it must have been disconcerting for a man who had grown up dreaming of military glory to see war in such a squalid and terrible form. De Gaulle never regretted his choice of career and seems never to have abandoned his view that France would have to fight Germany again. But from then on, he wrote about war in sober terms. Military life itself was often melancholy in France between 1918 and 1939. There was no dramatic conflict but the country was never completely at peace. There was fighting on its imperial frontiers – much extended by the mandates it had been granted by the League of Nations. There was also the continual prospect of further conflict with Germany.

De Gaulle's thoughts were always directed to the preparation for war but, for fifteen years after the armistice of 1918, the prospect of such a war was not imminent enough to imbue the French army with much prestige: 'Nothing is more secret than the army when war does not shine its bloody light on it.'[27] Apart from a couple of years in Beirut and some time in the Rhineland, de Gaulle's only posting outside France was a secondment to the French military mission that advised the Poles during their war against the Soviet Union in 1920. France had a conscript army and officers spent much of their time in a wearying round of initiating young recruits into simple military skills.

De Gaulle found relief in becoming a military intellectual. He was a student at the staff college in Paris, where his lack of respect for established military doctrine first seemed likely to damage his career. He was saved by the intervention of his then patron Marshal Pétain, a mere regimental commander when de Gaulle had first encountered him before 1914 but whom war had transformed into one of the most prestigious soldiers in France. De Gaulle served on Pétain's staff from 1925 until 1927. Among other tasks, he worked as a ghostwriter, producing work in Pétain's name. This duty eventually brought about a breach between the two men in 1928, when de Gaulle refused to agree that a work he had written be published in Pétain's name. De Gaulle wrote, in words that said much about himself, 'the book is the man'.[28] The book in question was eventually published in 1938 as *La France et son Armée*. De Gaulle wrote, again in terms that say much about him: 'This book is a biography. Its subject is France.'[29]

Writing was de Gaulle's most significant professional activity for almost twenty years. He produced articles for journals and a succession of books on military matters. Those who reviewed such works noticed that they evoked the 'tristesse et routine' of a peacetime army. Some thought that they recalled the works of Alfred de Vigny, a soldier in the aftermath of the Napoleonic Wars who published *Servitude et Grandeur Militaires* in 1835.[30] De Gaulle himself quoted another exponent of barrack-room *cafard*: Rudyard Kipling.

A few years after his return from captivity, de Gaulle married Yvonne Vendroux. Her family were prosperous Catholics from

Calais who had made their money in shipbuilding and more recently in biscuit manufacture. Apart from the fact that they were richer and more business-minded, the Vendroux were much like de Gaulle's own family and the marriage seems to have been partly arranged by relatives who took it for granted that de Gaulle should find his wife from his own milieu – his parents were cousins. In later life, Yvonne de Gaulle was an object of much mockery from fashionable Parisiennes and English socialites, who found her a 'shy mouse'. She seems, though, to have been unintimidated by her extraordinary husband and unafraid of his numerous enemies. De Gaulle was an uxorious man. One suspects that he had not been comfortable with the womanising culture of the French officer corps – a more worldly associate remarked that de Gaulle's laborious approach to flirtation reminded him of the heavy cavalry: 'De Gaulle seemed more intent on proving himself than enjoying the process.'[31]

Yvonne was the sentry who guarded the frontier between her husband's public and private lives. She once asked his aides to leave the room because she knew that Charles de Gaulle would not pick his grandson out of his cradle if he thought that he was being observed.[32] Occasionally, outsiders got a glimpse of domestic intimacy that was marked by an affectionate irascibility. They noticed the couple's enthusiasm for picnics in the country or recorded a scene in the late 1940s when Madame de Gaulle was driving while her husband navigated with a map spread out on his lap. When it became clear that they were lost, Yvonne suggested that Charles should ask directions of a peasant woman. He refused, claiming that women had to make the sign of the cross to remember the difference between right and left.[33]

The most important event in de Gaulle's family life, in some ways, the most important event in his life, occurred in 1928. He and Yvonne had already had a son (born almost exactly nine months after their wedding) and a daughter. Their third child, Anne, had Down's Syndrome. She never learned to talk. Charles and Yvonne kept Anne at home, an unusual decision at the time. De Gaulle was attached to the child – perhaps the only person who was unaware of, and uninterested in, his strange manner or changing public status. Anne's birth seems to have contributed to his own sense of the tragic and to have encouraged both he and Yvonne to value their privacy.

————

Before de Gaulle had decided on a military career, Churchill had resigned his commission to enter politics. For a man of his background, it was inevitable that he would do so as a Conservative and he was elected as an MP for Oldham in 1900. Lord Lindsay (later Lord Crawford) had met him shortly before this and recognised him as 'a coming man: pugnacious, obstinate and nervous'. He added that 'if he will consent to be humble and obscure for a few years there is no reason why he should not become a power in the land'.[34]

Churchill did not consent to be humble and quickly became a source of irritation for Lindsay and his colleagues. Their annoyance was much increased when Churchill crossed to the Liberal Party in 1904. Conservatives came to dislike 'his vain and priggish manner', his propensity for 'flatulent and rather vulgar' attacks on senior Tories[35] and the fact that he was 'without a glimmer of the comities of public reserve and deference'.[36] When it was rumoured that Churchill might form a centre party in 1914, Lindsay noted: 'our estimate of his character can be measured by this general belief that he is prepared to rat for a second time'.[37]

There was a degree of opportunism in Churchill's behaviour. He left the Tories when their electoral tide was going out. Had he not done so, he would probably have lost his seat with the spectacular Liberal victory in 1906 and would not have held ministerial office until at least 1915. As it was, he was a minister (undersecretary of state for the colonies) at the age of thirty-one, in the cabinet (as president of the board of trade) at thirty-three and appointed to a great office of state (home secretary) at thirty-five. By comparison, Stanley Baldwin and Neville Chamberlain, the

Conservatives who would dominate inter-war politics, were older than Churchill but did not enter parliament until Churchill was already a minister – Chamberlain did not do so until 1918. Two Liberal leaders – Herbert Asquith and David Lloyd George – sensed Churchill's unusual ability and treated him with warmth at a time when Conservatives, even before his departure from the party, were often condescending.

Churchill's politics were not entirely fake though. In some respects, liberalism (if not membership of the Liberal Party) was to be a dominant theme of his life. He felt no attachment to the privileges of the Anglican Church – a defining feature of Toryism for men such as his friend Hugh Cecil. Churchill was also a free-trader and reacted against Joseph Chamberlain's attempts to convert the Conservative Party to the support of tariffs. This was a strange reason for leaving the Conservatives, whose leader, Arthur Balfour, maintained a stance of studied ambiguity to avoid splitting the party. Perhaps Churchill chose Chamberlain, who unlike many Tories had always been civil to him, as his sparring partner because he recognised him as an equal and also because Joseph Chamberlain had been associated, alternately as adversary and ally, with his father.

Churchill's liberalism was underwritten by two personal relations. The first was with Eddie Marsh, who became his private secretary* when he was at the Colonial Office and then served in this capacity as Churchill passed through a succession of ministries. Marsh drew a small private income from the grant that parliament had voted to the family of his ancestor Spencer Perceval, the only prime minister in British history to have been assassinated. He never married and anyone who knew him must have guessed he was a homosexual. Aside from serving Churchill, his life was devoted to art and

---

*In this context, a private secretary is not simply a clerk but a civil servant assigned to work for a minister. In theory, posts such as this are assigned to able but relatively junior people; in practice, a private secretary can be one of the most powerful people in Britain, as was the case with John Colville when he worked for Churchill in the 1950s.

poetry – he moved on the fringes of the Bloomsbury Group. He was a self-effacing person and willing to work for little reward.

This was also the time of Churchill's marriage, in 1908, to Clementine Hozier. Like everything about his life, Churchill's marriage was a public event: Lloyd George signed the marriage registry. Marrying for love was a public statement. It broke with the conventions of nineteenth-century aristocracy, who had often married for money. Churchill contemplated a libel action against a journalist who suggested that his parents' union was a 'snob/dollar marriage'. Clementine was well-born but had lived in such straitened circumstances that she gave French lessons for half a crown. Churchill's affection for Clementine endured until his death but this was in spite, or perhaps because, of the fact that the marriage was rooted in a particular period of his life. As far as upper-class English women went, Clementine was on the left of the political spectrum. She was a Liberal and stayed one after her husband returned to the Conservatives. She was also an advocate of women's suffrage – she once wrote to a newspaper under a false name, mocking opponents of female suffrage and suggesting that they might consider 'abolishing women'. She, like Eddie Marsh, had a touch of the bohemian about her. In June 1911, the Churchills attended a fancy-dress party, he dressed as a cardinal, she as a nun. The second of these costumes attracted comment because Clementine was within two days of giving birth.[38]

Even during the fifteen years that he was a member of the Liberal Party, Churchill's politics were not fixed. For the first five or six of these years, he was at his most progressive. His interests were largely focused on domestic policy. Churchill seemed radical over the two great political dramas of Edwardian Britain. First, he countenanced Home Rule for Ireland, which would have meant Ireland being granted independence on the same terms as those enjoyed by, say, Canada, and even the coercion of unionists who sought to resist it – a striking position because his father had been a supported unionist and coined the phrase 'Ulster will fight and Ulster will be right'. Second, Churchill supported Lloyd George's budget of 1909 which proposed a 'war on poverty' and introduced new taxes to pay for this. When the House of Lords seemed minded to veto such legislation, Churchill went along with the threat that the government would ask the king to create additional peers to overrule the veto.

Churchill's private positions were more complicated than his public ones. He did not wish to coerce unionists in Ireland if it could be avoided and was already considering a compromise by which Northern Ireland (with a Protestant and hence unionist majority) would be separated from the South. As for the dispute with the House of Lords, there was also a contradiction between Churchill's public statements and his private feelings. He was attached to the idea of aristocracy even when he did not think that its political power should be given formal expression. With regard to taxes, Lloyd George was not being entirely flippant when he said that Churchill supported higher taxes as long as his own relatives were excluded from paying them.

Churchill's politics were also marked by a quest for excitement, and this was true especially when he held the usually staid position of home secretary. He deployed troops during labour disputes, though he did not, as was later alleged, have soldiers fire on striking miners at Tonypandy in Wales. When the Scots Guards were sent to besiege a house in Sidney Street, East London, where Latvian revolutionaries had taken refuge, Churchill was filmed at the scene obviously enjoying himself.

At the very moment when his enemies were most prone to denounce him as a dangerous radical, Churchill was already beginning to move in a different direction. Until then, his political interests had primarily been concentrated on domestic policy. However, conflict between France and Germany over North Africa (the Agadir crisis) seemed to bring Britain to the brink of war with Germany. This produced dramatic reversals in British politics. In

July 1911, Lloyd George, previously known largely for his opposition to the Boer War, made a speech describing German actions as intolerable. There was no obvious reason for Churchill, holding an office involved with domestic matters, to concern himself with foreign or military policy. This did not prevent him from doing so. He deployed guards to protect naval ammunition stores in London and he sent the Committee of Imperial Defence a memorandum about the prospect of a European war that would pit Britain, France and Russia against Germany and Austria-Hungary. Edward Grey, the foreign secretary, recalled that in the hot summer of 1911, Churchill 'kept me company for love of the crisis ... his high-mettled spirit was exhilarated by ... high events'.[39]

In the autumn of 1911, Churchill became First Lord of the Admiralty. The British navy was the largest in the world and of particular importance because Germany was seeking to match it. For the first time, Churchill was responsible for an aspect of military policy. Previously, he had sought to contain military spending – though, like many Liberals, he was more sympathetic to the navy, the armed wing of free trade, than to the army. Once at the Admiralty, Churchill increased spending, equipped battleships with 15-inch guns, a risky enterprise because no one was sure that such weapons would work, and converted ships from coal to oil. The Admiralty was fun. The First Lord had an elaborate uniform to wear on ceremonial occasions, he had a yacht (The Enchantress) that he could use to inspect the fleet and, though he had been a junior army officer not much more than ten years previously, he had the right to tell senior naval officers what to do. Churchill's relations with admirals – taciturn men used to giving orders in few words (appropriate for transmission by semaphore) – were rarely good. Jackie Fisher (1841–1920), gregarious and fascinated by novelty, was the one exception to this rule and Churchill brought him out of retirement to be First Sea Lord in 1914.

Churchill was probably the only member of the Cabinet who did not hesitate before supporting the British declaration of war on Germany in 1914. He knew that the war would be on a scale never seen before and he understood the destructive force of modern armaments. None of this dampened his excitement at the prospect of military action.

As it turned out, however, the beginning of the war was a disappointment. Churchill was the most enthusiastic and quick-witted warlord in Europe in 1914 – ensuring that the navy was not demobilised at the end of its summer exercises and was, therefore, ready for immediate action. But there was little for it to do; in fact, there was only one full-scale naval engagement (at Jutland in 1916) in the whole war. Churchill was jealous of the army. Asquith noted: 'His mouth waters at the sight and thought of K[itchener]'s new armies.'[40]

Churchill assuaged his frustration by creating an army of his own. Those who volunteered for service in the Royal Navy could not all be accommodated in a service that did not really need many new recruits. Instead of being sent to sea, they were put into a Naval Division – effectively an infantry unit. Most of the men in this division were not well trained for their new duties; some had never fired a rifle. However, they were quickly deployed because the Belgian port of Antwerp looked likely to fall to the Germans. Churchill went to Antwerp – his departure was so precipitous that Eddie Marsh was unable to accompany him because he was in evening dress and there was no time for him to go home and change.[41] The episode did not enhance Churchill's reputation. The town fell to the Germans, though holding it for even a few extra days may have served some military purpose. Churchill's suggestion that he should be given an appropriate military rank to take charge of the defence was greeted by the cabinet with hilarity.

No one laughed at the consequences of Churchill's next incursion into the land war. Believing that British resources were being wasted as soldiers were sent to 'chew barbed wire' in Flanders, he hoped to circumvent the western front with an operation that could be undertaken, at least in part, by the navy and would bring mobility to the war. Eventually he came to think that the ideal place for such an operation was around the narrow straits that separated Europe from

Asia: the Dardanelles. The idea was to subdue the Turkish forts with fire from warships and then take Constantinople. From this position the British and the French would control access to the Black Sea. They might remove Turkey (a German ally) from the war and encourage other Balkan countries to join the Allies.

The operation failed. Turkish forts were not subdued and, when troops were finally landed, they were pinned down close to the beaches. They were lucky to manage an evacuation without even greater casualties. The political consequences of the failure were made worse by the fact that Admiral Fisher resigned and disappeared in the middle of the operation. Churchill became obsessed with the vindication of his role in the Dardanelles operation but his claims – that it might have succeeded if given more time or if it had been pursued with greater vigour by the commanders in the field – have not met with much favour from recent historians. Even if Churchill was right to claim that he had been badly advised or failed by those who executed the plan, there was something distasteful about the sight of a minister, particularly one known for his determination to have his own way, seeking to shift responsibility on to his subordinates. When he accused Lloyd George of caring nothing for 'my personal reputation', Lloyd George replied that, in the desperate circumstances of the time, he cared nothing for Churchill's and nothing for his own.[42] In his memoirs, Sir Edward Grey refrained from criticism of Churchill but his understated insistence on taking his own share of the blame was more damning than any attack he could have made.[43]

Churchill was moved to be Chancellor of the Duchy of Lancaster, which meant that he was a minister without portfolio. He felt keenly the humiliation of both his failure in the Dardanelles and consequent demotion and when the committee responsible for directing the war was rearranged to exclude Churchill, he resigned his office in November 1915 and joined the army. He commanded a battalion of the Royal Scots Fusiliers, with the rank of lieutenant-colonel. He was a good commander who imparted cheerfulness and cared about the welfare of his men. He was also physically brave.

One should not make too much of Churchill's wartime command. He was in the army for a matter of months and at the front only for around a hundred days. There was no great offensive during his time and casualties among 41-year-old lieutenant-colonels (even brave ones) were lower than among twenty-year-old lieutenants or even among private soldiers. Unkind observers, and there were many who observed Churchill unkindly from the Conservative benches in parliament, thought there was something unseemly about his preoccupation with rank. The attention that was focused on Churchill and the restiveness of Conservatives made it impossible for Asquith to honour his promise that Churchill would be given command of a brigade. A man who had hoped to command an army at Antwerp and had gone to France hoping to command a brigade never commanded more than a battalion.

In 1916, Churchill returned to England and became minister of munitions, a post to which he brought considerable vigour. At the end of the war he moved to the War Office, which he combined with the Air Ministry. He was a successful minister of war – though in circumstances very different from those in which he might once have dreamed of occupying such an office. Instead of overseeing spectacular offensives, he was an administrator responsible for demobilisation.

During this period, there was a residue of military conflict for Churchill to concern himself with. Russian revolutionaries had deposed the tsar and, in March 1918, withdrawn Russia from the war. The British intervened against the revolution partly in the hope that they might keep Russia in the war, but Lloyd George lost interest in such intervention once the war was over. Churchill did not. He was bitterly opposed to the 'foul baboonery' of the Bolsheviks who had taken power in Petrograd and who were now fighting a civil war to impose their authority on the whole of Russia.

Churchill came to recognise that British sponsorship of counter-revolutionary 'White' forces in Russia was hopeless – partly because the Whites were so divided and disorganised. However, he thought that intervention had been useful as a means of excluding Bolshevism from central and western Europe: 'Russia has been frozen in an indefinite winter of a subhuman doctrine and superhuman tyranny. But Finland, Estonia, Lithuania, and, above all Poland, were able during 1919 to establish the structure of civilized States.'[44] He had particular admiration for the role that French military advisers had played in the 'miracle of the Vistula' when the Poles had burnt back the Red Army – though, of course, he had no knowledge of Captain de Gaulle's role in these events. Anti-Bolshevism was central to Churchill's outlook until at least the mid 1930s. It partly underlay his desire to avoid imposing excessively harsh peace treaties on the defeated central powers, which he hoped might be allies of the West against Bolshevik Russia.

British politics were in flux soon after the First World War. In October 1922, the coalition, formed under Lloyd George in December 1916, broke up when the Conservatives, who made up most of its supporters in parliament, withdrew and formed their own government under Andrew Bonar Law. The coalition had masked the decline in electoral support for the Liberal Party but this now became apparent in the general election of November 1922 when the two strands of the Liberal Party (that loyal to Lloyd George and that loyal to Asquith) between them won fewer seats than the Labour Party. There were two further general elections in the ensuing two years.

Churchill lost his seat in Dundee in the general election of 1922. He fought one more election, at Leicester in the general election of December 1923, as a Liberal. He fought the Abbey Division of Westminster (probably the constituency that he would have most liked to represent) as an anti-Socialist Constitutionalist in a by-election of March 1924. He failed to be elected partly because he was opposed by the official Conservatives, but most Conservatives recognised by this time that he was one of them. Finally, Churchill won Epping in the general election of October 1924. He was still a Constitutionalist but this time he had no Conservative opponent.

He rejoined the Conservatives in 1925 and held the seat until it was divided in 1945.

Liberal ideas were important in twentieth-century Britain – Keynes and William Beveridge (who wrote the report that laid the basis for the Welfare State) were both Liberals. But the Liberal Party was in decline. If he had stayed with the party after the break-up of the Lloyd George coalition in 1922, Churchill, like Lloyd George, might never have held office again. As it was, Churchill was back in the cabinet soon. The Conservative leader Bonar Law, who disapproved of Churchill, resigned in May 1923 and was replaced as leader of the Conservative Party and prime minister by Stanley Baldwin. In the long run, Baldwin was to prove a dangerous enemy of Churchill. But he was a shrewd man who understood the uses of bringing Churchill back to the front rank of Conservative politics – particularly, one suspects, because Baldwin was keen to ensure the sharpest possible separation between Churchill and the politician whom Baldwin most hated: Lloyd George. Baldwin made Churchill Chancellor of the Exchequer. This may have been a gracious personal gesture (Randolph Churchill had been chancellor) and it may have been a skilful political move. Baldwin probably guessed that Churchill might launch troublesome initiatives in almost any other office but that he would be controlled by self-confident functionaries when it came to financial matters – Clementine Churchill later astonished civil servants by saying that Sir James Grigg, private secretary to the chancellor, had bullied her husband in the 1920s.[45]

Churchill once wrote of Philip Snowden (his successor as chancellor, whose austere approach to public finances helped split the Labour Party and lay the way for the National Government of 1931): 'The Treasury mind and the Snowden mind embraced each other with the fervour of two long-separated kindred lizards.'[46] Churchill did not have a 'Treasury mind'. His style was expansive, and in his private life he was an enthusiast for deficit spending. However, he did not have any alternative to offer the Treasury view. He often described himself as a Victorian and in no respect was this truer than in his economic attitudes. He believed, as fervently as Gladstone, in balanced budgets and sound money. He also went along with the decision to return to the Gold Standard (the policy, abandoned during the war, that sterling should be convertible to gold at a fixed rate) and to do so at a level that valued the pound sterling relatively high against other currencies. Keynes believed that Churchill had been badly advised by his officials but also that 'he has no instinctive judgement to prevent him from making mistakes'.[47] Perhaps it would have been fairer to say that Churchill was unwilling to trust his instincts in economics, and felt obliged to defer to his civil servants in the end.

In other domains, Churchill did trust his instincts. After 1918, they were usually reactionary ones. His guiding principle now was a fear of disorder. In 1926, he was a bitter opponent of the General Strike and seized printing presses to produce his patriotic and anti-strike *British Gazette*. Churchill's wider fear of disorder was seen in his attitude to Ireland where, in spite of having negotiated with Irish nationalists, he deployed the brutal auxiliary police force known as the Black and Tans.

Churchill extended a dislike of disorder to take in a hostility to socialism, including the democratic socialism of the British Labour Party. Early in his career Churchill had made much of his willing-ness to maintain friendly personal relations with politicians from both major parties and contemplated alliances that would transcend parties. But socialism had no part in his political world. Even during his most progressive period, Churchill believed in the rights of property and the social hierarchy. Indeed, it was precisely because he had been a Liberal and was still a liberal that Churchill regarded the rise of the Labour Party with such disquiet: 'The destruction of Liberalism by the Labour movement, and the ranging of the less contented and less prosperous millions of our countrymen under the foreign and fallacious standards of Socialism, has been a disaster for the British people.'[48]

Churchill and de Gaulle presented an interesting contrast in 1930. Having been brought up a reactionary, de Gaulle had begun to think of himself, at least in the military sphere, as a moderniser (see Chapter 2) and was increasingly willing to make common cause with people from outside his natural milieu if they would help advance that cause. Churchill, on the other hand, sometimes seemed to be looking backwards. His writings at the time were suffused with nostalgia for the pre-1914 world. This was true of *My Early Life* but also true of the biographical essays he published between 1928 and 1931 and eventually gathered together in the collection *Great Contemporaries* (1937). These essays were mainly about contemporaries of his father – men whom Churchill had met when he was young, and who now served to imply that their successors (men of Churchill's own generation) were lesser figures.

The difference in mood between de Gaulle and Churchill at the end of 1930 was partly a matter of age. De Gaulle was forty. He could hardly have anticipated the extraordinary future that lay ahead of him, but it was reasonable to suppose that he was in the early stages of a promising career. Churchill turned fifty-six in 1930. His promising career was behind him and it seemed likely that, having enjoyed high office in his thirties, he had passed the point at which he could expect to attain the very highest of offices. Churchill's parliamentary colleagues, people who had perhaps resented his early successes, began to make pointed remarks about his age. His closest friend in politics – Lord Birkenhead (F. E. Smith) – drank himself to death at the age of fifty-eight in 1930. Churchill was painfully conscious that his father had died young. De Gaulle and Churchill were also conscious – in Churchill's case, almost obsessively so – of another model. Napoleon had won the battle of Wagram, in 1809, when he was the same age as de Gaulle in 1930. But Napoleon had lost the Battle of Waterloo in 1815, when he was ten years younger than Churchill was in 1930.

Age in itself did not explain the stasis of Churchill's career around 1930. The three prime ministers of the 1930s – Ramsay MacDonald,

Stanley Baldwin and Neville Chamberlain – were older than him. Part of the problem lay in the fact that he was so ill-suited to the role of elder statesman. He had extraordinary self-confidence but his colleagues did not always trust him.[49] The 1920s had been the time when Churchill came closest to being conventional. Even his mistakes (particularly the restoration of the Gold Standard) sprang from following received wisdom rather than rebelling against it. But his manner suggested intemperance and excess. During the General Strike, for example, his policy was the same as that of his cabinet colleagues, but he approached social conflict with an apparent zest that some found distasteful.

Comparison with de Gaulle reveals another of Churchill's problems. The first thirty years of de Gaulle's adult life were spent thinking about a single great problem – how France was to be defended against Germany. Churchill's life was not animated by any single problem. He did not fear Germany – though he did eventually come to fear Nazism. For a time, it seemed the dear of socialism might dominate his life, but, by 1929, the Soviet Union did not pose much threat outside its own frontiers. As for the British Labour Party, it was hard to claim that MacDonald or Snowden were dangerous in 1929, and even harder to sustain such a claim after they joined the National Government in 1931.

In 1930, it would have been difficult to foresee Churchill's role as the anti-Nazi prophet at the end the decade. It would have been impossible to foresee the extraordinary circumstances of 1940, when the governing classes would decide that the very qualities that they had distrusted in Churchill – disregard for convention, manic energy and childlike buoyancy – were what their country needed.

2

Gathering storms, 1930–39

Who would have believed seven years ago that
Winston Churchill had any kind of future before him?
George Orwell, 10 June 1940[1]

Surprise, brutality, speed ... A people that wishes to
survive must thus organize their own force to be able *to react*
in the same conditions as the agressors will act.
*Note by de Gaulle after German reoccupation
of the Rhineland in 1936*[2]

In the 1930s, Churchill and de Gaulle were thinking along similar lines. Having helped forces fighting against the Red Army in the aftermath of the Russian Revolution, de Gaulle as a military adviser in Poland and Churchill as a provider of aid to counter-revolutionary forces, both decided in the mid 1930s that their countries would be wise to ally with the Soviet Union against Nazi Germany. They denounced the Munich Agreement of September 1938 – by which Britain and France let Hitler occupy the German-speaking parts of Czechoslovakia. Churchill likened the Western powers to someone who feeds a tiger in the hope that it will eat them last. De Gaulle compared them to the elderly aristocrat during the Terror who had turned to the executioner on the scaffold and said: 'Just one more moment please.'

De Gaulle was rising in the world. In 1937, he became the youngest colonel in the French army – not that colonels in the peacetime army were very young. Churchill's star was falling. Having held high office almost continuously for a quarter of a century, he resigned from the Conservative front bench in December 1930 and would not return to it until September 1939. Churchill probably never abandoned the hope that he might somehow become prime minister but his involvement in politics was oddly detached at times. He had lost badly on the New York Stock Exchange in the crash of 1929 and needed to restore his fortunes, so he spent much of the next decade writing. The four volumes of his biography of the Duke of Marlborough were published between 1933 and 1938 and he was still trying to finish his *History of the English-Speaking Peoples* even after he had returned to government in 1939. He was also a journalist. Some of his articles were frivolous but, especially after 1936, he wrote much on international affairs. In 1937, he met Emery Reves, a Jewish literary agent of extraordinary energy who had fled from Hitler's Germany. Reves placed many of Churchill's articles with foreign publications – including, for example, both the Lithuanian and Yiddish newspapers in Kaunus. By the late 1930s, a single article appeared thirty times and Churchill's writing was published in 750 newspapers in a year.[3] His views were better known than those of most government ministers.

Even as a failure, Churchill was world famous; de Gaulle was still an obscure success. It is conceivable that Churchill had heard de Gaulle's name, but, if so, he took no note of it and had no recollection of knowing anything about him until they met on 9 June 1940. One assumes that de Gaulle had heard of Churchill, but he made little of Britain in his published writings. His first written reference to Churchill came in a letter to his wife on 8 May 1940.[4]

In retrospect the two men came to be seen as prophets who anticipated the advent and nature of the Second World War. But there was a difference between them. De Gaulle had been born to fight Germany. In the French Third Republic geography was the twin sister of history and much was made of French frontiers, especially after Germany annexed Alsace and Lorraine in 1871. De Gaulle began one of his books with a meditation on the geography of France and drawing attention its vulnerability to invasion from the east. It opens with the words: 'Just as the sight of a portrait suggests a destiny, so the map of France tells our fortune.' For him, Franco-German antagonism was permanent and only briefly interrupted by pauses like those that came when two exhausted wrestlers lean on each other.

As a young man de Gaulle had learned German. He spent two years in German prisoner-of-war camps and had much opportunity to observe the country as his frequent escape attempts meant that he was often moved from camp to camp – one wonders what passengers on the railway thought of this figure who towered over his guards and stared at them with the intensity of a man who was determined to learn about his enemy. He regarded everything about Germany – even its public toilets, 'like gothic palaces'[5] – with a horrified fascination.

For Churchill, in contrast, conflict with Germany was not inevitable. The title of the first volume of his history of the Second World War – *The Gathering Storm* – implies fatalism but this title was conferred on the volume at the last moment by others.[6] Churchill's own favourite phrase for the Second World War was 'the unnecessary war'. Eventually, Nazism changed his view but, as late as 1935, he hoped it would be possible to reach a peaceful accommodation with Hitler.

Churchill's admirers came to talk of the 1930s as the 'wilderness years' and to imply that he had consigned himself to this wilderness on account of his opposition to the appeasement of Germany. In fact, the matter that exercised Churchill most in the first half of the 1930s, and that provided the occasion for his resignation from the Conservative front bench, was not Germany but India. Churchill took exception to plans that India should eventually enjoy dominion status – i.e. that it should have the same power to manage its own affairs as Canada or Australia. The proposals, which culminated in the Government of India Act of 1935, were conservative ones.[7] The bill envisaged an expanded electorate but one that would still comprise only about one in six of the population. Lord Linlithgow, who did much to frame the bill and then served as viceroy from 1936 to 1943, wrote in December 1939, after having taken India into the Second World War by fiat that involved no consultation with Indians, 'we framed the constitution as it stands in the Act of 1935 ...[as] the best way ... of maintaining British influence in India'.[8]

Churchill spoke repeatedly against reform in India and claimed to regard it as the 'culminating issue in British politics'.[9] When he had made his last speech in opposition to the Government of India Act, Leo Amery (who would be secretary of state for India in Churchill's wartime government) could only laugh: 'Here endeth the last chapter of the Book of the Prophet Jeremiah.'[10]

Why did Churchill make so much of India? Sometimes, he emphasised British economic interests, especially those of the Lancashire cotton industry. At other times he talked of the fate of India itself. He claimed that self-government would mean domination by a Hindu Brahmin caste. The Muslims and Untouchables would be excluded. The princes would be swept away.

Stanley Baldwin thought that Churchill's attitude to India was that of a 'cavalry subaltern in '95'. It was an interesting remark because everything that most people knew of Churchill's life in India came from his account of his early life, published just as he began his campaign against the India Act. Churchill actually knew *less* about India than most officers. He believed, wrongly, that the bulk of soldiers in the Indian army were Muslims.* Many British officers learned Indian languages. In May 1940, civil servants transmitted

*In 1938, the establishment of the Indian army amounted to 55,000 British troops, 20,000 Gurkhas and 120,000 Indians. Among the latter were 51,000 Muslims, 46,000 Hindus and 23,000 Sikhs.

a secret message to Churchill in Paris by sending it in Hindustani, which general Ismay, Churchill's aide, was able to translate.[11] Churchill learned only three Indian terms of command: 'forward', 'retreat' and 'tally ho'. In the pages of *My Early Lives* devoted to his time in India, he mentions just one Indian (a polo playing prince) by name. Many British Conservatives – Lord Curzon or Enoch Powell – were fascinated by the ritual, tradition and hierarchy of India. Churchill had no interest in Indian culture and spent his afternoons there reading about British and European history. After he left India in 1899, having returned briefly to play in the Inter Regimental Polo Cup, Churchill never went back. His bill for drinks at his club in Bangalore – thirteen rupees – remains unpaid.

Churchill's actions produced the outcomes he claimed to fear most. He made it less likely that the princes would engage with the India Act, and thus more likely that they would lose their power in an independent India. He encouraged the intransigence of Muhammad Ali Jinnah, the leader of the All-India Muslim League, and thus made the eventual partition of India more likely. Lord Crawford, no friend of Indian nationalism, thought that Churchill was 'using the Princes to play into the hands of Gandhi and co'.[12] Churchill could be a monstrous hypocrite with regard to India. In the 1920s, he told his friend Sir Bindon Blood that Indianisation of the Indian army (i.e. the granting of commissions to Indians), a policy ostensibly pursued by the government of which Churchill was a member, would be 'nullified in practice'.[13]

Churchill's opposition to Indian self-government fitted in with an apocalyptic sense that a certain kind of world was coming to an end around 1930. He wrote to Linlithgow:

The mild and vague Liberalism of the early years of the twentieth century, the surge of fantastic hopes and illusions that followed the armistice of the Great War have already been superseded by a violent reaction against Parliamentary and electioneering procedure and by the establishment of dictatorships real or veiled in almost every country. Moreover, the loss of our external connections, the shrinkage in foreign trade and shipping brings the surplus population of Britain within measurable distance of utter ruin.

...

In my view England is now beginning a new period of struggle and fighting for its life, and the crux of it will be not only the retention of India but a much stronger assertion of commercial rights.[14]

It is remarkable that Churchill should associate British rule in India with liberalism. His campaign over India often brought him into alliance with the most reactionary Tories. However, he himself had been a Liberal, and in particular a 'Liberal Imperialist' for almost twenty years. When he spoke of the illusions of liberalism he did so not as an enemy who gloated but as a friend who grieved. There was a general sense around this time that liberalism was in crisis (or that a crisis that dated back to before 1914 could now be discerned). This sense was reflected in George Dangerfield's *The Strange Death of Liberal England*, published in 1935.

Churchill's position in these debates was an interesting one. He began to move away from aspects of liberalism, reluctantly accepting that the economic recession made it impossible to maintain free trade. But his historical vision still revolved around a belief in the progress of liberty ('Whig history' as it was sometimes called) that had been so important to nineteenth-century Liberals. He continued to expound Whig history even after Lewis Namier fired the first shots in the revolution that would sweep such an interpretation from universities.[15]

The Liberal Imperialists had been willing to grant self-government to the white dominions, but they had done so partly because they took it for granted that such reforms were inconceivable in other parts of the empire. India – a place that seemed to epitomise backwardness and superstition – was troubling to the Liberal mind, perhaps for the same reasons that India, though not Indian nationalism, was often an object of fascination for intelligent Tories. John Morley was the last and most intransigent representative of Gladstonian Liberalism in British politics. He had resigned from the government rather than support war in 1914. In spite of their differences, Churchill continued to think fondly of him. He also recalled that the reforms Morley (then secretary of state for India) and Earl of Minto (then viceroy) had introduced in 1909 were designed to contain nationalism rather than promote it. He wrote of Morley:

> He, the ardent apostle of Irish self-government, felt no sense of contradiction in declaring his hostility to anything like 'Home Rule for India'. He went out of his way to challenge Radical opinion on this issue ... he warned his supporters of the perils of applying to the vast Indian scene the principles which he applauded in Ireland and South Africa ...[16]

Churchill's politics in the 1930s owed much to his distaste for two men. The first of these was Mohandas Gandhi – the most prominent figure in the nationalist Congress Party. Churchill sometimes expressed sympathy for tribesmen on the imperial frontier who fought against British rule, but Gandhi was an educated man, who had had a successful practice at the Bar, a profession once deemed too demanding for Churchill. In 1931, Churchill said:

> It is alarming and also nauseating to see Mr Gandhi, a seditious Middle Temple* lawyer, now posing as a fakir of a type well known in the east, striding half naked up the steps of the Viceregal palace, while he is still organising and conducting a defiant campaign of

*Ghandi was at the Inner Temple.

civil disobedience, to parlay on equal terms with the representative
of the King-Emperor.'

In fact, the representative of the King-Emperor, still at this time Lord
Irwin (soon to take the title Earl of Halifax), was on cordial terms
with Gandhi. The fox-hunting English nobleman and the leader of
Congress were both men of deep religious piety, social conservatism
and considerable cunning. Irwin understood, as British officials had
done for some time, that Gandhi was playing complicated political
games with other leaders of the nationalist movement and was often
a 'retarding agent' in his dealing with more radical figures.[17] During
one of the moments when it looked as if they might have reached an
agreement, Gandhi told Irwin that he expected to be denounced by
Nehru (a leader of the 'left Congress' with stronger socialist incli-
nations) for having 'sold India'. Irwin replied: 'I should be getting
cables from England telling me that in Churchill's opinion I had sold
Great Britain.'[18]

Churchill's other defining enmity of the 1930s was for Stanley
Baldwin. Baldwin was the most influential Conservative and
the central figure in the British government from 1931 until
1937 – though he was prime minister only for the last two of these
years. He affected to be a slow-witted country gentleman, but was
actually a successful industrialist who understood the realities of his
time – radio, the newsreel and the influence of newly enfranchised
female voters – better than almost any other politician. Baldwin
had looked vulnerable after the Conservatives lost the 1929 election, and some believed that India would allow Churchill to seize
the leadership of his party and country, but, with his back to the
wall, Baldwin fought. An anti-Baldwin candidate who stood in a
by-election in Westminster St George's in central London in 1931
was defeated. In 1931, Baldwin allied with elements of the Liberal
and Labour parties to form a National Government that was dominated by the Conservatives – even though Ramsay MacDonald, of
what was now called the National Labour Party, remained Prime

Minister for several years. In 1935, the government of India Act was passed and Churchill pretty much ceased to talk about the matter, which strengthened the suspicion of many that his professions of interest in India had merely been a cover for an assault on the leaders of his party.

The youngest and/or most intelligent politicians, who were sympathetic to Churchill over European policy in the late 1930s, were hostile to his views on India. Austen Chamberlain, who had been foreign secretary in the 1920s and was an opponent of appeasement in spite of being the half-brother of Neville Chamberlain, wrote: 'Winston is inclined to make mischief but he is winning no influence with the younger men ... They begin to ask what his game is.'[19] This was true of Anthony Eden, Harold Macmillan and Duff Cooper. Cooper was the Baldwinite candidate in the St George's by-election. He was not an idealistic supporter of Indian nationalism, but thought: 'The idea of the inhabitants of an island in Europe governing against their will an Asiatic population ten times more numerous is not acceptable to the modern mind.' Most of all, he regretted Churchill's stand over India: 'the most unfortunate event that occurred between the two wars'.

> It reduced Winston Churchill to impotence for ten years and deprived the Government of the services of a man who plainly saw the growing German menace, and who, with his great gifts and dynamic personality, might have averted and certainly would have prepared to meet the disaster.[20]

Even Churchill's family were divided by India. His son, Randolph, a man with all his father's faults and none of his virtues, became an aggressive opponent of reform in India. He fought a by-election against the official Conservative candidate and against his father's wishes; in another by-election he supported an 'independent conservative' candidate who belonged to the British Union of Fascists. On the second of these occasions, the successful pro-government candidate was Duncan Sandys, another of those who were alienated by Churchill's attitude to India but later supported him against appeasement. Sandys also married Churchill's daughter Diana.

From 1935, Churchill's interests focused increasingly on the threat posed by Nazi Germany. After the First World War, Churchill had been in favour of magnanimity towards Germany and did not blame the Germans for trying to escape from some clauses of the Versailles settlement. He felt a touch of nostalgia for the German monarchy and for the aristocratic military leadership that had gone with the monarchy. He regretted the fact that the Paris peace settlement had brought the 'apotheosis of nationalism' without the 'discipline of great empires' – he meant the European empires of Germany, Austria-Hungary and Tsarist Russia.

In the 1920s, war had not been Churchill's major preoccupation. As secretary of state for war between 1919 and 1921 he had presided over the abolition of conscription, which was not reinstated until 1939. As Chancellor of the Exchequer from 1924 to 1929 he sought to contain military spending and decided that the Ten-Year Rule, which decreed that Britain should not anticipate a war with a major power for ten years, should be renewed automatically every year. The Ten-Year Rule was not abolished until 1932, by which time Churchill was out of government. Some commentators, exasperated by his later reputation, blamed him for having neglected British defences. The military historian Basil Liddell Hart cited the former cabinet secretary Maurice Hankey's remark about the Ten-Year Rule, that '"that damned fellow Winston" had been largely responsible'.[21] In fact there was nothing surprising about the Chancellor of the Exchequer wishing to contain military spending, which was higher in Britain in the late 1920s than in any other country, at a time when there was no obvious military threat on the horizon.

With regard to Europe, Churchill was sometimes sympathetic to right-wing dictatorship. He welcomed rulers who stood up to communism and who seemed to offer order. He met, and was impressed by, Mussolini. Hitler was different. Churchill felt little sympathy for Nazism and was moved to tears by the suffering of the Jews under the regime, but this did not mean that he decided straight away that Britain would have to fight Nazi Germany. He published a profile of Hitler in 1935.* It finished with the words: 'Thus the world lives on hopes that the worst is over, and that we may yet live to see Hitler a gentler figure in a happier age.'[22]

Whatever hopes he may have entertained of Hitler, Churchill believed in the military containment of Nazi Germany. He urged the British government to join with France in preventing the remilitarisation of the Rhineland in 1936. He said, as early as November 1933, 'Germany is rearming. That is the great new fact which rivets the attention of every country in Europe.'[23]

Two countries mattered particularly to Churchill: the first was the United States. America played a peculiar role in British diplomacy. On the one hand, it had failed to join the League of Nations after the First World War and it had largely withdrawn from intervention in the world, or at least in Europe. On the other hand, American leaders had views about what other democracies should do – perhaps views that were rendered all the more vehement by the fact that the United States was not likely to be directly involved. The Americans were worried by the threat to their position in the Pacific, which made it harder for the British to reach some accommodation with Japan. Roosevelt sought to organise an international conference in early 1938. Churchill later blamed Chamberlain for not having

*Churchill acceded to the request of the Foreign Office that he should refrain from being too aggressive in this essay.

seized this last chance for peace. There was certainly a difference between Churchill, who was pro-American, and Chamberlain, who regarded the United States as a 'nation of cads'.[24] The difference between the two men was less apparent in the 1930s, however, than it came to seem in Churchill's retrospective writings.

The ally that counted for most to Churchill was France. Faith in the French army was the cornerstone of his military thinking and the reason why he believed that Britain could get by with a relatively small army. He was dismayed by the consequences of the left-wing Popular Front government that was elected in the summer of 1936; he thought that trade unions were 'bullying' employers and weakening rearmament. Unlike Chamberlain, though, he did not regard political instability or the strength of the left as reasons to dismiss the French. He distinguished the left-wing government in France from that in Spain. France was more socially advanced: it had already had its revolution (in 1789) and consequently there would not be the attacks on the Church or landowners that marked the beginnings of the Spanish Civil War. Furthermore, France was locked into the international system in a way that Spain was not.[25] Churchill saw some French left-wing politicians as natural allies in the containment of Nazi Germany. Léon Blum, the Socialist prime minister, and Pierre Cot, the minister of the air, who was close to the Communist Party, were both received at Churchill's country house.

Sometimes dislike for Nazi Germany cut across what had formerly been Churchill's beliefs. He invested much hope in building an alliance against Germany, which meant working through the League of Nations. This was not an institution in which he had previously shown much interest, though his friendship with Austen Chamberlain – who, as British foreign secretary, had been an architect of the Locarno Pact of 1925 – may have underlain his attempt to present himself as a defender of international treaties. Churchill's enthusiasm for Franco cooled when it became obvious that Germany expected to profit from a nationalist victory in the Spanish Civil War.

Most strikingly, around 1935 Churchill began to contemplate the possibility of alliance with the Soviet Union. The evolution of his thinking on this matter derived partly from his cordial relations with Ivan Maisky, who became Soviet ambassador in London in 1932. He told Maisky in September 1938 that he was keeping a bottle of wine from 1793:* 'We'll drink this bottle together when Great Britain and Russia beat Hitler's Germany!'[26] Churchill was also influenced by a shrewd grasp of the animosities that divided the communist world. Leon Trotsky had been driven out of the Soviet Union by Stalin in 1929. Intelligent people in the West often assumed that any enemy of Stalin must be a friend of their own values. Churchill, who had not forgotten Trotsky's role as the warlord who had defeated the forces of counter-revolution, hated him. He did not see the conflict between Trotsky and Stalin as one that pitted 'good' Communists against 'bad' ones. Rather, he saw it as one that pitted Trotskyite support for international revolution against a Stalinist tyranny in one country. He had no illusion about the unpleasantness of Stalinism for those who had to live under it: in particular, he drew attention to the persecution of Jews in both Russia and Germany. However, he recognised that Russia might be a military ally, and the terms in which he expressed himself were more explicit than those he was able to use after June 1941 when he finally did lead Britain into an alliance with Stalin:

> It may well be that Russia in her old guise of a personal despotism may have more points of contact with the West than the evangelists of the Third International. At any rate it will be less hard to understand. This is in fact less a manifestation of world propaganda than an act of self-preservation by a community which fears, and has reason to fear, the sharp German sword.[27]

*The year, as both Churchill and Maiksy would certainly have known, Louis XVI had been guillotined.

A little later he wrote again of the 'Communist schism' noting that the Parti Communiste Français, slavishly loyal to Moscow, did 'nothing to hamper the preparations of the French army', while the POUM in Spain, which contained many Trotskyites was 'achieving the quintessence of foetidity and surpassing all others in hate'.[28]

Rearmament became the main theme in Churchill's political interventions, but he was distracted by one episode. In 1935, King George V died and was succeeded by his son: Edward VIII. The new king was in love with Wallis Simpson, an American divorcée. Bishops and religiously minded politicians (Baldwin especially) understood that the king, who was head of the Anglican Church, could not marry a divorcée. Churchill took the king's side. Perhaps this was partly because he had little feel for religious belief; perhaps it was partly because he was sentimental about love and marriage and prone to assume, in a way that would have amused many members of his own class, that these two things went together. He certainly relished any chance to discomfit Baldwin. Baldwin was not discomfited. As was often the case, he had judged the mood of the country right and the king abdicated. Churchill, by contrast, seemed unbalanced. Many felt it frivolous to turn away from grave matters and devote attention to a middle-aged love affair. Churchill also looked silly. He asked plaintively of the popular playwright Noel Coward, 'Why can't the king have his cutie?' Coward shot back, 'England doesn't wish for Queen Cutie!'[29]

After 1945, Churchill's admirers sometimes talked as though debates on foreign policy had pitted him and a few loyal associates against the government and a wider establishment that exercised influence in, say, the editorial offices of *The Times* or at All Souls College Oxford. Nothing could be further from the truth. Churchill and Baldwin were closer to each other than either was to George Lansbury, who led the Labour Party from 1932 to 1935, and who was near to being an outright pacifist. 'Appeasement' became a term of political abuse after the Second World War, but all politicians believed in seeking better relations with some potential enemies.

Churchill was sometimes an appeaser with regard to Italy and Japan because he wished to focus on the threat of Germany. Furthermore, appeasement and rearmament were not mutually exclusive policies. The British government increased arms spending at the same time as it appeased Hitler at Munich and some sought to defer war in order to be better prepared when it came.

Often the conflict between Churchill and the government was not one that pitted two different policies against each other. Rather it pitted a man who could express himself with the freedom offered by the back benches against those constrained by holding high office. Baldwin remarked, in words given to him by his cousin Rudyard Kipling, that 'power without responsibility' was the 'prerogative of the harlot'. He was referring to the press lords Beaverbrook and Rothermere, who were intermittently allied with Churchill, but he might as well have been talking of Churchill himself.

For all the scorn that Churchill later heaped on him, Baldwin did rearm and made sure that the victory of the National Government in the general election of 1935 provided a mandate to do so. Some who were later known as opponents of appeasement – Duff Cooper and Anthony Eden – served in Baldwin's cabinet. Churchill himself had hopes that he might be appointed to a Cabinet position. These hopes explain why he often toned down his attacks on the government in the short term; the fact that the hopes were repeatedly dashed explains his bitterness towards it in the long term.

Even out of office Churchill was never entirely removed from government. He was extraordinarily well connected. The most senior official at the Foreign Office saw nothing strange in the fact that 'Winston' (a backbench MP) should drop round and expect to be provided with information for a newspaper article in July 1938.[30] Churchill was appointed to a committee on air defence. Until his death in 1936, Ralph Wigram from the Foreign Office visited Churchill regularly, as did some officials from the Air Ministry. Wigram was acting without authority but sometimes the government accepted it as reasonable that Churchill should be shown confidential documents so that his discussion of military matters should be better informed. Neville Chamberlain, who succeeded Baldwin as prime minister in 1937, placed more faith in appeasement than his predecessor but even he recognised that circumstances might arise in which Churchill would be recalled to office.

Churchill's courage was admired by opponents of appeasement but many of these people were also troubled by the unmeasured terms in which he often spoke and by the sense that he was not, to use a term that mattered a good deal to the English ruling class of the time, a 'gentleman'. These considerations limited Churchill's influence. Leo Amery, Austen Chamberlain and Anthony Eden all had reason to consider themselves at least as important as Churchill. Even Duff Cooper, now mainly remembered in footnotes to biographies of Churchill, held significant offices at a time when Churchill had been out of power for almost a decade. Being in office gave opponents of appeasement a spectacular weapon to deploy: they could resign. Eden resigned as foreign secretary in February 1938, in protest against the government seeking to draw closer to Mussolini's Italy. Duff Cooper resigned six months later as First Lord of the Admiralty, in protest against the Munich Agreement. Eden and Cooper were much younger than Churchill; they had reason to suppose that they were at the start of brilliant careers at a time when Churchill was coming to the end of a chequered one.

Eden, more than Churchill, was the figure around whom the ablest of anti-appeasement Conservative politicians – Harold Nicolson, Duff Cooper, Ronald Cartland – first gathered. Churchill had few real allies. Austen Chamberlain, distinguished but past the peak of his career, died in 1937. Harold Macmillan would prove his mettle during the war and have a spectacular career after it, but in the 1930s he was regarded as a faintly absurd figure. Robert Boothby was a man of brilliant flamboyance but did not achieve much in politics and is now remembered largely for having cuckolded Macmillan. In any case, Boothby admired Churchill but did not entirely trust him. Brendan Bracken (1901–58) was a man of mysterious origins who had made a fortune and been elected to parliament in 1929. His support for Churchill was unconditional but, since almost no one, including Clementine Churchill, trusted him, this devotion was a mixed blessing.

———

Unlike Churchill, de Gaulle never doubted that his country would have to fight Germany. The important question for him was simply how France should do so. He studied these matters from a relatively privileged position because between 1931 and 1937 he was a staff officer working for the secretariat of the Conseil Supérieur de la Défense Nationale. This meant that he was in Paris – the longest period he lived in the capital before he moved into the Élysée Palace at the age of sixty-eight. He took well to life in the capital. He gained much from the company of two unconventional military men – Lucien Nachin and Émile Mayer. Perhaps these were the only real friends de Gaulle ever had.[31] The mid 1930s provided de Gaulle with a brief holiday from being de Gaulle. For most of his life he was a solitary man. He read and wrote on his own. His ideas, like the cards of a poker player, were kept hidden until they might produce the right effect. French army officers were better educated than their British counterparts, but they were unlikely to provide de Gaulle with many intellectual equals. Now, for a few years, he plunged into the company of people who were as intellectually adventurous as himself. A discussion group met at Mayer's flat on Sundays in a haze of cigarette smoke – de Gaulle chain smoked then. Gaston Palewski, who was later to join de Gaulle in London in 1940, first met him in 1934. He recalled an intense conversation that began with a formal meeting in an office and ended several hours later after lunch in a cheap restaurant.[32]

De Gaulle wrote about a wide range of matters – particularly relating to military history. In terms of practical proposals, there was an air of fantasy to some of his projects – though he had never set foot in Indochina, he wrote that Annamite auxiliary soldiers were particularly gifted in the use of camouflage.[33] The most striking feature of de Gaulle's work was how he failed to anticipate the nature of the Second World War. For him, the age of unrestricted warfare was over. He thought that states would fight over precise and limited objectives: 'the Sarre, the Dalmatian coast, a fragment of the Transylvanian lands'. Quick military operations – perhaps 'to maintain the hypocrisy' without formal declaration of war – would characterise future operations.[34] He presented himself as a technician who anticipated limited engagements with clearly defined aims and the latest equipment to fight them. He believed that nations were now well established and therefore the existential struggles that marked earlier wars were finished – a curious view for one who had watched the Polish nation define itself on the battlefield less than fifteen years earlier. But he also recognised that the absence of heroic causes might present problems for nations, especially his own.

After the French defeat of 1940, de Gaulle's admirers made much of one of his books – *Vers l'Armée de Métier* (Towards a Professional Army) (1934). There were frequent, and implausible, suggestions that German commanders, such as General Heinz Guderian, had learned their Blitzkrieg tactics from reading it.[35] Albert Speer wrote that Hitler had said: 'I have time and time again read Colonel de Gaulle's book on methods of modern warfare employing fully motorized units and I have learned a great deal from it.'[36] Philippe Barrès claimed that he first heard of de Gaulle from Germans who regarded him as a brilliant exponent of armoured warfare. Alain de Boissieu, an officer with the Free French and later de Gaulle's son-in-law, claimed to have seen a translation of *Vers l'Armée de Métier*, with 'annotations that were undoubtedly in the writing of Hitler', in Hitler's Austrian lair at Berchtesgaden in 1945.[37]

It is easy to see why *Vers l'Armée de Métier* achieved such fame in 1940. This was the moment when rapid attacks by armoured units seemed to have demonstrated their success in spectacular fashion;

it was also a time when de Gaulle was still regarded primarily as a soldier. But the book had a comparatively limited influence when it was first published. The German edition was abbreviated to remove much of the technical detail and concentrated instead on de Gaulle's anti-Germanism — besides German reviewers suggested that de Gaulle had been influenced, or at least anticipated, by German authors rather than the other way round.[38]

Even in its original French version, *Vers l'Armée de Métier* contained relatively little detail about the deployment of armoured forces. It was a political work as much as a military manual and this was reflected in the title — though the book did not actually propose a purely profes-sional army. Professionalism would have seemed an uncontroversial idea among British soldiers, and the English edition of de Gaulle's book was published in 1940 under the title *Towards the Army of the Future*. However, the French army was founded on universal military service. As an idea, this dated back to the 'nation in arms' that had defended France against foreign invasion after the Revolution of 1789. Conscription came with political baggage. Conscripts could be used for defensive wars more easily than for offensive ones. It was assumed that a conscript army would not seek to overthrow democracy in France itself. By associating his ideas about new military techniques with the need to create a professional army, de Gaulle was inviting attack from left-wing politicians as well as conservative soldiers.

De Gaulle sought to impose his ideas on the French army partly by seeking political sponsors. Some of those he approached were marginal or eccentric figures — such as Marcel Déat, a former socialist who would become a collaborationist during the war. The socialist Léon Blum was sympathetic to new military technology but not to the professionalisation with which de Gaulle associated it — he was one of those who believed that de Gaulle's notion would create an army that was 'always ready for a coup'. De Gaulle's most important patron was Paul Reynaud, a member of the centre-right Alliance Démocratique. Reynaud was a brave and unconventional politician; he was an ally of Churchill's in opposing Munich. But he had offended bourgeois opinion with his support for devaluation and was excluded from ministerial office until 1938.

Churchill and de Gaulle were working on parallel tracks with regard to Germany by the late 1930s, but they were different kinds of military thinkers. De Gaulle was almost entirely concerned with warfare on land. In spite of the fact that he had been minister of war, he had comparatively little to say about the army – partly because he placed such faith in the large French conscript force. He assumed that the coming war would be a relatively static one in which trenches would be at least as important as tanks. In 1939, he promoted an armoured 'mole' that would dig tunnels towards enemy fortifications. In spite of having been First Lord of the Admiralty, Churchill said relatively little about the navy. Overwhelmingly, his eyes were turned upwards in the defence debates of the 1930s. He thought that the most important military developments would take place in the air. Much of his energy was given to drawing attention to the growth of the German Luftwaffe and to the need for the Royal Air Force to match this expansion.

Since de Gaulle and Churchill would become so important to the post-war history of their countries, it is hardly surprising that much was made of their supposed prescience about changing warfare in the 1930s. But the truth was that the changes in military technology made it hard for anyone to anticipate how the next war would be fought. Some argued, like de Gaulle, that tanks would be important but others – including Churchill who had been an early advocate of armoured warfare – maintained that better anti-tank guns would give defenders the advantage. Equally, Churchill believed that better anti-aircraft guns and submarine detection systems would make warships immune to attack from above and below.

The Germans intended that their bombers should be used largely in support of operations by the army. The RAF wanted to employ strategic bombing – by which they meant attacks on targets in

Germany by long-range bombers – though they did not have the heavy bombers needed to sustain such a policy until after the war had started. No one really knew what a bombing raid would look like. There were many apocalyptic predictions. Churchill claimed that a week of bombing might cause 30 or 40,000 serious casualties in London alone. (The figure for the whole of the United Kingdom for the whole of the Second World War was in fact less than 150,000.[39]) It was hard to predict how civilian populations would react. British Conservatives – never prone to place much faith in the urban working class – often believed that there would be panic, disorder and uncontrolled flight from cities.

Basil Liddell Hart was the most widely read British military thinker of the 1930s. De Gaulle knew his work and Churchill knew him personally. In later years Liddell Hart was given to undignified displays of pique when he felt his importance was not being acknowledged. In 1945, keen to obscure the extent to which he himself had backed away from his initial belief in the importance of tank warfare in the late 1930s, he listed Churchill's false prophecies – on the protection of warships from attack by planes or submarines, on the strength of the French army – with glee.[40]

When de Gaulle returned to power in 1958, Liddell Hart wrote to the obituaries editor of *The Times* urging him not to:

[R]epeat the widespread wartime story that his little book *Vers l'Armée de Métier* (1934) was taken up by the Germans and influenced the pattern of their armed forces. That was a completely unfounded myth, put out by Gaullist propagandists here. The pattern of their armoured divisions and tactics was settled well before his book appeared and followed British ideas – as Guderian and others have amply acknowledged.[41]

For all his vanity, Liddell Hart was not entirely wrong about the military ideas of Churchill and de Gaulle; most of all, he was not wrong to point out the difference between stating general ideas in this domain and implementing them in practice. Liddell Hart's pencilled annotations in his copy of *Vers l'Armée de Métier*, written before he had any reason to be jealous of de Gaulle, are revealing. He noted that the book devoted only three pages to the air force and only about eight or nine pages to armoured warfare. He scribbled 'The right idea but wordy and woolly. No clear and precise strategical and/or tactical suggestions.'[42]

When it came, war transformed the fortunes of Winston Churchill. He went back into government in September 1939, as First Lord of the Admiralty – the position that he had held in 1914. It might have seemed a strange appointment because his first term of office had ended so badly and because he had paid little attention to naval affairs in the intervening period, but the position suited Churchill well. The navy was active in the early stages of the war – at a time when land war seemed frozen by the Maginot Line.

Many other senior ministers – Chamberlain especially – lived through this period as one of bitter disappointment. Their efforts to avoid war had come to nothing. Chamberlain's failure made life easier for Churchill. It meant that his show of deference to the prime minister seemed to be a sign of magnanimity rather than real subordination. But government policy on appeasement had changed in March 1939, when Hitler broke the Munich Agreement by sending troops to occupy Prague. The following months saw the signature of anti-German pacts, most notably that with Poland. Churchill was able to present this as triumph for the policy he had advocated all along. He wrote in an introduction to a collection of his articles in May 1939: 'It is a gratification to me that His Majesty's Government have at length by leisurely progress along their own paths of thought adopted even in detail the policy and theme set forth.'[43]

By September 1939, most of the British governing classes (and probably most of the British people) had reconciled themselves to war and accepted it as a necessary evil. They understood all too well that it would have unpleasant – perhaps terrible – consequences for themselves and all that they loved. James Pope-Hennessy wrote a book – *London Fabric*[44] – in which the hero wanders around the capital with Perdita (a character based on Churchill's niece Clarissa) contemplating buildings threatened with destruction. Harold Macmillan was an opponent of Munich – he threw an effigy of Chamberlain on the bonfire at his country house on Guy Fawkes' day 1938. Nonetheless, Macmillan – haunted by the death of so many friends in the First World War – felt guilty relief at one consequence of the settlement. It meant that his son would finish his time at Eton and get at least a few months at university.[45]

The horrors of war troubled Churchill little. His optimism and, to use one his favourite words, 'relish' were refreshing – perhaps particularly for those who were themselves pessimistic and fearful. Lord Crawford had often been critical of Churchill – especially during his period as a Liberal but also over India, the abdication and appeasement. But he changed with the outbreak of war. One of the last entries in Crawford's diary – rendered all the more poignant by the fact that it was written two weeks before his death and that he never lived to see Churchill's apotheosis – was written on 18 February 1940:

Churchill's speech to the officers and company of the *Exeter* on her return to Plymouth was splendid ... People say Churchill is tactless, that his judgement is erratic, that he flies off at a tangent, that he has a burning desire to trespass upon the domain of the naval strategist – all this may be less or more true but he remains the only figure in the cabinet with the virtue of constant uncompromising aggressive quest of victory ... the more I see and hear of him the more confident I become that he represents the party of complete totalitarian victory![46]

Particularly after his patron Paul Reynaud became prime minister in March 1940, de Gaulle's fortunes were also transformed by war. He was lucky to survive his last experience of leading men in battle. John Verrier Glassbrook was serving with a Scottish regiment near the Somme in 1940, under the command of a British lieutenant with a French liaison officer. They had been ordered to shoot anyone who appeared in front of them. Close to midnight they heard movement and thought 'this is it'. Then they saw two tanks and a car. A very tall man got out of the car. Glassbrook had his finger on the trigger of his Bren gun, aimed at the chest of the tall man. Suddenly the liaison officer shouted to them to hold their fire. Glassbrook gathered that the tall man was de Gaulle: 'I always thought how close I was to changing the course of the war – but somebody else would have taken his place I don't doubt.'[47]

3

The Fall of France

If France broke, everything would break,
and the Nazi domination of Europe, and potentially
of a large part of the world, would seem to be inevitable.
Winston Churchill, 1938.[1]

In 1940, for the first time, we acted as though
we were not a great power.
Charles de Gaulle, 1946.[2]

The defeat of France was the first episode in the premiership of Winston Churchill and the last episode in the conventional military career of Charles de Gaulle. Both lived through a period of extraordinary drama from the moment German troops entered Belgium on 10 May 1940 until the moment on 17 June when the French enquired about the terms on which they might seek an armistice. It was during these weeks that the two men first met. Churchill crossed the Channel five times to confer with his French colleagues. De Gaulle went to Britain twice in the ten days that led up to his final departure on 17 June. Both were deeply marked by the fall of France, but for different reasons. Churchill was shocked that an army in which he placed such faith collapsed so fast, but he saw this as a primarily military event. De Gaulle was less surprised by events on the battlefield. The most important feature of the defeat for him was the way in which it was marked by a broader crisis (a 'shipwreck' to use one of his favourite images) of the French state.

For eight months after the Franco-British declaration of war on Germany in September 1939, the French and German armies faced each other on France's eastern frontier, where French fortifications had been built along the Maginot Line. The French understood that the German attack was likely to circumvent the Maginot line and come through Belgium – though they did not anticipate where it would be or how quickly it would proceed. The French planned to meet a German advance in Belgium, but this strategy was thrown into disarray in 1936 when Belgium declared itself neutral. This meant that the French could not enter Belgium until after the Germans had done so.

British and French attention in the period from September 1939 until May 1940 was focused on theatres of war that in retrospect appear to be irrelevant to the coming conflict. Churchill wanted to drop mines into the Rhine to impede the transport of goods. The French were nervous about this – France was exposed to retaliation by German bombers – but they were keen to cut the transport of iron ore from Sweden to Germany and in pursuit of this wanted to put mines in Norwegian fjords. Churchill also supported the mining of Norwegian waters. R. A. Butler, under-secretary of state at the Foreign Office, objected to this in a memorandum that made sly reference to the reputation of the 'brilliant ... mind' that had conceived the operation: 'I dislike action for action's sake ... [it] may rank in history with the ... Dardanelles.'[3]

The British and the French also offered to send troops to Finland, which had been invaded by the Soviet Union. The Soviet Union was not at war with Britain and France but had signed a non-aggression pact with Germany and helped itself to part of Poland after the German invasion. There were some on the political right who would have preferred to be at war with the Soviet Union than with Germany. The Anglo-French interventions in Finland and Norway failed. The Finns were forced to make peace with the Soviet Union in March, but they later joined the Germans in fighting the Soviet Union. As for Norway, the British did lay mines in early April and then launched what they intended to be a preemptive occupation of Norwegian coastal towns on 8 April, which turned out to be the day before the Germans invaded Denmark and Norway.

Events in Scandinavia brought political changes in both France and Britain. In March 1940, the right became dissatisfied with the French prime minister, Édouard Daladier, because they considered him insufficiently vigorous in providing help to Finland. He was overthrown and replaced by Paul Reynaud. In Britain, Churchill might easily have been blamed for the unsuccessful intervention in Norway, but Chamberlain had made a complacent speech in which he said that Hitler had 'missed the bus', and this drew the ire of the House of Commons. On 10 May, he resigned and Churchill replaced him. Churchill communicated a mood of determination and optimism that had been conspicuously absent under Chamberlain. In private, though, Churchill had few illusions. His niece Clarissa saw him immediately after his appointment as prime minister. She recalled: 'He was terribly pessimistic – not at all virile and courage-giving as he was usually. Lloyd George ... wanted to sue for peace but Winston thought there was just a chance that we would pull through.'[4]

Political change was accompanied by military turmoil. On 10 May the Germans invaded Luxembourg, the Netherlands and Belgium. Now Britain and France could act on their plans to confront the Germans in Belgium. German forces, however, circumvented the British and French by cutting through the Ardennes Forest in the south, which some had assumed to be impassable for tanks. British and French troops in Belgium and northern France were now threatened with encirclement. This marked the beginning of a chaotic retreat.

The two men who had to deal with military disaster (Reynaud and Churchill) had much in common. They had both been excluded from power for much of the 1930s partly because they had defied political orthodoxy – Reynaud on devaluation and Churchill on India. Both had supported rearmament against Germany. Churchill (still First Lord of the Admiralty) rejoiced at Reynaud's appointment as prime minister.'⁵ But Reynaud's reputation was not enhanced by his tenure in the post. He was unlucky that his brief time at the centre of the historical stage invited comparisons with Churchill and de Gaulle. But there was also a sense in which he failed as a wartime leader because of the virtues he had displayed as a peacetime politician – particularly his capacity for compromise. In the late 1930s and perhaps until Churchill became prime minister, Reynaud had been the more powerful of the two. Furthermore, he regarded Churchill's determination as a sign of poor judgement rather than moral steel. In early 1940, Sumner Welles toured Europe as an emissary of the American president Franklin Roosevelt. He met and was impressed by Reynaud, who despite having been the 'hardest' member of the government with regard to Germany, now spoke in a 'temperate, moderate and constructive fashion'. Reynaud told him that he had recently received a 'midnight visit' from Churchill:

> Mr. Churchill's point of view was utterly intransigent. M. Reynaud felt that while Mr. Churchill was a brilliant and most entertaining man, with great capacity for organization, his mind had lost its elasticity. He felt that Mr. Churchill could conceive of no possibility other than war to the finish—whether that resulted in utter chaos and destruction or not. That he felt sure was not true statesmanship.⁶

Reynaud had returned to office as minister of finances in the Daladier government of 1938, and was therefore associated with unpopular decisions. Believing that the social reforms the Popular Front government had introduced in 1936 were impeding rearmament, he limited some of them and then crushed the General Strike that the main trade union launched in protest – one wonders how Churchill would have fared in 1940 if memories of his career as a strikebreaker had been so fresh. The fact that Reynaud became prime minister before Churchill also worked against him. Churchill took over at a moment of supreme crisis when most of his compatriots appreciated that desperate measures were required. Reynaud took over in the last month of the phoney war – soon enough to take the blame for what was about to happen but too late to do much about it.

Both Churchill and Reynaud had to deal with the chaotic circumstances that followed the German invasion of France. However, from the French point of view this period was one of unrelieved disaster. The British experience was more complicated and the difference between the two is summed up in one word: Dunkirk. It was from Dunkirk in northern France that a large part of the British Expeditionary Force and many French soldiers were evacuated in late May and early June 1940. No one pretended this was a victory. The British were in desperate retreat and left much of their equipment behind. All the same, Dunkirk was a relief for the British because the destruction of their army had seemed so likely just weeks before. Eventually, the British troops eventually returned to the fight.

Dunkirk had no such meanings for the French. Fewer of their soldiers escaped – the great movement of the summer of 1940 involved almost 2 million Frenchmen being taken as prisoners to Germany rather than a little over 100,000 being taken to England. The majority of those who did get away went back to France. The historian Marc Bloch arrived at Dover from Dunkirk on the morning of 1 June and embarked at Plymouth for Cherbourg on the evening of the same day. He joined the resistance and would be shot by the Germans in 1944. The town of Dunkirk itself was pretty much destroyed by fighting in 1940. It became a battlefield again because it was the stronghold of a German garrison that held out after the rest of France had been liberated and did not surrender until 8 May 1945. Dunkerque was also the name of a French battleship, badly damaged by a British attack in July 1940 and then scuttled by her own crew in 1942. De Gaulle was indignant when Dunkirk was the site for the signature of an Anglo-French treaty in March 1947: 'When one remembers what Dunkerque was.'[7]

The period immediately after Dunkirk was a particularly bleak one for France, marked not just by military defeat but by the *exode* of 8 or 10 million refugees who fled the advancing Germans, by the collapse of the government and by the disappearance of the state in parts of the country as officials simply vanished. As for Britain, the first two or three weeks of June 1940 were often remembered by the British, at least by influential British people, as a time of growing optimism. This was because the successful evacuation of Dunkirk had saved the country from the worst. The writer and soldier Peter Fleming recalled the atmosphere: 'When men escape from mortal danger, the mere act of survival has a curiously moving and even exhilarating effect on them.'[8] It was also because France had come to seem such a centre of chaos and despair that many British people were glad to escape from involvement in its affairs. The mood was captured in the diary of Alexander Cadogan, the permanent head of the Foreign Office: 'an awful day' (15 May); 'the blackest days I have ever lived through' (16 May); 'Situation less awful, but still pretty grave' (18 May); 'News pretty bad' (19 May) 'awful tale of woe (21 May); 'black as black' (22 May); 'News awful' (23 May); 'pretty gloomy' (24 May); 'Just as gloomy as usual' (25 May); 'as gloomy as ever' (27 May). Cadogan's first flicker of optimism in many weeks came on 31 May: 'we have taken off 165,000 men [from Dunkirk]: a miracle.'[9]

General Alan Brooke had lived through a particularly tense few weeks in France and Belgium – apart from his crushing military responsibilities he did not know what had happened to his son, whom he had last seen about to undergo an operation in a Belgian military hospital. Getting back to England was a relief. He wrote:

I was still overcome by the wonderful transformation from war to peace. The awful load of responsibility had been laid aside, the nightmares of anxiety were gone, roads were free from refugees, demoralization no longer surrounded me on all sides, it was another glorious English spring day. From every point of view life had suddenly assumed a very rosy outlook.[10]

He was horrified to be ordered back to Normandy where he spent a desperate week trying to stiffen French resistance. His first encounter with Churchill came on 14 June on a bad phone line when the prime minister questioned Brooke's desire to withdraw: 'The strength of his power of persuasion had to be experienced to realize the strength that was required to counter it.'[11] Brooke would have a hard war – preparing to face invasion as commander of forces in Britain and then, as chief of the Imperial General Staff, having repeatedly to pit his will against Churchill's. All the same, nothing that happened subsequently matched the horror of his experiences between the German invasion of Belgium and his final departure from France on 18 June 1940.

Churchill and Reynaud did not just come to power at different times (separated by a few extraordinarily dramatic weeks); they also assumed power in different ways. The difference was illustrated by an incident in March 1940. Madame de Portes, Reynaud's mistress, went to see Paul de Villelume, one of his aides. She told him that Churchill, then still First Lord of the Admiralty, had given Reynaud, then still finance minister, some advice – she believed that Churchill had come to Paris for this specific purpose. He had said: 'We are at war. I do not want to work to overthrow Chamberlain. I hope that you will behave in the same way towards Daladier.'[12]

Churchill's words reflected the difference between the two political systems. In Britain, governments usually commanded an absolute majority in the House of Commons and measured their lives in years. Churchill was astute enough to guess that Conservative MPs would not forgive him if he upset this stability and that his best hope of obtaining power lay in an ostentatious show of loyalty to Chamberlain. French politicians, by contrast, were like music hall artists performing one of those tricks (spinning plates or riding a unicycle) that require constant movement. Because no single party commanded a majority, Reynaud needed to form a coalition to become prime minister. He could not just wait to be offered the post. His parliamentary position was delicate. His government was elected by a majority of one and even this may have required some generous arithmetic on the part of the president of the Chamber of Deputies.[13]

Because Reynaud's political balancing act was so complicated, he felt obliged to appoint people who might prop up his government. He brought back Marshal Pétain, sent as ambassador to Franco's Spain in 1939, and appointed him as deputy prime minister on 18 May. Pétain enjoyed an extraordinary public status in France. His appeal was enhanced by the fact that no one knew exactly what he stood for and consequently many projected their own hopes onto him. He was the last surviving French marshal from the First World War, and there had been a project in the 1930s to have him drafted as head of the French government. Reynaud hoped that Pétain would lend the government his prestige but not interfere much in the making of policy. He was disappointed because Pétain became the most important figure pressing for an armistice with the Germans and then himself became prime minister on 16 June.

Reynaud also replaced the French commander-in-chief – Maurice Gamelin – with Maxime Weygand. This change might have done some good if made several months earlier – because Weygand, though seventy-three years old, was a more aggressive general. However, changing commanders in mid battle wasted time. Furthermore, Weygand was a royalist. His strong anti-German feelings were matched by his distaste for parliamentary government. He might have been the right man to defend France against the Germans before the defeat, but was not likely to defend the republic against right-wing Frenchmen after the defeat. He also added to the political instability of the government and there were some who thought that Weygand might replace Reynaud as prime minister.[14]

Churchill was the product of a coalition rather than being a leader who needed to pull a coalition together. In arithmetical terms, it would have been possible for Chamberlain to stay in office with the large majority that the Conservatives and their allies had obtained in the 1935 general election. However, in May 1940, Chamberlain decided that the prime minister would need the authority that derived from the support of all parties and recognised that Labour would not serve under him. Churchill did not have to cobble together a parliamentary majority or ask for anyone's support. He did not need to do anything. Lord Halifax, the foreign secretary, might have had more support than Churchill among the parliamentary Conservative Party. But, when the two met Chamberlain, Halifax, who probably appreciated that there were many reasons why Churchill would have to be prime minister, did not press his case. For once Churchill said nothing and simply let Chamberlain draw his own conclusions about who should succeed him.*

Strictly speaking, the British prime minister was appointed by the monarch and Churchill sometimes described himself as 'the King's First Minister.' George VI summoned him and said: 'I suppose you know why I have sent for you.' Churchill replied: 'I have no idea' and both men laughed. It was convenient to Churchill that he should come to power in this *ancien régime* manner. The prime minister derived authority from the fact that he had been chosen without the vulgar counting of heads. It suited him too that the king was a shy man with a pronounced stammer. There was never any risk that he would overshadow his prime minister or challenge his authority. Things might have been different if the opinionated and vain Edward VIII had remained on the throne in 1936 as Churchill had wished.

*Some accounts dispute Churchill's claim not to have spoken on this occasion – though it is certainly true that he did not have to say very much.

In any case the House of Commons rallied behind Churchill in 1940 and there was not, until at least 1942, much chance that he would fail to command a parliamentary majority. In spite of his anti-socialist past, Churchill could rely on the support of the Labour Party. He also benefited from the fact that he had known many of those with whom he worked for years or decades – at the age of fourteen he had pushed Leo Amery into the Harrow School swimming bath. There was almost no one in the political class who had not had dealings with him and, though he had been out of office for almost a decade, his newspaper articles, books and speeches ensured that he was better known in May 1940 than at any previous point in his life.

None of this meant that Churchill was universally admired. The key to his success was not that the governing class regarded his virtues with unqualified admiration but rather that they had a realistic appreciation of his vices. For them, Churchill's appointment was a desperate measure for desperate times. They also understood from the start that Churchill would need special kinds of support. Those around him had to be prepared to put up with hard work, humiliation and ingratitude., and would sometimes have to steel themselves to argue their case against a storm of objections. Halifax appears to have decided not to be prime minister partly on the grounds that 'Churchill needed a restraining influence', which he, Halifax, could better exercise as a minister in Churchill's government than as prime minister.[15] There must have been dozens of former ministers and officials who read Churchill's post-war remarks about how his whole life had been a preparation for taking power in 1940 and muttered 'my whole bloody life was a preparation for dealing with Winston as PM.'

Reynaud's position was more awkward than Churchill's. His private office (his *cabinet* in the French sense of the word) was as divided as his government. It contained two men – Yves Bouthillier and Paul Baudouin – who would soon hold office at Vichy, but the most awkward figure in it was Charles de Gaulle. In the mid 1930s, de Gaulle had been the supplicant. Even out of office, Reynaud could provide him with useful support. Oddly, as Reynaud rose, the balance of power between the two moved in de Gaulle's favour. This may have been because the war made military advice more important, but it was also because de Gaulle had what Reynaud most lacked in 1940: utter confidence in the rightness of his own judgement. In January 1940, when still a serving officer, de Gaulle sent politicians, including Reynaud, a memorandum on the correct use of armoured force. It was an extraordinary document, which began with an allusion to the Battle of Crécy (1346) and finished with the prediction that 'a new order would be forged in the crucible of war'. In May 1940, de Gaulle got a chance to put his ideas into practice as a commander of a tank unit. Though he fought with courage and determination, he was not very successful in military terms. He would have argued that he had not been given enough time to make his ideas work and that he fought with inadequate resources. His many enemies would have pointed out he ran into problems that anyone reading his confident assertions of earlier years might have anticipated: his heavy tanks ran out of petrol.

De Gaulle was promoted to the rank of *général de brigade* on a temporary basis and then, on 3 June 1940, appointed under-secretary of state for war. This was a more important position than it sounded because his immediate superior, the minister of war, was also the prime minister, Reynaud. Reynaud's military *chef de cabinet*, Paul de Villelume, distrusted de Gaulle's judgement and disliked his arrogance. Reluctantly, he rang the military authorities to ask them to release de Gaulle for his new duties. Hardly had he put the telephone down when de Gaulle erupted into his office with the words: 'I am glad to have you under my orders.'[16]

Ever since his lectures in a German prison camp during the First World War, de Gaulle had insisted on the importance of civilian control over the military. For this reason, accepting political office meant the beginning of a new life. For the rest of his career, de

Gaulle's authority was to come from his political position (even when that position was insecure and ill-defined) rather than his military rank. At a time when almost everyone else hesitated, de Gaulle gave orders. When General Weygand, the most senior officer in France, referred to a remark by de Gaulle, the most junior minister in the government, as a 'suggestion' he was slapped down: 'The government does not make suggestions; it gives instructions.' De Gaulle briefly toyed with the idea of having Weygand dismissed. Some of Reynaud's aides eventually asked him to limit de Gaulle's encroachments on their authority. Reynaud asked them what de Gaulle wanted and they replied: 'Your job, Prime Minister.'[17]

The diplomat Roland de Margerie accompanied de Gaulle to London on 9 June. De Margerie spoke English and knew the city well; de Gaulle had never set foot in England. Nevertheless he took charge of their mission. The two men met Churchill, the first time de Gaulle had done so. De Margerie recalled the prime minister pacing up and down the Cabinet room 'like a caged lion'. De Gaulle assured the Prime Minister that France was now resolved to fight on. Churchill gave the war cabinet a brief account of the meeting and told his colleagues that de Gaulle 'had recently been appointed to an important position on General Weygand's staff'[18] – the exact opposite of the description de Gaulle would have given of himself. De Gaulle found time to inspect troops and tell the chief of the Imperial General Staff that his tanks were not heavily armoured enough. De Margerie and de Gaulle then flew back. They were exhausted and were therefore horrified when the pilot told them that he could not land at Le Bourget airport, which was littered with unexploded bombs. The pilot proposed to land at Caen, which would mean an extra five hours of journey by road. De Gaulle ordered the pilot to land at Le Bourget regardless of the bombs. When he saw the pilot wipe the sweat from his face after they landed, de Margerie realised the risk they had taken.[19]

If managing a divided government had not posed enough problems, Reynaud eventually had to perform this feat while on the run. The Germans were now approaching Paris and the French government left its capital. At 10 p.m. on 10 June, de Villelume saw from his office window Reynaud and de Gaulle getting into a car. Though everyone knew that the government was going to leave Paris, most of Reynaud's entourage had not been warned of the prime minister's imminent departure. De Villelume threw his cases (already packed) into his car and followed – though, as it turned out, the convoy of cars then drove in the wrong direction for twenty minutes. In the next few days, Reynaud spent much of his time in the back of a car bumping along minor roads, which the party took in order to avoid the refugee columns that blocked the *routes nationales*.[20]

It was during this extraordinary period that Churchill met the leaders of the Third Republic for the last time at a succession of improvised headquarters. On the evening of 11 June, Churchill and his entourage arrived at a château in Briare; on the French side were Reynaud, Weygand and de Gaulle. Weygand looked meaningfully at de Gaulle and said that if anyone thought they could do a better job than himself then they should take over. He added, presumably with another glance at de Gaulle, that he would serve them as loyally as his own subordinates had served him.[21] De Gaulle sat next to Churchill at dinner. He spoke little: his relative silence seems to have been one of the qualities that impressed the British contingent. The following day the British party flew back. Interviewed for the French film *The Sorrow and the Pity* in 1969, Eden, the secretary of state for war who had accompanied Churchill, recalled that their plane flew low over the Norman countryside and that 'there is nothing more beautiful in June'. He wondered whether he would ever see it again.

On 13 June, Churchill returned to meet the French leaders at Tours, landing on an airstrip that had just been bombed. De Gaulle had not been told about the meeting but turned up halfway through it. Reynaud asked the British whether they would release the French from the undertaking of March that neither side would seek a separate peace – an undertaking that Reynaud himself had suggested. Churchill remarked that he would 'understand' if the French were forced to sue for peace. In July 1942, de Gaulle said that it was during this meeting that he decided to continue the fight from Britain.[22]

In spite of Reynaud's request for France to be released from her commitments to Britain, he had not taken a final decision about whether France would try to make peace with Germany. It is hard to tell whether Reynaud's apparent shifts of policy as he faced German invasion in May and June 1940 were the result of an indecisive mind or the product of his attempts to persuade the different members of his divided government that he agreed with them all.

Everyone knew that the Battle of France was lost and that the French army could not continue fighting on the mainland. The question was what to do next. Pétain and Weygand did not wish the army to endure the humiliation of defeat. They hoped that an armistice would put the responsibility on the government and (a particularly important consideration for Weygand) that it would leave an army in existence to maintain order in France. The alternative was a 'capitulation', in which French soldiers would lay down their arms but the government would have no dealings with the enemy and might move overseas. Even those who left France to continue the fight did not necessarily oppose the armistice. The philosopher Raymond Aron went to London in June 1940, but he thought that the armistice served the useful purpose of preventing French suffering, until the end of 1942.

Charles de Gaulle was an unqualified opponent of armistice. He had written in 1934 that modern wars did not threaten the existence of countries. These words must have aroused bitter amusement from, say, Czechs who read them in 1940 but they did apply to France. In spite of Louis-Ferdinand Céline's claim that the word 'merde' would be the only remnant of Gallo-Roman civilization after the defeat, there was no real chance that France would cease to exist. German victory meant the loss of Alsace-Lorraine. There might have been other small transfers of territory to Germany or to Italy, which to the fury of even the most defeatist French leaders, had declared war on France on 10 June. France, though, would have been recognizably the same country after a peace treaty with Germany.

Others wanted an armistice because it might spare French lives or the French way of life. They often had a visceral attachment to institutions (especially the army) or to particular parts of France. None of this meant much to de Gaulle. His conception of France was an abstract one. He had little emotional attachment to places. Even his country house at Colombey-les-Deux Églises had been bought for practical reasons rather than because of affection for the landscape or population. De Gaulle's concern was to save an 'idea of France' rather than to protect a piece of land or a group of people. He hated the idea that the greatness of France would be sacrificed to the comfort of the French. He feared in 1940 that the latter would survive as 'hairdressers and cooks.'[23]

In June 1940, de Gaulle invested his hopes in the possibility that the fight might be continued in Brittany. He talked of defensive lines that might be established on the rivers Redon and Vilaine, and of the prospect that a 'Breton redoubt' might encompass the peninsula stretching from Rennes to Brest. This was unconvincing. The battered remnants of the French army would have had to defend a front that extended over 150 kilometres. An army that had swept through the Ardennes Forest was not likely to be stopped by a couple of minor rivers. De Villelume told Reynaud that Brittany would provide a 'beautiful backdrop' for a last stand that would be a 'twilight of the Gods'. He then regretted his sarcasm – thinking that Reynaud, by now in an unpredictable mood, might be attracted by the prospect of a dramatic end.[24]

De Gaulle was sent to investigate the possibilities of defence in Brittany and left Bordeaux on 14 June, reaching Rennes the following morning. Just before he left Bordeaux, in the dining room of a hotel, he saw Pétain for the last time. De Gaulle shook the marshal's hand without a word. The following day he had another last meeting – this time with his mother, who had taken refuge in Brittany. De Gaulle later claimed that his approach to the Breton redoubt was rational because provided easy access to the sea and would therefore make ultimate evacuation to either Britain or North Africa relatively easy. It also fitted with his all-or-nothing approach to the war. The Germans needed to occupy Brittany if they were to mount an assault on Britain and so there was no possibility that this area (unlike the south of France) might be left as somewhere for a French government to operate in after an armistice.

However, the Breton redoubt made sense only if it fitted into a wider allied strategy and provided a place from which contact could be maintained with the British. They were dismissive. Eden reported to the cabinet:

> It had been explained to General de Gaulle that both General Weygand and General Georges did not regard the project as feasible. In any case, it did not cover Nantes, and at least 10 divisions would be required to hold it. These troops were not available. General de Gaulle had been informed that it had been arranged with General Brooke to evacuate from Cherbourg any French troops who would be willing to come away with ours.[25]

Perhaps de Gaulle had already abandoned hope of fighting in Brittany because he boarded a British destroyer bound for Plymouth. Driving all night, he arrived in London on the morning of 16 June. At the Hyde Park Hotel he met André Corbin, the French ambassador, and Jean Monnet, charged with negotiations with the British over armaments. Corbin and Monnet presented him with an extraordinary idea, a *coup de théâtre* which they hoped might restore the French will to fight: France and Britain were to be united into a single country.

The idea was eccentric. One has only to say the words 'subject of the British Crown' to appreciate the difficulties of blurring this status with that of 'citizen of the French republic'. De Gaulle, however, persuaded Churchill to take it seriously, and telephoned Reynaud in Bordeaux to put the proposal to him. Reynaud relayed it to his aides. When he told them he was to be prime minister of the new united country, they said 'you will soon be overthrown by the House of Commons', a remark that reveals much about the political turbulence of wartime France. After this everyone laughed and continued to laugh every time anyone mentioned the proposal.[26]

Probably some of those who pressed for union saw it as a means to promote internationalism – Monnet was the founding spirt behind a united Europe after 1945. He may also have seen union as a means to address the asymmetry of the French and British war effort. The British often presented the relative calm of their country in June 1940 as a sign of their superior character; from the French point of view, it was the product of outrageous hypocrisy. At a time when they were asking the French to fight a last desperate battle on their own soil and then to abandon the mainland of the country to the mercy of Nazi Germany, British politicians were fussing about the rationing of tea or whether to open the grouse shooting season early. The difference between the two ways of thinking was reflected in the terms of the proposal for Franco-British unity. The first draft contained a suggestion, presumably from Monnet, that the British would raise an army of 'several million men'.[27] The war cabinet dismissed this suggestion almost straight away. British ministers, on the other hand, spent time discussing the minutiae of tariff agreements and currency.[28]

Churchill appreciated that the Franco-British union was a 'dramatic announcement ... to keep the French going.'[29] Most importantly the project was a means to try to salvage the French fleet and some French overseas possessions from the catastrophe that was about to engulf France. But by the time the project was announced in the British newspapers on 18 June, Pétain was prime minister of France and had declared his intention to ask about terms of an armistice. Extraordinarily, in the chaos of the French defeat a functionary of the French post office commissioned a design for a stamp that would feature the head of George VI alongside that of Albert Lebrun, the French president. The sketch for this would be the only lasting legacy of the project.

On the evening of 16 June, de Gaulle returned to Bordeaux in a plane the British lent him. It was understood that the aircraft would remain at his disposal in case he needed to get out again. On his arrival late that night he was told Reynaud had resigned and Pétain was now Prime Minister. De Gaulle risked arrest if he stayed in Bordeaux. On the morning of 17 June, he reboarded the British plane and flew to London with Churchill's emissary General Edward Spears. Spears wrote a dramatic account of de Gaulle hiding in the shadows as he sought to dodge arrest until Spears himself pulled him aboard the plane at the last moment. De Gaulle was to become bitterly hostile to Spears. Perhaps because of this, or perhaps because he disliked the British propensity to recount military and political events as though they were part of an adventure story, de Gaulle wrote simply that his departure took place 'without romance or difficulty'.[30]

Romanticism was not the same as mysticism and there was certainly something mystical about de Gaulle's willingness to leave his native country in such circumstances and at a time when his prospects seemed so bleak. De Gaulle was often cruel about Paul Reynaud, but wrote with sympathy of their last meeting on the evening of 16 June: 'it was a tragic spectacle that was offered by this great figure shaken by impossible events'. Perhaps de Gaulle also recalled Reynaud's words spoken a month previously in the different age, when the government had still been in Paris: 'If it takes a miracle to save France then I believe in miracles.'

4

London Calling, 1940

'The Battle of France is over ... the Battle of Britain
is about to begin'
Winston Churchill, 18 June 1940.

'On the 18 June 1940, answering the call of the eternal fatherland,
which had no other recourse to save its honour and its soul,
de Gaulle, alone, almost unknown, had to take up France.'[1]
Charles de Gaulle, 1969

On the evening of 18 June 1940, Charles de Gaulle walked into a BBC studio. One assumes that no English person there was tactless enough to remind him it was the anniversary of the Battle of Waterloo – though he is hardly likely to have forgotten the fact. The engineers asked him to test the microphones and he uttered two words: 'La France.' In his hand he held the draft of a speech. He read it with no apparent nervousness though this was only the second broadcast that he made in his life.* He called on the French to continue the fight against Germany and on soldiers to join him in Britain for this purpose. He concluded by saying that he would speak again the following day.

---

*De Gaulle had spoken on the radio on 21 May 1940, though, in his memoirs, he writes that he had never broadcast before 18 June.

This became the most famous speech in French history. Its anniversary was celebrated by the Free French from 1941 onwards. In 1945, the Socialist leader Léon Blum, recently returned from imprisonment in Germany, wrote that the speech alone would have been enough to earn de Gaulle a place in history 'alongside [George] Washington.'[2] Though 18 June has never been a public holiday in France, partly because de Gaulle chose for it not to be, the date is burnt into French public consciousness. There are streets in almost every large town in France named rue du 18 Juin. In Paris, the Place du 18 Juin, so named since 1951, stands at the intersection of the Boulevard Montparnasse and the rue de Rennes. It is from a window overlooking this square that the assassin aims, and misses, his shot at Charles de Gaulle in Frederick Forsyth's novel *The Day of the Jackal*. Even de Gaulle's enemies marked the anniversary of 18 June. It was an occasion for republican (which in this context meant anti-Gaullist) demonstrations after de Gaulle's return to power in 1958. The best-known leader of student rebellion, Daniel Cohn-Bendit, had been expelled from France and was in London on 18 June 1968 – the British Foreign Office seriously feared he might try to broadcast an 'appeal' to France over the BBC.[3]

De Gaulle's speech was almost not delivered. Speaking on the radio on 17 June, Pétain had told the French army they must cease fighting and that he had contacted the enemy to enquire about the terms on which they might 'end hostilities'. No one was sure what these words would mean and uncertainty was particularly marked in the days between Pétain's speech and the signature of an armistice between France and Germany on 22 June. Some in Britain hoped that at least some of the French might return to the fight when the Germans presented them with the terms for the armistice or when it became clear how ruthlessly the Germans would exploit those terms. Maxime Weygand, Minister of War and probably the most important member of the Pétain government, was known to be anti-German. Though he had supported an armistice, it was not clear how far he would seek to subvert it. Just a few weeks earlier, he had called for French soldiers to 'defend the honour of their flags by disassociating themselves totally from the Belgian armistice'.[4]

Many Frenchmen assumed that an armistice with the Germans in mainland France did not preclude a continuation of the struggle from overseas. For a time, it seemed likely that the President and the members of the National Assembly would move to North Africa, where they might form an alternative government. A small group of politicians – notably Georges Mandel, until recently Minister of the Interior – sailed to Morocco aboard the *Massilia*. They did so with official authorization, but by the time they arrived the political currents had changed direction again and they were now blamed for having deserted their country.

Because of these uncertainties, the British War Cabinet decided on the afternoon of 18 June that de Gaulle should not be allowed to speak on the BBC. Churchill had not been present at the meeting of the War Cabinet but Edward Spears, the member of parliament who had accompanied de Gaulle from France, persuaded the Prime Minister that it would be a mistake to prevent de Gaulle from broadcasting. With Churchill's authority, Spears approached individual ministers in the afternoon and convinced enough of them to change their minds. Even then the British authorities were uncertain about letting de Gaulle use the BBC to address France. Despite the promise that he made at the end of his speech of 18 June, de Gaulle was not allowed to broadcast again until 22 June.

The speech of 18 June was improvised at short notice. Recollections of simple matters, such as what time it was delivered or who was present during its delivery, varied. In fact, it seems to have been recorded around six and broadcast at ten o'clock British time, though the recording was not kept. Later published versions were slightly different from the words that de Gaulle actually spoke and the most reliable version was a transcription (translated into German) made by Swiss radio.

Who heard de Gaulle's broadcast? There was no particular reason why anyone in France should have been listening to the BBC on 18 June. More than a quarter of the population were absent from their homes, and, therefore, away from their radio, because they were in the armed forces, in the holding camps to which the Germans had assigned almost 2 million prisoners of war before shipping them to Germany or because they had taken to the road to escape the advancing German armies.

Many people – including some, such as Raymond Aron or René Cassin, who would soon reach London – found out about the speech without having heard it.[5] Claude Hettier de Boislambert had already reached England and was on a train from Falmouth to London on the evening of 18 June when a woman in his carriage told him that de Gaulle, whom he knew, was there.[6] Some read versions in French newspapers. On 18 June, de Gaulle's mother, his brother, Henri, and his niece Geneviève were heading west towards what some still imagined would be the Breton redoubt. The family did not listen to the BBC.[7] In the village of Locminé in the Morbihan, a priest emerged from his presbytery and began to talk about a speech that he had heard on the BBC, but he could not remember exactly what had been said. An officer asked if he had caught the name of the speaker and the priest replied: 'I think it was someone called de Gaulle.'[8]

Most French people knew nothing about de Gaulle. Maurice Garçon was a Paris lawyer with good political connections – he was to be Georges Mandel's defence counsel when the former minister was put on trial by the Vichy government. Garçon had never heard of de Gaulle and did not even know how to spell his name. He was told about de Gaulle's broadcasts of June 1940 (he believed, wrongly, that de Gaulle was broadcasting every evening) but did not listen to them himself. He dismissed the general as a 'tinpot dictator' and regarded as mad the suggestion that French people should move to London mad.[9]

De Gaulle said in his broadcast of 18 June 'the flame of French resistance must not and will not go out.' But he was not talking about resistance as it would be conceived in, say, 1943 when partisans in mainland France fought against both the Germans and the agents of the Pétain government. De Gaulle's call was addressed to soldiers and armaments workers and he asked them to join him and come to Britain. As for Pétain, de Gaulle did not mention him by name until 26 June. Many thought there was no contradiction between supporting Pétain in France and supporting armed resistance to Germany abroad. Emmanuel Berl heard, and approved of, de Gaulle's speech but this did not stop him from writing speeches for Pétain.[10] It was he who coined the most memorable phrase the Marshal ever uttered 'the soil does not lie'.

De Gaulle's first speech on the BBC was overshadowed by another event that seemedmore important at the time. It was on 18 June that Winston Churchill delivered the most historically resonant speech of his life. It finished:

What General Weygand called the Battle of France is over. I expect that the Battle of Britain is about to begin. Upon this battle depends the survival of Christian civilization. Upon it depends our own British life, and the long continuity of our institutions and our Empire. The whole fury and might of the enemy must very soon be turned on us. Hitler knows that he will have to break us in this Island or lose the war. If we can stand up to him, all Europe may be free and the life of the world may move forward into broad, sunlit uplands. But if we fail, then the whole world, including the United States, including all that we have known and cared for, will sink into the abyss of a new Dark Age made more sinister, and perhaps more protracted, by the lights of perverted science. Let us therefore brace ourselves to our duties, and so bear ourselves that, if the British

Empire and its Commonwealth last for a thousand years, men will still say, 'This was their finest hour.'

Unlike de Gaulle, Churchill was an experienced broadcaster – though some of his most famous wartime speeches were made in parliament and not, therefore, broadcast.* He had been speaking on the radio for more or less as long as radio had existed. Churchill's voice was strange. The residue of a lisp, a propensity to slur his words and his growling tones made some listeners assume, usually without justification, that he was drunk. His message, though, was perfectly comprehensible. He expressed himself in short words of Anglo-Saxon origin. Foreign terms – such as 'Narzi' – were mispronounced in the way that most English people would have mispronounced them. Churchill's appeal sprang partly from the fact that he sounded so different from the kind of people who were usually heard on the BBC. George Orwell wrote of Churchill: 'too old to have acquired the modern "educated" accent he speaks with the Edwardian upper-class twang which to the average man's ear sounds like cockney.'[11] In 1940, a large proportion of the British population listened to Churchill's speeches. The telephone exchange in Southampton once did not have to field a single call during the fifteen minutes that Churchill was speaking.[12]

The fact that Churchill commanded such attention did not mean that he commanded unqualified approval. Outright denunciation was rare, and probably made rarer by the fact that a few people who did talk in such terms were sent to prison. But many expressed reservations. Brenda Cobbett, a masseuse from Surrey, said: 'I wish I didn't remember so clearly the intervention in Russia and the general strike of 1926.'[13] Churchill's patrician entourage often imagined a gulf

---

*In January 1942 Churchill asked that in exceptional circumstances his parliamentary speeches might be recorded for later broadcast. He told the House of Commons: 'I am entirely in the hands of the House. If they do not feel they can give me easement on this occasion as an experiment, I shall not take it amiss in any way, and shall do my best over the broadcast that evening to repeat what I have said.' His request was refused.

between themselves and a large part of the population. John Colville, Churchill's private secretary, noted on 1 August 1940: 'it is already being said in the provinces that Churchill is "played out".'[14] One assumes that 'provinces' in this context meant industrial cities rather than the places that Colville went to hunt or shoot. There were, though, plenty of people from his own class who had doubts. Colville himself had previously been private secretary to Neville Chamberlain, to whom he remained loyal, until the new Prime Minister won him over. David Fraser was nineteen years old in the summer of 1940. An Etonian from an aristocratic family, he joined the Grenadier Guards and eventually rose to be a general. In his memoirs, he wrote: 'Churchill's great speeches ... acted as a memorable tonic. His effect on England was magical, although to my father (who had known him well in the First World War) and that generation there were always question marks over Churchill's judgement.'[15]

In the summer of 1940, it would have seemed unimaginable that de Gaulle would one day be considered as important as Churchill. Nothing is more deceptive than the title *général* de Gaulle. De Gaulle was a *général de brigade*. But the rank of brigadier general did not exist in the British army. It had briefly been used during the First World War to align British ranks with French ones. For the British, de Gaulle was a brigadier. He held the same rank as the 600 brigade commanders in the British and colonial armies during the First World War,[16] many of whom were younger than General de Gaulle was in 1940 and some of whom were younger than Captain de Gaulle had been in 1918. Churchill, still smarting that he had not commanded a brigade in France in 1916, referred to de Gaulle as 'this lanky brigadier'.

There were three other French *généraux de brigade* – Antoine Béthouart, Pierre-Paul Lelong and Jean Charbonneau – in Britain on 18 June 1940.[17] They were anti-German and the British hoped that they might lead French troops against Germany. Some British soldiers thought more highly of them (they described Charbonneau as a 'good chap') than of de Gaulle. As it turned out, all three returned to France – Béthouart, and Lelong joined de Gaulle later in the war; Charbonneau never did so. He later alluded to the luke-warm support the British had given the Free French in 1940 and the determination of de Gaulle, but also hinted at the awkwardness of de Gaulle's personality.[18]

De Gaulle's rank mattered because British officials assumed that his significance derived from his military abilities. One wrote that de Gaulle:

> [H]as so far shown little aptitude for political art, whatever his merits as a soldier. His character gains the respect of those Frenchmen with whom he comes into personal touch, but lacks charm and makes no popular appeal. It seems certain that before he can grow in stature in the eyes of his countrymen he must achieve some significant personal military success.[19]

Desmond Morton, the Prime Minister's intelligence adviser, thought that de Gaulle would play a military role, probably a subordinate one. He wrote to Churchill: 'I still wonder if we could find a potential Napoleon among the French Armed Forces. I doubt if de Gaulle is more than a Marshal Murat.'[20] As late as 1942, Alan Lascelles, the King's secretary, wrote of de Gaulle 'What he ought to be doing is commanding an Armoured Division in Egypt.'[21] Edward Spears wrote later: 'When he [de Gaulle] first arrived he had no other idea than to go on fighting under a higher-ranking soldier than himself. The military hierarchy was part of his bone structure.'[22]

Spears could not have been more wrong. Even before his flight to London, de Gaulle had repeatedly sought to circumvent officers more senior than himself. By 1940, he did not think of himself primarily as a soldier. Though he used his military title, rank meant little to him. When General Catroux, who had been governor of Indochina and who was senior to de Gaulle in rank, rallied to the Free French, de Gaulle accepted this as a sign that 'De Gaulle was ... outside the scale of ranks and endowed with a power that had nothing to do with hierarchy.'[23] When the socialist Jules Moch met de Gaulle in April 1942, he told him that his comrades in the French resistance admired him 'in spite of the fact that you are a general not because of it.' De Gaulle replied: 'I am above the hierarchy of the army'.[24]

The comparison between de Gaulle and Churchill is revealing. While Churchill had been a civilian for forty years but could not resist interfering in military matters, harassed his generals and made detailed suggestions about strategy, de Gaulle never wanted to lead men in battle after the defeat of France. He accompanied troops to Dakar in West Africa in September 1940 (see chapter 5) but did so in the hope that French forces there would abandon their allegiance to Vichy without a fight. De Gaulle's son considered incongruous the idea that his father might have taken to the battlefield after June 1940 'in boots and steel helmet'.[25] De Gaulle quarrelled with senior officers when they threatened to usurp his political authority, but he gave them a free hand in battle.

The difference between Churchill and de Gaulle was partly rooted in different military circumstances. Churchill could not be detached about the performance of commanders because, until at least 1942, the survival of his country depended on them. De Gaulle, on the other hand, knew that the victories and defeats of the Free French, until at least 1943, had a mainly symbolic importance. But there was more to it than this. De Gaulle defined a leader as someone who left details to other people and military matters were details to him. Though he would not have liked the word 'politician', de Gaulle had effectively become one in 1940. General Alan Brooke met him on 19 August 1940. His verdict that de Gaulle wanted to be a 'dictator' was, as it turned out, unfair, but he captured the relative indifference with which the Frenchman (junior to Brooke in military terms) regarded the conduct of war: 'in all discussions he assumed that the problem of the liberation of France was mine, while he concentrated on how he would govern it, as dictator, as soon as it was liberated.'[26]

The problem for de Gaulle was that the British were not remotely close to admitting that he was the symbol of French political legitimacy. On 28 June, Churchill recognised de Gaulle as the leader of 'the Free French wherever they may be', but this recognition was the result of failure rather than success. It was granted to de Gaulle as an individual because attempts to create more formal structures to lead the Free French had come to nothing. Other prominent Frenchmen in London were reluctant to join a committee under the aegis of a relatively junior officer. The recognition that Churchill afforded to de Gaulle was limited and ambiguous. The term 'Free French' did not mean much at this stage. Some European countries – Poland, Czechoslovakia, Holland, Norway, Belgium, Luxembourg – had governments in exile in London in 1940. This was because ministers (in some cases monarchs) from these countries had taken refuge in Britain. No one recognised de Gaulle as a head of government until 1944.

And there was still a government in France. Marshal Pétain's appointment as Prime Minister was the result of French political processes. It was a response to German military success but owed little to direct German intervention. French democracy was suspended on 10 July 1940 when Marshall Pétain was granted full powers. But since the National Assembly, meeting in the Grand Casino at Vichy, had voted by an overwhelming majority to award him those powers, the suspension of democracy had itself been underwritten by a democratic institution. The British did not like the Pétain government (and liked it less and less as time went on) but they accepted that it was the legal government of France and expressed this opinion as late as September 1941:

His Majesty's Government are unable to recognize General de Gaulle as the head of the Government of France. Neither His Majesty's Government nor any other government has challenged the legality of the French government at Vichy and most countries, including the United States and the South American countries, maintain diplomatic representatives at Vichy. There is at present no legal basis for the recognition of an alternative French Government, and His Majesty's Government are unable to assess how far General de Gaulle may be considered representative of the French people.[27]

Vichy was recognised by the Vatican and the Soviet Union as well as the United States, which kept an embassy of Vichy until November 1942, after they had been at war with Germany for almost a year. In May 1942, Eden acceded to an American request that he should express public approval for the retention of diplomatic relations between the United States and Vichy.[28] Two Commonwealth countries – Canada and South Africa – kept ambassadors at Vichy until 1942, in part because the British government wished to keep channels of communication open.[29] The British ambassador and his staff left Bordeaux on 24 June but the French embassy in London remained open until 8 July. De Gaulle was informed of the first sanctions the Vichy government had imposed on him (he was sentenced to four years imprisonment on 4 July) by the Marquis de Castellane who had become the French chargé d'affaires and whose post-war career did not benefit his performance of this duty. Britain and France came close to war in early July 1940 after the British sank part of the French fleet (see chapter 5), but war was not declared and British consuls and military liaison officers remained in French territories even after this date. This led to a surreal episode when a British consul in French-ruled Dakar was asked to ascertain the damage British naval guns had done to a French ship moored there.[30]

De Gaulle claimed that Vichy was subservient to the Germans, but this was only partly true. By definition, an armistice involves two sovereign governments and, since Vichy never signed a peace treaty with Germany, technically speaking, the two countries remained at war. The Pétain government gave up some of its territory and accepted a limit on the number of soldiers it could maintain in the army in mainland France. Vichy, though, was not just a German instrument. It controlled the southern part of France – the so-called 'free zone' – until the Germans occupied the whole of mainland France in November 1942. Pétain sacked Pierre Laval – the most pro-German of his ministers – on 13 December 1940. The Germans intervened to rescue Laval from house arrest, but he then moved to Paris. He did not return to the Vichy government until April 1942. Some of the regime's most distasteful policies – including its early anti-semitic measures – were French initiatives not German impositions. The police and law courts in the non-occupied zone functioned with a degree of independence: some Frenchmen convicted of spying for the Germans were executed. The military tribunal that sentenced de Gaulle to death *in absentia* in August 1940 (thus revising the original sentence of imprisonment) was not acting under German orders. General Frère, who presided over it, later joined the resistance and died in German captivity.[31]

At first, the British hoped that Pétain himself and most of his government might move to North Africa and resume the war with Germany. Failing this, they thought it possible that Pétain might give tacit approval to initiatives by other people. Churchill wrote in July 1940:

> I want to promote a kind of collusive conspiracy in the Vichy Government whereby certain members of that Government, perhaps with the consent of some of those who remain, will levant to North Africa in order to make a better bargain for France from the North African shore and from a position of independence.[32]

The British also sought to contact individual French leaders in North Africa. On 25 June, Duff Cooper, accompanied by General Lord Gort, went to Rabat in a seaplane to meet General Charles

Noguès, the French resident general in Morocco, whom they hoped might fight on after the armistice. Cooper discovered that the French politicians who had travelled from France on the *Massilia* were in Casablanca. He was keen to meet Mandel but was refused permission to do so.[33] Cooper thought that a military intervention in North Africa might bring some senior generals over to the British side – though the chiefs of staff refused to authorise such an intervention. His report did not mention de Gaulle.[34]

Mandel was particularly important to Churchill. The two had known each other since the First World War, when the former had been deputy to Clemenceau. A man of great courage and patriotism, he was, according to Churchill, 'the only one [of the leaders in 1940] who never swerved'. He was imprisoned by the Vichy government and ultimately killed by collaborationists – though the British were still considering projects to rescue him as late as July 1942.[35]

De Gaulle claimed that he would have been willing to place himself under the authority of some more senior figure. He contacted Noguès, Weygand and Marcel Peyrouton, the French resident in Tunis who was soon to become Vichy's Minister of the Interior. There was duplicity in de Gaulle's actions. He could hardly have expected a cordial reply from Weygand, whom he had recently sought to have dismissed as Commander-in-Chief. In any case, none of these men joined the fight against Germany; all served Vichy until the end of 1942.

Roland de Margerie, the diplomat who had accompanied de Gaulle on his first visit to London on 9 June, illustrated the complexity of Anglo-French relations in the summer of 1940. He was opposed to the armistice and travelled to London in late June. He met de Gaulle who made no effort to recruit him. Churchill did not encourage him to join de Gaulle either. De Margerie believed that this was because Churchill assumed that de Gaulle was simply a soldier and would therefore have no need for diplomats. On 26 July, de Margerie was summoned for a late-night meeting with Churchill, who suggested that it might be possible to form an alliance with Pierre Laval, who was Pétain's deputy and regarded as the leader of the pro-German faction in the Vichy government. Churchill said: 'I will do business with the devil himself if it is useful to beat Hitler.' De Margerie regarded the suggestion as mad. He was relieved to find that Churchill's advisers shared his view and that Churchill himself had abandoned his project the following day. De Margerie suggested a list of alternative French politicians and generals the British might contact.[36]

Eventually de Margerie decided that it was his duty to serve the Vichy government and accepted a posting as French consul in Shanghai. In April 1941, the British managed to convey a message from de Gaulle to de Margerie. The last sentence of the message, in which de Gaulle urged his 'dear friend' to join him, did not get through, but de Margerie understood the gist and replied:

> Your message moves me deeply. It puts a question which I debated within myself at length last year. Like you I see no future for France except in a German defeat, and, consequently, in England's victory. But I think that I can more usefully serve this cause here in post which I occupy and by methods other than yours … may we meet soon in a liberated France which each of us will have served according to his conscience.[37]

De Gaulle and de Margerie did not meet again until 1958.

At first, few rallied to de Gaulle. By July, a total of just over 6,000 French people (overwhelmingly men) had joined Gaullist forces in Britain and a further 800 had done so in other parts of the world. By September, the number in Britain had risen to a little over 7,000 and that elsewhere to over 5,000. Those who came to London took a risk. Many left their families behind. One returned in 1944 to find that his two daughters had been raised by his own parents in a house with a bust of Pétain on the mantelpiece.[38] Some assumed false names in the hope that this would spare their relatives from reprisals. André Dewavrin took the name Passy, after a Paris metro station. Philippe de Hauteclocque was a captain when he left France in 1940; he was a general when he led Free French forces back into Paris in 1944 – though he had now adopted the more plebeian name of Leclerc.

Those Frenchmen who joined de Gaulle were younger and better educated than most of their compatriots.[39] The quintessential recruit was a man from a bourgeois family who had not yet acquired the kind of professional or family obligations that might keep him in France.* They were not generally left-wing but they were often rebellious. This did not always make them good soldiers. Daniel Cordier arrived in England in June 1940. He seemed like a character from a novel by Roger Peyrefitte or a Louis Malle film. He was twenty. His romantic ideas of military life had not been tempered by experience of the army. He had no practical skills. He had been expelled from more than one school. He had, at that stage, right-wing and anti-semitic opinions that, as he later recognised, might have taken him into the collaborationist Milice if he had stayed in France. He was much given to romantic fantasy and passionate attachments to people of both sexes. As it turned out, Cordier was heroically brave and, even more importantly, an efficient administrator. In 1940, he must have seemed a recruiting sergeant's nightmare.

The Free French were less significant to the British war effort than the Poles or the Czechs, both of whom provided what Britain needed most at the time: fighter pilots. There were 186 French pilots in Britain by September 1941 –compared with 546 Czechs and 1,800 Poles. A significant minority of those who joined de Gaulle were in

*In 1958, de Gaulle asked Anthony Montague Browne, Churchill's private secretary, what he would have done if he had been French in 1940. Montague Browne, who had been a gallant pilot with the Royal Air Force, replied that if he had been seventeen he would have joined de Gaulle in London but if he had been in his forties he would have supported Pétain. 'C'est une réponse,' said de Gaulle.

fact Czechs, Poles, Spanish republicans or even Germans. Some came after joining the French Foreign Legion or having otherwise passed through French forces. Some simply admired France. Rolf Weinberg was a Jew from Westphalia who had been washed up by the tides of war in Montevideo. He managed to get to England and joined the Free French forces. He recalled his first meeting with de Gaulle in terms that, like many such accounts, may owe something to retrospective exaggeration. De Gaulle asked him only one question: 'Why do you want to join?' Weinberg replied: 'I have lost everything dear to me, I had to run. I think the same happened to you.' De Gaulle shook his hand and said: 'I trust you.'[40]

De Gaulle was allowed to approach French servicemen in Britain, but the British military authorities were ill at ease encouraging men to disobey their own commanders and were often sceptical about the military value of the French. Churchill complained that they gave many potential volunteers a discouraging reception.[41]

The British wanted to avoid offending officers who remained loyal to the Pétain government. The balancing act was particularly delicate in the Middle East. French soldiers came over from the Levant (controlled by the French) to Palestine (controlled by the British). On 2 July 1940, at the meeting at which it was decided to seize or destroy much of the French fleet, the War Cabinet ordered that the following message be broadcast on the radio from Palestine

> The British have undertaken not to encourage desertion from the French Army. At the same time, it is false that volunteers whose honour forbids them to obey the dictates of the Bordeaux Government are not welcome, or that they are returned to the French authorities. No volunteers have been or will be turned back.[42]

De Gaulle arrived in London with four shirts, a spare pair of trousers and a photograph of his family.[43] He had 100,000 francs (about

2,000 dollars at the time), which he had been given from secret service funds, and the keys to a two-bedroom flat at 8 Seamore Grove in Mayfair. His wife and children were extracted from France on a British ship. His mother died in July 1940. His disabled brother was carried across the Swiss frontier in 1942. Another brother and his niece were left to the mercy of the Pétain government and eventually the Germans.

Everything else was lost. On 22 June de Gaulle's promotion to *général de brigade* was revoked, on 23 June he was forcibly retired from the army. On 8 December, he was stripped of his French nationality. De Gaulle's political survival in London hung by some frail threads. One was the personal support of the Prime Minister, who admired de Gaulle's courage and paid less attention to questions of formal diplomatic status than did his more orthodox colleagues. But Churchill could be a dangerous associate. His long attachment to France meant that there were many Frenchmen whom he knew well, and who were more important than de Gaulle in his eyes. Furthermore, Churchill believed in the loyalty others owed him more than he believed in the loyalty he owed them – which partly accounts for the savagery with which he sometimes later turned on de Gaulle.

De Gaulle had the support of some Francophile British officials and politicians. These included the Minister of Information, Duff Cooper, and his deputy, Harold Nicolson (both former diplomats who had been elected to parliament), Edward Spears (who acted as liaison officer between Churchill and de Gaulle). Robert Vansittart (the former Permanent Secretary to the Foreign Office who, for a time, chaired a committee on European resistance); and Anthony Eden (Secretary of State for War until December 1940 and then Foreign Secretary).

For these men the fall of France was like the amputation of a limb. They continued to feel the sensations associated with it even when contact had been severed. They had spent some of their formative years training for diplomatic careers at language schools of the kind parodied by Terence Rattigan in *French Without Tears* (1936). Their lives were closely intertwined with those of the French ruling classes. In 1928, Nicolson had employed Maurice Couve de Murville (who was later to become de Gaulle's last Prime Minister) to act as a tutor to his sons during their holidays from Eton.[44] These men cast long shadows in the history books because they left striking memoirs or diaries. Apart from Eden, however, none of them was as influential as they would have liked to have been and all of them often seemed eccentric and inconsistent to people who exercised greater authority. Vansittart had been eased out of his position as head of the Foreign Office in 1937.

De Gaulle was isolated and uncomfortable. Other Frenchmen found consolations in London. Jean Monnet had been involved in Anglo-French negotiations since the First World War. Raymond Aron picked up a working knowledge of English within a few weeks. Soon he was dining at the Reform Club with the economist Lionel Robbins. Frenchmen took solace in the company of British women – especially at a time when some British men were absent. Lucien Neuwirth, who, as a Gaullist member of parliament, sponsored the legalization of contraception in France, had his first experience of birth control when a cheerful and drunken Irish female soldier took him to Hyde Park, where she handed him a condom and relieved him of his virginity.[45]

De Gaulle had no English friends and no English mistress. Even during their bitterly anti-Gaullist phase in the early 1960s, British diplomats did not believe the rumour that he was going mad as a result of syphilis caught in London.[46] French prostitutes in London do seem to have admired de Gaulle, though, and Jean Oberlé claimed that he met one who kept a photograph of the general above her bed.[47] De Gaulle took no pleasure in the city. At first he lived in unfashionable suburbs – Petts Wood and Berkhamsted. Finally he acquired a house in Hampstead. Perhaps he liked it because the proximity of the Heath made him feel that he was not in a city at all, but he never seemed at home even here.

By contrast, in a strange way, the summer of 1940 was the happiest time of Churchill's life. His child-like quality was never more evident than when he assumed the heaviest responsibilities. He often wore an overall or 'siren suit', which almost everyone around him referred to as his rompers. He took afternoon naps and seems, however grave the decisions he had taken, would fall asleep almost as soon as his head touched the pillow. He ate and drank as much as he wanted. He threw tantrums when he did not get his way. He enjoyed childish films – Donald Duck was briefly interrupted in 1943 by the announcement that Italy had requested an armistice. Churchill had a child's energy and optimism. The petulant question 'why not?' was a useful one to ask of generals and officials – provided that those on the receiving end of the question had the patience and determination to fight their corner when necessary.

De Gaulle wrote of Albert Lebrun, the last President of the Third Republic: 'As a head of state he lacked two things – being a head and having a state.' No one could deny that Churchill was a head (albeit not a head of state in constitutional terms). On arrival in Downing Street he made it clear that important decisions were to be authorised by him. This might have made for an impossibly rigid style of government but for the fact that Churchill took decisions quickly. In early August, he sent a note on the subject of 'brevity':

> The aim should be Reports which set out the main points in a series of short, crisp paragraphs ... Let us have an end of such phrases as these: ... 'Consideration should be given to the possibility of carrying into effect' ... Let us not shrink from using the short expressive phrase, even if it is conversational.[48]

Brevity was not always a virtue that Churchill himself practised but in the summer of 1940 Cabinet business was conducted at a brisk pace. Churchill sent back documents with a phrase he had printed on stickers that could be deployed like the seal of a medieval king: 'ACTION THIS DAY'.

To take the second part of de Gaulle's jibe about Albert Lebrun, Churchill was not merely a 'head' but he also had a state. The monarchy, the armed forces, the civil service, parliament and the Cabinet all worked in 1940. French political scientists often say that the British have no conception of the state. It would be fairer to say that the British take elements of the state so much for granted that they are barely conscious of their existence. As the last Prime Minister of France before the defeat, Paul Reynaud could not trust his military commanders or his officials. Civil servants who were brought into the last government of the Third Republic then conspired to overthrow it. One of these men, Yves Bouthillier, was later to claim that Vichy represented 'the triumph of administration over politics'. This would have seemed a meaningless remark to British civil servants. They had political views. They were mostly Conservatives and mostly supporters of Chamberlain against Churchill. But none thought they had the right to undermine the legitimate government once it was constituted. Men who wrote in their private diaries to express their bitterness at Chamberlain's overthrow then set themselves to being loyal servants of Churchill's government.

One person above all others helped Churchill: Chamberlain. Chamberlain's association with the failure of British military and diplomatic policy since the mid 1930s reinforced the sense that every option other than those advanced by Churchill had been explored. Churchill was the anti-Chamberlain – flamboyant and vigorous where Chamberlain (known to his enemies as 'the coroner') was cold and formal. Chamberlain also provided Churchill with direct support. Discredited in the country, Chamberlain still commanded loyalty in the parliamentary Conservative Party. He might have made life awkward for his successor if he had set himself up as a leader of opposition. As it was, Chamberlain kept the formal leadership of the Conservative Party when Churchill became Prime Minister. He agreed to serve as minister without portfolio in the Cabinet. In fact, he did exactly what Reynaud had hoped Marshal Pétain would do when he appointed him as deputy Prime Minister:

lent his prestige to the government without seeking to interfere in its decisions or challenge its authority. Furthermore, Chamberlain was sick with cancer and died in November 1940. Churchill's gracious eulogy in the House of Commons did more for Churchill's reputation than it did for that of Chamberlain.

The relative unity of the British political classes was marked in comparison to France. French politics was sucked into a whirlpool of recrimination in 1940. Politicians blamed for having started and/or lost the war were imprisoned, tried and eventually murdered in some cases. On the other hand, in Britain there were few reproaches. Churchill said he would feel no bitterness if those who could not support his policy left the government. Those who stayed were not blamed for what they had done in the past. In his speech to parliament on 18 June 1940, Churchill stated there should be no inquest into mistakes that his predecessors might have made:

> Of this I am quite sure, that if we open a quarrel between the past and the present, we shall find that we have lost the future. Therefore, I cannot accept the drawing of any distinctions between Members of the present Government .... Its members are going to stand together, and, subject to the authority of the House of Commons, we are going to govern the country and fight the war.

The politician whose behaviour was most vulnerable to criticism in the summer of 1940 was R. A. Butler, Under-Secretary of State at the Foreign Office, who had made unwise remarks to a Swedish diplomat about the possibility of a negotiated peace. His punishment was to endure some mockery from Churchill – who compared his contribution to the war effort unfavourably to that of the Downing Street cat. Butler stayed in government and was appointed to the Cabinet in 1941 as President of the Board of Education. He became an important architect of post-war Conservatism.

Churchill's buoyancy could not disguise the desperate state of the country he ruled. Fighting spirit was part of Churchill's nature but it had to be inculcated into those around him. Churchill sent a famous memorandum (Harold Macmillan kept a framed copy) in which he wrote:

> In these dark days the Prime Minister would be grateful if all his colleagues in the Government, as well as high officials, would maintain a high morale in their circles; not minimizing the gravity of events but showing confidence in our ability and inflexible resolve to continue the war till we have broken the will of the enemy to bring all Europe under his domination.

This was a moment of terrible peril for Britain. Its most important ally had been crushed. German forces were now twenty miles away from the Kent coast, which meant that British cities were more vulnerable to the threat of German bombers. Churchill addressed the House of Commons in secret session on 20 June 1940. In his notes he wrote: 'if we get through the next three months, we get through the next three years'.[49] But nobody was sure that Britain would get through the next three months.

It has become fashionable among historians in recent years to suggest that there was no serious prospect of German invasion of Britain in 1940. It is hard to say whether this was true. Crossing the sea in the face of British naval power would have been a difficult operation but driving tanks through the Ardennes Forest also seemed difficult, until the Wehrmacht did it. The Admiralty pointed out in July 1940 that the 'Hitler regime ... [has shown] complete disregard of losses to be expected if this will facilitate the attainment of the objects. We cannot therefore assume that ... past military rules as to what is practicable and what is impracticable will be allowed to govern the action undertaken.'[50] Many British people feared invasion. Alan Brooke, commander of United Kingdom Home Forces, wrote several diary entries in the summer of 1940 on days when he thought invasion 'imminent'. On 3 October, he noted: 'Still no invasion … I am beginning to think the Germans may after all not attempt it. And yet! I have the horrid thought that he may still bring off some surprise on us.'[51] He referred to rumours of imminent invasion twice again in October,[52] and once in January 1941.[53]

At least some of the time, Churchill professed not to believe in the possibility of invasion. He insisted soldiers and tanks should be sent from Britain to fight the Italians in the Middle East in the summer of 1940. His sanguine declarations should be put in context. There were times, though, when Churchill anticipated fighting on British soil.[54] He was not just using a figure of speech when he told the Cabinet that they should not let 'our island story' end until they were 'choking in their own blood'. He knew there was a prospect that he would die violently within months of taking office. Tidying her husband's possessions after the war, Clarissa Avon (Churchill's niece and Anthony Eden's second wife) found an ugly, discoloured lozenge. He told her it was a cyanide pill: 'Both he and Winston had been given them in the war in case they were captured.'[55]

Even if Britain avoided defeat and invasion in 1940, it was unclear what the alternative might be. Churchill talked of 'victory' but what would victory look like? It was not until early 1943 that Britain and her allies fixed their aim as being the 'unconditional surrender' of the Axis powers. The notion that the Allied armies would march on Berlin, hang the surviving Nazi leaders and then rebuild Germany according to their own design would have seemed fantastical in 1940. In July 1941, Eden, then Foreign Secretary, gave a speech at Leeds football ground in which he said more or less spontaneously that the government would never 'on any subject or at any time treat with Hitler'. The Cabinet approved his statement retrospectively, though it turned out that they had not previously discussed the matter.[56]

Privately Churchill seems to have envisaged three possibilities. The best was that the Germans would suffer such military reverses that Hitler would be overthrown and Britain might conclude a peace with his successors — presumably authoritarian, but not Nazi, army officers. Churchill had told French leaders at their meeting on 11 June. 'In spite of everything, let us maintain an absolute confidence that Hitler will fall, even though we do not know how it will happen.' Reynaud replied: 'That is what one calls an act of faith.'[57] The second possibility was that Britain might conclude a deal with its enemies or at least with some of them. Churchill had said in late May that he would be happy 'if we'd get out of this jam by giving up Malta and Gibraltar and some African colonies'. However, he did not think that such an offer was likely to be accepted. The third possibility was defeat. At least when he was trying to scare the Americans into giving more aid, Churchill allowed for the prospect that Britain might be invaded and that there might be a British Vichy. He wrote to Roosevelt: 'If members of the present Administration were finished and others came in to parley amid the ruins ... I could not answer for my successors, who in utter despair and helplessness might well have to accommodate themselves to the German will.'[58] De Gaulle was brutal in his view of what would happen if British forces were driven from the mainland. He anticipated that the government would take refuge in Canada: 'The well-informed murmured the names of politicians, bishops, writers and businessmen who, in this eventuality, would come to terms with the Germans to assure, under their aegis, the administration of the country.'[59]

The gravity of Britain's military situation in the summer of 1940 raises some questions. Why were the governing classes so calm? Why were there so few calls for negotiation with Germany? Why, in short, was Britain in the summer of 1940 so different from France? A simple answer is that there was a world of difference between the prospect of invasion, which pulled Britain together, and the fact of invasion, which pulled France apart. It is worth comparing the life of Paul Reynaud in the last few weeks of his premiership with that of Churchill in the first few weeks of his. Reynaud faced enemy troops advancing across France as his own government retreated. This meant that he often had difficulty communicating with his own subordinates and foreign allies. Reynaud's war ended with a crash on 28 June. He was travelling with his mistress Madame de Portes towards the Spanish frontier in the hope of crossing to North Africa. Their car hit a tree and de Portes was killed by a suitcase that hit her in the back of the neck.

By contrast, Churchill lived in 10 Downing Street during this period. An alternative base for the Cabinet was established in North London, in case bombing should make life in central London impossible. Ministers went there once, had a 'convivial lunch' and returned to Westminster. Churchill often spent the weekend at Chequers (the official country residence of the Prime Minister) or at Ditchley Park (another country house that was deemed safer) and sometimes went to inspect troops in other parts of the country. Otherwise he stayed put. The time between his return from France on 13 June 1940 and his departure (for a secret meeting with Roosevelt in Newfoundland) on 4 August 1941 was the longest period in his adult life that Churchill had not left Britain. Churchill's household – his wife, his servants and Nelson, the cat who had come from the Admiralty and whom Churchill occasionally held personally responsible for the failings of the Royal Navy – was secure. Apart from the civil servants who surrounded him, he had a group of efficient secretaries – accustomed to his odd hours and colourful oaths – as well as the Downing Street telephonists, famous for their ability to reach almost anyone in the country at short notice.

The summer during which Churchill established himself in power had an air of curious unreality. On the one hand, the country was threatened with the terrible prospect of invasion, defeat and occupation; on the other hand, the immediate consequences of the war were almost trivial. De Gaulle had a sharp appreciation of the paradoxes of the British mood. He commented on the 'vibrant atmosphere' as everyone waited 'at any moment' for the German offensive. It was, he said, 'a truly admirable spectacle' to see 'every English person behaving as if the salvation of the country depended on them'. He added drily: 'This universal feeling of responsibility seemed all the more moving because, in reality, it was on air power that everything depended.'[60] Once the soldiers were home from France, there was no land front on which the British were fighting the Germans until Hitler invaded Greece in 1941. The Battle of Britain was dramatic and dangerous for the small number of pilots involved. But it too had an unreal quality for most people. Children watched enemy planes overhead and collected fragments of German bombs. Churchill, ever the child, went out to watch bombing raids as though they were firework displays.

Perhaps, Churchill's child-like qualities commended themselves to some of the British in the summer of 1940 partly because some of the country lived that summer as a kind of second childhood. Peter Fleming oversaw measures by which the British might, after invasion, fight behind enemy lines. This was a serious business – especially to anyone who knew what was likely to happen to those captured behind German lines. All the same, when Fleming came to write his book on the period, *Invasion 1940*, he often seemed to regard it as a kind of child's adventure story. His book is laced with quotations – from *Alice in Wonderland*, *The Adventures of Sherlock Holmes* and *Peter Pan*. He wrote:

On the British the threat of invasion had a … vivid, direct and comprehensive impact, for the danger, and precautions taken to avert it, affected the whole population. Yet legend plays a large part in their memories of that tense and strangely exhilarating summer, and their experiences, like those of early childhood, are sharply rather than accurately etched upon their minds.

———

Fleming came from a patrician family. There must have been many less privileged people who felt – as they worked long hours in factories or spent squalid nights in bomb shelters – that the war was all too real. The government itself did not always take an optimistic view of the national mood in 1940. On 16 June, Eden had told his Cabinet colleagues that he had been worried by a report on the state of public opinion. 'Bearing in mind the stern times ahead of us he would like to have seen a firmer note of resolution in the people of this country.'[61] Conservative ministers often believed that order might break down even without German invasion. They feared that civilians would abandon cities to escape bombing raids or that work would cease in factories. Churchill talked of putting men at the Spitfire factory in Castle Bromwich under military discipline.

The 'child-like' state of part of the British ruling class in the summer of 1940 derived from the fact that they were relatively immune to normal political pressures. Nothing marked the humiliation and chaos of France in 1940 more than the fact that its government left the capital city. In Britain, on the other hand, London's status was reinforced. Power was more centralised than ever before as 'regional commissioners' circumvented elected local authorities. It is no accident that Churchill's accession to power coincided with the eclipse of the one political dynasty in Britain, the Chamberlains, who had built their power on municipal government. For those in London, the rest of the country sometimes seemed remote. New Zealand, which had an independent government and controlled its own armed forces, sometimes impinged on the thinking of the government more than Birmingham or Manchester.

In peacetime British governments had to worry about elections but there was no general election between 1935 and 1945 and the major political parties did not contest by-elections. Conservatives (who made up the majority of MPs) were particularly isolated – partly because so many of their electoral agents were serving in the armed forces. They were probably wrong to claim that this accounted for the scale of their electoral defeat in 1945 but it certainly did account for the fact that the defeat came as such a surprise. If Britain had been invaded, or even if large numbers of British troops had been fighting abroad, then the government might have had to worry about a breakdown of order among civilians or mutiny among soldiers. As it was, dissatisfaction with government policy, particularly regarding victims of air raids, seems to have contributed to the quiet revolution that eventually brought the Labour Party to power, but it had remarkably little short-term impact.

———

De Gaulle did not fit into the story the British ruling classes told about themselves in the summer of 1940. They could not understand how a man who was dependent on their favour could show himself so haughty and ungrateful. But that was the point. De Gaulle knew all too well that he did not have a single strong card to play and that his only hope was to bluff. As he later conceded, he was 'too weak' to compromise. In these circumstances, the peculiarity of de Gaulle's manner was an advantage: it was useful to him that the British should find him mysterious and even exasperating. A 'reasonable' man would have either adjusted himself to the reality of his weak position – what reasonable men, such as Jean Monnet, reproached de Gaulle for not doing – or despaired, which de Gaulle did more often than he cared to admit.

Churchill was sometimes reduced to incoherent fury by de Gaulle's behaviour, but this was partly because he believed in the myth of de Gaulle – perhaps, in his romantic way, believed in it more than de Gaulle believed in it himself. Churchill could be earthy and funny but there was always a part of him that yearned to be a 'chevalier sans peur et sans reproche'. He once said of de Gaulle: 'He thinks he's Joan of Arc but I can't get my bloody bishops to burn him.' It's a typical piece of Churchillian wit but it gains an extra twist when one remembers that Churchill was almost obsessively interested in, and admiring of, Joan of Arc.[62]

———

Even among those French people who stayed in Britain, not all were Gaullists. Some simply did not wish to live in occupied or

Vichy France but took no political stance. Some bitter opponents of Vichy were not Gaullists. The newspaper *France* was established in London by the French journalist Pierre Comert. It was not explicitly opposed to de Gaulle – he visited its offices and it published his communiqués – but it was emphatically not Gaullist. Elaine Barr worked for the paper, finding that the French spoken by journalists did not much resemble the language she had learned in an Ursuline convent. She recalled that the political composition of the staff was 'very open, left-wing, anti-fascist, anti-Pétainist, very anti the sort of thing de Gaulle was wanting to set up'. Barr said that the paper did not attack de Gaulle but found him 'horribly embarrassing ... one simply raised one's eyebrows'. The one thing that united journalists on *France* was Anglophilia: for them, Churchill was 'a God'.[63]

The journal *La France Libre* published its first issue in November 1940. Its title made it sound like a mouthpiece of Gaullism but it was an independent publication. Its founder, André Labarthe, became violently hostile to de Gaulle. Its most eminent contributor – Raymond Aron, who wrote under the name of Robert Avron – was more guarded in his views. He had wanted to join a fighting unit of the Free French. Had he done so, he would have been included among Gaullist forces whatever his private opinions. As it was, he was sometimes expressed reservations about de Gaulle's policy.

De Gaulle would later write bitterly of 'parallel movements that were in reality movements of opposition'. In fact, the lines between his own movement and other groups of anti-Vichy French people were not as sharply drawn in 1940 as they were to become later in the war and this was fortunate for de Gaulle because it concealed the weakness of his position. In the small world of French people and their associates in London in the summer of 1940, it was impossible for separation to be complete. Robert Mengin was a diplomat at the French embassy in London. He opposed the armistice and resigned his post on 17 June. Two days later he presented himself to de Gaulle. However, he decided that the undertaking that volunteers for Free French forces were required to sign was 'an oath' to de Gaulle personally. Consequently, he did not join the French navy until 1943, by which time the statement of personal allegiance was no longer required. In spite of this, he did work for a time at Gaullist headquarters in Carlton Gardens – refusing to go to the shelter during bombing raids in order to avoid an uncomfortable encounter with the general himself. Many of his closest associates (including his wife, whose political opinions were much to the right of his own) were Gaullists.[64]

The central institution around which early Gaullism revolved was the BBC and especially the evening broadcast 'Les Français parlent aux Français'. Those listening in France probably assumed that all French people whose voices were heard on the BBC belonged to the same group and were united around de Gaulle. In fact, there were divisions inside what seemed to listeners to be a single programme. The French news was produced by the BBC itself. Only a part of the evening's broadcast was specifically devoted to information from de Gaulle – this was usually relayed by Maurice Schumann, a socialist politician whose disconcertingly high-pitched voice became that of the Free French. When he was in London, de Gaulle himself broadcast around once a week: 'with the moving sense that I was undertaking, for the millions who listened in anguish and through terrible jamming, a kind of sacrament'.[65] Staff at the BBC came to admire de Gaulle: 'one of the few prominent figures in the war who came here knowing nothing about broadcasting and yet took the trouble to improve and perfect his technique'.[66] Reports from France suggested there was a correlation between Gaullist sentiments and the possession of modern radios.[67] In September 1941, a British official recognised that one of the reasons why the British could not afford to dispense with de Gaulle lay in the fact that he had become a 'broadcasting genius'.[68]

There was also entertainment in French-language broadcasts, which featured people who did not regard themselves as Gaullists. Michel Saint-Denis, a theatre director who operated under the pseudonym of Jacques Duchesne, was central to this part of the programme. He worked, as he put it, 'with neither the Croix de Lorraine [the symbol of de Gaulle] nor the Francisque [the symbol of Vichy]'.[69] If anyone was the hero of 1940 for Duchesne, it was Churchill. Duchesne translated the speech Churchill delivered to the French people on 21 October 1940. He was told to make the text sound authentic rather than grammatically correct. Later he wrote a moving account of Churchill's kindness and good humour. Both men were amused when Duchesne overheard Churchill refer to 'my frog speech'. The Prime Minister insisted that his guest be served wine – though, for once, he himself did not drink with dinner. Finally, they dashed through a bombing raid to a tiny studio under the War Office. There was no space for two chairs in front of the microphone and Churchill suggested that Duchesne should sit 'on my lap'. The French people who listened to the crackling broadcast might have been surprised to learn that the man who introduced it was crouching awkwardly between the Prime Minister's thighs.[70]

De Gaulle himself often moved among French people who were not Gaullists. He dined with Jean Monnet on his first night in London after his flight from Bordeaux. Monnet, like Raymond Aron, admired de Gaulle but had reservations about him. He was disconcerted by the intemperate quality of de Gaulle's language and particularly by the fact that he denounced Pétain as a 'traitor'. He thought de Gaulle's policy was 'too authoritarian and too personal' and too rigid at a time when everything seemed in flux.

Perhaps Gaulle's critics understood him better than his supporters. Comert, Aron, Monnet and Mengin were wary of de Gaulle because they were alarmed by his will, his authority and his confidence in his own judgement, whereas prominent men who threw in their lot with the Free French sometimes did so because they assumed de Gaulle would be malleable or even naive. At the end of December 1940, Robert Vansittart had lunch with Admiral Muselier, who had joined de Gaulle in July. Vansittart wrote:

there is not the least doubt in my mind that he [Muselier] is a far cleverer man than de Gaulle ... an intelligence not only technically but psychologically a great deal ahead of de Gaulle. He is convinced that de Gaulle must be maintained and built up, but he recognizes, as a great many of us do, that this will not be possible if de Gaulle continues to make the mistakes that he is doing now.[71]

As late as January 1943, General Catroux told Anthony Eden: 'De Gaulle easily took offence and was a vain man, but he could also be handled.'[72]

Looking back at the summer of 1940, de Gaulle's apparent confidence in his own destiny seems even more extraordinary than that of Churchill. If the British had come to terms with Hitler in 1940, de Gaulle would have finished his life in a bedsitter in South Kensington giving French lessons to schoolgirls who would have giggled at his appearance and manner. If the Germans had invaded Britain, de Gaulle would, if taken alive, have been sent back to France and shot. If Pétain had rebelled against the conditions the Germans imposed on France and called on his forces in North Africa to fight, or if French commanders there had decided on their own authority to continue the war against Germany, de Gaulle might, if he was lucky, have been given the command of a division. Beneath the carefully cultivated air of assurance, de Gaulle understood the terrible odds against him. In his memoirs he likened his position during his first weeks in London to that of a man who stands on the edge of an ocean and steels himself to swim across it. The image is striking because de Gaulle, unlike Churchill, who was also fond of marine metaphors, could barely swim and had had difficulty in passing the twenty-five-metre test imposed on cadets at St Cyr.[73]

5

Modus Vivendi,
July 1940–December 1941

> The conversations with Vichy, if they take place, may reach
> a *modus vivendi* .... Of course, if we could be assured that Vichy,
> or part of Vichy, were genuinely moving in our direction, we could
> ease up on them to a very large extent ... the tide in our favour
> will master and overwhelm the disturbing eddies of the blockade,
> De Gaulle and possible sea incidents.
> *Winston Churchill, 15 October 1940*[1]

Until the end of 1941, the British often sought some gentlemen's agreement that would define their relations with the Pétain government – though de Gaulle later suggested that the British understood such agreements counted for little 'because this war was not a war of gentlemen'.[2] In the short term, however, Britain and France came close to war in July 1940. The object of their dispute was the French Fleet. At the beginning of June 1940, the British had the most powerful navy in the world. The United States and Japan – respectively the second and third largest naval powers – were neutral in the European war. Germany's navy ranked sixth in the world. However, Italy entered the war on the German side on 10 June 1940 and brought the world's fifth largest fleet with it.

Worst of all, at a time when British survival depended on command of the seas, was the prospect that the French fleet, the world's fourth largest, might fall into German hands. The French promised that this would not happen, but the British remained nervous. They issued an ultimatum. French ships must either be handed over to the British, scuttled or sailed to the Caribbean and placed under American control. If the French did none of these things, the British would attack. On 3 July, they seized French ships that were in British ports. The French commander in Alexandria, in British-controlled Egypt, agreed that his ships would remain neutralised in harbour. Elsewhere, the British fired on the French navy. This caused most damage at Mers-el-Kébir near Oran in Algeria – where almost 1,300 French sailors were killed. It was an act of spectacular cold-bloodedness. French sailors were playing ball with English girls in Hyde Park as the government took the decision to open fire. Roger Cambon – French chargé d'affaires in London and the nephew of the long-serving ambassador to Britain, Paul Cambon, who had been a friend of Churchill's since before 1914 – resigned his position because he feared that he might have to convey a French declaration of war on the British.[3] The French did not declare war but some never forgave Churchill. In the 1950s, he received venomous letters on each anniversary of Mers-el-Kébir.[4]

Cold bloodedness was not a bad quality in wartime, though. Even French people who resented the attack sometimes recognised it as a sign that Britain would fight on and that, therefore, the Pétain government's expectation of a quick peace with Germany would be confounded. The French diplomat Robert Mengin wrote that the British action was 'grim and ruthless against a grim and ruthless enemy'.[5] De Gaulle knew that at least for a time Mers-el-Kébir would make it hard for the British to come to terms with the Pétain government, which suited his purposes. He broadcast five days after the attack, expressing his 'grief' and 'anger'. But he added that he regarded the act as a necessary one in a war where 'each nation staked its life'. A few months later he had lunch at Downing Street and came close to expressing admiration. Churchill's private secretary reported him as saying: 'We should make more of the fact that we stood alone, "*le champion du monde*" against Hitler, and, if we were accepted as such all our actions would be excused; Oran would seem natural, merely because the world was at stake.'[6]

The British mounted another operation against Vichy forces a few months later. 'Operation Menace' was designed to capture the port of Dakar in Senegal. It was to involve both British and Free French forces and, if it succeeded, Dakar would be placed under de Gaulle, who accompanied the expedition. Until and unless the colony was taken, the British remained in control. They rejected de Gaulle's suggestion their own troops should be 'dressed in uniform bearing some resemblance to the French' to convey 'the impression that the landings were being carried out by French Forces'.[7]

De Gaulle had much to gain. Senegal would provide him with his own territory. The stakes for the British were lower. It would suit them to be able to use the naval base at Dakar and to undermine Vichy's authority. The latter purpose would be particularly well served if the garrison at Dakar welcomed de Gaulle as a liberator. However, the British commitment to Dakar was limited. It was never as important as the simultaneous operations they were mounting in the Middle East.

For all the hopes de Gaulle and the British entertained, Dakar did not rally to the Free French. Vichy had sent ships to reinforce their garrison shortly before the British arrival. In spite of this, Churchill was persuaded to let the operation go ahead. Spears, travelling with de Gaulle, signalled 'if he [de Gaulle] fails to seize opportunity so obviously within his grasp of rallying West Africa ... his power to rally any other part of the Empire is lost for ever'.[8] When the British fleet arrived at Dakar, troops loyal to Vichy fired on it. De Gaulle, horrified at the prospect of shedding French blood, now favoured withdrawal, but the British insisted on a continuation of the operation until one of their warships was damaged.

For the British this was a minor annoyance; for de Gaulle, Dakar was a crushing humiliation. He had been obliged to show himself dependent on British military support andhe had failed even with this support. Spears thought that de Gaulle had lost his confidence and was 'curiously reluctant to be drastic save in word at moment. Fear of failure lies heavily with him. Leclerc attempts to relieve him by assuming total responsibility.'[9] De Gaulle was indeed shaken by Dakar – though he may have ceded some control to Leclerc simply because he did not see himself as a military commander or because he was already displaying a capacity, very evident in his later life, to let subordinates take responsibility for enterprises that might go wrong.

De Gaulle went to Cameroon, via Freetown and Nigeria. He was now in territories that had rallied to him without coercion. This included Chad, which had come over on 26 August. Africa exercised no romantic appeal for de Gaulle, and this desperately poor part of French Equatorial Africa, offered few material advantages to anyone. Nevertheless, the transformation in de Gaulle's fortunes was spectacular. When he left London in August, he had been able to command the loyalty of a few thousand troops and had the use of some borrowed offices. Now he ruled over millions of people (he was vague about how many millions) and territory that was larger than the whole of mainland France. He also had an independent base in which he was no longer required to ask for the permission of the British before every important decision. The notion of volunteering in French Africa was a helpfully ambiguous one: instead of having to persuade every soldier to join their forces, Gaullist officers dealt with tribal chiefs who would deliver hundreds of recruits at a stroke.

The very remoteness of Equatorial Africa suited de Gaulle. He found, more than he cared to admit, dealing with his British allies and French subordinates difficult. It was hard to maintain the air of remote mystery on which his appeal depended if he had to haggle every day to get what he wanted. During debates about the Levant in May 1941 (of which more below) de Gaulle withdrew to what he described as 'his cloud' in Brazzaville. When a British diplomat tried to persuade him to return to London, he objected that 'in London he would be caught in a network of problems'.[10]

The failure of the Dakar operation did not discredit de Gaulle in the eyes of the British, but it marked a new stage in their relations with Vichy. Just as Mers-el-Kébir had shown Vichy that the British meant to fight, so Dakar showed the British that Vichy would do so. It meant that there was going to be no easy way to take Vichy territory, but it also suggested that Vichy might defend this territory against the Germans as well as British-backed forces. Halifax recognised that Dakar would increase 'French self-confidence' and added: 'It should be our aim to see that this rising self-confidence developed in an anti-German, rather than anti-British sense'.[11] The Admiralty were concerned at the damage that the Vichy forces might do in the Mediterranean: 'the result of Dakar is to make more necessary than before that we should arrive at such a modus vivendi, even though it may be more difficult to achieve'.[12] The Foreign Secretary also wrote of a possible 'modus vivendi' with Vichy while adding: 'It must be understood that HMG cannot withdraw their support of General de Gaulle's movement and must give him such support as he requires to maintain his authority in those French Colonies which rally to his cause.'[13]

There was another important change in September 1940 that influenced Franco-British relations. Maxime Weygand ceased to be Minister of National Defence at Vichy and was appointed Delegate General in North Africa. This suggested he was not comfortable in Vichy. It also meant that he now controlled large forces because the French army in North Africa (unlike that in mainland France) was not restricted by the terms of the armistice. The British transmitted a message to Weygand that they would send six divisions to support him 'if he unfurled his flag again in North Africa'.[14] British people who encountered Weygand during the early stages of the Second World War were mainly struck by his vanity. British politicians, though, remembered a younger more vigorous man, whom they had first encountered in the First World War. He had then been the aide of Marshal Foch – the most aggressive of French generals and one who was often seen as the opposite of Pétain. Admiral

Keyes,[15] Leo Amery (secretary of state for India)[16] and Desmond Morton (Churchill's adviser)[17] had all known Weygand before 1918 and all placed some hope in him. Most importantly, Churchill had written in 1929 of Weygand: 'At the head of Marshal Foch's "famille militaire" stood a soldier of subtle and commanding military genius veiled under an unaffected modesty.'[18] On 8 November 1940, Churchill suggested that de Gaulle might be prevented from going to Cairo because doing so 'might arouse the antagonism of General Weygand.'[19]

De Gaulle conducted a balancing act. Dismissing attempts to bring Weygand over would have angered his British supporters and perhaps some of his potential supporters in France or North Africa too – though de Gaulle must also have realised that his own eclipse would have been a condition of Weygand joining the British. In October 1940, de Gaulle wrote to General Ismay (Churchill's most important military aide) that if Weygand or Noguès were to approach the British they should receive expressions of sympathy but be reminded of the British commitment to de Gaulle and asked to get in touch with him 'with view to forming a war government'.[20]

On 28 November, Catroux, then in Egypt, sent Weygand, in Algeria, a 'neighbourly letter', presumably approved by de Gaulle. De Gaulle himself wrote to Weygand as late as March 1941 telling him that he was now in the last few days of the time when he might be able to play a 'great national role'.[21] In reality, de Gaulle must have known that invitations were unwelcome to Weygand – partly because they aroused German suspicion and partly because they implied that de Gaulle would be the senior partner in any future relationship. The second of these points was underlined by the fact that de Gaulle said he would welcome men 'whatever their past faults.'[22]

Matters were complicated by the fact that the British did not see a simple division between Vichy and its opponents. On the contrary, their justification for dealing with Vichy hinged on the idea that the government was not homogeneous and that elements in it might be persuaded to adopt a more anti-German line. At one extreme they saw Pierre Laval as an arch collaborator; at the other extreme they placed most confidence in Weygand. Between these two they took a particular interest in Paul Baudouin (Foreign Minister at Vichy in the summer and autumn of 1940): their ambassador in Spain heard that Baudouin was increasingly anti-German, while their ambassador in Washington heard that he was the 'chief Anglophobe element at Vichy'.[23] It suited people on both sides to avoid a complete breach and to shroud their relations with a degree of ambiguity. Such ambiguity was increased by the fact that communication between London and Vichy depended on informal contacts and unauthorised emissaries – such as the law professor Louis Rougier, who came to London and saw Churchill on behalf of Pétain in October 1940.

In October 1940, John Colville wrote:

Halifax comes perilously near advocating appeasement, saying that all we require is an assurance that the French Colonies are 'healthily anti-German and anti-Italian'. We must be careful not to let de Gaulle down ... but perhaps there is no harm in our flirting with M. Baudouin, through the embassy at Madrid, about questions of interest to both countries.

However, he added: 'Should the Germans decide to take over the whole of France, it looks as if the Vichy government – presumably minus Laval – might fly to North Africa; and then of course the whole of the French Empire would rejoin us in active resistance to the enemy.'[24] The British sometimes told de Gaulle about their dealings with Vichy.[25] They did not appreciate that he might be offended – partly because it did not cross their minds that de Gaulle might consider himself as equal to a government.

Churchill disliked Vichy and despised most of its leaders, but he too recognized the uses of ambiguity. He told the Cabinet that Britain should 'adopt a mixed attitude and not play out our hand against the Vichy French to the uttermost'.[26] He was also brutally realistic about the prospect that Britain might have to do some kind of deal with the Pétain government or that opinion inside Vichy might change. He sometimes urged robust policies towards Vichy precisely because he thought that they might speed such evolution. He counselled against a 'nice, soft, cosy, forgiving England': 'it would be a mistake to suppose that a solution of our difficulties with Vichy will be reached by a policy of mere conciliation and forgiveness.' He denounced Laval 'filled by the bitterest hatred of England'; Darlan 'mortally envenomed by the injury we have done to his fleet'; and Pétain 'always ... an anti-British defeatist ... now a dotard'. However, he also recognised that '[t]hey may be forced by rising opinion in France, and by German severities, to change their line in our favour'. He hoped to force the French government 'into a more serviceable mood.'[27] As late as December 1941, Churchill was willing to countenance a personal message from himself to Darlan (at that time the senior figure in the Vichy government after Pétain), promising 'an honourable place in the Allied ranks' to anyone who was able to bring the French fleet over to the British side.[28]

The British still recognised Vichy as the legitimate government of France and considered it better that French overseas possessions should be under the control of Vichy rather than of the Germans. On the other hand, they also appreciated that de Gaulle had acquired de facto authority in the parts of Africa that were now under his control. Some officials could see that de Gaulle's constitutional position had changed. He had 'become the administrative head of large territories outside the United Kingdom'. They foresaw the possibility that a government might eventually be established outside mainland France but they were keen that power over the Free French should be exercised by a council based in London – perhaps chaired by Catroux. They still entertained the fantasy that de Gaulle would return to being a simple soldier 'whose position would probably, for the immediate future, be that of Commander of the Free French Forces in Africa, subordinate to the British High Command.'[29]

De Gaulle preempted British moves to establish structures that might govern the Free French. On 27 October 1940, he set up a Council for the Defence of the French Empire in Brazzaville. The British could hardly object though they regarded it as 'tiresome' that he had done this without prior consultation and emphasised that the Council could not be a 'rival Government'.[30] De Gaulle also issued an Organic Declaration on 16 November. This had something to offend everyone because it denied the legitimacy of Vichy without promising to establish a democratic regime in Vichy's place.

In late November 1940, de Gaulle returned to London much stronger than when he had left in September. Britain too had changed in his absence. The Battle of Britain was over and the atmosphere of strange exultation that had sometimes marked the summer of 1940 had dissipated. Everyone understood that there was a long and difficult war ahead of them. As de Gaulle put it: 'At the beginning of this winter, fog shrouded souls.'[31]

De Gaulle's return to London meant he had to face awkward questions about his own organisation there. He had written about the nature of leadership but his experience of command was brief, and he had spent long periods of his adult life mainly in reading and writing. In any case, he had argued that the leader should delegate administrative details (*'l'intendance'*) to subordinates. The problem in London was that de Gaulle had few subordinates with administrative ability. The embarrassing truth was not just that de Gaulle's forces got their weapons and money from the British. They would probably have had no one capable of organising an office if it had not been for the help of some energetic and francophone young English women. Furthermore, those who joined de Gaulle in London during his first few months there were often awkward characters. De Gaulle described his supporters to Churchill in terms that might equally well have been applied to himself: 'He begged the Prime Minister to understand that the leaders and members of the Free French Movement were necessarily somewhat difficult people; else they would not be where they were.'[32]

Almost as soon as de Gaulle returned to London, the British began to wish he was somewhere else. Relations with de Gaulle were particularly tense because, at the beginning of 1941, the British arrested Admiral Muselier – head of the Free French navy – whom they alleged was passing secrets to the Germans. De Gaulle was furious but behaved, as Churchill put it, 'like a gentleman' when the British admitted that they had made a mistake.[33] In truth de Gaulle was probably not sorry to see Muselier, who had begun to emerge as a potential rival to himself, discomfited.

In March 1941, de Gaulle left for East Africa wherehe hoped initially to recapture the French port of Djibouti from Vichy forces. The British were badly stretched in the region and had no interest in supporting this operation. De Gaulle's hopes turned to the Middle East. Some French troops had managed to join the British forces in Palestine after the armistice of June 1940. There was also a French civilian population (made up of those who administered the Suez Canal) in Egypt and there was the tantalising prospect that the French fleet, immobilised in Alexandria, might be brought back into the war.

Most of all, de Gaulle's interest was focused on the Levant – Syria and Lebanon. After the First World War, the League of Nations had awarded these to France as mandates. In theory ,t his meant that they were to be prepared for independence; in practice France had often treated mandates as an extension of its empire. The acting secretary of the League of Nations (not someone to whom the world paid much attention at the time) had received a telegram from de Gaulle in October 1940 announcing that Cameroon, another mandate, would henceforth be administered by the Free French.[34] De Gaulle and Catroux (who had himself been high commissioner in the Levant in 1926) hoped that the Free French might take control of Syria and Lebanon and that French soldiers there would rally to their cause without a fight. This hope became increasingly unrealistic as Vichy strengthened its control in the region.

In pursuit of his Middle Eastern project, de Gaulle arrived in Cairo on 1 April. A band struck up the 'Marseillaise' as the plane door opened but it was a pretty dark-haired woman who emerged. This was Mrs Brittain-Jones, the mistress of the king of Greece, who had been brought by the British in the hopes that she might improve the morale of her lover. De Gaulle and she had been put on the same flight and he had waved her to go first – perhaps out of gallantry or perhaps because he had noticed the date.

The incident provided a rare moment of mirth in what were otherwise desperate days. The British had achieved some success against the Italians in North Africa, but the Germans had come to the aid of their allies and the Afrika Korps, commanded by Erwin Rommel, had begun to push the British back. Soon Benghazi was evacuated in the face of German advance. The Italians had also invaded Greece in October 1940 and, when it looked as though they might be unsuccessful there too, the Germans intervened again and invaded Greece (along with Yugoslavia) on 6 April 1941. Churchill insisted that the already stretched forces in the Middle East should now help the Greeks.

The British commander in the Middle East, Archibald Wavell, opposed de Gaulle's projects for a Free French advance, which would have imposed strains on British forces. In spite of this De Gaulle admired the 'noble serenity' of Wavell. He wrote with sympathy about Wavell's plight – supervising operations over a vast area at a time when he was subject to 'all sorts of political interference' – and even appreciated that his own arrival, 'inconvenient and pressing', added to Wavell's problems.[35] De Gaulle, obsessed with precise definitions of sovereignty was sensitive to the difficulty of trying to marshal Australian, South African and Indian forces – all made up of soldiers who were subjects of the British crown but controlled by governments that were at least partly independent of London.

This was probably the only occasion in de Gaulle's political career when he was gracious about someone who had thwarted him. Perhaps this was simply because he saw at first hand the circumstances in which Wavell had to work. Perhaps it helped that Wavell – an erudite poetry-reading Wykehamist – was the kind of scholar soldier who was more familiar in France than in Britain. Relations between de Gaulle and Wavell were also smoothed by the latter's aide-de-camp, Peter Coats, a self-effacing Etonian (remembered today largely as the lover of the MP and diarist Chips Channon). Though he talked like Bertie Wooster, he acted like Jeeves, displaying much tact in dealing with the powerful. Coats seems to have been the only adult man allowed to see de Gaulle naked. He called on him at Shepheard's Hotel to explain that almost all the senior British figures in Cairo, who were locked in frenetic discussions about the German advance, would be unable to attend the dinner de Gaulle had planned. De Gaulle was in his bath and Coats passed him 'an elegant blue and red silk dressing gown which, as I handed it to him, I saw had been bought at Hawes & Curtis in London.'[36]

After failing to obtain Wavell's support for a Free French assault on the Levant, de Gaulle retired to Brazzaville to ponder his next move. Events soon turned in his favour. In April, a coup in Iraq had given more power to a pro-Axis prime minister. German planes, flying to help Iraqi forces fight the British, were refuelled in Syria and this provided a *casus belli*. Churchill, pressed by Spears, insisted that an assault on the Levant be mounted. On 29 May, de Gaulle and Spears arrived in Jerusalem where the latter conveyed to the British commander Maitland 'Jumbo' Wilson that 'one should defer to his [de Gaulle's] wishes as much as possible'. Wilson was a less sophisticated person than Wavell but even he grasped that 'this was not going to be a straightforward military operation as there were already signs of political implications attached to it'.[37]

The political implications concerned the regime that would prevail in the Levant after the Vichy French were driven out. The British wanted a declaration that Syria would be granted independence without reservations and that the Lebanon would be granted a constitution 'subject to French interests'. Though the French were in theory committed to the independence of both countries, de Gaulle was suspicious of anything that might infringe on French power or prestige.

On 8 June, Free French troops moved into Syria while British and Australian forces moved into Lebanon. Far from giving in without a fight, the Vichy forces fought the Free French with more ardour than they fought the British or Australians: Frenchmen on both sides were killed. De Gaulle appointed Catroux as high commissioner of the Levant – an appointment that worried the British because it suggested French imperial ambitions for the region and was likely to offend Arab opinion. Maitland Wilson signed an armistice with the Vichy commander on 14 July. Catroux was present as the armistice was negotiated but not allowed to determine its form. To add insult to injury, his gold-leafed kepi was stolen by a souvenir hunter.

The Free French wanted the longest possible time to try to win over soldiers in the Levant to their side. Wilson considered: 'It was to our advantage to get those tainted with Vichy and collaboration out as soon as possible.'[38] The British refused to allow direct recruitment without the presence of British officers but conceded that Free French barracks might be placed near those of the Vichy loyalists in the hope that this might help the former to rally the latter to their cause. Unsurprisingly, this produced undignified scenes as the two sides abused each other. In the end, 30,000 French soldiers in the Levant went back to France; only 5,000 joined de Gaulle.

De Gaulle was angry and believed that the armistice was designed to weaken himself and France. He was also struck by the hypocrisy of the British position. Churchill could hardly claim to be an opponent of imperialism and had seemed indifferent to Arab nationalism until 19 May when he had declared: 'the invasion of Syria must take first place in our thoughts. For this we must have an Arab policy.'[39] The British insisted on the rights of the local population in the Levant but, as de Gaulle noted, their ambassador turned up with an escort of tanks when it seemed the king of Egypt might act in ways that would have run against British interests. De Gaulle overstated the importance of the whole affair to the British who had more pressing worries than 'a desultory war ... between the Free French and the French who had rallied to Vichy'.[40]

Three years later, Harold Macmillan, by then British pro-consul in the Mediterranean, wrote a memorandum for his colleagues explaining de Gaulle's resentment about the Lebanon. Macmillan could not hide his amusement at the combination of moralism and cynicism in the British position: ['T]he whole French policy towards native ambitions has what we should now call reactionary but used to believe normal.' Furthermore, the British themselves had been continuously sucked into the imperialist endeavours that they denounced:

> Of course a series of British Governments declared their intention to leave Egypt, but somehow or other Lord Cromer brought us back there. We are always on the point of evacuation, but always return with greater authority. This, which according to our political beliefs we regard either as the wicked and cruel fate which dogs us and forces us against our will to be a great Imperial race, or know to be the result of the mysterious workings of Providence, anxious always to give the British a second chance, the French believe to be due to more sinister, less hallowed and in any case less fortuitous causes.[41]

De Gaulle confronted the British ambassador in Egypt, Miles Lampson, and the british minister-resident in the area, Oliver Lyttelton, in Cairo on 21 July. After a heated conversation, things calmed down and an agreement was signed, effectively over-ruling the terms of the armistice signed by Wilson. Catroux was to be granted the title of delegate general in Syria and the Free French were allowed to retain a substantial number of French civilians whom they needed to administer the area – though not all were required to rally to de Gaulle.

The immediate result of the arguments in Cairo was a breach between Spears and de Gaulle. Spears had been de Gaulle's most enthusiastic supporter in June 1940 and worked closely with him since then — though he was increasingly prone to condescension, which was the one thing that de Gaulle would never forgive. The acrimony of disputes in the Middle East turned the two men definitively against each other. The transformation was tragic for Spears. A man who had devoted much of his life to promoting good relations between Britain and France would be an object of de Gaulle's contempt for the rest of his life.

Syria and Lebanon were a disappointment to de Gaulle, but he had, nonetheless, extended the territory under Free French control. De Gaulle's own approach had changed. In the summer of 1940, his mysticism had obscured, perhaps for himself as much as anyone else, what practical measures he might take to advance his cause. By the autumn of 1941, things were clearer. De Gaulle recognised that he still had limited military forces at his disposal. Rather he urged the British to accept that his strength was a moral one, associated with the need to reverse France's humiliation.[42]

De Gaulle returned to England in early September and Churchill insisted that he be treated with ostentatious bad manners: 'No notice will be taken of General de Gaulle's arrival, and it will be left to him to make any overtures.'[43] He was finally allowed to meet Churchill again on 12 September 1941. In his diary John Colville anticipated 'sparks' and in his memoirs (published many years later) he claimed that the meeting had been so stormy that he and then another interpreter had been thrown out of the room. Finally, fearing that the prime minister and de Gaulle might physically assault each other, Colville nerved himself to go back and was amazed to find them both smoking cigars and on apparently amicable terms. The formal minutes suggest something less dramatic. They record a conversation in which Churchill expressed 'very great sorrow' at de Gaulle's attitude and de Gaulle regretted anything he had said that offended the British.[44] The meeting appears to have finished on a cordial note. Churchill said he would be happy to see de Gaulle again. He told the cabinet: 'there could now be some relaxation in the attitude of caution that had been enjoined upon Departments in their dealings with the Free French'. Those who had followed the acrimonious negotiations of the previous few months would have been surprised at how low it featured among British priorities. The cabinet reached de Gaulle only after having exhausted an agenda that included Persia, Afghanistan and the state of Finnish social democracy.[45]

There was greater calculation in de Gaulle's approach than the British realised. He remarked: 'In normal circumstances difficulties of this sort between two countries would be smoothed out in a moment by their Ambassadors.' This implied that he saw his own movement as one that might have the diplomatic status of a sovereign state. At the end of the meeting Churchill suggested 'a formal Council ... which would have an effective voice in shaping the policy of the Movement of which General de Gaulle was the head as the recognized leader of all Free Frenchmen'. De Gaulle's response was a sly one: he 'agreed that there would be some advantage in him having about him some body analogous to a government.'[46] It would be more than two years until anyone recognised de Gaulle as head of a government, but it was clear how his mind was working.

After the meeting between Churchill and de Gaulle, a group of Frenchmen, including André Labarthe and Admiral Muselier, met at the Savoy hotel in the presence of British officials to devise a committee that might exercise control over de Gaulle. They failed because de Gaulle himself assumed control of the committee. The British had fallen into what one of them recognised to be 'a carefully prepared trap'.[47] Churchill was disappointed: 'We did not want General de Gaulle to create a shadow French government with offices to individuals at the present stage.'[48] When told that the new council was made up of 'yes men',Eden wrote in exasperation that it was unclear 'where "no men" are to be found' among the French in London.[49] Perhaps it crossed his mind that British government worked effectively because there were men, such as himself, who said 'no' to the prime minister.

In the summer of 1940, many members of the British ruling class had regarded de Gaulle as a minor figure, primarily useful as a soldier. A year later, after the arguments over the Levant, they had wondered whether he might be 'crazy'.[50] But some of them were beginning to understand the extraordinary person that they were up against. The prime minister's adviser Desmond Morton wrote:

> In my opinion de Gaulle is a very clever man. It is wrong to assume that he is not a politician, if the word be used in a debased sense. He is not a diplomat, but there lies a calculating brain behind that curious countenance, and though absolutely sincere and honest, he is undoubtedly swayed by deep prejudices ... He is not mad. If he raves like a lunatic at one man and attempts to charm another by quiet reasonableness, it is because he thinks that such an attitude is more likely to gain his ends with the person in question.[51]

6

'Les Jeux Sont Faits': World War

'In the third spring of the war, destiny gave its verdict,
les jeux sont faits.'
Charles de Gaulle.[1]

On 7 December 1941, the Japanese attacked the US fleet at Pearl
Harbor. Four days later, Germany declared war on the USA.
This was the most important single event in the Second World
War – perhaps in the twentieth century. Churchill and de Gaulle
always understood that the outcome of the war would be decided by
the industrial might of the United States. America had already helped
Britain before a formal declaration of war. The US navy fired on
German submarines that threatened American merchant ships and
American munitions were provided to Britain under arrangements
that were generous, at least in the short term. De Gaulle recalled
a visit to Chequers in March 1941 when Churchill had woken him
'literally dancing with joy' to announce that the American Congress
had authorised the Lend-Lease programme.[2]

The transition to world war had dramatic effects on the lives of
Churchill and de Gaulle. No two leaders were more defined by their
relation to the aeroplane. De Gaulle began his political career with
the flight to London on 17 June 1940; Churchill had been flying
since before the First World War. Now they both flew around the
world to stiffen the resolves of their subordinates and negotiate with
allies. Roosevelt and especially Stalin were less willing to endure the

danger and discomfort of travelling outside their own countries. In January 1942, Churchill became the first important politician to fly the Atlantic. No one commented on the fact that he left on a British battleship and came back on an American aircraft: only American planes could undertake such long journeys. De Gaulle was more alert than Churchill to the symbolism of aircraft and obsessively concerned to ensure that he flew in planes with French insignia – he was willing to risk his life rather than board a more sophisticated machine that required a British crew.[3] De Gaulle was also painfully aware that British control of aircraft gave them the power to confine him to, or exclude him from, the British Isles.

The formal entry of the United States into the war seemed to make the defeat of the Axis powers certain in the long term. Churchill said that, after hearing about Pearl Harbor, he 'slept the sleep of the saved'. There was, though, another dimension to the event. For decades, Britain and France had been living under a kind of suspended death sentence. They ruled huge empires. Because of the mandates they had been awarded by the League of Nations after the First World War, the territory under their aegis in the 1920s and 30s was more extensive than ever before. But their real power was in decline and this decline had been masked by the fact that no single country challenged them across the world. The United States had not translated its economic power into military strength after the First World War. In December 1941, Dwight Eisenhower was, like de Gaulle, fifty-one years old. He had spent several years in the Philippines and undertaken a one-year posting to France in 1928. Other than this, he had never served outside the United States and never seen military action.

Once America went to war in 1941, everything changed. Churchill – distracted by immediate military concerns – was slow to appreciate this. De Gaulle understood straight away:

In Washington, the President, the ministers, the great leaders felt themselves to have become the masters of the coalition. Their tone and their manners made it clear enough ... The streets, the shops,

RICHARD VINEN

the cinemas, the pubs of London were full of yankee soldiers ... The
English .... [were] no longer masters in their own house.[4]

Churchill's exultation at American entry to the war obscured something that had a more immediate impact on the British empire: it was
now at war with Japan. The British government, unencumbered by
the need to consult Congress, declared war on Japan a few hours
before the United States did so. The Far East had featured little
in Churchill's thinking. His extensive travels never took him east
of Calcutta. He understood many of the theatres in which British
troops fought and had fought in some of them himself.. He found
it harder to imagine the vast distances involved in the Pacific war,
which were, as one commander drily remarked, hard to grasp 'in
portions, from small scale maps'.[5]

The Japanese did not fit neatly into Churchill's racial dichoto-
mies. They were not white, but they were hardly tribal warriors
either. Japan was itself the capital of an expanding empire that was
ruled with particular brutality. In the 1930s, Churchill had written
with some admiration of the Japanese as a 'proud race' and had
sometimes seemed to value them as potential allies. In 1940, he was
reluctant to allow the supply of anti-Japanese forces from Burma for
fear that this might antagonise the government in Tokyo. Whatever
illusions Churchill had entertained about the Japanese, he was
quickly disabused by what Orwell was to call 'the worst ten weeks
of the British Empire'. On 10 December, Japanese aircraft sank the
Prince of Wales (a modern battleship) and *The Repulse* (an older
heavy cruiser) in the China Sea. It was a shattering blow. Churchill
had ordered the two ships to the area to communicate a 'sense of
menace', but they had not been covered by an aircraft carrier. Eve
Curie, the Free French journalist, heard the news in Egypt. She was
with a British naval officer who turned white. She later wrote: 'To
lose a 35,000-ton man-of-war was of far more consequence than

to lose a town, a province.'[6] Churchill recalled 'In all the war I never received a more direct shock ... Over all this vast expanse of waters Japan was supreme, and we everywhere were weak and naked.'[7]

The loss of the ships had a special twist for Churchill. Despite having twice been First Lord of the Admiralty, he was often at odds with the navy. To Churchill, brought up in the simple world of the cavalry regiment, the calculations of naval commanders about whether and how to risk their ships could seem like cowardice. He thought they ought not to shrink from battle whatever the odds: 'What do you think we build ships for?', he asked when his private secretary expressed regret for the loss of two cruisers off Crete in May 1941.[8] He had reproached Leach (the captain of the *Prince of Wales*) for lack of fighting spirit only months before he went down with his ship in the Pacific.

The final catastrophe in this period was the fall of Singapore to the Japanese on 15 February 1942. Singapore was the site of a large naval base, finished in 1937 at a cost of 25 million pounds. However, the base depended on British naval supremacy rather than bringing that supremacy about. Furthermore, Singapore, for all the talk about it being a 'fortress', was not secure since it could be attacked from land via Malaya, and this was what the Japanese did.

The defence of Singapore was damaged by overlapping commands. No one was sure who exercised authority – though everyone knew Duff Cooper, sent out by Churchill, did not. Australian soldiers – particularly their commander Major-General Gordon Bennett – were reluctant to accept subordination to the British. Reinforcements arrived but were unfit and demoralised after long sea voyages in squalid conditions. Ships – including the *Empress of Japan* – went on bringing troops to Singapore after it was obvious that it would fall: the last contingent arrived on 13 February. When the end came, one officer recalled that units were not 'in a coherent mood ... and a lot of individuals were doing odd things'.[9] Officers smashed whisky bottles from the yacht club to stop them being looted by the soldiers who were still nominally under their command. As the Japanese approached, the British blew up part of the causeway that linked Singapore to Malaya. Someone asked the eighteen-year-old Lee Kuan Yew (later prime minister of Singapore) what the sound was. He replied: 'The end of the British Empire.'

Churchill ordered that 'Senior officers must die at their posts.' Wavell, briefly transferred from India to command Allied forces in the Pacific, softened the order and eventually told the British commander that he must make his own judgement about when further resistance was useless. The Japanese insisted that Lieutenant-General Percival, the most senior British officer to stay behind, surrender under a white flag. Over 80,000 British, Indian and Australian servicemen in Singapore and another 50,000 in Malaya were captured. In his memoirs Churchill wrote about the defenders of Singapore in ungracious terms. Those defenders had no great admiration for Churchill. One parodied his speech of 20 August 1940: 'Never before have so many been ****** about by so few.'[10]

Singapore in February 1942 seemed, as one diplomat noted, to have '[m]any disturbing resemblances with the fall of France'.[11] There was the same desperate flight that had been seen in the French *exode*. There was the same sense that institutions had broken down and authority itself had collapsed. There were the same bitter inquests as those responsible for the defeat blamed each other. Gordon Bennett had begun negotiations with the Japanese but then, leaving his deputy to handle matters, made good his escape. The cabinet considered his report 'unsuitable for publication.'[12] Officers began to use the word 'Singapored' to describe an abject capitulation.[13]

At the end of February 1942, the MP and writer Harold Nicolson had a nightmare (after doing 'a talk on Winston for the Empire programme') in which a 'wraith' put its hand on his shoulder and said: 'I am Defeat.' When he woke, he wrote the following words:

The Singapore surrender has been a terrific blow to all of us. It is not merely the immediate dangers which threaten in the Indian Ocean and the menace to our communications with the Middle East. It is the dread that we are only half-hearted in fighting the whole-hearted. It is even more than that. We intellectuals must feel that in all these years we have derided the principles of force upon which our Empire is built. We undermined confidence in our own formula. The intellectuals of 1780 did the same.[14]

Even when he was battered by events in the Pacific, Churchill's attention stayed focused on the Atlantic. Days after the sinking of the *Prince of Wales*, he boarded its sister ship, the *Duke of York*, and set sail for Washington. Personal relations between Roosevelt and Churchill had not always been good; when Churchill visited the United States in 1932, Roosevelt avoided meeting him. Once the war began, however, Churchill had cultivated Roosevelt – 'no lover ever studied every whim of his mistress as assiduously as I did those of President Roosevelt'.[15] It suited both men to give the impression that they enjoyed easy, informal relations. Arthur Schlesinger (whose views on the matter owed something to his friendship with Pamela Harriman, once Churchill's daughter-in-law) suggested that the president and the prime minister 'liked the theory of liking each other in the great historical context'.[16] Churchill seems to have genuinely admired Roosevelt – sometimes claiming that he was the 'greatest man I have ever known'. Roosevelt had a cooler view of Churchill. Beneath his charm, he had a cooler view of most things.

———

At times de Gaulle invested hope in the United States – because it might counter balance the influence of Britain. A British diplomat wrote in July 1941 that de Gaulle 'is under the impression that within a fairly short time the United States will have decided to enter the war as a belligerent, and it would seem he hopes in such an event to diminish his dependence on Britain'.[17] However, the United States kept its ambassador at Vichy even after it was at war with Germany. The American diplomats who dealt with France – Admiral Leahy, the ambassador in Vichy, and Robert Murphy, who became chargé d'affaires after Leahy's departure – were conservative Catholics who were sympathetic to some aspects of Vichy's internal policy, and who aroused complaint from de Gaulle.[18] Like many in Britain, American diplomats sought to prevent Vichy France from moving to outright collaboration with Germany. Unlike the British, they were not moved by memories of 1940 and did not feel bound by undertakings given to de Gaulle.

Particular tension was generated by those French colonies in the Western hemisphere – those near to the United States. De Gaulle offered America access to bases on those islands that rallied to him but was alarmed by the extent to which the Americans made use of this facility on New Caledonia in the South Pacific, to which they sent 40,000 troops. De Gaulle blamed the governor (who had brought the island into the Gaullist camp in the first place) and eventually dismissed him. For his part de Gaulle had offended the United States government when he sent Admiral Muselier to liberate the islands of Saint Pierre and Miquelon, off the coast of Newfoundland. The islanders were keen to rally to de Gaulle (and had been prevented from doing so by their Pétainist governor), but it was tactless that the operation was carried out in December 1941, just as the United States entered the war. Cordell Hull, the American secretary of state, was particularly exasperated and became a relentless enemy of de Gaulle's.

The Far East, so important to the British, meant relatively little to de Gaulle. The French authorities in Indochina were supporters of Vichy and had allowed the Japanese to station troops there from September 1940. In the long term, de Gaulle was to complain that the Americans showed no enthusiasm to restore French authority in Indochina, but in the short term there was nothing that Gaullist forces could do to advance their cause in the area. There were Gaullist representatives in parts of the Far East, but these were not significant people[19] and, as far as the Japanese were concerned, neither was de Gaulle. In early 1941, the Japanese ambassador in

London told R. A. Butler, then a junior minister at the Foreign Office, that he proposed to send a counsellor to discuss New Caledonia with de Gaulle. Butler agreed to this 'providing it did not imply that HM government were in control of General de Gaulle or New Caledonia. The Ambassador said he would accept the fact … he seemed to find it very amusing that he should have to speak to General de Gaulle.'[20]

The one area where Gaullist interests intersected with the war against Japan was Madagascar, in the Indian Ocean, a French colony under Vichy rule. If the Japanese had invaded, they might have used it to harass Allied shipping on its way to the Far East. De Gaulle was keen to take control of the island but the British were wary of such operations – partly because they believed that Vichy forces were more likely to fight against the Free French than against soldiers from the British Empire. On 5 May 1942, a South African force invaded Madagascar in an operation the British and Americans had authorised without telling de Gaulle. To their surprise, Vichy soldiers resisted them – or at least mounted a fighting retreat as they pulled back across the island. When the Vichy French finally gave in on 6 November, their commander told the South Africans that six months of active service earned soldiers an enhanced pension.

De Gaulle was furious at the landing in Madagascar, though perhaps consoled by the fact that Vichy forces had resisted the South Africans with even more determination than they had shown against the Free French in Dakar or Syria. He called on Eden on 11 May and explained after a disconcerting period of silence that he understood the military necessity of the British undertaking operations alone and 'he might himself one day undertake an operation without consulting anybody'.[21]

More important than Madagascar was French North Africa. It offered a base from which to attack southern France, Corsica and Italy, and there were many French troops there who might be rallied to the Free French cause. It, or more particularly Algeria, also had political importancein that it contained a million inhabitants of European origin and was part of France in terms of constitutional theory rather than a colony. A British official in Brazzaville had reported de Gaulle's interest in North Africa in July 1941:

> Were he to succeed in establishing his base in Tunisia or Algeria he could then, when the moment came, cross from French territory to the relief of France, and such an operation would be, on political grounds, far preferable to a landing in Brittany from a base in the United Kingdom.[22]

De Gaulle was also suspicious of the intentions of his allies with regard to North Africa. Some in Britain and America had always hoped that they might establish a French leader in North Africa who would replace or counterbalance de Gaulle. At first their hopes had been invested in Weygand but he had been recalled to mainland France. In April 1942, another potential French leader appeared on the horizon when General Henri Giraud escaped from a German prisoner-of-war camp. Giraud was older than de Gaulle (he was sixty-three) and very senior to him in military rank. In political terms, he was a conservative who had spent the first month of his imprisonment writing a document – blaming the defeat of 1940 on silk stockings and left-wing politicians – that might have come from the pen of one of Pétain's own speechwriters.[23] After his escape aided by Vichy agents, Giraud went to meet Pétain. Vichy did not return prisoners of war who managed to reach the unoccupied zone of France, though an officer as senior as Giraud caused them embarrassment. The Americans reported that Giraud did not like de Gaulle and did not want to be involved in politics.[24] Gaullists discussed what to do with Giraud if he left France. Some proposed sending him to lead a Free French mission in the United States. De Gaulle apparently favoured making him commander of French troops in the Middle

East with a base in Cairo. The British, who detected 'a flicker of apprehension' in de Gaulle's attitude,[25] followed Giraud's movements with interest. Eden wrote in July 1942:

> It is not impossible that some other leader, such as General Giraud, will eventually emerge, who will enjoy greater support in France than General de Gaulle and be able to challenge his position. But there is no sign of such a rival at present. In spite of his collaborationist policy, Marshal Pétain has hitherto managed to retain the loyalty of the Generals, including General Weygand, and there is no sign yet of any break-away, even on the part of those whom we know to be anti-German and well-disposed to us.[26]

This does not mean that the British were seeking to displace de Gaulle. Rather they believed that no single figure could claim to be the sole legitimate representative of France:

> General de Gaulle is the only leader of French resistance who has emerged since the collapse, but he cannot substantiate a claim to be regarded as France or as the head of the Government of France ... France was shattered at Bordeaux and it will be a long time before the pieces can be joined together again.
>
> General de Gaulle's failings are well-known. His sudden actions can at times be dangerous. He is intensely suspicious and, like all true Frenchmen, suffers deeply the humiliation of his country. Many of his own followers find him just as difficult to deal with as we do. Yet, we must give him credit for having kept the flag of France flying by our side since June 1940. We have been largely responsible for building him up in France, and it is clearly impossible for us to drop him now.[27]

Giraud was contacted by the Allies and agreed to cooperate with them to support landings in North Africa provided that the troops involved were exclusively American (he was bitter about the British attack on Mers-el-Kébir) and that he was given command of troops there within forty-eight hours of the landings. Neither of these conditions were likely to be met but the Allies proceeded with the operation. Giraud was collected by a British submarine, masquerading as an American one, and taken to Gibraltar. He arrived too late to accompany the landings in North Africa, which involved both American and British soldiers. The Allies had made prior contact with Frenchmen in North Africa (mainly from right-wing circles), but in spite of this Vichy troops fired on the Anglo-American forces as they landed.

At this point, an unforeseen opportunity arose. Admiral Darlan, who had been a senior figure in the Vichy government, happened to be in Algeria, visiting his sick son. Darlan signed a cease fire with the American general Mark Clark, and for a time it seemed that Darlan himself would become the main French interlocutor of the Americans. De Gaulle was hardly likely to welcome this arrangement and the British were also unhappy with it. Eden thought that Darlan might be a worthwhile ally if he could bring the French fleet in Toulon with him: 'If he cannot render this service, his inclusion in a French administration ... would cause more trouble than it would be worth.' As for Giraud, they were willing to recognise his authority in North Africa but not over 'the many important colonies which own allegiance to de Gaulle and have been with us through all the dark days'.[28]

Darlan disappeared from the scene as unexpectedly as he had arrived because he was assassinated on Christmas Eve by a French royalist – who was himself then executed almost immediately. Not surprisingly these deaths gave rise to dark suspicions. There is no evidence that de Gaulle or his agents were behind the assassination, but he greeted it with grim satisfaction. He sent Giraud the following message:

The assassination at Algiers is an indication and warning; an indication of the exasperation into which the tragedy of France has thrown the mind and soul of Frenchmen; a warning of the consequences of every kind which necessarily result from the absence of a national authority in the midst of the greatest national crisis in our history.[29]

All concerned now agreed that de Gaulle and Giraud should meet, but there was no consensus as to what the purpose such a meeting should serve. De Gaulle wanted to unify French forces under a single authority. The British hoped that some real agreement might be reached. The Americans sought to ensure that all action by the French should be subordinated to military needs, to be determined by Eisenhower, now the American commander-in-chief in the area.

De Gaulle was persuaded to come to Casablanca in Morocco in January 1943. Here Churchill and Roosevelt met for a conference, and a meeting was contrived on its margins between Giraud and de Gaulle, who were photographed shaking hands. Roosevelt continued to treat the matter with levity – referring to de Gaulle as a reluctant bride – though some believed that the president's entourage took de Gaulle's hostility so seriously that they posted guards armed with sub-machine guns, behind a curtain when de Gaulle and Roosevelt met.

After the meeting, de Gaulle was stuck in London because the British refused him the means to travel. In March 1943, he enquired 'whether he was to regard himself as a prisoner in this country'. Since the war cabinet decided that the home secretary should 'consider what special measures were required to ensure that General de Gaulle would not leave this country under his own arrangements',[30] the answer to this question was clearly 'yes'.

In fact, de Gaulle's alliances in British politics had been reversed since 1940. At first, his most important ally had been Churchill. Most ministers had been indifferent to him. The Admiralty and the Foreign Office (both keen to maintain some kind of relation with Vichy) had been hostile. However, as de Gaulle's position became more established, British diplomats were cold-blooded enough to see the advantages of working with him and their views were reinforced in December 1940 when Anthony Eden (the cabinet minister most favourable to de Gaulle) replaced Halifax as foreign secretary. Churchill was not cold-blooded about de Gaulle and was increasingly irritated by his conduct. Sometimes the divergence of opinion between Churchill and Eden over France produced odd contortions as the former presented himself as the exponent of diplomatic subtlety. He wrote to Eden in June 1942: 'The position is so anomalous and so monstrous that very clear-cut views such as you are developing, do not altogether cover it.. There is much more in British policy towards France than abusing Pétain and backing de Gaulle.'[31]

For Churchill, relations with de Gaulle and Roosevelt were intertwined. Because he considered the second of these relations so important, Churchill was exasperated when he felt that de Gaulle crossed the Americans. Matters reached a head when Churchill visited Washington in May 1943. Roosevelt and also Cordell Hull complained about de Gaulle's conduct and showed Churchill documents that seemed to reflect de Gaulle's hostility or lack of grace towards his English and American allies. Eden, who might usually have calmed Churchill and defended de Gaulle, was in London. The prime minister telegraphed: 'I ask my colleagues to consider urgently whether we should not now eliminate de Gaulle as a political force.'[32] The cabinet considered the matter and disagreed. They allowed de Gaulle to go to Algiers at the end of the month.

Churchill was more exercised by the offence that de Gaulle supposedly caused to Roosevelt than Roosevelt was himself. The president controlled the greatest military power the world had ever seen and he was fighting a war that stretched across most of the world. In these circumstances, the vital fact about de Gaulle was his unimportance. Why should the Americans bother about a man who had a relatively small military force at his disposal? Roosevelt pointed out that the British provided de Gaulle with his money and weapons and asked why they did not just cut off his supplies – an interesting point to make at a time when America was providing Britain with money and armaments. Roosevelt was a cultivated man who spoke better French than Churchill but he did not share Churchill's emotional attachment to France. Churchill swung between admiration for de Gaulle and anger at him. Roosevelt regarded him just as a faintly comic figure or as a mystic[33] – two categories that did not necessarily exclude each other. Regardless of his private feelings Roosevelt's policy towards de Gaulle was driven by the wider requirements of war. When Eisenhower suggested, first in North Africa and after June 1944 in mainland France, that working with de Gaulle might be militarily convenient, Roosevelt was willing to do so.

De Gaulle was also more detached than Churchill about Roosevelt and America. He had never been to the United States and would not do so until July 1944. He met Roosevelt only twice. Churchill admired the United States as a torchbearer of liberty; for de Gaulle, it was simply a huge war machine – notable mainly for its industrial production. He did not see it as the representative of high ideals and was not shocked when it acted as ruthlessly as any other great power in pursuit of its interests. He even came to understand Roosevelt's irritation with him. In 1955, he talked to the American ambassador in Paris:

I remember my difficulties with Roosevelt. In retrospect, I think we were both right. I was led to act in a way that, I recognize, was intransigent to maintain the recognition of France as a power ... But on the other side I can understand that Roosevelt, the leader of the greatest nation in the coalition struggle for the survival of the free world was exasperated by my attitude.[34]

When de Gaulle reached Algeria, he and Giraud became joint chairs of a new body – the Comité Français de Libération Nationale (CFLN). This was composed of Gaullists and those supporting Giraud but, if one includes Catroux who had originally brokered the negotiations between the two sides, Gaullists outnumbered Giraudists. Furthermore, Jean Monnet – who had come from the United States to North Africa and who was ostensibly associated with Giraud – was intelligent enough to appreciate de Gaulle's qualities. Alphonse Georges, a retired general who had been spirited out of France, was imposed on the committee largely because Churchill admired him. But he was so politically inept that his support for Giraud probably worked in de Gaulle's favour.

At first the forces loyal to the two men were brought under central authority, then de Gaulle argued that military and political authority should be separate and that he should exercise the latter – a fact that said much about his belief in the subordination of military to civil power. Finally, Giraud was stripped even of his military function and offered the honorary position of inspector of the army, which he refused.

De Gaulle was assisted by the fact that the greater part of the resistance in mainland France rallied behind him (see chapter 7). In June 1943, an intelligence report to Churchill described the balance of forces. The British had helped Giraud to make contact with 'specialized military groups' drawn from the army in France but 'this movement never will have a "popular' backing'. The report added:

> The name of Giraud counts for very little indeed in France. The name of Georges is mud. The name of anyone else in power in 1940 is manure ... It follows from the above that it would be very difficult to persuade the heads of the Resistance Movements to transfer their present allegiance to any other authority except a French Committee of National Liberation in which de Gaulle had his due place.[35]

De Gaulle had other advantages. Some of the French army in North Africa, initially under Giraud's command, defected to join the Gaullist Leclerc, who had fought his way across the Sahara to reach Tunis. The English-language press was largely sympathetic to de Gaulle; in the United States there was a sharp divide between

government policy and the Gaullist opinions of prominent journalists, most notably Walter Lippmann.[36] De Gaulle was also helped by
Third Republic parliamentarians. A British agent relayed the view of
Jules Jeanneney (the president of the French Senate) that 'de Gaulle
was by far the superior man ... Giraud was brave but not brainy.'[37]
Those parliamentarians who reached Algeria gave de Gaulle their
support and imparted a degree of political finesse to his cause.
Some of de Gaulle's new supporters were incongruous in view of
his right-wing past. The British assumed that the former minister
Henri Queuille incarnated everything about the Third Republic that
they and de Gaulle despised. Duff Cooper was incredulous when
he reported that Queuille was acting for de Gaulle while the latter
was ill: 'Queuille is a nice friendly little old gentleman who has held
office in, I think, eleven French governments, and who would have
made an admirable President of the Republic of the Le Brun type.'[38]

De Gaulle's most effective ally against Giraud was Giraud.
Someone with republican views might have outmanoeuvred him
on the left. Giraud, on the other hand, was a person of such obvious conservatism that he made de Gaulle's professions of loyalty
to the French republican tradition seem convincing. Giraud did not
cultivate the politicians who might have provided him with useful
support. After meeting Giraud in January 1943, Duff Cooper's wife
Diana described him as 'a more wooden Kitchener of Khartoum'.[39]
She added:

> Never in the history of politics has a man frittered away capital so
> quickly ... he has been driven, or rather voluntarily retreated, from
> every bastion of his fortress. He has been exploded by mines of
> his own making, he has himself dug and opened the trenches that
> besieged his citadel.'[40]

With all French territories in Africa and the Americas under
Gaullist control, Algeria transformed de Gaulle's status: he now
had an independent territory relatively close to Europe. He had

established something that looked like a government and, more surprisingly, something that looked like a parliament because a provisional Consultative Assembly (made up of representatives of the resistance along with some deputies and senators who had got out of mainland France) met in Algeria from late 1943.

Between 1940 and 1943, de Gaulle had travelled more than ever before, but the most striking feature of his travels was his apparent indifference to the places he visited. He saw sub-Saharan Africa for the first time, but Brazzaville and Algiers mattered to him primarily as stages on which dramas relating to mainland France were played out. Empire featured little in de Gaulle's thinking before 1940; he had served outside mainland France only briefly. Many French soldiers were moved by the romance of the empire – especially in North Africa. For de Gaulle, the empire mattered primarily because it provided him with an area in which he could exercise a degree of autonomy and gave him a base from which he might move to the mainland.

De Gaulle's relative indifference to empire was underwritten by two things. First, the French empire was compact. France had possessions in Asia and the Americas but these were mostly small – the French-ruled area around Pondicherry (which rallied to de Gaulle in September 1940) was hardly comparable to the British Raj. The parts of the French empire that mattered most, especially in North Africa, were close to mainland France in geographical terms and – as far as the European population of the coastal cities was concerned – close in cultural terms too. Second, by comparison with its British rival, the French empire had been politically quiescent. There had been modest, and unsuccessful, moves to grant the indigenous population of Algeria greater political rights in the 1930s but little serious change in the status of any French colony for over a hundred years.

Because he presided over decolonisation after his return to power in 1958, it is tempting to assume that de Gaulle thought deeply about the future of empire during his wartime travels. In fact, most of de Gaulle's remarks on Africa and empire were banal. He talked of modernisation and reform but never suggested that he anticipated independence. Significantly, he said more about sub-Saharan Africa than Algeria – perhaps precisely because the prospect of independence seemed even more remote in the former than the latter. On the day the Second World War in Europe ended, there was a rebellion in Sétif in Algeria, which the authorities and settlers crushed with great brutality. Algerians sometimes define this as the beginning of their war of independence. An official inquiry into events at Sétif was stopped on the orders of de Gaulle.[41] In his memoirs he devoted one sentence to Sétif.

The British empire together with the Commonwealth was bigger, richer and more far-flung than the French. Whereas the French empire was of *political* significance to de Gaulle in his struggle against Vichy, the British empire was *militarily* significant in the war against Germany and Japan. Troops, munitions and money came from the colonies and dominions to the metropole or the various theatres in which the British were fighting. The white-settler colonies, by now self-governing dominions, were also independent military powers. India was politically subordinate to the London government but it had its own army, its own government and its own budget. Britain's political position was weakened by the fact that it owed the Indian government money for Indian troops who served abroad. Churchill was tempted by the suggestion of Maynard Keynes (bitterly opposed by the India Office) that the British government should simply renounce its debts to India.[42]

Sometimes it seemed as though the dominions were operating a reverse imperialism as their role in the formulation of strategy gave them power in London. The South African Jan Smuts was particularly important. In November 1943, he made a speech in which he commented on the decline of the European powers, especially France. De Gaulle took great offence – and was even more offended when Churchill invited Smuts to the Normandy beaches on 12 June 1944, before de Gaulle himself had returned to France. Shrewd observers understood that what Smuts had said about France might equally well have applied to Britain.[43]

De Gaulle felt uncomfortable with the Commonwealth; its existence would be one of the reasons why he opposed British accession to the Common Market in the 1960s. During the war, it was painfully obvious that the Commonwealth countries were more important in military terms than the Free French. One of Churchill's private secretaries listed Bernard Freyberg, commander of New Zealand's forces in Britain, as one of the important generals to visit the prime minister's residence at Chequers in 1940. He recorded de Gaulle's name among 'various lesser fry.'[44] Exasperated with de Gaulle, Churchill wrote to Eden in 1945 about representation at conferences to plan the post-war world. He said that France's contribution to the war was small and added: 'Canada has more right than France.'[45]

De Gaulle believed in clear definitions of sovereignty. The French empire was made up of people who were French or people who were ruled by the French. The Commonwealth, in which nations might owe allegiance to the British head of state without being subordinate to the British government, aroused his disquiet. Everything that troubled de Gaulle about the status of the self-governing dominions was epitomised by the fact that Canada and South Africa retained diplomatic relations with Vichy France until 1942.

As far as the British were concerned, the ramshackle quality of the empire and Commonwealth partly concealed their decline. Since the white-settler colonies were already self-governing, there was to be no dramatic break with the mother country until Rhodesia declared itself independent in 1966. The British assumed that a variety of political regimes would survive inside their Commonwealth for decades to come. Duff Cooper suggested that Britain was uniquely qualified to lead a united Europe after the war because 'the smaller nations of western Europe might themselves request to be taken into the British Commonwealth, which has, more successfully than any other institution, dealt with the dilemma of the creation of union and the retention of sovereignty'.[46]

Churchill – admiring of, and admired in, the settler colonies – did not fully grasp the implications of their growing autonomy. He was also prone to assume that the settler colonies were part of a wider group of English-speaking peoples. He regarded the United States as a natural ally of the British empire, perhaps even its successor, rather than being its nemesis. In June 1939, when an American journalist asked him about the prospect of British defeat in the coming war, he replied: It will then be for you, for the Americans, to preserve and to maintain the great heritage of the English-speaking peoples. It will be for you to think imperially, which means to think always of something higher and more vast than one's own national interests.[47]

But Churchill could not fail to appreciate the importance of diminishing British power in the part of the empire that mattered most to him: India. Even during the first year of the war and when, as First Lord of the Admiralty, he might have had other matters to engage his attention, Churchill fussed about India.[48] In July, by which time he was prime minister, he returned to the issue of dominion status. Ostensibly, Churchill did not break with the commitments given by his predecessors, but he sought to slow the progress towards Indian independence. He advanced two characteristic arguments. The first related to India and to the defence of 'minorities' – 'including, of course, not only the Hindus and Moslems but the Princes, the Depressed Classes, the Sikhs, the Anglo Indians and others'. The second related to Britain and reflected Churchill's deference to the House of Commons – though also, one suspects, his failure to predict what would happen in 1945: 'It would only be misleading our Indian friends if we led them to believe that we had any power in our free democratic system to prescribe in advance the composition or temper of a future House of Commons'.[49]

The viceroy took India into the war in 1939, but the immediate consequences were limited. Until December 1941, blackouts, rationing and evacuation were things that the British in India knew about only from reading newspapers in their club. Indian soldiers were sent abroad – to Africa, the Middle East, Malaya and Singapore – but it did not seem likely that there would be fighting on, or even close to, Indian soil. The Indian National Congress opposed participation in the war, but Indian men joined up in greater numbers than ever before.

Japanese entry into the war and the fall of Malaya changed everything. Soon the Japanese were marching through Burma. They occupied the Andaman and Nicobar islands – used by the British authorities as a penal colony for Indian prisoners – in 1942. Ceylon was also threatened and Calcutta was bombed. More important was the arrival of refugees from Burma – starving, exhausted people who staggered into Darjeeling in what some believed to be, at the time, the largest migration in human history. Around 600,000 people had arrived from Burma by the autumn of 1942. Most of these were Indians and around 80,000 died on their journey.[50] In Malaya and Burma Europeans were given more help to escape than either the native population or the large Indian communities in these countries. This caused resentment among those left behind, but it also meant that Indians, used to dealing with the British as self-confident men, suddenly saw them as fleeing women and children.

The British fought a rearguard action across Burma and eventually began to fight their way back. Burma was remote from Britain. It was the site of a long, grinding campaign that never yielded the clear-cut success obtained elsewhere, nor even the clear-cut avoidance of catastrophe that had marked Dunkirk. Conditions were hard and fighting was brutal. The writer George MacDonald Fraser fought through Burma as a private in the Border Regiment, which was absorbed into a ragbag army of British and Indian soldiers. In his old age MacDonald Fraser became a ferocious Tory but not an admirer of Churchill. He recalled a confused attack in which 'Grandarse lost his upper dentures ... [[and]] ... little Nixon disturbed a nest of black scorpions in the dark': 'the general feeling was that the blame for the whole operation lay at the door of, first, Winston Churchill, secondly, the royal family, and thirdly (for some unintelligible reason), Vera Lynn'.[51]

Military reverses intertwined with India's internal politics. In March 1942, the Labour MP Stafford Cripps went to India to try to trade Indian support for the war for the promise of dominion status. He failed. Gandhi remarked that he offered 'post-dated cheque on a failing bank' – perhaps giving rise to memories of the money-lenders in Bangalore with whom lieutenant Churchill had endured some uncomfortable interviews. In August, the Indian National Congress launched the Quit India movement and its leaders were imprisoned. One Congress leader – Subhas Chandra Bose – had already escaped from house arrest and fled India. He went, via Afghanistan and the Soviet Union, to Germany where he met Hitler. He was then transported by submarine to Japan – once Germany and the Soviet Union were at war, this was the only way to make the journey.

Bose sought to raise an Indian National Army (INA) that would fight against the British. He recruited mainly among Indian soldiers who had been taken prisoner by the Japanese. The INA was not successful in military terms. The number of soldiers that it recruited was relatively small, given that the alternative was starvation in a Japanese prison camp. But Bose's initiative intersected with developments in India among nationalists who had not taken up arms against the British. When the surviving leaders of the Indian National Army* were tried at the Red Fort in Delhi, Nehru himself served as one of

---

*Bose himself died in a plane crash days after the Japanese surrender.

their defence counsel. The men were convicted but their sentences were commuted by the commander-in-chief of the Indian army, who recognised that executing them would cause more trouble than it was worth. This was the moment when the British writ ceased to run in India. By inciting prisoners of war to fight for the Axis, John Amery, son of the secretary of state for India, had committed the same offence as the officers of the Indian National Army. He was hanged.

The problem for the British, though, was not simply military defeat – in the end they won the war against the Japanese – or political opposition to their rule, which was hardly new. Rather, it was that the war brought such social and economic upheaval. The most spectacular manifestation of this was the Bengal famine of 1943. According to some estimates, 3 million people starved to death. There is debate about whether the famine reflected a real shortage of food, though no one denies that things were made worse by the war. The fall of Burma deprived India of rice imports. The British had impeded fishing and transport by destroying boats that they feared might be used by the advancing Japanese. British soldiers consumed beef, which meant killing animals that might otherwise have been used to produce milk or to pull ploughs.

Were the British, especially Churchill, responsible for the famine? The British did not want Indians to starve to death. Wavell, by this stage viceroy, pressed the government in London to provide more food for India and to speed up the replacement of the governor of Bengal, whom he regarded as inefficient. There was, however, a difference between the way in which India was treated and the way in which Britain itself, or even defeated Axis countries in Europe, were treated. The British shipped grain to Italy, though starvation levels there never approached those in India. In 1940, at a time when a bombed-out family in Bethnal Green lived better than an average Indian peasant, the Viceroy's War Purposes Fund had given £150,000 raised in India for victims of the Blitz in Britain.[52]

There were extraordinary features of Churchill's attitude to famine in India. A man who repeatedly fussed about the need for British workers and soldiers to be provided with beef and cheese, and whose own gargantuan appetites were satisfied without regard to rationing, thought about food for India only when it intersected with military considerations. On 12 January 1943, the war cabinet discussed India. Churchill expressed vigorous opinions about the detention of Gandhi but remained silent while his colleagues discussed famine.[53] Churchill's request to Roosevelt for extra ships to convey grain from Australia to India justified this on the grounds that it would contribute to 'war efficiency' rather than because it might save lives.[54]

Economic and social change ate at the foundations of the Raj. The India of the 1890s had already largely disappeared when Churchill evoked it in his autobiography of 1930; it had certainly gone by 1945. Bangalore had been mainly a garrison town. When Churchill was stationed there, it had a population of around 150,000. By 1930, this had doubled. War brought rapid industrialisation. A local businessman obtained some derelict land outside the city. After clearing the cobras and the termites, he built the first factory of the Hindustan aircraft company.[55] Between 1941 and 1951, the city's population increased from a little over 400,000 to almost 800,000. The current population of Bangalore is around 8 million. Parade Row, by the old British barracks, is now Mahatma Gandhi Road.

Churchill was still sentimental about the Indian army – though also prone to brood on 1857 and fear the consequences of 'putting modern weapons in the hands of sepoys'.[56] When Subadar Richhpal Ram won a posthumous Victoria Cross in Eritrea, Churchill wrote to the viceroy that the feat brought back memories of his youth 'as one who has had the honour to serve in the field with Indian soldiers from all parts of Hindustan.[57] But the Indian army changed. In October 1939 it had just over 200,000 soldiers; by July 1945, this figure was two and a quarter million.[58] Fewer Indian soldiers were drawn from what the British considered to be 'martial races'; the Punjab was still the single most important recruitment ground but no longer accounted for a majority of soldiers.

The hierarchies of the Indian army that Churchill had seen in the 1890s were shaken by the Second World War. Once there had been a clear distinction between officers, invariably white, and other ranks. Between the wars, and in spite of Churchill's efforts to impede the process, some Indians had been commissioned. But distinctions remained. Most Indian officers held a Viceroy's Commission while their British comrades held a King's Commission. Until 1943, Indian officers were forbidden to impose punishments on white soldiers. When the matter was discussed in cabinet, the secretary of state for India recorded: 'Winston let himself go with a flood of all the most childish out of date objections to the poor much harassed British soldier having to face the extra humiliation of being ordered about by a brown man.'[59] By 1945, however, British commanders appreciated that Indian officers would soon be commanding their own army. In any case, the British soldiers posted to India during the war – men such as the communist historian John Saville – were very different from those who had been celebrated by Kipling.

By the end of the war, Churchill himself recognised that India was lost. He told de Gaulle on 11 November 1944 that 'colonial possessions might sometimes be more of a liability than an asset, as Great Britain's balance sheet with India now showed'.[60] In the long term, industrialisation, the militarisation of politics and the political separation of Muslim and Hindu destroyed the India of Gandhi as much as that of Churchill. In the short term, however, it looked as though Gandhi had won during the war. Bose, who might have been his rival, was dead. Nehru had not been comfortable with the idea that Congress should play no part in a war against fascism, but he had gone along with Gandhi's views and the British had simplified matters by locking both men up. Churchill constantly complained about favourable treatment for Gandhi. But it was not just left-wingers, such as Stafford Cripps, who respected Gandhi. Lord Mountbatten, the last viceroy of India, attended Gandhi's funeral after his assassination by a Hindu extremist in 1948. Mountbatten's predecessor, Wavell, had long been intrigued by Gandhi and eventually met him at the Simla conference in June 1945. Wavell's aide, Peter Coats, in military uniform, bowed his head as Gandhi passed. Gandhi signed a photograph of the scene for Coats.

Most of all, Churchill's India was destroyed by the United States. This was partly because Roosevelt liked to portray himself as the representative of national freedom pitted against the caricature imperialism of Churchill – de Gaulle thought the Americans were merely launching a new kind of imperialism. Most important, though, was the tangible reality of American power. By 1945, India contained hundreds of US bases. The Americans provided work for Indians – though they also disrupted their lives, for example by draining paddy fields to eradicate mosquitoes. The British refused to let the Americans maintain a formal presence in India after the war, or to keep bases in Bombay and Calcutta, but nothing could disguise the fact that parts of the Indian state, especially the railway system in the east of the country, had effectively been taken over by the United States. Peter Coats recalled the moment in 1943 when Linlithgow was about to step down as viceroy. Few guessed that Coats' own chief, General Wavell, would be appointed to the post; most thought that London might send out Halifax, Eden or Butler. One day, Coats's Indian bearer reported a rumour from the bazaar that, while factually incorrect, suggested many Indians had a firm grasp of geopolitical realities. The next viceroy, said the bearer, would be an American.[61]

7

A War of Peoples and of Causes?

This is no war of chieftains or of princes, of dynasties or
national ambition; it is a war of peoples and of causes.
Winston Churchill, 14 July 1940.

Churchill and de Gaulle were both men of the right who formed
alliances with the left during the Second World War. In the long
run, de Gaulle adjusted to the transition better. He sat in government
with Communists and Socialists in 1945, after Churchill had been
evicted from power by a Labour election victory, and, even after he
broke with the Communists, de Gaulle kept some contact with the
left. Until 1969, leading French politicians described themselves as
'left-wing Gaullists' and assumed that the general had sympathy for
their position. Though Churchill had admirers on the left after 1945,
none of them imagined that he, or his closest political associates,
shared their views.

Things did not seem so simple in 1940. Denouncing the Third
Republic almost as vigorously as he denounced Vichy, de Gaulle
often seemed at his most reactionary in that year while Churchill,
ferociously opposed to the Nazis and comparatively uninterested for
the time being in British internal politics, sometimes appeared indul-
gent towards the left – both in Britain and abroad.

At least from the mid 1930s, Churchill's view of politics was
closely associated with his view of Britain's diplomatic and military position, and there was always an element of realpolitik in his

attitude to potential allies. He was a democratic conservative in British politics, but his conservatism often made him undemocratic when he looked at other countries, especially if he thought that undemocratic regimes (even the Soviet Union at times) might serve British interests. Churchill's shifting view of Spain was particularly revealing. He was most sympathetic (or at least most prone to say sympathetic things in public) to the anti-Franco republican forces when they were directly engaged with troops from Germany or Italy and then, in 1940, when it seemed possible that Franco might join the Axis. He even slipped a favourable reference to republican Spain ('the brave men of Barcelona') into his 'Finest Hour' speech of 18 June 1940.. Later in the war, when Franco had made it clear how far realpolitik governed his own policy, Churchill's view of Spain (at least the view he expressed in private) shifted again. In July 1943, he told the Spanish ambassador in London that he was sympathetic to Franco's authoritarianism, though sure that such a regime was unsuitable for Britain. Knowing that such remarks would not be well received by his colleagues, he talked to the ambassador alone in the garden at Chequers. But his attempts to avoid leaving a record of the conversation were thwarted because the British security services intercepted and transcribed the account that the ambassador sent back to Madrid.[1]

France, though, was different. Churchill did not see it as another backward country that might be suited to authoritarian government. The Frenchmen whom he knew best and admired most were democratic politicians. The kind of French patriotism Churchill admired (that of Clemenceau) was intimately associated with republicanism.

De Gaulle also admired Clemenceau, but he was less sympathetic to the republican tradition and was particularly unsympathetic in the summer of 1940 – when he argued that the whole political system of the Third Republic had failed. Listening to the BBC in occupied France, the economist Charles Rist noticed that references to 'liberté, égalité, fraternité' on the French language broadcasts had been replaced by the words 'honneur et patrie'. He wrote in his diary: 'the Republic is in decline – even in England'.[2]

Many British people shared de Gaulle's hostility to French parliamentarianism. Robert Vansittart, the diplomat who for a time chaired the British committee on relations with the Free French wrote:

> No Frenchman at all wants to go back to their old unhappy branch of Parliamentary democracy. Some are ready for a totalitarian regime, some for a halfway house authoritarian regime. It is some regime of this latter kind that will almost certainly emerge from the turmoil. But all hate the Germans.[3]

It was sometimes alleged that French royalists seized on the defeat of 1940 as a chance to destroy the republic. This is not true. Some monarchists – notably General Weygand and Charles Maurras – supported Vichy but they had not welcomed the defeat and remained bitterly anti-German. In any case, Vichy did not restore the monarchy. The French journalist Geneviève Tabouis told John Colville: 'the Pétain Government will make every mistake except that one'.[4]

The people who took the restoration of the French king most seriously were often British. For them, monarchy was natural and they also hoped that the prospect of restoration might encourage Weygand to join the war against Germany. In November 1940, Desmond Morton suggested that the Comte de Paris (the pretender to the French throne) might set himself against Vichy and the Germans in North Africa and then Weygand would rally to him. He also reported that the Comte de Paris 'fears de Gaulle as a rival ... but would be delighted to recognize him as "Constable" [i.e. the king's lieutenant]'.[5] The most important British opponent of monarchical restoration in France was Churchill. He wrote: 'It would be a great mistake for de Gaulle at the present time to take any action or associate himself with the restoration of the Monarchy in France, and it would be intolerable if he did so without prior consultation with us.'[6]

For at least a year after he arrived in London, de Gaulle's own politics remained those of the royalist right – which is not quite the same as saying that he was a royalist. The language of Maurras's Action Française – 'la France seule' or 'le pays réel' – came so naturally to de Gaulle that it was hard to know with what degree of self-consciousness or irony he used such terms.[7] His abstract notions of how France might be governed in an ideal world were always undercut by realism about what was politically feasible and he would probably have been disconcerted if there had been any serious effort to restore the monarchy. In July 1942, he told a private meeting that only around 5 per cent of the French population were royalists and added that the pretender to the French throne had missed 'a priceless opportunity' by not coming out in favour of resistance.[8] He himself never proposed the restoration of the monarchy during the war but two Gaullists – Maurice Dejean and René Pleven – had an odd conversation with the British minister R. A. Butler in February 1941. They suggested that a monarchical restoration might provide a means of rallying the French people and that supporting such a restoration would show the British did not 'desire a return to the Popular Front in France.' They may have been seeking to sound out British intentions, in which case they were disappointed because Butler made no comment on their proposal. He gave no indication as to whether he believed them when 'they made it clear that they were not speaking on behalf of General de Gaulle'.[9]

De Gaulle's political position – at least his public expressions of that position – evolved during the war. This was a slow process. On 15 November 1941, he used the phrase 'liberté, egalité, fraternité' to define the Free French. These words, though, did not replace 'honneur et patrie' but were set beside them, along with 'libération'. De Gaulle found it easier to embrace revolution than republicanism – the word 'revolution' and especially the association of revolution and war featured in his speeches from 29 November 1940. In April 1942, he talked of 'national insurrection'. He found the notion of revolutionaries fighting against foreign armies at

Valmy in 1792 more appealing than the portly and bearded parliamentarians of the 1930s.

De Gaulle was playing a complicated game. An expression of republican or democratic principles would please important powers, especially the United States. Twice – on 14 July 1941 and again a year later – de Gaulle delivered speeches for broadcast in America, in which he said 'this national festival is the festival of liberty'. These speeches may have reflected an evolution in his thought or simply an ability to direct his remarks to particular audiences. On 1 August 1940, he had addressed French Canadians (a population that traced its origins back in part to those who had emigrated to escape the French Revolution) 'as a soldier, a Catholic and a Frenchman' – all terms that hinted at right-wing proclivities.

De Gaulle's own supporters in London were a coalition drawn from different political tendencies. Some of the army officers who had joined him were right-wing nationalists hostile to the republic. But René Cassin – his adviser on constitutional matters – was an emphatic supporter of the republic, though not particularly left-wing. Men like Cassin wanted a statement of republican principles from de Gaulle because it would underline a commitment to restore democracy after the liberation of France. This was also a point made by emissaries of the resistance who reached London.

It is hard to plot de Gaulle's moves on the political spectrum because the spectrum itself moved during the war. The divide between resisters and Pétainists sometimes supplanted existing political categories, or cut across them. A group of early resisters – Jacques Lecompte-Boinet, Henri Frenay, Philippe Viannay – had associations with the extreme-right. Such people usually began to think of themselves as 'socialist' during the war – though this did not always mean they espoused policies that a pre-war socialist would have approved. Pierre Brossolette and André Philip, on the other hand, had been socialists before the war but sought in 1943 to introduce Charles Vallin (who had been a member of the right-wing Croix de Feu) into the Free French leadership in London. They defended this move (resented by other pre-war socialists in London) on the grounds that the old parties were now discredited. Attacking political parties was the kind of right-wing argument that would once have been made by de Gaulle, but he stood aside and allowed Brossolette to be 'more Gaullist than de Gaulle' without expressing his support.

De Gaulle was a master of studied ambiguity. 'Republicanism' and 'democracy' were vague terms. De Gaulle could claim to be a republican without supporting the Third Republic and could distinguish the Third Republic of Clemenceau in 1918 from that of Lebrun in 1939. He could claim to be a democrat without supporting parliamentarianism. Those who met him often admitted that they did not know his real thoughts. Desmond Morton (Churchill's adviser) wrote to René Cassin (de Gaulle's adviser) on 14 July 1941:

> You and a few of General de Gaulle's close associates — even I myself — may think we have had some indication of the General's political views in private. In point of fact, have we? Anyway, when has he made any political declaration in the usually accepted meaning of the term?[10]

As late as January 1944, Harold Macmillan believed that de Gaulle was 'in a position of intellectual confusion: 'He has thought out no clear lines. He is partly reactionary and partly progressive.'[11] De Gaulle regarded the confusion about his real intentions with mischievous pleasure. He said on 15 November 1941:

> One of the rare distractions accorded by my present task is the reconciliation of varying affirmations. Because it is amusing to observe that the Free French are judged, at the same moment, to be inclined to fascism or preparing a restoration of constitutional monarchy or seeking the complete re-establishment of the parliamentary republic.[12]

There was an important difference between Churchill and de Gaulle. Churchill saw himself as fighting an ideological war against Nazism; de Gaulle had shown almost no interest in the rise of Nazism during the 1930s. For him, the Second World War was simply a continuation of the First – a 'thirty-year war', as he would sometimes refer to it. Even when inaugurating a monument to the resistance in 1946, he insisted on the continuity between the two world wars: 'Foch, Clemenceau, de Gaulle, it is the same thing.'[13] The difference between Churchill and de Gaulle emerged when they talked over lunch in December 1940. De Gaulle objected to Churchill's view that he was fighting the Nazis rather than the Germans and on the contrary insisted that Hitler was the heir to the Hohenzollerns 'toujours le militarisme allemand'. The conversation must have made Churchill think because later that afternoon he said: 'Germany existed before the Gestapo.'[14]

For Churchill, one aspect of Nazism had special importance. On the whole he admired Jews – a less unusual position among the English upper classes than is sometimes supposed. The idea of the law-abiding Jew who could expect protection from the state was important to his conception of British virtue, and also explains his hostility to Jews who rebelled against established authority. He was horrified by Nazi persecution and his objection to anti-Semitism (or Hitler's objection to his objection) seems to have lain behind the fact that a projected meeting between the two men in 1932 did not take place.

Unlike many people from his milieu, de Gaulle was not anti-Semitic, or at least he did not act in an anti-Semitic way as leader of the Free French. He welcomed Jews who joined him in London and condemned the treatment of Jews in Nazi-controlled Europe. His view of anti-Semitism was less straightforward than that of Churchill's, though. There were times when de Gaulle used anti-Semitic terms (to describe Jews in Russia or Poland rather than those in France) and he suggested that the Jewish Georges Mandel (whom he admired) would be less effective as a war leader than Clemenceau had been because he 'had not the same deep roots in the soil of France'.[15] Whereas Churchill saw the suffering of the Jews as a wrong to be righted, de Gaulle sometimes seemed to see it as an aspect of the human tragedy. When serving as a military adviser in Poland in 1920, he watched what was in effect a pogrom. He described it in vivid terms. The Poles blamed the Jews, who made up more than half the population of a town that had been occupied by the Red Army, for having collaborated with the enemy. A number of Jews were taken to be shot and then buried quickly: 'When a Jew dies, I was told, one must put the body underground before a Christian bell sounds. Otherwise a demon will torment them and cause a sea of troubles to those around.'[16]

De Gaulle did not approve of the killings, though he did not suggest that he or anyone else should intervene to stop them.

De Gaulle occasionally alluded to the moral dimensions of the war when he wanted to enlist Churchill's support. Seeking to prevent the British and Americans from supporting Darlan, he said: 'Today we make war with the soul, the blood, the suffering of peoples.'[17] But de Gaulle's references to morality in war were rare. Commenting on attacks by the resistance in France, he said on 23 October 1941: 'If the Germans want us to stop killing them, they have only to stay at home' – as though the Third Reich would have been of no concern to anyone else if its crimes had been confined within its own frontiers.

At the end of the war and after it, de Gaulle was moved by what he discovered about Nazi crimes. He stood on the platform of the Gare de l'Est on 14 April 1945 to greet 200 women prisoners returning from Ravensbrück concentration camp. He told his niece Geneviève that her account of Ravensbrück, where she had been imprisoned for being a member of a resistance network, 'cut into my soul' and he dedicated the first volume of his war memoirs to her. In 1967, he visited Auschwitz; once again, he seems to have been moved almost beyond words. However, his expressions of moral indignation about Nazism were not as frequent or as vehement as those of Churchill.

He was also prone to see the extermination of the Jews as a purely German crime. He said little about French participation in it.

Churchill sometimes claimed that Hitler was the only person he hated. De Gaulle's attitude was less emotional – or perhaps rooted in more troubling emotions. In his memoirs de Gaulle included a long meditation on the death of Hitler that teeters on the edge of admiration.

> It was suicide and not treason that put an end to Hitler's enterprise. He had embodied it. He ended it. To avoid being chained, Prometheus threw himself into the chasm ... Hitler's enterprise was superhuman and inhuman ... The Titan who had striven to raise the world could never flinch nor soften.

De Gaulle finished this passage with a curiously sympathetic sentence, one that illustrated his sense of the public masks that leaders wear: 'But, beaten and destroyed, perhaps he became a man again, just for long enough to shed a tear at the moment when everything ended.'[18]

De Gaulle's attitude to the Vichy government could also seem divorced from moral or ideological considerations. For him, Pétain's crime was submission to the Germans, not the establishment of a repressive regime, and the crime of the National Assembly lay in having accepted the armistice rather than having voted full powers to Pétain.[19] He complained that the French did not rebel against the defeat as such and would have tolerated the Vichy regime had it not 'disturbed their habits' with anti-Semitism and authoritarianism.[20]

In the long term, de Gaulle's political persona became intimately associated with the French resistance. At first, though, it sometimes seemed as though Churchill was more enthusiastic than de Gaulle about resistance. Churchill had begun his career as a soldier fighting rebels on the frontiers of the British empire. He expressed a grudging admiration for his opponents – lightly equipped forces fighting with guerrilla tactics close to their own homes. His admiration for the Boers in South Africa was particularly marked: 'If I were a Boer, I hope I would be fighting in the field.'

Churchill anticipated partisan warfare in 1940. He urged the French to continue guerrilla operations against the Germans in mainland France even after their armies had been defeated. Some of his colleagues anticipated sabotage in France and Belgium after German occupation. Such operations were to be coordinated by a specially created body in Britain[21] and associated with preparations made under the aegis of Lord Hankey for resistance and sabotage by the civilian population on British soil after German invasion.[22] Jean Monnet, sceptical about the extent to which the British really understood the implications of the 'total war' they sometimes advocated, conveyed messages about the organisation of guerrilla armies between the British and French governments. Perhaps he hoped that the British official mind would be concentrated by the discussion of such plans.

In the short term nothing came of discussions of guerrilla fighting in France. After the French defeat, however, Churchill anticipated that there might be fighting on British soil and talked more than ever of irregular warfare against the Germans. Indeed, his enthusiasm for resistance in occupied Europe – exemplified by his instruction that the Minister of Economic Warfare should 'set Europe ablaze' – sprang partly from the fact that, in 1940, he had contemplated the most desperate kind of resistance in occupied Britain. He sought to obtain dumdum bullets for his own pistol on the grounds that fighting in Britain was unlikely to be regulated by the Geneva Convention – which forbade such ammunition. He believed that the city of London would provide a good battle-ground because its narrow lanes lent themselves to the construction of barricades. He said on 14 July 1940:

Should the invader come to Britain, there will be no placid lying down of the people in submission before him, as we have seen, alas, in other countries. We shall defend every village, every town, and every city. The vast mass of London itself, fought street by street, could easily devour an entire hostile army; and we would rather see London laid in ruins and ashes than that it should be tamely and abjectly enslaved.

Churchill contemplated resistance that might take place in Britain in highly coloured terms. He said: 'here we want every citizen to fight desperately and they will do so the more if they know that the alternative is massacre ... even women must, if they wish, be enrolled as combatants.'[23] But Churchill never had to face the horror of what it was like to organise resistance activity among the civilian population and under the noses of a brutal enemy. There was an element of fantasy to many schemes for resistance in Britain. Peter Fleming, always alert to the child-like quality of British reactions in the summer of 1940, later suggested that the hides, from which it was intended that guerrillas would emerge to fight the Germans in the Home Counties, felt like the 'lost boys' castle' in Peter Pan.

Various kinds of irregular warfare caught the imagination of the British public in 1940. One of them involved specially trained and selected soldiers – commandos – who would be detached from their usual units and sent to 'butcher and bolt'. The commandos were intended to fight at first in Britain against invasion and then land on the coasts of occupied countries.

The excitement of commando raids appealed to Churchill. He wrote regretfully of war in the western desert:

Descriptions of modern battles are apt to lose the sense of drama because they are spread over wide spaces and often take weeks to decide, whereas on the famous fields of history the fate of nations and empires was decided on a few square miles of ground in a few hours.[24]

Commando raids offered quick bursts of decisive violence. Churchill was stirred by the raid on the coast of North Africa in which thirty men, only two of whom got back to their own lines, sought to capture Rommel and after which Geoffrey Keyes (the son of Admiral Sir Roger Keyes) was awarded a posthumous Victoria Cross. Churchill dreamt of attacks by '300 determined men, with blackened faces, knives between their teeth and revolvers under their tails.'[25] In his enthusiasm, he was prone to blur the boundaries between three different things: commandos, partisans and resistance seen in the early part of the occupation of France. Commandos were uniformed soldiers. If captured they were, in theory, protected by the Geneva Convention. Partisans, who operated in Yugoslavia and Greece and, by 1944, in parts of France enjoyed no such protection, but they were full-time combatants living in the woods or hills and organised into something resembling military units. Resistance of the kind seen in France in the early stages of the occupation was usually a matter of organisation, propaganda and information-gathering. Those involved rarely touched a gun.

For the French in 1940, the prospect of guerrilla warfare felt horribly real. They knew what devastation it would bring to their country and resented the relish with which Churchill contemplated it. Weygand had made a perceptive remark when Churchill suggested that the French should mount a 'guerrilla action' against the Germans in June 1940: 'It is a story [roman]. M. Winston Churchill is a very gifted writer ... but he has too much imagination. The German armoured divisions will make light work of the great guerrilla operation.'[26]

In London in July 1940, a British official showed the French diplomat Roland de Margerie a lurid pamphlet to be dropped into occupied France advocating attacks on Germans by civilians. De Margerie was horrified and asked who had written it. The answer was H. G. Wells.[27] Plans for some operations did often resemble the fantastical stories that Churchill so much enjoyed. De Gaulle noted the link between adventure stories and the resistance. He believed that recruitment for 'clandestine action' was made easier by the fact that, between the wars: 'Books, newspapers, theatre and cinema were largely devoted to the adventures of more or less imaginary heroes who undertook extraordinary exploits in the shadows for the service of their country.' De Gaulle, however, did not approve of the results of such reading, which risked introducing fraud, frivolity and, worst of all, 'romanticism' into the resistance.[28]

In 1940, the resistance de Gaulle had in mind was to be undertaken outside France and by uniformed soldiers. Unlike Churchill, he had little regard for irregular warfare and had written contemptuously that the Bolshevik forces he had encountered in Poland in 1920 were a 'mob' rather than an army. De Gaulle was troubled by the idea of resistance that might be based on ideology (by which he meant left-wing ideology) rather than patriotism. After the war, he spoke of a division between 'resistance to the enemy and then a politicians' resistance that was anti-Nazi but in no way national'.[29] Uncertainty about what resistance might mean was common among the French in both London and in France. Daniel Cordier came to Britain in June 1940 and was eventually parachuted back to help the resistance in occupied France, but at first he regarded fighting without uniform as dishonourable and hoped to serve as a conventional soldier.

The first resistance groups in France were small and isolated. Those in the north and west of the country (directly occupied by the Germans) had little to do with those in the southern or 'free' zone – de Gaulle later suggested that resistance in the north was more 'real' and less political than in the south. There was almost no contact between London and the early resistance movements in France.

Once contact was established, relations between the Gaullists in London and the resistance in France were handled by André Dewavrin ('Passy'),[30] who dealt with information, and Raymond Lagier, who dealt with 'action'. On the British side, the French (or F) Section of the Special Operations Executive (SOE) was based in Baker Street, which seemed appropriate to those who thought that the British way of clandestine action owed something to the stories of Sherlock Holmes. From early 1941, Section F of SOE was directed by Maurice Buckmaster, a former businessman and intelligence officer who had found his way back to Britain after Dunkirk. SOE and the Free French agencies existed in an uncomfortable forced intimacy. The French were trained and equipped by the British and depended on the RAF to get their agents in and out of France. Buckmaster and Passy worked together – sometimes negotiating as they paced up and down the mews street between their offices. In 1941, SOE established another section (RF), primarily composed of French agents who answered to Passy. Relations with de Gaulle, who occasionally visited Baker Street, were uncomfortable. Buckmaster recalled: 'I did not like him because he was not a likeable man, but I admired him.'[31]

The resistance did not start killing Germans until a Communist (Colonel Fabien) shot a German officer at Barbès-Rochechouart metro station in August 1941. At first, de Gaulle seemed minded to welcome the attack on the grounds that 'rivers of blood' would have to flow before France was liberated. He then took a more calculated position. While stressing that he had no moral objection to killing Germans, he felt that attacks were premature and might invite reprisals. On the BBC, Maurice Schumann, de Gaulle's spokesman, discouraged the French resistance from individual and 'dispersed' acts of violence. Rather, Schumann counselled a slow and patient obstruction and sabotage of German war production. Churchill was disconcerted and wrote: 'Is it true that the BBC deprecated the killing of Germans in France last night? Let me see what was actually said.'[32] British officials were, in fact, sympathetic to de Gaulle's position.[33] They favoured 'passive resistance' but counselled 'prudence' with regard to attacks and wished to avoid the suggestion that sabotage was 'under the control of a central organisation, British or French'. They understood that 'The General's point of view is that the assassination of individual Germans gives to the German authorities in France the opportunity of killing off his supporters and destroying his secret organisation.' At least in theory, the war cabinet supported Churchill's position and decreed: 'it is not the policy ... to discourage individual acts by French patriots against their German oppressors.'[34]

Churchill's views on resistance can be summed up with the instructions that he gave to his emissaries to wartime Yugoslavia who were charged with deciding whether the British should support the Communist Tito or the royalist Serbs of Draža Mihailović: 'Find out who is killing most Germans and how we can help them to kill more.' British support went to Tito and officers (including Churchill's son Randolph) were sent to liaise with Communist forces in Yugoslavia. Mihailović – accused of having fought against Tito's partisans and sometimes of having cooperated with the Germans – was executed under the post-war Communist regime in 1946. De Gaulle regarded Mihailovic with sympathy and sometimes reflected bitterly on his fate. Alain Peyrefitte, the minister of foreign affairs, recorded the following conversation in the 1960s: 'The real national hero was Mihailović. He was not fighting for an ideology, nor for the Soviet system. He did not launch into action because a foreign country pushed him to do so. He was simply a patriot. He had no goal but to liberate his country.' Peyrefitte added: 'It is a portrait of de Gaulle, of a de Gaulle who failed.'[35] De Gaulle had been even more explicit a few years earlier. The denouement of events in wartime Yugoslavia was 'a little as though Thorez [the Communist leader] had had de Gaulle shot'.[36]

For all his doubts, de Gaulle recognised that the resistance might serve his purposes because it could prove that he had support in mainland France. Indeed, the resistance in France mattered to de Gaulle partly because it mattered to the British. Desmond Morton wrote to Churchill in August 1942: 'General de Gaulle has formed the opinion that the degree of support H.M. Government will afford to his political ambitions will vary with the views held by

H.M. Government on the extent to which the French people are behind General de Gaulle.'[37]

In September 1942, Morton wrote a report on opinion in France and the Vichy colonies. He argued:

'Support for' de Gaulle means different things to different Frenchmen at different times. The extent of their support for him varies with their thought of him as a symbol of resistance, as a military chief or as a political leader. Unless helped to clear their own minds, Frenchmen often confuse the issue by giving a false impression of their attitude when they really support de Gaulle in one capacity, but condemn him in another. A further source of confusion is the term 'Gaullisme', purposely applied by Vichy and the Germans to any sort of resistance to collaboration. 'Gaullisme' is not necessarily 'de Gaullisme'.

A majority of the French people support de Gaulle as a symbol of their own desire to see French soil cleared of the enemy, though there is a new tendency to substitute the Croix de Lorraine for the person of de Gaulle.[38]

For those who dealt with him every day in London, de Gaulle was all too real. It is easy to see why they were exasperated by the perception that he enjoyed such an exalted status in France. But those who knew de Gaulle only through BBC broadcasts were bound to have an abstract image – often an image that was so abstract that it served as a screen onto which they could project their own values. Seeking to persuade Churchill not to discard de Gaulle in May 1943, Eden stressed his support among the French but added: 'The de Gaulle whom they follow is of course an idealized semi-mystic figure very different from the man we know.'[39]

Some senior resistance leaders understood the difference between the man whom they met on their visits to London and the myth of de Gaulle they cultivated in France. When in London in November 1942, Pierre Brossolette wrote de Gaulle an aggrieved letter complaining about his brusque and authoritarian manner. Back in France, on 2 March 1943, Brossolette published a 'Homage to General de Gaulle' in a resistance newspaper.[40] Henri Frenay manoeuvred to free his resistance movement from dependence on Gaullist agencies but still insisted that he was loyal 'to de Gaulle as a symbol'.[41]

Morton interviewed a succession of men who arrived in London from France and reported to Churchill on the conversations. The arrivals often did not know much about de Gaulle but they were emphatic, at least by 1941, that he had come to represent resistance in the eyes of most French people. 'Claudius' – the resistance nom de guerre of Eugène Petit, a Catholic but left-wing trade union leader, spoke to Morton in November 1943. The latter reported:

'Claudius' has never met General de Gaulle but insisted that his name is the only one with any power in France. After the fall of France, the French were suspicious of de Gaulle, believing him to be either another Boulanger, a self-seeking politician or a British tool. Now all in France, except an insignificant percentage who adhere to Vichy, have found in de Gaulle's public utterance the only voice which exactly represents their sentiments. His known differences with Mr Churchill have increased the prestige of both.[42]

A naval airman told Morton that 80 per cent of France was Gaullist.[43] Jacques Kayser, a politician and member of the Radical Party, said: 'General de Gaulle as a person is known to very few people. On the other hand, he is the embodiment of the spirit of resistance.' Kayser added, implausibly, that Édouard Herriot, leader of his own party, was the only man whose prestige might rival de Gaulle but then added, even more implausibly, that Herriot's ideas and those of de Gaulle were the same.[44] The journalist Jean Mousset called Gaullism a 'mystique', a religion founded and 'revealed' by de Gaulle's speech of June 1940. Its connection with de Gaulle is fortuitous'.[45]

Frenchmen who came to London often distinguished between the mystical image of de Gaulle, communicated to France via the BBC, and the conservative figures who gathered around him in London. However, they also recognised that the relationship between Gaullism as mystical idea in France and Gaullism as political reality in London was symbiotic: 'De Gaulle would "not be what he is" without resistance inside France, it is also true to say that resistance in France would not have been what it is without de Gaulle.'[46]

De Gaulle's greatest contribution to the resistance in France was unity. It was an advantage that he was not associated with any pre-war political party – though the most sophisticated French people would have understood that de Gaulle's variety of 'apoliticism' was, in practice, another way of saying that he was right-wing. It was also an advantage that he spoke in abstract terms and rarely anticipated a particular kind of post-war political order.

The German invasion of the Soviet Union in June 1941 threw Stalin onto the same side as Britain and the Free French. Like Churchill, de Gaulle had been willing to embrace a Soviet alliance against Nazism in the 1930s. De Gaulle saw Stalin as simply another leader of 'Russia', which might have strategic interests in common with France. Unlike Churchill, he was not concerned by the horrors that Stalin might unleash against his own people. De Gaulle also recognised that the Soviet Union might be useful in his wartime diplomatic manoeuvres. There was even a moment when de Gaulle seems seriously to have contemplated moving his headquarters to Moscow. In truth, Stalin, who cared greatly about weapons and troop numbers and nothing for mystical appeals, had a low regard for de Gaulle. De Gaulle's visit to Moscow in December 1944 was an occasion for humiliation. Mercifully, he did not know Stalin had telegraphed an account of their meeting to Churchill and Roosevelt and assured them that he would not discuss the question of the French frontier on the Rhine 'without the knowledge and agreement of our chief allies whose armies are waging a battle of liberation on the territory of France'.[47]

However, Stalin's cynicism could serve de Gaulle's interests. After the German invasion of the Soviet Union, he subordinated everything to the defeat of Germany – Alexander Bogomolov, who had been Soviet ambassador at Vichy, was sent as a representative to de Gaulle. If a united resistance in France could advance the cause of Allied victory in even a small way, then Stalin would support that unity and, if de Gaulle looked like the most plausible figure around whom a united resistance might rally, then Stalin would order Communists in France to give their loyalty to him. Stalin, for whom the notion of 'restoring democracy' was very strange, was mystified that his American and British allies should consider anything other than military interest when defining their relations with de Gaulle.[48] Communists threw themselves into the resistance in 1941 and bore the brunt of the consequent reprisals. The Communists swelled the ranks of those who were, at least nominally, de Gaulle's supporters, and in April 1944 Communists joined the Committee of National Liberation in Algeria.

De Gaulle benefited from Communist support and from the general perception that the resistance with which he was associated stood on the left. But he also gained from the fear of Communism. The more powerful Communists became, and the more violent their behaviour, the more de Gaulle seemed a guarantee of stability. Claudius of the Francs-Tireurs told Morton that if de Gaulle was excluded from power 'there will be Civil War and perhaps a sort of Communism'.[49] In November 1943, René Massigli, de Gaulle's commissioner for foreign affairs, told Harold Macmillan 'the only hopes of preventing a complete seizure of power by the Communists would be for the Allied armies to work in the closest harmony with the Committee (i.e. the Free French) with a view to imposing immediately on liberated territories the Prefect of the Committee's choice'.[50]

One resistance figure was to have particular importance for de Gaulle. Jean Moulin had been born in 1899 and spent most of his adult life in the prefectural corps. He was a cheerful, athletic man of seductive charm and a gifted caricaturist with an interest in modern art. Even in the desperately dangerous conditions of a resistance leader in occupied France, he contrived to enjoy life – almost the first thing he did after parachuting into France in 1942 was to go on a skiing holiday. He was, as the French say, but as no one ever said of de Gaulle, 'bien dans sa peau'. Whereas de Gaulle was raised in the austere Catholicism of northern France and brought up to regard the republican state with suspicion, Moulin came from the south. He was the son of a freemason and his own career had been built largely on the political patronage of figures from the Radical Party. He was close to Pierre Cot, a left-wing Radical, minister in the Popular Front government of 1936 and the one person whose support de Gaulle had refused in 1940. Moulin had also met Churchill (in 1939) before either man had met de Gaulle – though the encounter does not seem to have made much of an impression on Churchill.

Unlike de Gaulle, Moulin had not sought to leave France in 1940. He had stayed in Chartres (he was prefect of the Eure-et-Loir) and done his best to administer the region. He had a brief conflict with the Germans when they made a violent effort to get him to blame French Senegalese soldiers for killings that had been carried out by their own forces. After this, however, Moulin worked with the German authorities. He considered it his duty to stay at his post and do his best for the people of his region. A number of prefects who started out with similar intentions were eventually sucked into outright collaboration. Moulin, however, was dismissed by the Vichy government on account of his pre-war associations with left-wing politicians. He began to seek out resistance organisations and he reached England in October 1941.

Desmond Morton interviewed Moulin and reported on him to Churchill. He was impressed by his personality and especially by his discretion – in the view of the British, a quality the French often lacked. Moulin had not met de Gaulle before coming to London. However, he now told Morton that 'whereas up to a few months ago General de Gaulle's role was largely only a symbol of resistance in France, General de Gaulle's person has now become real to a large majority of Frenchmen owing to the great decline in the prestige of Pétain'. Moulin added that 'if the enthusiasm for the organisation of resistance on the part of hundreds of thousands of young men in France were to lack response, there is the gravest danger that they will turn from General de Gaulle to the Communists'.[51]

There was a good deal of bluff in Moulin's position. There were not hundreds of thousands of young men in the resistance in 1941 and, even if there had been, Moulin would have been in no position to speak for them. It was not clear why someone from Moulin's political milieu would attach himself to a right-wing army officer. Equally, it is not clear what de Gaulle made of Moulin. Perhaps he just welcomed a man who had enjoyed a relatively high official position in the French state and perhaps too he recognised that Moulin had a degree of intellectual lucidity and practical experience often conspicuous by its absence among the Free French in 1941.

Moulin returned to France as de Gaulle's emissary on the night of 1 January 1942 – apparently having had a last private meeting with de Gaulle on New Year's Eve.[52] He came back briefly to London in early 1943. He negotiated to unite the main resistance movements and political parties under the aegis of the newly constituted Conseil National de la Résistance, but soon afterwards was captured and died under torture. After this, the resistance leaders in France made a renewed effort to assert their independence with regard to London, but their efforts were thwarted because so many of them fell victim to the Germans. Moulin had brought de Gaulle considerable advantages. The resistance was more united than ever before and had now pledged loyalty to de Gaulle in explicit terms. In a grim way, Moulin's death suited de Gaulle. Alive, Moulin, an astute political operator, might have created all sorts of difficulties; dead, he became a Gaullist icon.

———

De Gaulle never had unchallenged authority over the resistance; some *résistants* looked to his conservative rival General Henri Giraud. However, support for Giraudist resistance never matched that for Gaullist resistance and Gaullism had acquired such an aura in France that many assumed that Giraud himself would accept that this was simply a synonym for resistance and that he would, therefore, describe himself as a 'Gaullist'. François Mitterrand and one of his comrades from the resistance were interrogated in Britain in January 1944. In 1981, Mitterrand would become the Socialist president of the Fifth Republic but, at this stage, he was still attached to the conservatism of his youth. He and his companion described themselves as 'Giraudists' but recognised that Gaullists and Giraudists were closely intermixed in practice and 'they would have to combine on D-Day if not before it'.[53]

From early 1943, the numbers joining the resistance (more particularly, the rural maquis) increased as young men sought to escape from the compulsory labour service in Germany imposed from February of that year. Numbers increased even more sharply in the spring and summer of 1944 – because the imminence of liberation meant that maquisards would no longer have to survive a winter. De Gaulle's view of resistance was based on a chronological hierarchy in which those who had stood against Germany in 1940 were placed above those who had joined the fight later. This was unfair. As anyone who has examined a war memorial in small-town France knows, resistance was most dangerous in 1944 – the year when there was most fighting and in which German troops, often brought back from the eastern front, were most brutal.

De Gaulle appreciated that he needed to make a show of support for the maquis and wrote to Churchill in March 1943 asking him to arm 50,000 men for a 'general insurrection'.[54] But he can hardly have been surprised to be told in reply that mass action would be premature until the Allies landed.[55] De Gaulle later admitted that his wartime statements on the maquis had been the product of political calculation: 'Free France had an interest, at that moment, in exalting the role of the resistance to reinforce its own influence with the allies.'[56] In private de Gaulle said that the uniformed soldiers of the Free French ran higher risks than the resistance inside France. His disdainful view of the internal resistance was sometimes close to that which evoked indignation from conservative French people when expressed by the American historian Robert Paxton in the 1970s. Like Paxton, de Gaulle believed that Jean Dutourd's cynical novel *Au Bon Beurre* (1952) was a good depiction of life in occupied France.[57] De Gaulle seems to have believed that the 'real resistance' was small and that the ranks of the maquis in 1944 were swelled by men who sought to avoid being sent to work in Germany. De Gaulle's son remembered his father's 'bitter laugh' as he described those who took to the hills: 'They avoided going to Germany, which was bombed and invaded, but they did not agree to join the resistance in any way and often they explicitly refused to do so.'[58]

Churchill became most interested in the French resistance at the moment (early 1944) when de Gaulle was most dubious about it. Until then, Churchill's interest in irregular warfare had mainly concentrated on Greece and Yugoslavia where large guerrilla forces operated. He was sympathetic to the more low-key activities of the early French resistance – organisation and intelligence gathering – but less excited by them. However, by 1944 he began to see a use for large-scale resistance in south-eastern France as a means of supporting the Allied advance through Italy, an operation that was dear to Churchill's heart. Furthermore, the maquis began to look like the kind of guerrilla army that excited him. It even seemed possible that maquisards might seize and hold a whole area of France. This was also the time when Churchill met Emmanuel d'Astier de La Vigerie, whom he described in characteristically dramatic terms:

This is a remarkable man of the Scarlet Pimpernel type and fairly
fresh from France, which he has visited three or four times. He has
made very strong appeals to me to drop more arms by air for their
resistance movements. ... As you know I am very anxious to see a
guerrilla à la Tito started up in Savoie and the Alpes Maritimes ... He
is a fine fellow, very fierce and bitter but one of the best Frenchmen
I have struck in these dark times.[59]

De Gaulle's relations with British members of the Special Operations
Executive, or Frenchmen who had been associated with British
agencies, were awkward. His words to Roger Landes (an SOE officer) in Bordeaux in September 1944 became notorious: 'You are
English. You do not belong here.'[60] From the British point of view,
the exchange illustrated de Gaulle's lack of grace towards his allies.
From de Gaulle's point of view the most important point about the
incident was probably that Landes ignored de Gaulle's instruction
that he should leave France and that de Gaulle was in no position to
impose his authority on British officers in his own country. SOE was
dissolved in January 1946, at almost exactly the moment when de
Gaulle resigned as head of government.

Other French politicians, including Gaullists, found it easier to
accept the British role in the resistance. Vincent Auriol, who had
been elected president of the republic in 1947, awarded Landes
the Croix de Guerre; the decoration was presented at a ceremony
presided over by Jacques Chaban Delmas, the Gaullist major of
Bordeaux. It is fortunate that de Gaulle never realised that the diplomat Anthony Montague Browne (attached to the British embassy in
Paris and soon to become Churchill's private secretary) was touring
France in the late 1940s and distributing money to people who had
been members of British-sponsored resistance networks.

British writing about relations with resistance in occupied Europe
often had the boys' adventure story quality that mattered so much to
Churchill and so exasperated de Gaulle. Harold Macmillan, who had
shuttled between Churchill and de Gaulle during the war, produced

such works in his capacity as a publisher. As prime minister, Macmillan also sponsored the official history of the SOE in France. This history was justified partly on the grounds that the British wanted to emphasise their own role at a time when European Communist parties were making much of their contribution to wartime resistance movements. Diplomats anticipated that the book would annoy de Gaulle.[61] It did. It was translated into French but then mysterious 'political difficulties' interrupted the process, and the book was not published in France until after de Gaulle's death.[62]

The relation between de Gaulle and the resistance was somewhat strange. On the one hand, he had been the figurehead of the resistance and it was from the resistance that he derived his legitimacy as a man who could claim to represent France. But his vision of the resistance was an abstract one, detached from acts by particular individuals or groups. Similarly, it sometimes seemed that members of the resistance in France had an abstract vision of de Gaulle – whom they knew only as a name and a voice on radio broadcasts.

After the war, the breach between de Gaulle and the Communist Party (which was at its most intense in the late 1940s) created a squabble about who was the rightful heir to the legacy of the resistance. The attitude of Communist leaders to resistance was similar to that of de Gaulle: the party celebrated the memory of resistance but disciplined resistance veterans who showed themselves to be too independent. De Gaulle too often found that his opponents used the memory of resistance to justify defying authority. Daniel Cordier, who had been Jean Moulin's aide, in 1958 helped found the Club Jean Moulin, which was intended to resist what its members believed to be the dictatorial quality of de Gaulle's rule.[63] George Bidault had succeeded Moulin as head of the Conseil National de la Résistance. In the 1960s, Bidault was living outside the law again – this time as an opponent of de Gaulle's decision to take France out of Algeria – and the body he founded to advance his cause was again called the Conseil National de la Résistance. Some of de Gaulle's most determined opponents – notably François Mitterrand – had had distinguished careers in the resistance.

The memory of resistance (or guerrilla warfare) was simpler in Britain because such warfare had never been conducted on British soil. The sharp divisions between left and right mattered less in Britain – where a desire to resist Nazism did not imply any choice about the regimes that would follow the war. Fitzroy Maclean was Churchill's emissary to the Communist Tito in Yugoslavia; Monty Woodhouse was sent to Greece, where the British backed the political right at the end of the war. Both men became Conservative MPs.

The British often suggest that post-war France was built on a 'myth' of resistance. But resistance could be an uncomfortable presence in French public life. It raised awkward questions about, for example, how much French people had acted against each other during the war. It suited de Gaulle that discussion of resistance should become a formal and pious commemoration of dead heroes and that most French people should regard their own wartime lives as marked by neither great courage nor complicity in the crimes of Vichy and the Germans. De Gaulle liked heroism, but he did not always like heroes and he liked France's heroic past to stay where it belonged – buried beneath granite monuments.

8

Shadows of Victory, 1944–55

'This leader, who had been invested by no sovereign, no parliament
and no plebiscite and who had no political organization of his own
at his disposal – would he be followed for long by the most fickle and
unmanageable people on earth?'
Charles de Gaulle on his return to France after the liberation[1]

'It seems quite effectively disguised.'
*Winston Churchill on being told, by his wife, that his defeat in the general
election of 1945 was a 'blessing in disguise'*

'How terrible it is that all we were able to achieve is now plunged in the
deepest peril, I have ever known, and that is saying a good deal.'
Churchill to de Gaulle, 22 August 1950[2]

The end of the Second World War was a triumph for Churchill
and de Gaulle, but both men were out of power just months after
the German surrender. Furthermore, the final victory in the Second
World War came with a display of American power that sometimes
overshadowed both Britain and France. The might of the United
States was seen during the Normandy landings of June 1944. The
landings might have happened earlier but for the fact that Churchill
feared that Allied troops would endure heavy casualties if they
engaged the Germans in northern France. He had hoped to circumvent the most obvious front lines by invading southern Italy – an

operation he described in characteristically vivid and misleading terms, as 'putting a wildcat' into German occupied Europe. About half of the soldiers who landed on D-Day itself (6 June) were British but most of the Allied equipment was directly or indirectly provided by the United States. Americans (Canadians as well as those from the United States) came to make up a large proportion of the troops in France. By the end of the war, Camp Lucky Strike in Normandy extended over 600 hectares and accommodated 58,000 Americans as well as the 3,000 German prisoners of war who worked for their captors. Such places would remain a feature of the French landscape until Charles de Gaulle withdrew France from NATO's command structures in 1966.

De Gaulle was in North Africa until shortly before D-Day. The British told him nothing of their plans and did not allow him to return to Britain until 4 June. He was taken to see Churchill, installed in a train near Portsmouth, who told him about the forthcoming operation. There was then a bitter argument. The British wanted de Gaulle to broadcast to the French people and wanted French liaison officers to be sent with the advancing troops. The Americans had come close to cutting the French out of the operation entirely and had trained some of their own men to manage an Allied Military Government of Occupied Territories (AMGOT), the mechanism through which they had administered Italy since their landings there in 1943. The British too had trained civil affairs officers, who cooperated with the French but who might, in slightly different circumstances, have supplanted them. De Gaulle was willing to broadcast but wanted the initial announcement by Eisenhower, the military commander of the liberating force, to be amended to say that the French authorities would re-establish civil government rather than 'When France is liberated from her oppressors you yourselves will choose your representatives and the government under which you will live.'[3] When this was not done, de Gaulle refused to broadcast and threatened to withdraw his liaison officers.

The British also tried to persuade de Gaulle to visit the United States and establish good relations with Roosevelt. The official transcript stated:

> He [Churchill] must tell him [de Gaulle] bluntly that, if after every effort had been exhausted the President was on one side and the French National Committee of Liberation on the other, he, Mr Churchill, would almost certainly side with the President and that anyhow no quarrel would ever arise between Britain and the United States on account of France. As regards the Civil Affairs agreement, he would sum up the view of His Majesty's Government as follows: 'If General de Gaulle wanted us to ask the President to agree to give him the title deeds of France, the answer was "No". If he wanted us to ask the President to agree that the Committee of National Liberation was the principal factor with whom we should deal in France, the answer was "Yes".'[4]

The British, desperately anxious about what would happen in the following few days, probably did not give much thought to the long-term implications of Churchill's words. But de Gaulle always thought about long-term implications and immediately repeated what he took to be the essence of Churchill's remarks: 'he quite understood that in case of disagreement between the United States and France, Great Britain would side with the United States'.[5]

Churchill was hysterical with fury. He drafted a letter to de Gaulle:

> I regret very much that you have refused to join with other United Nations concerned in the broadcasts which are to be delivered at the opening phases of this great, and in many ways, unique battle. I have tried very hard on many occasions, during four years, to establish some reasonable basis of friendly comradeship with you. Your action at this juncture convinces me that this hope has no further existence.[6]

He asked his aides to ensure that the general was removed from the country 'in irons if necessary'.

Some fast work by those around Churchill and de Gaulle produced a compromise and Churchill himself seems to have thought better of his letter to de Gaulle, which was not sent. A small number of French liaison officers went to Normandy. De Gaulle did broadcast – though he did not do so immediately after Eisenhower. The British discreetly ignored the fact that de Gaulle referred to the 'Government' – meaning his own authority – in his broadcast. Emmanuel d'Astier de La Vigerie said that he could tell from de Gaulle's voice 'what an exploding rage he was in'.[7] Churchill's resentment was not completely abated. On 16 June 1944, even after having received a conciliatory letter from de Gaulle, Churchill wrote:

> Ever since 1907 I have, in good times and bad times, been a sincere friend of France, as my words and actions show, and it is to me an intense pain that barriers have been raised and are being raised to an association which to me was very dear. Here in this visit of yours, which I personally arranged, I had the hope that there was a chance of putting things right. Now I have only the hope that it may not be the last chance.[8]

Addressing the cabinet, 'Winston again delivered a tirade against de Gaulle and, his eyes flashing with fury, warned us all against this enemy of England as he had warned us against Hitler.'[9] Leo Amery believed that most ministers disagreed with the prime minister but did not think it worth arguing.

In private, de Gaulle was surprisingly sympathetic (perhaps pitying) in his reaction to Churchill's anger. He told his son that the prime minister was 'the genius of this war but an old man made too irritable by exhaustion and a little too prone to take refuge in whisky'.[10] But the encounter between the two men over D-Day was to cast a shadow over Anglo-French relations for decades.

De Gaulle recalled Churchill saying that 'between France and the open sea Britain will always chose the open sea.' It was a phrase that de Gaulle was to repeat frequently and use as a justification for excluding Britain from the Common Market in the early 1960s. Indeed, de Gaulle sometimes seemed to grow more bitter about the events of 1944 as the years passed. He refused to visit the Normandy beaches on the twentieth anniversary of D-Day. He told one of his ministers that Churchill had summoned him 'as a Lord rings for his his butler', adding: 'And now you want me to celebrate *their* landing, when it was a prelude to a second occupation.'[11]

De Gaulle was allowed to go to Normandy on 14 June, two days after Churchill had done so. Escaping from his British escort, he visited Bayeux. For all his confident statements, he could not really know how he would be received. Normandy was a conservative and Catholic area, which would become an electoral bastion of Gaullism for much of the post-war period. Perhaps just because the population had other things on their mind, de Gaulle's initial reception appears to have been cordial rather than ecstatic — 'as though a republican dignitary … had come to open a Sunday fair'.[12] Unsurprisingly, de Gaulle remembered with emotion his first contact in four years with mainland France — maybe sharpened by the fact that he had dosed himself with a drug that prevents sea sickness and induces mild euphoria.[13] De Gaulle left two aides behind to establish his authority in the liberated area of France.

Allied troops from North Africa landed in the south of France on 15 August. The French contingent in these forces was larger than in those that landed in Normandy, and German opposition was less formidable. Parts of southern France were liberated by the resistance, or, at least, resistance forces were the first to arrive after the Germans had left. For all his complaints, de Gaulle probably faced more problems as a result of what the French did in the south than what the British and Americans did in the north of France. It was not always clear that areas liberated by the resistance would yield to the authority of a newly constituted French government.

Once they landed in France, British and Americans played little part in the country's civilian administration. Their soldiers were under orders not to become involved in 'internal' disputes among the French. Eden had written in early May that the Committee of National Liberation – first established by de Gaulle and Giraud in Algiers, and which Eden believed exercised a restraining influence over de Gaulle – 'had given us a pledge that there would be elections once France was re-occupied and that while Allied forces were occupying France, there would not be executions.'[14] No doubt De Gaulle would have seen sinister significance in the use of the word 'occupied' but, as it turned out, there were executions while Allied troops were still fighting on French soil. Anglo-American forces rarely intervened to stop violence among the French because they saw France as a battleground, a place through which they wanted to move as quickly as possible as they advanced towards Germany. They cared little for the symbolic importance of towns that had no particular military value. If it had not been for de Gaulle's intervention, Allied forces might have circumvented Paris and abandoned Strasbourg in the face of a German counterattack. The military authorities were concerned with French civilians only, in so far as those civilians helped or impeded their advance. Indeed, the Allied commanders were not even particularly concerned with German forces unless those forces blocked their route east. For this reason they did not bother with German garrisons on French coasts (or, for that matter, on the British Channel Islands), some of which did not surrender until after Hitler had killed himself in Berlin. Poorly equipped French units were left to try to take these citadels.

In June 1940, de Gaulle had left France at a time when the state seemed to have collapsed. Things were worse when he returned. The Vichy government's writ had ceased to run in much of the country. It was challenged by the resistance and, as the maquis grew in 1943 and 1944, this meant increasingly that the French state exercised authority only in towns, where it was often overridden by the Germans or the collaborationist groups they supported.

The German retreat left a vacuum. The lines of legality were blurred as people accused of collaboration were punished without formal process or after summary trials.

For de Gaulle, the most important moment in the liberation of France came in August 1944 when the Germans left Paris. He arrived in the city on 25 August. Asked to proclaim the republic from the town hall, he replied that the republic had never ceased to exist – presumably meaning that the Free French had incarnated the republic since 1940. He then made a famous speech. He spoke of 'Paris broken, Paris martyred but Paris liberated, liberated by itself'. None of this was quite true. Parisians had suffered during the occupation but the city itself was intact. It had not been damaged in 1940 because the French had abandoned it without a fight, it had been little damaged during the war (partly because it contained few industrial targets for British and American bombers) and it was not blown up by the retreating Germans because the commanding officer disregarded Hitler's order that he should do so. This was a considerable advantage for de Gaulle. His notion of the dignity of the state was closely associated with the city and the ceremonies of the liberation revolved around ancient buildings – notably Notre Dame Cathedral – and grand avenues – notably the Champs Élysées. The ceremonies would have been less impressive if Paris had been a city of bombsites and ruins. For the first time since 10 June 1940, France had a capital city worthy of the name. A chapter in de Gaulle's *Mémoires de Guerre* is entitled simply 'Paris'.

An unexpected moment of drama came during the service of thanksgiving in Notre Dame Cathedral when shots were fired. De Gaulle's apparent impassivity impressed those watching. Some believed that the shooters were collaborationists. In his memoirs (published when his politics were largely defined by the Cold War) de Gaulle implied that the Communists had started the shooting – not because they wanted to hit anyone but because they wanted to foster a revolutionary atmosphere.[15] At the time, he took a more prosaic view. The British chargé d'affaires reported: 'de Gaulle said that nobody had tried to shoot him. "It was simply a case of one man letting off his rifle, possibly accidentally, and everybody firing in the direction of the first shot.'" De Gaulle added that 'the English and Americans loved beautiful stories'.[16]

It was only partially true that Paris had 'liberated itself'. There had been an insurrection, but this alone would hardly have been enough to drive out heavily armed German troops if the American army had not been close. French soldiers, under General Leclerc, entered the city but they did so because the British and Americans recognised the symbolic value of this rather than because the French had fought their way to Paris. Though the French army did not make much difference in military terms in 1944, it was important for political reasons. It is revealing that, though de Gaulle was now head of the government, he established his headquarters in Paris in the Ministry of War in the rue Saint Dominique, where he had had his office during his brief tenure as a minister in 1940. The army mattered because it was the one force in France during the liberation that was clearly subordinate to the state and because it provided the means of controlling other forces. This was why the integration of the resistance into the Forces Françaises de l'Intérieur (FFI) and the subsequent integration of the FFI into the regular army mattered so much to de Gaulle. He also ensured that regular, uniformed French soldiers were fighting the Germans in Europe. Frenchmen shedding their blood was what earned France her right to be considered one of the victor powers.

De Gaulle restored authority in France between June 1944 and May 1945, though his task was extraordinarily difficult. Britain, America and the Soviet Union did not formally recognise de Gaulle as head of a government until October 1944. France was divided by battle lines, which meant that some regions (especially in the southern part of the country) were almost autonomous. Parts of northern and eastern France were placed under the direct control of the Allied military authorities. De Gaulle's emissaries described chaotic circumstances. Claude Bouchinet-Serreulles toured parts of southern

France in August, sleeping in official buildings in the rooms that had, until recently, been reserved for Marshal Pétain. His visit to Vichy was dispiriting. He was greeted by a 'pitiful local committee' and shown an improvised effigy of a general (still wet with glue) which was meant to represent de Gaulle. He felt there was a revolutionary atmosphere 'that of [17]92' in Montpellier, Limoges and Toulouse. The Limousin was the area most obviously independent of central authority. 'Boys' who had just come down from the maquis and took orders only from their own leader were reluctant to allow him into the prefecture.[17] Michel Debré had an easier time in Angers. He succeeded in installing himself in the prefecture before the Americans arrived 'It is still not eight o'clock in the evening on 10 August 1944. I control the prefecture and have become the state.'[18]

De Gaulle and his agents had some advantages in their struggle to reestablish authority. For one thing, there was a subterranean state already in existence. Some of those who had rallied to de Gaulle were senior civil servants or drawn from institutions that had close links with the state. Such men understood how administration worked. They could sometimes impose their authority simply by walking into the appropriate office. Many from the senior ranks of the civil service had made discreet contact with the Free French before the liberation.[19] A Canadian diplomat reported from Vichy in September 1941 that officials of the Ministry of Finance had taken a vote and that 90 per cent of them had been 'opposed to collaboration'.[20] Some important figures worked for the resistance even while holding positions in Vichy institutions. The Organisation Civile et Militaire resistance network was composed largely of such people. One of its members, Aimé Lepercq, moved from being the head of the Vichy body that ran the French coal industry, to being an open resistant who participated in the liberation, to being minister of finances in de Gaulle's first government.

De Gaulle had a symbiotic relation with those who might have been assumed to be his most dangerous rivals – the Americans and the Communists. Roosevelt had been hostile to de Gaulle in 1943 but the relative indifference of American military authorities in France was an advantage for de Gaulle. American generals wished to keep their relations with the French civil authorities as simple as possible and to avoid impeding the war effort. Once it became clear that de Gaulle was likely to be the most important single source of authority, they dealt with him and, on 12 July, the American command recognised 'the French Committee of National Liberation as qualified to exercise administrative responsibility in France'. Similarly, the Communist Party was generally keen that the war be pursued as effectively as possible to relieve pressure on the Soviet Union – especially after the Communist leader Maurice Thorez returned to France from Moscow. However, de Gaulle also benefited from the fact that he was defending French sovereignty against the Americans and defending the French property-owning classes against communism. Many rallied to de Gaulle in 1944 because they believed that the alternative might be worse.

Churchill's position looked more secure than de Gaulle's during the last year of the Second World War. He did not have to worry about whether foreign powers would recognise him as the legitimate head of a government or whether he would be able to exercise power over parts of his own country. His reputation in the world stood higher than ever before or would ever do again. He was particularly admired by the French. Churchill visited Paris on 11 November 1944 and, now that they were no longer locked in day-to-day conflict, de Gaulle was remarkably gracious. He ordered the band to play 'Le Père la Victoire' (a song usually associated with Clemenceau) and said to Churchill, in English, 'For you.'

Churchill wrote to Roosevelt that he had had a 'wonderful reception' in Paris and had 'reestablished friendly private relations with de Gaulle, who is much better since he has lost a large part of his inferiority complex'.[21] But Churchill was never completely reconciled to de Gaulle, in spite – or perhaps because – of the fact that the French seemed to accept de Gaulle as their leader. In January 1945, Churchill wrote to Eden about whether France should participate in the forthcoming conferences at which the state of the post-war world would be discussed by the victorious powers: 'I fear we shall have the greatest trouble with de Gaulle, who will be forever intriguing and playing off two against the third.'[22]

There were ways in which the experience of Churchill and de Gaulle ran parallel in the last stages of the war and immediately after it. Both men discovered their own countries. This was true for de Gaulle because he had not been to France for four years. There was also a sense in which Churchill was cut off from the British population. He prided himself on being used to the rough and tumble of parliamentary democracy, but he had never led his party into an election. In any case, there had been no general election since 1935. Part of the horrified fascination with which he regarded Stanley Baldwin derived from his awareness of Baldwin's skill in reading and managing the electorate. After the Conservative electoral defeat of 1945, one Tory notable recalled: 'He [Churchill] kept comparing himself to SB and finally posed me the question, "What was it that enabled SB to win elections while I always lose them?"'[23]

During the war, the political class had wrapped Churchill had been wrapped in a cocoon of admiration that partially insulated him from the atmosphere in the country, but the coalition government gave Churchill an artificial view of the popular mood. The fact that Labour ministers sat with him in cabinet did not mean they or their supporters approved of everything he said and did. Ernest Bevin was Churchill's favourite Labour politician and stood for his idealised view of a certain working class – patriotic, unintellectual, trade unionist, without being really socialist. He sometimes distinguished 'my friend Ernie Bevin' from the left-wing Aneurin Bevan, but it did not occur to him that Bevan – who once remarked that in the Welsh valleys he came from, Tories were regarded as 'lower than vermin' – represented a significant strand of opinion.

Churchill's ignorance of the lives led by most British people was comic. After visiting the Manchester slums when he was a Liberal minister before 1914, he remarked: 'Fancy living in one of those streets – never seeing anything beautiful – never eating anything savoury – *never saying anything clever*!'[24] He talked of workers as 'artisans'. He disliked the villa houses of suburbia and was disconcerted when it was pointed out to him that the inhabitants of such places were the bedrock of Conservative support or, as a right-wing civil servant put it, 'the anti-Bolshevik host'.[25] During the war, he complained that resources were being wasted on the provision of mobile baths for troops – which was a bit rich from a man who spent a significant part of his life soaking in warm water and who regarded it as normal that officers should take their valets to war. Even when he admired those from outside his own class, Churchill rarely knew much about them. He repeatedly insisted that the success of the RAF sprang from the plebeian origins of its recruits. He claimed that only 30 per cent of RAF pilots were public school boys – 'the remainder being products of the Elementary Schools and professional classes. It was striking that none of the aristocracy chose the RAF – they left it to the lower-middle class.'[26] Lumping the products of elementary schools (mostly working class) with the lower-middle and professional classes suggested that Churchill had a weak grasp of social distinctions in Britain. In any case, he was wrong. The upper classes were over-represented among aircrew, though not as over-represented as they were among officers in smart regiments.

Churchill's ignorance had an important effect on the 1945 election. He had hoped to continue as leader of the wartime coalition and the fact that he was surprised when the Labour Party did not allow this reflects his distance from political reality. He became notorious for one speech during the campaign in which he alleged that a future Labour government would need a 'Gestapo-like' organisation to assert state control, but the most revealing moment came when he referred to the British people in their 'cottages' – a remark that would have astonished those crammed into urban tenements at a time when bombing had destroyed so many houses.

The Conservatives lost the 1945 election to Labour. This was a surprise. Churchill's political hegemony seemed so absolute to the political classes that even the Labour leaders had hardly dared hope that they would win. People from Churchill's own class were shocked. The historian Michael Howard spent most of the Second World War as an officer with the Coldstream Guards. The Coldstreams had been deployed early in the war to protect the prime minister at Chequers – the officers, drawn from privileged backgrounds, were considered smart enough to be invited in for dinner. Howard remembered an evocative moment when he had entered Churchill's bedroom 'which smelt deliciously of lavender toilet water and Havana cigars, the smells, I thought, of the belle époque'.[27]

In 1945, the Coldstreams were fighting in Italy. The officers believed the other ranks ought to be informed about the coming election. Howard remembered the scene:

A senior officer spoke for the Conservatives shrewdly downplaying domestic politics and emphasizing the need to keep Churchill in power to help shape the postwar world. I could find no officer in the battalion prepared to speak for Labour, so I had to import an earnest Wykehamist from the Scots Guards who was unfortunately a hopeless speaker. I myself spoke eloquently on behalf of the Liberals ... Then a young sergeant got up. 'This is all very well' he said, 'but the likes of us – we're all Labour aren't we? So we'll vote Labour.' There was a deep growl of agreement.[28]

Given that the Coldstreams' traditional recruiting ground lay in the north-east of England and that the soldiers of 1945 would have grown up in the shadow of the General Strike, the officers ought not to have been surprised by the result, but they were. For many British aristocrats, the 1945 election was, as the Dowager Duchess of Wellington put it, a 'monstrous calamity'. She wrote to Churchill that she had felt sure she would never weep again after her son (the sixth duke) had been killed in action in 1943 but that 'because of the ingratitude shown towards you I weep with shame and grief'.[29]

Churchill had told the Spanish ambassador in 1943 that 'I might disappear and things would take their course without confusion or shocks harmful to this country.'[30] He was disconcerted to find that this was more or less true. The smooth-running British state, which had operated to Churchill's advantage in 1940, now operated to the advantage of his successor. Churchill flew home in the middle of the Potsdam Conference and when its discussion resumed Clement Attlee, the new Labour prime minister, replaced him.

De Gaulle adjusted more easily than Churchill to post-war politics. His political skills had been sharpened by several years of manoeuvre at a time when his position was weak. Whatever he said about his own authority, he understood that, in practice, his power derived from the willingness of politicians to let him exercise it. Churchill was evicted from power when his wartime coalition broke up; de Gaulle assumed power as the head of a coalition. In social terms, de Gaulle was less removed from the lives of ordinary people than Churchill. He was not as rich, his family was less grand and he cared little for money. De Gaulle was never a socialist but there were times when he seemed to welcome some apocalyptic transformation that might sweep economic privileges away. Writing about the United States in the 1930s, Churchill had worried that Roosevelt seemed to 'hunt down rich men as if they were noxious beasts'.[31] De Gaulle, on the other hand had anticipated, around the same time, that mobilisation for war might destroy notions of private property in America – a prospect he seemed to regard with grim relish.[32]

Churchill campaigned against nationalisations in 1945; de Gaulle's government carried out nationalisations – sometimes to punish collaborators but sometimes for reasons of economic efficiency.

The word 'state', pronounced with distaste by British Conservatives, was one of the most important in the Gaullist political lexicon. De Gaulle did much to refashion the civil service. In 1945 he created the École Nationale d'Administration (ENA) – designed to train men and women for the most important positions in the administration – and refounded the Institut d'Études Politiques – designed to prepare students for entry to ENA. The two schools were sufficiently important in de Gaulle's mind for him to include the decrees establishing them as annexes to his *Mémoires de Guerre*. De Gaulle was in power for only around eighteen months after the liberation but the French state that survives to this day was created during those months. It is a state in which a relatively small, tightly knit group of civil servants, politicians and managers exercise powers that transcend the division between the public and private sector and in which the state enjoys great prestige.

However, though de Gaulle may have recast the state, meaning the civil service, in his image, he conspicuously failed to do the same with the republic, meaning the political system. He had no experience of democratic politics. The British had grudgingly come to recognise that he was the symbol of French resistance but they had noted that this symbol was an abstract one, which often did not survive personal contact with de Gaulle. They had also been struck by the frequency with which their French interlocutors assumed that de Gaulle's role would be temporary – that it might last only 'until the new constitution is drawn up after the liberation'.[33]

De Gaulle faced the same problem as many resistance leaders – including those, such as Henri Frenay or François Mitterrand, who were not well disposed to de Gaulle. All of them had acquired their reputations at a time when ordinary politics was suspended. They often had origins on the political right but had come to assume that association with the resistance would make others accept them as left-wing. De Gaulle himself seemed to share this assumption, at least for a time. In 1944, he told a delegation of socialists that he believed France to be 'on the left', 'social or socialist' and '*socialisante*'. The socialists had more precisely defined notions of what their political beliefs meant and would certainly have regarded de Gaulle's remark that the country was 'democratic rather than parliamentary' as characteristic of the extreme-right.[34]

Desmond Morton reported to Churchill in September 1944 on the awkwardness of de Gaulle's position:

> The attitude of Paris and I think of France toward de Gaulle and the Administration [Morton meant the government] is very curious. The Administration is at present popular, and doing its work well where its writ runs. De Gaulle himself is looked on as something different from the Administration. He is venerated as the standard-bearer of French liberation. At the same time, should de Gaulle wish to descend from his unique pedestal to become a political leader when times are more normal, even de Gaulle's closest friends say that he will have to prove his ability in this role before the French accept him at his own valuation.[35]

The truth is that de Gaulle did not want to 'descend from his unique pedestal'. He wanted the political system to adjust to him rather than vice versa. He was caught in an odd trap. He had obtained everything he had claimed to want. France was liberated. He was recognised as head of government by the French people and his government was recognised as legitimate by the other Allied powers. In theory he had enormous power in the autumn of 1944. The Assembly set up in Algeria, which now came to France, was consultative. It could not control de Gaulle. In effect, he could rule by decree.

But de Gaulle now had to translate his idea of France into reality. The country over which he ruled was poor and militarily weak. The latter was made painfully clear when the British intervened to prevent the French from imposing their power in the Levant. The Americans treated France as what it was – a middle-sized European country that needed their economic aid. Returning from the Yalta Conference, at which the French had not been represented,

Roosevelt invited de Gaulle to come and see him on a US battleship off Algeria. Furious at the implication that he might be treated as a guest on his own country's territory, de Gaulle refused.

De Gaulle had no experience of peacetime politics. He knew what he disliked in constitutional terms – the parliamentary instability of the late Third Republic – but had no precise sense of what he would like. In spite of all the fears that had been expressed during the war, he did not contemplate making himself a dictator. Parliamentary elections were held in October 1945.* At the same time, there was to be a referendum (a mechanism that had last been deployed in France to underwrite the coup of Napoleon III in 1851). Voters were asked, first, whether the National Assembly they elected should be given powers to draw up a new constitution and, second, whether that constitution should then be put for approval by another referendum. De Gaulle wanted the answer 'yes' to both questions and he obtained it by an overwhelming majority to the first question and a substantial majority to the second. The Assembly elected in October had a large representation from a new Christian Democrat Party, the Mouvement Républicain Populaire, which was relatively sympathetic to de Gaulle, and the old Socialist Party. The largest single group was the Communists. The Assembly confirmed de Gaulle's position as head of government. He managed to prevent the Communists from taking any of the most important ministries – Defence, Foreign Affairs or Interior – and he got his way when he insisted on large defence spending.

In spite of all this, De Gaulle resigned in January 1946. No one quite knew why. Perhaps he sensed that the Assembly and the electorate would produce a constitution much like that of the Third Republic – which they did in due course. Perhaps he appreciated that it would be hard to govern unless he himself became a party

*The Third Republic law that serving soldiers could not vote was abolished only in August 1945. The legislative elections of October were, therefore, the first in which de Gaulle himself cast a vote – his wife had voted in the municipal elections of April 1945.

politician. Perhaps he hoped that a dramatic gesture would quickly allow him to return to power. Perhaps he was just tired.

Duff Cooper, the British ambassador in Paris, wrote:

> There seemed to be no reason why de Gaulle, who at the end of the year had won a victory in the Assembly in the matter of army estimates, and whom the members of that Assembly had accepted unanimously a few weeks before, should voluntarily throw away the greatest opportunity ever offered to a Frenchman since Napoleon Buonaparte picked the crown of France out of the gutter on the point of his sword ... On January 20th, the eve of the anniversary of Louis XVI's execution, General de Gaulle cut off his own head and passed into the shadow-land of politics.[36]

As it turned out, neither de Gaulle nor Churchill disappeared from politics after their post-war defeats but they seemed to live in a shadowland for the second half of the 1940s and most of the 1950s. They looked like men whose best days were behind them. Churchill was seventy in 1945. The extraordinary energy that had sustained him during the war had largely dissipated. He had had a minor stroke during the war and his lifestyle was hardly calculated to keep him fit. At a time when food was still rationed for most people, Churchill began his day with breakfast in bed, which he would top off with a cold partridge or grouse during the appropriate seasons; this would be washed down with a weak whisky and soda. De Gaulle's eclipse was political not physical or psychological. In 1945, he was still ten years younger than Churchill had been in 1940. Smoking had been his only vice, and, in a characteristic act of will, he broke the habit soon after the war – his aides were disconcerted to see him chewing gum.[37] His daughter, Anne, died in February 1948. He grieved deeply but the death did not dent his will or sense of his own destiny – perhaps the contrary.

The political position of the two men was also very different. Churchill had been leader of the Conservative Party since the death of Neville Chamberlain in late 1940. There was no serious challenge to him. The main opposition parties had not run candidates against Churchill in his own constituency in 1945 – though shrewd observers might have noted that an independent candidate, whose only appeal was that he was not Churchill, received a quarter of the vote. If he wanted to be prime minister again, then all Churchill had to do was float until the electoral tides washed him back to government. He had little interest in party organisation and played no role in the restructuring of the Conservative Party in the late 1940s.

Churchill spent a good deal of his time outside Britain – sometimes on holiday and sometimes playing his new role as the grand old man of the Western alliance. The most resonant speeches he made after 1945 were the ones he delivered at Fulton Missouri in March 1946 – when he spoke of an 'Iron Curtain' that now divided eastern (Communist) Europe from the West – and that which he delivered at Zurich in September of the same year, when he said 'We must build a kind of United States of Europe.' Conservative support for west European unity was closely associated with fears of the Soviet Union. As Churchill put it: 'Nothing but the dread of a Stalinised Russia could have brought the conception of a united Europe from dreamland into the forefront of modern thought.'[38] In Strasbourg in 1950, Churchill called for the creation of a European army.

All this went with some extraordinary fantasies about the role Churchill personally might play in the future. Paul Reynaud suggested in August 1950 that Churchill might be minister of war in a European government.[39] Colonel Monty Woodhouse, who was soon to be a Conservative MP, was attached to the Western Union planning staff in February 1951. He anticipated that the West might respond to Soviet invasion by withdrawing to a mountainous redoubt that encompassed the Alps and extended as far perhaps as Greece and Yugoslavia: 'the Government of Europe would actually come into being in this mountain redoubt. Mr Churchill might decide to leave the government of Britain to Mr Eden in order personally to preside over the government of Europe.'⁴⁰ Harold Macmillan regarded Woodhouse's remarks as 'both obvious and zany'. The zaniness will be particularly apparent to those who recall, first, that Churchill was seventy-five years old and, second, that he was not prime minister of Britain at the time.

Unlike Churchill, de Gaulle did not have an established place in the political system of his country. He had never been a member of a party. He recognised, though, that he needed some movement to propel him back to power and, in April 1947, he founded the Rassemblement du Peuple Français (RPF). The Rassemblement was, at least in de Gaulle's mind, not a party. It was intended, at first, to rally Gaullists from existing parties, but it was confounded by the decision of the major parties not to allow this sort of double affiliation. Some left existing parties – even the Communists – to join de Gaulle but most significant politicians did not do so. This pushed the RPF into contesting elections under its own colours and against other parties. De Gaulle launched a ferocious campaign, travelling round the country to address large rallies – the government had taken away his most effective weapon of the past by depriving him of the means to broadcast. The RPF was not a comfortable party. De Gaulle said relatively little about his past. He had told an aide in 1946: 'they bore me with their call of 18 June ... the political parties want to reduce my role to that call'.⁴¹ He looked forward rather than back – though the future was not painted in optimistic terms. He made much of the Soviet threat and, soon after his bitter arguments with Roosevelt, stressed the importance of the western alliance. His wartime companions were largely gone. Passy was briefly imprisoned after a scandal about the misuse of secret service funds in 1946. Gilbert Renault ('Rémy'), the most dramatic of the agents sent to

France on behalf of de Gaulle, was an early leader of the RPF but de Gaulle dismissed him after he suggested that France had needed Pétain as well as de Gaulle – though it suited de Gaulle in the late 1940s that his party should appeal to Pétainists.

Unlike Churchill, de Gaulle did not surround himself with familiar faces after 1945. The most important person in the RPF who had been in London was Raymond Aron – though in his London days he had not really been a Gaullist. Many of de Gaulle's associates now were young. Olivier Guichard, born in 1920, and Pierre Lefranc, born in 1922, joined the RPF and soon became important members of de Gaulle's entourage. Such people could not claim the independent authority that might derive from a resistance record. Their only previous encounter with de Gaulle came from listening to BBC broadcasts during the war. Claude Mauriac, who became de Gaulle's aide, wrote to André Gide about the emotional impact of living alongside a man whom he had previously known as 'a voice and a myth'.[42]

At first the RPF was extraordinarily successful. In the 1947 municipal elections, it gained control of Bordeaux, Marseilles and Strasbourg. De Gaulle's brother Pierre became head of the Paris municipal council. In the legislative elections of 1951, the RPF displaced the Communist Party as the largest single group in the National Assembly. However, without having an absolute majority in parliament, being the largest single party was no use unless the RPF allied with other parties. De Gaulle was bitterly opposed to such alliances. Furthermore, the other political parties had manoeuvred effectively against the RPF – changing the electoral system to disadvantage the Gaullists. De Gaulle had underestimated his opponents. Vincent Auriol, the first president of the Fourth Republic, who served from 1947 to 1954, was a tough and vigorous man – he had voted against granting full powers to Pétain in 1940 and subsequently escaped to London and then Algeria. Henri Queuille, who served as prime minister three times between 1948 and 1951, was also an effective operator. Though he had worked with de Gaulle during the war, he refused ministerial office in de Gaulle's post-war government and then kept the Gaullists out of his own fiefdom in the Corrèze. After the 1951 elections, in which de Gaulle had failed to break the Fourth Republic's political system, Queuille was succeeded as prime minister by René Pleven. A Gaullist might have argued that the fact that Pleven was leader of the political party (the Union Démocratique et Socialiste de la Résistance), which had won only fourteen seats in the elections, illustrated the perverse results of electoral coalitions. Gaullists, though, also had to face the uncomfortable fact that Pleven (unlike many of those who joined the RPF) had been with de Gaulle in London in 1940.

De Gaulle was bitter at the failure of the RPF and bitter at those candidates who had defied his orders and formed alliances with other parties. Talking to his aides, he dismissed his own political movement as 'your RPF'. In 1953, he withdrew from politics and, to a large extent, from public life. In 1955, he dissolved the RPF.

───────

Churchill won the general election of October 1951 – though the Conservative parliamentary majority was just seventeen seats and the party had actually received fewer votes than Labour. But where de Gaulle, thwarted by the 1951 legislative election in France, had had a clear idea of what he would do if he attained power, Churchill's return to Downing Street was accompanied by uncertainty about what he had been elected to do. The interests of the electorate and the Conservative Party had now turned largely to domestic policy – in which Churchill had little interest. The crushing weight of his prestige was not always matched by faith in his ability. A civil servant recorded the remarks of Jane Portal, one of the prime minister's secretaries, in March 1954:

She now admits that the old boy, whom she loves dearly, is getting senile and failing more and more each day ... Life is a misery to him; he half kills himself with work, cannot take in the papers he is given to read and can hardly get up the stairs to bed ... It is impossible for him to resign, because he can no longer write, dreads solitude and oblivion, fears rest. But he will soon die.[43]

Describing Churchill as senile was unfair – at least in 1954. In his idiosyncratic way, he was still intellectually alert. He read a good deal after 1945, perhaps more than he had done since he left India in 1899 – though he disconcerted his private secretary in 1952 by claiming never to have heard of E. M. Forster.* But his intellectual powers were diminished. For most of his life he had been a brilliant but unsystematic thinker who depended on the discipline that was imposed by argument with confident interlocutors who hammered his ideas into shape and forced him to discard some of his more dangerous notions. After 1945, the brilliance dimmed and the discipline of argument disappeared.

Churchill's politics had been reactionary in many respects since the aftermath of the First World War. But this had been partly masked by the admiration that many progressive Conservatives, and some on the left, felt for his opposition to appeasement and then for his conduct of the Second World War. After 1945, the mask dropped. Churchill was more right-wing than ever before – hardly

*The story was reported by John Colville to Evelyn Shuckburgh. Churchill is unlikely to have been telling the truth. Forster was one of most famous writers in the world and one of the half dozen candidates considered for the Nobel Prize for literature in 1953 whose claims on purely literary grounds would have been better than those of the winner: Winston Churchill. In 1922, Forster had written a poem attacking Churchill's role in the Gallipoli campaign – perhaps this was why Churchill feigned ignorance.

surprising in an old man from his background. He supported the death penalty – though he had been sparing in its use when home secretary in 1910–11. He was also troubled by the prospect of racial equality. Though Churchill had said in one of his wartime speeches that the courage of the Confederacy was marred by 'the stain of slavery' (he then worried that this remark might offend American opinion),[44] the prospect that black people might be treated as equals by white Americans hardly crossed his mind. When he gave his Iron Curtain speech at the University of Westminster in Fulton, Missouri in March 1946, he referred to the 'strong parent races' of Europe without apparently regarding it as significant that every face in his audience was white – the educational authorities in Missouri enforced racial segregation with obsessive zeal. An American journalist recorded Churchill's views in 1956:

> America should be temperate and wise about taking time to solve its negro problem. 'After all, you can't take twenty million of them into your belly just like that. Nonsense to say the black is the same as the white.' He called for a copy of this morning's *Daily Sketch* with a picture of a Negro Salvation Army singer followed by a white Salvation Army lass. 'Is that what they are going to have in Heaven?' he asked ... 'If so, it is no place for me.'[45]

Britain itself began to be changed by non-white immigration from the late 1940s. Churchill had some respect for Africans and Afghans against whom he had fought during his youth. He admired warrior virtues. He also came to have cordial relations with some of the non-white leaders of the Commonwealth – including Nehru in India. He was photographed in apparently animated conversation with Eric Williams – the first prime minister of independent Trinidad and Tobago and the author of *Capitalism and Slavery* (1944). Churchill was more uncomfortable with people, especially from the West Indies, who arrived in Britain from the late 1940s onwards. His discomfort seems to have derived not from difference but from similarity. These were not tribesmen on a remote frontier. They were frequently men who had first come to Britain to serve in the armed forces (the RAF especially) during the Second World War. Many boys born in the West Indies after the war were christened 'Winston'.

Churchill's views on race had been recognised, while he was still prime minister, as a topic that might embarrass the government. He refused to answer a parliamentary question on 25 February 1954 about whether he would discourage colour bars in hotels. Harold Macmillan noted after a meeting of the Cabinet in January 1955: 'More discussion about the West Indian immigrants. A Bill is being drafted – but it's not an easy problem. PM thinks "Keep England White" a good slogan!'[46]

In a curious way, the extremeness of Churchill's views on some subjects prevented them from having much effect. 'Keep England White' was never a Conservative slogan – party leaders knew how much trouble they might cause if they poked the sleeping monster of popular racism. There was no serious effort to resist granting independence to India. Churchill was disconcerted when Enoch Powell, then a member of the Conservative Research Department, told him how many divisions he would need to reconquer the subcontinent.[47] The most important difference Churchill made to British politics in the early 1950s pushed it to the left. He had a sentimental regard for trade unionists (partly because he regarded them as a brake on middle-class intellectuals in the Labour Party) and he was keen that the illusion of social consensus that had surrounded him during the war should be sustained. For these reasons, Walter Monckton was appointed as minister of labour with instructions that there was to be no confrontation with organised labour. Some in Churchill's entourage opposed his policy on trade unions and he himself seems to have regretted it in retirement.[48] In

1957, Harold Macmillan wrote: 'We are now paying the price for the Churchill-Monckton regime – industrial appeasement, with continual inflation.'[49]

There were two, perhaps related, respects in which Churchill appeared to depart from things he had advocated in opposition. First, reference to European unity largely disappeared from his public statements. Second, in opposition Churchill had advocated firm treatment of the Soviet Union. In public, he insisted that peaceful coexistence with communism was possible – the official title of the 'Iron Curtain' speech was 'The Sinews of Peace'. In private, he had sometimes suggested that the West might make a preemptive strike against the Soviet Union while it still enjoyed military advantage.[50] However, perhaps precisely because he had been attacked for bellicosity, he was particularly hurt by a *Daily Mirror* headline that asked 'Whose finger on the trigger?' during the 1951 election, Churchill was keen to present himself as a more pacific figure in office.

Churchill's most plausible justification for staying in office lay in his supposed personal relations with other leaders, and, for this reason, he became a keen advocate of summit diplomacy. He wanted 'a small meeting between heads of Governments, without agenda, without Press, without communiqués ... a simpler, more primitive meeting'.[51] Churchill went to America in early 1952 to see Truman and then again a year later to see the newly elected Eisenhower. A three-power conference in Bermuda in December 1953 brought together France, Britain and the United States. Churchill made much of the fact that the conference took place on British soil. It was marked by a succession of indignities. The French prime minister (at that point René Mayer) had originally suggested it as a means of reining in Churchill's enthusiasm for meeting Soviet leaders.[52] It was delayed twice – once because the instability of Fourth Republic France produced a period in which it was not clear who would be prime minister (in the end, it was Laniel who attended the conference) and once because of Churchill's health. When it finally took place, Churchill was photographed reading a novel by C. S. Forester entitled *Death to the French*.

Churchill's great desire was to arrange a meeting that would involve the Soviet Union or, even, that he might go alone to Moscow and negotiate a settlement of the Cold War. This never happened. Members of his own cabinet rebelled when he sought to arrange such a meeting in 1954. In any case, the deference with which Churchill was treated on his visits to Washington only partially disguised the fact that he (and Britain) now counted for little in American eyes. Macmillan had written of Anglo-American relations in 1950: 'We are treated worse than de Gaulle or exiled governments during the war!'[53]

Churchill's desire to live in the past drew the teeth of his government. He was sentimental about his own youthful liberalism and always hoped to draw Liberals into an anti-socialist alliance. Some of his most shocking political statements derived from his understanding of liberalism – and of what he thought to be the threats to liberty – as much as conservatism. His 'Gestapo speech' of 1945 was partly inspired by Friedrich Hayek's *The Road to Serfdom*.[54] But sometimes 'liberalism' came to mean that nostalgia for the governments of the Edwardian era influenced him almost as much as nostalgia for those of the war. He appointed David Lloyd George's son as home secretary. He offered to make Asquith's son Lord Chancellor. He was close to Asquith's daughter Violet Bonham Carter and supported her when she ran as a Liberal candidate for parliament (she had no Conservative opponent).[55]

The Churchill government laid the pattern for a style of politics that would dominate British Conservatism until the second Thatcher government of 1983. Many close to the party espoused very right-wing views, but they rarely did much to enact such views when in government. The paradox was incarnated by the

Daily Telegraph, the only quality newspaper with a circulation of more than a million. It was closely associated with Churchill, who had not forgiven *The Times* for its support of appeasement, and it serialised his history of the Second World War. The *Telegraph* was very right-wing – particularly on matters such as race and the death penalty – but it was hard to tell how far its journalists were indulging in a deliberate parody.* Malcolm Muggeridge was deputy editor of the paper and it was he who liaised with Churchill over the serialisation of his book – though, at first in private and eventually in public, he mocked many Conservative pieties including the cult of Churchill: 'a slightly ridiculous figure, mouthing the rhetoric of a past age to sustain the fantasies of the present one'.[56]

Churchill's government was old. The average age of members of the 1951 cabinet was fifty-nine. Some were in poor health and Churchill, sensitive about his own physical state, was ostentatious in his solicitude about the ailments of his younger colleagues. He still hankered to be leader of a government that was above parties and many of his appointments were not really politicians. A significant number of his cabinet were peers.

In the 1950s, officials felt, or were made to feel, that they owed a personal loyalty to the prime minister – though in private some of them did not express unqualified admiration for Churchill. Sir Edward Bridges, fifty-nine years old, was due to be replaced as cabinet secretary but was kept on because Churchill had become accustomed to working with him during the war. Norman Brook, forty-nine years old, was permanent secretary of the Treasury and head of the civil service. Churchill referred to them as 'the boys'.[57]

In earlier years, Churchill had sought out companions who would make up for his own educational shortcomings and challenge his opinions. Now those around him were expected to provide reassurance. During the war, officials had served the state and recognised

---

*Parody was most evident in the Peter Simple column that began in 1957. Michael Wharton, the column's author, was a right-wing Tory but no great admirer of Churchill.

that the interests of the state required them to support Churchill, which did not always mean letting him get his way. John Colville, who had been a junior private secretary in the war, was brought back as joint principal private secretary to the prime minister. The difference between Colville in 1940 and Colville in 1951 said much about how Churchill himself had changed. In 1940, Churchill had simply inherited Colville from his predecessor and not troubled himself about the fact that Colville was still personally loyal to Chamberlain at first. In 1951, Churchill tried to ensure that the civil servants with whom he worked should be ones with whom he felt personal affinity and insisted on Colville's return to Downing Street. In 1940, Colville had been an ingénu who described his own mishaps with disarming modesty as though he had been a character out of P. G. Wodehouse. In 1951, he was more assured and well connected (he had served as private secretary to Princess Elizabeth). His political views, like those of Churchill, were now emphatically on the right. He had also come to regard himself as a kind of liegeman for Churchill. When the prime minister had a severe stroke in June 1953, which looked likely to incapacitate him, Colville helped cover it up.

The long-term shift in Churchill's attitudes can be illustrated by comparing his first and last private secretaries. Eddie Marsh, who had worked for Churchill before 1914, was an intellectual with progressive opinions and close links to Bloomsbury. Anthony Montague Browne was appointed in 1952 as the prime minister's private secretary for foreign affairs, on Colville's recommendation. He was a dashing ex-RAF pilot who had never finished university. Though he was barely thirty, some of his political views were to the right of those held by Churchill at the age of eighty. He recorded Churchill's remarks with mischievous pleasure: 'Homosexuals often feel themselves alien and apart from the mainstream of the country, like a black in a white country or a white in a black country.'[58]

Sometimes Churchill implied that his victory of 1951 was a symbolic one and that he would retire after a year or so in government. In practice, however, he repeatedly found some reason why it was necessary for him to stay. Churchill claimed to have doubts about his successor. During the war, Anthony Eden enjoyed a special status as heir apparent. Churchill wrote to the king saying that Eden should be prime minister in the event of his own death. Given the unusual circumstances, no one complained about the intrusion on the royal prerogative and, given the risks that Churchill took on his travels, it seemed eminently possible that the king might have to act on his advice. Things began to change after 1945. Eden was in poor health and shattered by the death of his oldest son in the last year of the war. Churchill had found it easier to contemplate death in wartime than to contemplate retirement in old age. The more Eden pressed him to resign, the more Churchill resisted – in the summer of 1954 he almost flew back from a meeting with Eisenhower rather than spend five days sailing on the *Queen Mary* with the certainty that Eden would use the occasion to nag him about resignation.[59] Churchill fussed about whether Eden would be up to the job.

Churchill's colleagues fussed about whether *he* was up to the job. Discussions began early in his government in Harry Crookshank's house. Crookshank, a Conservative MP and minister, had been emasculated by his wounds during the First World War and assumed that Churchill's offer of a peerage – made in 1942 to a man who could have no heirs – was a calculated insult rather than being an example of Churchill's carelessness.

No one thought that Churchill was capable of achieving the diplomatic triumphs that he hoped would cap his career. An official at the Foreign Office wrote in his diary in 1953:

> The more I think of it, the more I disapprove of WSC fostering this sentimental illusion that peace can be obtained if only the 'top men' can get together. It seems an example of the hubris which afflicts old men who have power, as it did Chamberlain when he visited Hitler … It is hard to avoid the conclusion that WSC is longing for a top level meeting before he dies – not because it is wise or necessary but

because it would complete the pattern of his ambition and make him the Father of Peace as well as of Victory.[60]

Harold Macmillan was even more brutal:

> The curious thing is that he has made no plan as to what he will talk about. He is, of course, physically and mentally incapable of a serious negotiation. In Washington or Ottawa, among friends, they tolerate the endless repetitions and the frightful waste of time, out of loyalty and respect ... But with the Russians up against him, he would, of course, be absolutely lost.[61]

Relations between Churchill and the British establishment were painful precisely because there was such a gulf between what they wanted to believe about the prime minister (and, perhaps, about the country) and what they knew in their hearts to be true. Soon after Churchill retired, Peter Fleming published his book about Britain in 1940, in which he remarked that the country then had a 'story book leader'. The problem in the 1950s was that the old stories were less convincing and the most significant storyteller was now Peter's younger brother Ian. Ian Fleming's first James Bond novel, *Casino Royale*, was published in 1953 and introduced a world – of sex, snobbery and obsession with national decline – that differed sharply from the stories of G. A. Henty, John Buchan* or C.S. Forester, which had so marked Churchill's view of the world. Churchill knew the Fleming family well. The Bond novel *Moonraker*, published in the year of Churchill's retirement, contains a vivid evocation of the Prime Minister – made all the more disconcerting by the fact that we never hear his voice. Bond has saved London from nuclear annihilation and the Prime Minister wishes to give him a medal. M, the head of the Secret Service, a former

*A line from Buchan's *Greenmantle* would surely win the prize for the words least likely to be spoken by James Bond. 'I had never before', says Richard Hannay, 'got into a motor car with a lady.'

admiral and perhaps, like many naval officers, qualified in his admiration for Churchill, is polite but firm in his refusal. One can imagine the old man at the other end of the phone – obsessed with decorations, uniforms and ceremonies involving the young queen – pleading to have one last public celebration of gallantry.

Of course, Churchill and de Gaulle spent a good part of the years between 1946 and 1958 writing their own stories in that both men published their accounts of the Second World War. Their books differed in revealing ways. Churchill's *History of the Second World War* was a vast enterprise. It was published in six long volumes. Churchill dictated to teams of secretaries. Assistants did the research and sometimes suggested initial drafts of passage. Documents and memoranda were reproduced at length. The books were a commercial success. They were serialized in eighty magazines and newspapers around the world and sold in great numbers – though, judging from the pristine copies that turn up in second-hand books shops, not read by every buyer. They made Churchill's family rich and complicated manoeuvres ensured that he paid as little tax as possible – the amount that these saved Churchill was much larger than the sum that he gave up when he asked for his Prime Ministerial salary to be lowered from £10,000 to £7,000 per year.

Discerning judges – including Harold Macmillan, who looked at matters with a publisher's eye, and Charles de Gaulle – thought that Churchill's book on the Second World War was too long, too unwieldy, too full of documents. The award of the Nobel Prize for literature to Churchill 'for his mastery of biographical and historical detail' was laughable and greatly annoyed Churchill, who thought that he ought to have been given the prize for peace.[62] Churchill produced an account that was accurate – in that his assistants had checked the facts. But it was often untrue. Churchill was, for example, much given to quoting communications that he had made to commanders or pro-consuls but then omitting their replies to him. His memoirs were a justification for his own past but also a contribution to current politics. Discussion of Hitler in the 1930s was designed to evoke thoughts of Stalin in the late 1940s. References to grey men, such as Baldwin, may have been designed to evoke thoughts of Attlee.[63] There were flashes of petty malice. The description of Rudolf Hess, 'a good-looking youngish man', whose actions were partly motivated by 'jealousy' and by his 'neurotic' character, must have made many readers think of Churchill's own protégé/rival Anthony Eden. In case the point needed reinforcing, Churchill wrote: 'It was as if my trusted colleague the Foreign Secretary, who was only a little younger than Hess, had parachuted from a stolen Spitfire into the grounds of Berchtesgaden.'[64]

De Gaulle, by contrast, wrote memoirs rather than a history and was intensely conscious of a distinct French tradition of memoir writing. This is not to say that he always wrote in imitation of those he admired – one wonders whether Chateaubriand's memoirs, a romantic adventure story, served as a kind of anti-model. Occasionally, de Gaulle read parts of the draft of his memoirs to distinguished visitors: René Pleven got the description of Marshal Pétain. But generally, de Gaulle wrote alone in an almost illegible long-hand that was given to his daughter to be typed. His pre-war books had been those of a young man straining to make a reputation – they were stuffed with literary quotations. His memoirs rarely refer to other authors. They are the work of a man who knew that he must write a work that would itself be quoted. The burden of the duty to be de Gaulle never weighed heavier than during the composition of his memoirs. He found writing painfully difficult but hated the idea that anyone should know about his struggle with the blank page – he was said to have copied a final version of one volume in his own hand so that a copy was left with no corrections.[65]

De Gaulle's memoirs were intended to be literature – an artistic creation – in a way that Churchill's work was not.* De Gaulle made

---

*De Gaulle was considered as a candidate for the Nobel prize for literature in 1963 but rejected by the jury 'for obvious reasons.' The prize that year went to the Greek poet Georgios Seferis.

mistakes; in his first draft, he even got the date of his first meeting with Churchill wrong.[66] But de Gaulle's memoirs were, in their way, true, if not accurate. They encapsulated de Gaulle's view of history and the world. They were written for posterity and for France – not for money or short-term self-justification. De Gaulle disapproved of the fact that Churchill's book was serialized in newspapers: 'can you imagine ... Saint-Simon being published in little pieces in a Paris daily paper?'[67] The royalties from de Gaulle's memoirs were given away to the foundation that he had set up in the memory of his daughter Anne.

De Gaulle finished his war memoirs in the 1950s – the three volumes were published in 1954, 1956 and 1959. The first two volumes were written after the failure of the RPF and his own, apparently definitive, withdrawal from politics. They have an Olympian melancholy that was conspicuously missing from much of what Churchill wrote or did in the decade after 1945. Unlike Churchill, de Gaulle was not writing to a deadline. There were times when he suggested that his memoirs would not be published until after his death. De Gaulle wrote later, after having withdrawn from politics for a second time in 1969, that his resignation of 1946 had been intended to leave him 'intact' so that he might be of use to his county 'either in person or by example'.[68] By the time that he wrote the first volume of his memoirs, it seemed almost certain that de Gaulle's future influence would depend on example rather than personal intervention and that curating the memory of his past action was now his most important political activity.

Churchill finally retired on 6 April 1955, after having entertained the young Queen and some of her ministers to dinner in Downing Street. Churchill was dismayed that a printers' strike in London meant that few newspapers covered his departure – perhaps he was particularly dismayed that the only national newspaper to be published was the liberal *Manchester Guardian*. Relief swept through Westminster and Whitehall. It was partly rooted in the hope that the storybook Churchill might be revived now that the old man was out of the way. Evelyn Shuckburgh wrote:

It is a relief that one can now revert to admiring W. for what he has done and been, and not worry about what is doing or will do. I began to feel, as I listened to those speeches about 'the greatest Englishman of our time', that my diary contains a great deal of unworthy and even scurrilous criticism, and ought perhaps to be suppressed. 'The myth' will now take over, and none will want to listen to the carping voice or the awkward derogatory fact. But it doesn't matter, of course. The great thing is that he has gone from the active scene and can be a great man against without damage.[69]

9

Resurrection, 1955–1962

'But this crisis may also be the beginning of a kind of resurrection'
Charles de Gaulle, 19 May 1958.

Even since his return from captivity in 1918, Charles de Gaulle was haunted by the passage of time.[1] His historical vision swept across centuries but he was painfully aware that time to make his own contribution to history was short. After the dissolution of the RPF in 1955, he must have thought that his public life was over. He wrote later that he retired to his country house where the door was closed to all but his family and people of the village and that he seldom went to Paris 'where I only received rare visitors.'[2] The brutal truth was that few influential people wanted to meet de Gaulle in the mid 1950s. In their desperation, his aides turned to writers who might interview the general or, at least, endure his monologues. The novelist Jean Dutourd – who had made de Gaulle a character in his *Les Taxis de la Marne* (1956) – and the English journalist Malcolm Muggeridge were both to dine out for many years on the afternoons that they had spent in de Gaulle's company around this time.[3]

The high drama of international politics in the last years of Stalin's rule had given de Gaulle an invigorating burst of apocalyptic fervour. For a time, it seemed possible that the Soviet Union might invade and that the Red Army would reach the Pyrenees. The death of Stalin in March 1953 changed things. When the American anthropologist Lawrence Wylie began his study of a village in the

Vaucluse in the late 1940s, he found that the farmers had stopped planting fruit trees because they feared that their land would soon be a battleground in a nuclear war; by the time he finished his book in 1957, they were planting trees again.[4]

The politics of the Fourth Republic also changed in the mid 1950s. The desire to exclude Communists (and Gaullists) from power had imposed discipline on other politicians. They had formed complicated but effective alliances to exclude these two forces from power. Enemies of the political establishment referred to it as 'the system' and, for all the multiplicity of parties and frequent changes of government, the mainstream parties of the Fourth Republic did indeed function as a kind of machine.

After 1953, it was harder to keep the machine running and harder to hold political alliances together. The Communist threat diminished – partly because Communist leaders seemed less clear that they wanted to take power. This diminishing threat destabilized the system – because it made unity among non-Communist politicians less urgent. Amnesty laws of 1951 and 1953 brought Pétainists back to the forefront of political life and this created new fissures between, or within, political parties. In 1953, Pierre Poujade led a movement of shopkeepers and artisans to protest against value added tax. This mutated into a political party, the Union de Fraternité Française (UFF), which won over fifty seats in the legislative election of 1955. Poujadism – vulgar and materialistic – seemed the antithesis of Gaullism, but Poujade suspected that de Gaulle, furious at the Fourth Republic, might have voted for the UFF in 1955. In 1954, the Socialist Vincent Auriol finished his term as President. Presidents in the Fourth Republic served for a seven-year term. They were, therefore, more secure than Prime Ministers (who lasted only as long as they could sustain a majority in parliament). Furthermore, Auriol was a strong character who made the most of his powers to inject some stability into politics. His successor, René Coty, was less robust.

The instability of the Fourth Republic would not in itself would have brought de Gaulle back to power – the Third Republic, which had a similar constitution and the same instability, had lasted for seventy years. It seemed, briefly, possible that defeat of French forces in Indochina at Dien Bien Phu on 7 May 1954 might undermine the Fourth Republic. De Gaulle laid a wreath on the tomb of the unknown soldier on the following day (ostensibly because it was the anniversary of allied victory in Europe) and some demonstrators called for de Gaulle's return. As it turned out, Indochina brought down the government of Joseph Laniel – he resigned after having been Prime Minister for almost a year, which was a long time in the politics of the Fourth Republic – but did not bring the return of de Gaulle. Instead, Pierre Mendès France formed a government on 18 June.

Mendès had been elected to parliament at a young age. He was a member of the Radical Party (the quintessential party of the Third Republic) and, in his youth, he had been a Freemason. He was also Jewish. He had an agreeably ugly face and great charm. He stood for much of what de Gaulle had been brought up to despise. Yet he had also rejected the armistice of 1940, been put on trial by the Vichy government, escaped from prison and made his way to London where he joined the Free French air force. After the war, de Gaulle had appointed him as Finance Minister but Mendès resigned because he wanted more rigorous policies to contain inflation.

In spite of his roots in the Radical Party (associated with anticlericalism), Mendès attracted support from left-wing Catholics. He was also admired by many Gaullists – 59 Gaullist deputies voted in favour of his investiture. De Gaulle met Mendès in private and told him that he might achieve things in the short term but that the political system would defeat him in the long term. François Mauriac – an admirer of both men – said that an alliance between Mendès and de Gaulle was in the national interest but would be prevented by 'the very nature of PMF, in that inflexibility that is his greatness.'[5] It is revealing that Mauriac should identify inflexibility as being on the side of Mendès rather on that of de Gaulle. De Gaulle often talked in terms that implied inflexibility but frequently compromised to achieve his ends; Mendès seemed more emollient, but he could be brutally clear about choices. He came to power with a promise to extract France from Indochina within thirty days and was true to his word. De Gaulle, however, turned out to be right about the system and Mendès was overthrown in February 1955.

For all the political instability and international humiliations, the material interests of the French (which de Gaulle sometimes regarded with disdain) were well served by economic growth, an efficient state administration and peace in Europe. The farmers replanting their fruit trees in the Vaucluse – often men who had endured five years in a German stalag – were happy to swap grandeur for peace and prosperity. The shock that destroyed the Fourth Republic came from outside mainland France. Algeria had been a French colony since 1830 and had, since 1870, been formally defined as part of France. It was, like the mainland, divided into departments. Its voters sent representatives to the National Assembly. However, its electorate was more circumscribed than that of mainland France. A million people of European origin had the right to vote as did the indigenous Jewish population. The great majority of the nine million Algerian Muslims had few political rights. On 1 November 1954, the Front de Libération Nationale (FLN) launched an armed rebellion to secure independence for Algeria.

Almost all the leading politicians in France agreed that Algeria must remain French. Guy Mollet, the Socialist Prime Minister in 1956, was a defender of French Algeria and his convictions were strengthened rather than weakened when Europeans, who blamed his government for not being firm enough, pelted him with tomatoes during a visit to Algiers. Many French army officers believed in French Algeria and, indeed, its defence became a crusade for some who wished to assuage the humiliation of defeat in 1940 and their guilt at having abandoned Indochina in 1954.

The only significant person who had expressed no public view on Algeria was de Gaulle, who expressed no public view on most things after 1954. He did not, however, need to say anything for people to assume they knew what he would think. In 1947, the American ambassador in Paris had told the Gaullist Gaston Palewksi that 'many people were apprehensive lest de Gaulle return to power and put an end to the present French government's efforts at democratic reform in North Africa.'⁶ Some of de Gaulle's associates were supporters of French Algeria. Particularly important were two men. The first of these was Jacques Soustelle – an anthropologist (a specialist on the Aztecs) who had rallied to de Gaulle in 1940 and helped run his intelligence service. In 1955, Soustelle was appointed as Governor General of Algeria. Though he supported reforms that would improve the lives of the native population and hoped for more racial integration, he wanted Algeria to stay French. His removal from office in 1956 provoked protests from Europeans. The second important person was general Jacques Massu. He had served with the Free French for most of the Second World War and was sent to Algeria in 1956 to crush the FLN in the city of Algiers.

The public, which seemed almost to have forgotten de Gaulle in the mid 1950s, took an interest in him again as Algeria cast its shadow over French politics. Polls began to show a significant minority of the population would support de Gaulle's return to power. During his visits to Paris, the nature of the visitors that de Gaulle received changed. He saw people who were associated with Algeria or who were active in politics. Though he was sometimes dismissive of Gaullists who accepted office in the Fourth Republic, it suited him to have people who might advance his cause in positions of power – Jacques Chaban-Delmas, Minster of Defence in 1957 and 1958, was particularly important.

By 1958, many army officers and much of the French right had lost faith in the ability of the Fourth Republic to defend Algeria. In Paris, the government was weak. Félix Gaillard was overthrown as Prime Minister in mid-April but then, for some weeks, other politicians were unable to obtain a parliamentary majority to form a new government. In mid-May Pierre Pflimlin, a Christian Democract became Prime Minister – though his slim majority depended partly on the fact that many members of parliament abstained. Some supporters of French Algeria believed that Pflimlin had dangerously liberal views on Algeria. Enraged when the FLN killed three French prisoners of war, soldiers and settlers took over the government building in Algiers on 13 May and formed a Committee of Public Safety, presided over by General Massu: an obvious challenge to the authority of the government in Paris. The protesters did not all agree on policy – some wanted the Muslim Algerians to be more integrated into the French political system and some were bitterly opposed to such integration. In this opaque world of interlocking plots, Gaullists had an advantage. They alone had a single, simple and concrete aim: the return of de Gaulle to power.

Raoul Salan, the commander of the army in Algeria was not devoted to de Gaulle in that way that, say, Massu was – he had joined Free French forces part of the way through the Second World War. When Gaullists persuaded him to send a telegram to President Coty calling on him to establish a government of public safety – he removed the name 'de Gaulle' from the telegram and replaced it with reference to a 'national arbiter.' On 15 May, Salan, made a speech to the crowd assembled in Algiers that finished with the words 'Vive l'Algérie Française.' After a brief discussion with those around him, he then turned back to audience and added 'Vive de Gaulle.' De Gaulle now issued a laconic statement – just seven lines – saying that he was willing to form a government.

Was this a military coup? The army had effectively seized power in Algeria. Soldiers and Algerian settlers also took power in Corsica, where the local authorities made little effort to resist them. Officers discussed plans for 'Operation Resurrection' in which the army would seize the capital and install de Gaulle in power. Matters, however, were complicated partly by the fact that politicians in Paris were reluctant to impose their will – they feared bloodshed and also that a direct order to the army might be disobeyed. Before the investiture of Pflilmlin, Gaillard hovered like a political ghost – the nearest thing that France had to a Prime Minister but possessed of no real authority. He told Massu not to fire on the crowd of settlers in Algiers – an order to the contrary would almost certainly have been ignored. De Gaulle wrote contemptuously about the action, or inaction, 'of what, by force of habit, one referred to as authority,' in May 1958. He would have claimed that there was no *coup d'état* because there was no *état* to resist the *coup*.

In truth, it suited de Gaulle to pretend that the government had simply melted away because the alternative would have been to admit how far his return was forced by the army and how far his own manoeuvres undermined ministers in office. Pierre de Chevigné illustrated the complexity of relations between established politicians and de Gaulle in May 1958. De Chevigné was a Gaullist *de la première heure*. Wounded in the battle of France in 1940, he had discharged himself from hospital and talked his way on to a British boat. Still bandaged, he met de Gaulle in London on 25 June. In August 1944, marched down the Champs Elysée with de Gaulle. After the war, however, he joined the Christian Democrats rather than the Gaullist grouping in parliament and, in May 1958, he briefly replaced the Gaullist Jacques Chaban Delmas as Minister of Defence. De Chevigné tried to impose order on the army. However, he came to recognize that cutting all contact between de Gaulle and the army was impossible. He also made a discreet enquiry as to whether de Gaulle would approve of his action before he cancelled an aggressive operation against the FLN that the army planned to launch in Algeria. When de Gaulle was installed in power, de Chevigné refused to accept ministerial office. He said that he would not follow the general 'under the threat of machine guns.'[7]

De Chevigné told de Gaulle: 'You are no longer the man of 1940.' It sounds like an unforgivable insult. But, for once, de Gaulle was conciliatory – sending a footman to intercept de Chevigné after he had stormed out of their meeting and seeking to smooth things over. The truth was that de Gaulle understood all too well that 1958 was not 1940. He was no longer a lone figure making a heroic gesture of defiance. Rather he was a spider weaving his web around the whole

French state – a web that required patience and fine judgement about when it might be wise not to pull too hard on the threads.

De Gaulle wanted to return to power but, above all, he wanted to do so on his own terms. It is hard to know whether de Gaulle would, if all other options had failed, have agreed to take power after the army had overthrown the previous government – probably he did not know himself. He knew about the plans for an assault on Paris but was careful to avoid giving them explicit approval. Olivier Guichard, one of de Gaulle's aides, told one soldier, 'the general does not want an assault but he will take the situation as he finds it.'[8] The fact that conversations were secret and that de Gaulle's emissaries had no formal authority created confusion, which suited de Gaulle. One Gaullist told American diplomats that de Gaulle would, if necessary, accept Algerian independence – exactly the opposite of what the army was being told. He added that, as the diplomatic telegram put it, 'he had no "message" from General, but stated latter knows of his démarche and has given it tacit approval.'[9]

What de Gaulle really wanted was to return not as the leader of a coup, still less as the instrument of other leaders, but rather as the man who would protect France from a coup. The distinction was abstract. In the last volume of his memoirs, written ten years later, de Gaulle recalled having told the presidents of the two houses of the French parliament that, if he failed to extract the terms that he wanted for his return, he would 'shut myself away with my grief' and that they would then have to 'explain yourselves to the paratroopers.'[10] The two presidents, in accounts that they wrote immediately after the event, did not allude to these words having been spoken.[11] The truth is that that they did not have to be. Everyone knew what would happen if the army were not appeased.

With varying degrees of reluctance, leading politicians – the socialist Guy Mollet, the conservative Antoine Pinay and the former President of the republic Vincent Auriol – accepted that de Gaulle's return to power was inevitable. Coty appointed de Gaulle as Prime Minister – he was to be the last man to hold this office in the Fourth

Republic. At Coty's insistence, de Gaulle appeared before parliament to seek investiture. Parliament granted him full powers to produce a new constitution, which, after having been approved by referendum in September 1958, came into effect in January 1959. The constitution of the Fifth Republic was drafted fast by a small group of people. It gave much greater power to the President, who was granted, in particular, the right to dissolve the National Assembly. A group of notables, largely composed of men from the local *conseils généraux*, then voted to appoint de Gaulle as the first President of the Fifth Republic.

De Gaulle's return to power in 1958, unlike that of Churchill in 1951, was unexpected until shortly before it happened. Churchill returned in a haze of nostalgia that was, to some at least, reassuring. De Gaulle looked to the future rather than the past in 1958, and very few people, not even his supporters, found him reassuring. Churchill was treated with a degree of deference that sometimes made him look absurd; de Gaulle was treated with a degree of trepidation that he sometimes exploited to make everyone else look absurd. Jules Moch, the socialist Minister of the Interior, deployed the police in armoured cars along the banks of the Seine when de Gaulle convoked a press conference on 19 May. But the general turned up accompanied by no one except his chauffeur and his aide de camp. He issued a succession of brief declarations and then stood back in amusement as the political classes sought to make sense of his Delphic pronouncements.

Churchill's return had been the product of the British parliamentary system. He was scrupulous in his respect for constitutional proprieties in the treatment of the monarch and the House of Commons. De Gaulle, by contrast, came to power to sweep away the existing constitution. He addressed parliament on the 1 June 1958 and then attended the sitting of 2 June; after that he never set foot in the National Assembly again.

De Gaulle's return to power was made easier by the fact that the apparatus of the state was often Gaullist by 1958. The first graduates of the Ecole Nationale d'Administration began to reach influential positions. Maurice Papon – who became prefect of the Paris police in March 1958 was a Gaullist – in spite, or because, of having collaborated with the Germans during the occupation. But de Gaulle was not as strong as he pretended. There was, as in 1940, a touch of bluff in the way that he presented himself. For one thing, there was no Gaullist party. At first, de Gaulle headed a coalition drawn from the major existing parties – other than the Communists and the Poujadists. He had to deploy all his prestige and force of personality to impose his authority on his ministers.

The army also impinged on de Gaulle's authority. General Salan had abolished the distinction between civil and military administration in Algeria in May 1958 and de Gaulle confirmed this move in the following month – making Salan delegate general (effectively governor). For the rest of 1958, the army had extraordinary powers in Algeria. This was a delicate position for man who had always emphasised that the army must be the servant of the state not its master. De Gaulle worked quietly to weaken the power of the military and the settlers who were associated with them. A telegram from the American embassy in Paris relayed what a conservative politician, soon to be one of de Gaulle's ministers, believed to be de Gaulle's strategy: 'For present he will have to retain in office certain extremists in Algeria since they have power rather than he. He plans to treat them as he did resistance leaders by kicking them upstairs.'[12] Officers who had been associated with defiance of civil authority were discreetly posted away from Algeria in late 1958. Raoul Salan was 'kicked upstairs' by being made Military Governor of Paris. His replacement as commander in Algeria – Maurice Challe – was a less political figure, though not, as it turned out, entirely apolitical. Paul Delouvrier, a veteran of the resistance, was appointed as delegate general in Algeria – thus bringing its administration back under civilian aegis.

For his first few years in office, Algeria was at the centre of de Gaulle's thinking. He was later to imply that he understood from the start that Algeria would be granted independence and that his whole policy was designed to achieve this end. Some of his bitterest enemies did indeed conclude that de Gaulle had always plotted to betray *Algérie Française*. His associates thought things were more complicated – that de Gaulle had only gradually moved towards supporting Algerian independence as other options proved impossible.[13]

Three things governed de Gaulle's attitude to Algeria. First, he believed in the greatness of France and was, consequently, alarmed at the prospect that France might seem to retreat in the face of military defeat. However, the abstraction of de Gaulle's 'idea of France' meant that he could be detached about particular territories. In addition to this, his notion of national greatness changed with circumstances. If Algeria contributed to the power of France as a whole, he was in favour of keeping it; if it began to drain that power, he would not be. The journalist Raymond Cartier had suggested in 1956 that the economic costs of colonial possessions might be greater than the gains. At first de Gaulle distanced himself from this notion. He said, at a press conference of 10 November 1959, that France had a 'mission' that went beyond the mere calculation or profit and loss – though he also recognized that countries that had ceased to be colonies would have the right to reject French help. Later his position changed. He said in April 1961, 'the least one can say is that Algeria costs us more than it brings in.'[14] Most significant for de Gaulle was the fact that Algeria created a certain kind of army – one that revolved around infantry soldiers rather than jet aircraft and missiles. In 1960, 418,000 French soldiers were in North Africa – this compared to 253,000 in France and West Germany combined.[15] De Gaulle's desire for military modernization was impeded by Algeria.

Second, de Gaulle, unlike many French army officers, had no personal attachment to Algeria. He had never served there and his time there in 1943 and 1944 had left him with little affection for the European population – which was more Pétainist or Giraudist than Gaullist.

Third, de Gaulle did not believe in racial integration. His views on race were never as viscerally felt, or crudely expressed, as Churchill's. De Gaulle had worked with non-white people. He respected Felix Eboué, the governor of Chad who had rallied to the Free French in 1940. Gaston Monnerville, the president of the Senate, with whom de Gaulle negotiated in 1958, was the descendant of slaves from Martinique. Though de Gaulle disliked Monnerville, he did not see anything incongruous about a non-white man holding such an important position. But de Gaulle believed that racial mixing was possible only when small numbers were involved. For him, France was a white, Christian country.

The more that progressively minded defenders of French Algeria (such as Soustelle) talked of integration, the less de Gaulle liked it. He regarded the idea that nine million Muslim Algerians should be given citizenship on the same basis as forty-five million French people with horror. De Gaulle disliked the idea of 'assimilation' (he devised the word 'Francization' partly as a means of avoiding the terms 'assimilation or 'integration'). He particularly disliked the prospect of sexual relations between white women and non-white men – an interesting sentiment in someone who had portrayed relations between white men and non-white women as so alluring in his youthful stories. De Gaulle, in short, supported decolonization not in spite of being a racist but because of it.

None of this was clear to anyone, including, probably, de Gaulle himself, in 1958. In retrospect, the most striking feature of de Gaulle's Algerian policy was studied ambiguity. An American diplomat telegraphed on 1 June 1958: 'Silence of General de Gaulle over past few years plus contradictory and doubtful reliability of numerous self-appointed spokesmen for the General make it particularly difficult estimate in advance character of his regime and policies he will follow.'[16] The general understood that it would be useful to make as few commitments as possible and to maintain the widest possible margin for manoeuvre. Soon after he came to power, he visited Algeria and made a speech that began with the words 'Je vous ai compris' (I have understood you) – a phrase that might have meant many things. A couple of days later, perhaps overcome by the emotion that often seized him when he addressed enthusiastic crowds, he shouted 'Vive l'Algérie Française' at the end of a speech – it was the only time that he used the phrase in public. Other than this, his views of Algeria were expressed in a succession of scrupulously vague formulae.

The first of these came on 23 October 1958 when de Gaulle said that the Algerian rebels had fought courageously and proposed a 'Paix des Braves', by which men would return to their homes and work. No concrete political concession was offered – though thousands of FLN suspects were quietly released from custody. Nothing came of this gesture in the short term. The next year on 16 September 1959, de Gaulle talked of 'auto-determination' that would leave the Algerians free to choose their own destiny. He still expressed the hope that they would choose to remain closely associated with France and he accentuated the uncertainty around his proposal by emphasizing, or having other people emphasize, that 'auto-determination' was not the same as the English phrase 'self-determination'.

De Gaulle toyed with other means of settling the Algerian problem. He told the British ambassador in Paris that independence for Algeria would mean partition – 'since the French would never agree to evacuate 1,200,000 Frenchmen and would insist on their remaining, if they so desired, in some kind of strip along the coast.'[17] He seems to have derived the idea of partition partly from the Israeli Prime Minister Ben Gurion, with whom he had good relations.[18] Characteristically, de Gaulle did not advance this idea in public himself but got Alain Peyrefitte, at the time Minister of Information, to discuss it in newspapers articles and a book. The latter appeared just six months before an unpartitioned Algeria gained independence.[19]

With regard to means as well as ends, de Gaulle's views were often shrouded in mystery. It was no secret that the French army had tortured FLN suspects in Algeria. More generally soldiers had used violence (including rape) to try to terrify Algerians into submission. De Gaulle had cordial relations with some – such as the army officer Jacques Paris de Bollardière – who condemned torture, but he said almost nothing about the matter himself. In his memoirs, he remarked that French soldiers in Algeria were charged with 'the sometimes odious rigour of repression'.[20] Some of the officers who authorized torture in Algeria – Jacques Massu, Marcel Bigeard and Paul Aussaresses – were Gaullists.

In June 1958, André Malraux, the Minister of Culture, said that torture had stopped from the moment that de Gaulle visited Algiers at the beginning of that month. This was untrue – though the public disavowal of torture by someone close to de Gaulle was, in itself, significant. Attempts to impose rules on the army had more to do with the desire to asset the authority of the state than protect individuals. In May 1960, the father of the FLN militant Djamila Boupacha told a soldier 'De Gaulle has said that there is no more torture'; the soldier replied 'De Gaulle can do what he likes *chez lui* here it is us who are in control.'[21] In fact, abuses took place in the mainland too. In October 1961, the Paris police attacked Algerian demonstrators – killing some of them. In police stations, badly injured demonstrators were forced to stand up and shout 'Vive de Gaulle.'

In January 1960, general Massu gave an interview to a German newspaper in which he said that the army did not 'understand' de Gaulle's policy. Summoned to Paris to explain himself, he made it clear that he remained loyal to de Gaulle but was, nonetheless, transferred away from Algeria. Partly in response to this, Europeans in Algiers, with the complicity of some in the army, took to the streets and sought, as in 1958, to dictate policy to Paris during what became known as 'Barricades Week.' It was an awkward moment. For a time, the Paris government could not impose its will in Algeria. Fourteen gendarmes were shot dead by European settlers. The rebellion fizzled out – partly because heavy rain made presence on the barricades uncomfortable. De Gaulle, in military uniform, spoke on television on 29 January. His most important words were addressed to the army. It would, he said, be 'nothing but an archaic and absurd relic of feudal lords if it imposed conditions on its loyalty' and that loyalty must be to him.

The imposition of discipline on the army was less clear cut than de Gaulle made it seem. Settlers who had participated in Barricades Week were tried but soldiers who had shown their sympathy were, on the whole, spared. The army's obedience was obtained, in part, with discreet hints that there would be no further concessions to the FLN. In March, de Gaulle visited soldiers in Algeria. The tour was designed to reassure officers; some of those committed to French Algeria were later to look back bitterly on this as the last occasion when they might easily have assassinated de Gaulle.

There was an extraordinary moment in 1960 when a guerrilla commander in Algeria, Si Salah, discontented with the FLN leadership, contacted the French authorities to negotiate a peace directly on behalf of the forces under his control. Si Salah and some of his comrades talked to French negotiators and were eventually taken secretly to Paris where, on the night of 10 June they met de Gaulle himself in his office in the Élysée Palace. De Gaulle, considering it inappropriate to shake the hands of men who were fighting the French army, saluted them. The negotiations, however, came to nothing. Si Salah's superiors found out about the initiative and had him killed. It is possible that de Gaulle used Si Salah as an instrument to pressure the leaders of the FLN to come to the negotiating table. In December 1960, de Gaulle made his last ever visit to Algeria. It was considered too dangerous for him to go to the coastal cities where most European settlers lived. In spite of this, his presence was accompanied by violent demonstrations which, according to the British consul general, caused 125 deaths, mostly of Muslims.[22]

In April 1961, after it became clear that de Gaulle was moving towards the recognition of Algerian independence, part of the army rebelled in the so-called 'generals' putsch'. Generals Raoul Salan, Maurice Challe, Edmond Jouhaud and André Zeller sought to establish an independent authority in Algeria. They were not clear on their aims and particularly disagreed about whether they wanted simply to mobilise the whole European population of Algeria against the FLN or whether they would seek to overthrow the government in the mainland. They probably hoped that, as in 1958, the government in Paris would submit without a fight.

This time, however, there was no submission and none of the discreet compromises that had marked de Gaulle's response to Barricades Week in 1960. He appeared on television (in uniform) and dismissed his enemies as 'un quarteron de généraux en retraite' (bunch of retired generals) – 'quarteron' being one of those archaic words that he flourished when he wished to make an impression. The revolt in Algeria collapsed. Its leaders were arrested or went into hiding. De Gaulle, once the proponent of the *armée de métier*, benefited from the fact that conscript soldiers in Algeria were reluctant to follow their officers and elite units (mainly professional) in seeking to overthrow the government. Air force officers, excited by the prospect of technological modernisation that de Gaulle had begun to dangle in front of their eyes, were generally loyal to the regime, which was important because a single squadron of Mirage jets could have thwarted any attempt to transport soldiers from Algeria to the mainland.

Only one person (a sergeant who resisted the putschists) was killed during the rebellion – an astonishingly low figure when one considers the violence soldiers had deployed against Algerians. All the same, both sides were playing for high stakes. Gaullist officials in Algeria were imprisoned during the putsch and had the army succeeded in moving to the mainland, de Gaulle would at the least have been deposed. When Challe handed himself to the authorities just a few days after the rebellion had started, he expected to be executed. The authorities brought forward the date for testing an atomic bomb in southern Algeria because they feared the consequences if the weapon fell into the hands of the rebellious soldiers. An outright civil war had been averted, but there was a subterranean civil war for several years because defenders of French Algeria – grouped in the Organisation de l'Armée Sécrète (OAS) – launched a campaign of terrorism (directed against the French state as well as Algerian nationalists) in Algeria and then transferred this campaign to mainland France.

After the generals' putsch, no one had any doubt what de Gaulle's policy with regard to Algeria would be. French representatives negotiated with those of the FLN at Evian. De Gaulle took no direct part in the discussions but made it clear that he wanted France out of Algeria and had little concern for the consequences. It was agreed that there would be a ceasefire and, subject to a referendum of the Algerian population, France would leave. The negotiations and the implementation of the agreement were conducted against a terrifying backdrop. The OAS killed the mayor of Evian simply because the negotiations had been conducted in his town.

The divisions over Algeria were bitter. A whole section of the extreme-right – the 'opposition nationale' – came to define itself against de Gaulle, which meant that its supporters sometimes embraced policies, such as support for Israel or European integration, that would have seemed incongruous to an earlier generation of right-wingers. De Gaulle did little to appease anyone. He had always been ruthless but, during and immediately after the Second World War, he had been reluctant to shed French blood. Some around him thought that he found it particularly painful to authorise executions after the liberation; he spared about two thirds of those sentenced to death for collaboration, including all women and minors.[23] On the other hanf, in Algeria de Gaulle seemed contemptuously indifferent to the fate of many French people – or those who had reason to consider themselves French. He cared little for the million or so settlers (*pieds noirs* as they became known) who returned to France. He tried to prevent harkis – Muslim auxiliaries who had fought with the French – from being brought back to France. Some harkis left behind were killed by their compatriots; those who escaped to France spent years in squalid camps. If de Gaulle had had his way, the leaders of the generals' putsch would have been executed. An officer who presided over the military tribunal that sentenced the putschists committed suicide partly because he found his duties so painful. De Gaulle established a new military court because he was disappointed at the leniency of the sentences imposed on putschists.

Robert Buron, a minister with responsibility for Algeria, described de Gaulle during the Algerian War as the 'Prince of Equivocation'.[24] During the first three years of his presidency, de Gaulle conveyed an impression of resolution and certainty but, in reality, his own associates were often unsure about his policy. They did not know what he intended to do about Algeria or even whether he knew it himself. By 1962, the ambiguity was dissipated. Algeria was gone and the army was humbled. Ministers who disagreed with de Gaulle or simply showed themselves independent were eased out of office. The first prime minister of the Fifth Republic, Michel Debré, was a loyal Gaullist who had worked to bring about de Gaulle's return as a member of parliament in the 1950s. He might have claimed, with some justice, that de Gaulle owed his power partly to him. He was also distressed by the French departure from Algeria – though, unlike some of de Gaulle's ministers, he did not rebel against his master. In April 1962, Debré resigned. His replacement, Georges Pompidou, was an able man but one whose power derived almost entirely from de Gaulle. The authority of the state had been restored and de Gaulle himself was in command of that state.

Survival and Death, 1962–5

'The Greatest Dying Englishman'
Private Eye *magazine on Churchill (1963)*

'I am not too bad, but rest assured one day I will die.'
*Charles de Gaulle, when a journalist enquired after his health
in January 1965*

In the early 1960s, Churchill was dying. There were times, though, when it seemed that de Gaulle would predecease him: French departure from Algeria provoked at least a dozen serious assassination attempts against the general. At a time when Churchill's powers were so visibly in decline, de Gaulle's icy self-control was underlined by the contempt with which he treated threats to his own life. De Gaulle's mortality mattered in a way that Churchill's did not. The British political system was not going to be shaken by the death of a former prime minister, whereas the political theatre built around de Gaulle was rendered all the more compelling by uncertainty about how much of the system he had constructed would outlive him. The threat of assassination came to define the middle years of de Gaulle's presidency. It emphasised how different he was from other democratic leaders – except perhaps those of the United States. When he came to visit Harold Macmillan in 1963, the British prime minister noticed the vast number of policemen and the special fridge for plasma in case de Gaulle required an emergency transfusion.[1]

In fact, nothing became de Gaulle better than the hatred that he aroused. It saved him from looking ridiculous – perhaps, particularly, to himself. He was in his early seventies during the last stages of the Algerian War and was afflicted by some undignified physical frailties. He underwent a prostate operation in April 1964. His eyesight was weak – twice in the 1950s, he had had cataracts removed from them. British diplomats believed that he was not even capable of reading documents.[2] Most of the world more than a few metres from his face was a blur for much of the time but he refused to wear glasses in public. But attacks on de Gaulle turned him from a myopic old man with a weak bladder into the central figure in a great drama. A military doctor who had had occasion to observe him at close quarters, believed that the president was living under pressures that would have been 'a severe strain on a much younger man' and had 'come to rely on the stimulus of living in the public eye in order to keep going'.[3]

Protecting de Gaulle was difficult because he insisted that nothing should overshadow the dignity of the state. This had odd consequences. He thought policemen should not turn their back on the president, which made it hard for them to watch those who lined the roads.[4] His protectors took to hiding men in the bushes. One policeman, thus concealed, had an uncomfortable experience when de Gaulle's car stopped, the General got out and advanced towards the concealed man's hiding place – absent-mindedly undoing his fly buttons.[5]

The most famous attempt on the life of de Gaulle occurred on 22 August 1962 when gunmen fired on his car as it drove through the Paris suburb of Petit Clamart. An almost religious mythology grew around the attack. One minister absurdly claimed that the general had refused to duck and that a bullet would have hit him had he done so: 'his principles saved him – the general never bows down'.[6] There was a revealing moment in the trial of Colonel Jean Bastien-Thiry, the leader of the assassination team at Petit

Clamart. Bastien-Thiry insisted that they had intended to kidnap de Gaulle rather than kill him. The prosecuting counsel asked them how, if this was the case, they planned to keep their captive from escaping. Bastien-Thiry replied that they would have only to take away his braces and his glasses and he would be powerless. One of the defence lawyers whispered: 'He's just signed his own death warrant.'[7] De Gaulle might have spared a man who tried to kill him but never one who laughed at him. Characteristically, he thought that Bastien-Thiry, shot by firing squad in March 1963, had met a more dignified end than those more senior officers who survived 'playing ball in the prison yard at Tulle'.[8]

The Petit Clamart assassination attempt provided de Gaulle with an opportunity. The fact that he had come so close to death allowed him to insist that a means must be found to appoint a potential successor – someone who would not, like himself, have been anointed by history. From now on, de Gaulle wanted the head of state to be chosen by direct election rather than by a college of notables. This illustrated a more general principle of Gaullism which emphasised that legitimacy sprang from the direct relations between the ruler and the people; such relations should be unmediated by parties or other authorities.

De Gaulle's own direct relations with the people were supported by another constitutional innovation: the use of the referendum. Direct relations also went with a new party system. Instead of managing a ramshackle coalition of parties, de Gaulle formed (or allowed his supporters to form) the Union pour la Nouvelle République (UNR). It was a new kind of party – de Gaulle would have denied that it was a party at all. It was dominated by prominent national leaders, rather than by ordinary militants (as were the Communist and Socialist parties) or by local notables (as were the parties of the centre and right). The electorate of the UNR was closer to the average population of France than that of the existing parties, which meant that it was primarily female, though the party leaders were almost all men.

Did the French people buy de Gaulle's new vision of politics? They supported his constitutional innovations in a succession of referendums. The UNR was the largest single party in the National Assembly after the legislative elections of 1958; in 1962 it obtained almost half the seats. Forming an alliance with a few right-wingers meant that it was the first party in French history that could command an absolute majority in parliament. But there were few unconditional Gaullists. De Gaulle said of the referendum of September 1958, which approved a new constitution, that 'tous les oui ont été joyeux' (all the yes votes were joyful). This was untrue. Support for de Gaulle was often grudging and guarded. The proportion of the electorate that supported de Gaulle's positions in referendum was higher than the proportion who voted for Gaullist candidates in elections. Local political fiefdoms survived under the broad umbrella of Gaullist politics – the Communist Party controlled municipal government in many working-class areas. De Gaulle himself voted for a member of the Radical Party in local elections at Colombey-les-Deux-Églises, where there was no Gaullist candidate.[9]

The direct relations between ruler and ruled that de Gaulle desired were made easier by broadcasting and, particularly, by television. In the Third and Fourth Republics, French politics had been built around newspapers – *L'Humanité* for the Communists, *Le Populaire* for the Socialists and *La Dépêche* for the Radical Party. The monarchist Action Française was a party that served a newspaper more than a newspaper that served a party. In the late 1950s, this changed. The proportion of households that owned a television set increased from 5 to 62 per cent between 1958 and 1969. A million sets were bought in 1964 alone. More transmission stations meant that the broadcasts, available, at first only in large cities, reached 80 per cent of the population by 1963.[10]

De Gaulle worked hard to master this new medium. Television took him straight into most French households – meaning that he reached women as much as men. Black and white programmes conferred an appropriate air of gravitas as did the respectful presentations of a single state broadcaster. De Gaulle, who had been excluded from the airwaves by governments of the Fourth Republic, was ruthless in his exploitation of the state's monopoly over broadcasting. His physical oddity, so painful to him in earlier life, gave him an advantage. His self-consciousness made him an arresting performer – much given to extravagant gestures and obscure words that had foreign diplomats reaching for dictionaries.* The historian Emmanuel Le Roy Ladurie recalled the broadcasts:

> The image and the person of the General ... came down among us during those beautiful nights in Montpellier on our neigbours' television. [The historian] Kantorowicz had underlined that in the Middle Ages the body of the king much more than an abstract conception of the state was at the centre of the process of unification of the kingdom and even of nation formation. The corporality of power derived from the new medium generated a similar effect. The mass of the citizenry communed directly with the upper half of the presidential body, with the face, the voice and the facial ticks of the head of state transmitted by the television screen.[11]

De Gaulle watched a lot of television – his poor sight and refusal to wear glasses in public meant that he saw much of France only when it was portrayed on the small screen. Programmes were sometimes censored for political reasons but more important was the implicit control deriving from the fact that loyal Gaullists were appointed to senior positions in the state broadcaster and often asked themselves

---

*'Quarteron' (see above) or 'Bambocher' (see chapter 11). In 1968, the British ambassador wrote of the 'antique vulgarity' of 'chienlit' – the word de Gaulle used to describe the student disturbances.

what the general would think of their broadcasts. Even apparently apolitical programmes reinforced the Fifth Republic. Documentaries celebrated French history and culture. *Les Chevaliers du Ciel* (an adventure series for children broadcast from 1967 to 1970) was about the French air force and, implicitly, about Gaullist military policy – it once featured a discussion of the circumstances in which the heroes might deploy a nuclear bomb.

De Gaulle had written on the opening page of his memoirs that 'only great enterprises are likely to balance the festering propensity for division that [the French people] carry in themselves … In short France cannot be France without grandeur.' Grandeur sometimes came from spectacular displays of prowess in science and engineering. Huge hydroelectric plants transformed the French economy (by providing a new source of electricity) and enforced a brutal modernisation – because ancient villages were often flooded. Opening the dam that runs across the Rance estuary in Brittany in 1966, de Gaulle said: 'Just as the Rance flows to the sea because her source sends her there, so France is true to herself when she advances towards progress.'

The greatest of de Gaulle's 'great enterprises' involved foreign policy. He was much given to talking about eternal realities and interests in international relations. For him, everything revolved around the nation or the state – he regarded the terms as interchangeable. He disliked international bodies – especially the United Nations. He regarded the USSR as simply another name for Russia. He would have disapproved of the Commonwealth less if he had thought that it was just another name for the British empire.

The trenchant expression of de Gaulle's opinions concealed flexibility. His views – on the dangers of German power or the benefits to be drawn from American alliance – changed over time and according to circumstances. He knew that France was no longer a great power and sometimes seemed to feel that his most important duty was to conceal this fact from the French people. His diplomacy often displayed the very quality that his critics were least likely to attribute to him: moderation. He avoided expensive adventures in foreign policy and understood that the United States and the Soviet Union were over-extended. Balance mattered to him and he sought to play potential enemies off against each other. The 1960s was a particularly propitious time for a policy of equilibrium because the United States and the Soviet Union had reached a kind of stasis in their relations that made it easier for medium-sized powers to manoeuvre between them.

The American secretary of state Dean Acheson remarked in 1962 that Britain had lost an empire but not yet found a role. De Gaulle understood that giving up Algeria was useful partly because it allowed France to play a new role. No longer a colonial power, it had a freer hand in international diplomacy. France was the first western country to recognise Communist China in 1964; it made much of its relations with countries that were not clearly aligned with either the United States or the Soviet Union. De Gaulle's diplomatic flexibility was enhanced by his indifference to the degree of internal repression exercised by, say, Nicolae Ceaușescu in Romania. He sought to create good relations with the Arab countries and spoke of Israel after the 1967 war in terms that some saw as anti-semitic. De Gaulle himself probably regarded his remarks about the Jews being 'sure of themselves and dominating' as a compliment. In private he was contemptuous of Islam, though he admired the Arabs of the desert 'because they learn to enjoy their thirst'.[12]

During his last years as prime minister, Churchill had been obsessed with the need to establish 'intimate' relations with other leaders in the belief that such relations would then yield real changes in policy. De Gaulle's diplomacy was one of icy formality and it often seemed that official encounters were a kind of political theatre that served as an end in themselves rather than being the means to achieve a particular concession. This was apparent when a conference brought together the leaders of France, Britain, the United States and the Soviet Union in Paris in 1960. The Soviet Union had just shot down an American spy plane and captured its pilot. Khrushchev brandished this to humiliate Eisenhower and it was quickly apparent that there would be no serious negotiations. The British prime minister, Harold Macmillan, was distraught. De Gaulle took it better. For him what mattered was the fact of the meeting rather than its results – world leaders had come to Paris and recognized France as being, at least in formal terms, an equal.

Much of de Gaulle's foreign policy had a ritualistic quality. France's first atomic bomb was exploded in 1960 – making it the fourth nuclear power in the world (after the US, the USSR and Britain). But France's nuclear weapons were small (some commentators talked of the 'bombinette') and it was not certain that a single one of the Mirage jets charged with delivering them would have got through Soviet air defences. The French atomic bomb mattered as a symbol – that France was one of the great powers and its policy was independent of that of other western countries – rather than because there was much chance that it could achieve anything.

De Gaulle's attitude to America owed much to symbolism. Even though he bridled at American power and removed France from NATO's joint command structures in 1966 (see chapter 11), France was always part of the western alliance. De Gaulle's generals privately conceded that nuclear armaments did not really give France strategic independence. Its weapons were 'trip wires' that might start a nuclear war into which America would then be drawn on the French side. De Gaulle talked of his policy as reflecting the interests of an eternal France but his affectation of detachment from the great power blocs was possible only in the unusual circumstances of the 1960s. In the late 1940s, the Soviet threat had been too immediate to permit such an affectation – de Gaulle had then been a strong proponent of the western alliance. Equally, once the threat of the Soviet Union disappeared altogether, then the United States might have been in a position to take France at its word and abandon it to diplomatic isolation. De Gaulle's successors rejoined NATO command structures in 2009.

De Gaulle's spectacular gestures – such as his speech of 1966 in Phnom Penh, when he criticised American policy in Indochina – were often made in what the French demographer Alfred Sauvy had labelled the 'third world', but de Gaulle was a European. He read Conrad and Goethe as well as the great French authors. For him, culture meant European culture. He allowed the Louvre to release the *Mona Lisa* for a diplomatic visit to the United States but would have been lost for an answer if Jacqueline Kennedy, who helped broker this arrangement, had asked him what great American artistic object he would like in return. De Gaulle spoke of a Europe that would extend 'from the Atlantic to the Urals'. The notion implied a continent independent of America. But it seems to have aroused more concern in Moscow than Washington – since it implied that the Soviet Union itself would be divided. As was often the case, race played a part in de Gaulle's thinking. He had said at a press conference of 10 November 1959 that the Russians were a 'white' and 'European' people. He thought that Russia's Asian empire might cause it the same problems that Algeria had caused for the French.[13]

Europe was also important to de Gaulle for more mundane reasons. For all his insistence on the sovereignty of states, he knew that the Common Market, established in 1957, served French economic interests. He also understood that a united Europe might be an important means of balancing the might of the United States and the Soviet Union and that France might be the dominant power in western Europe.

Relations with two countries in particular mattered especially to de Gaulle. One was Germany. He had regarded Germany as France's most significant enemy until 1945 and, in some ways, as its most significant partner after this date. In his memoirs, first published in 1954, de Gaulle cited an unofficial message he received from Heinrich Himmler 'on the edge of the tomb' in May 1945. Himmler said that France risked being crushed by the Soviet Union or becoming an Anglo-Saxon satellite and that 'the only path that leads your people to greatness and independence is that of entente with defeated Germany'. De Gaulle acknowledged there was 'some truth' in this.[14] He had a high regard for what he saw as German virtues and contrasted these favourably with the characters of the British and the French in late 1965: 'Only the Germans have redis-covered a certain form of ambition. They want to get back their frontiers, their dignity and their unity.'[15] De Gaulle had contem-plated reconciliation with Germany almost as soon as the Second World War was over but, at first, had feared German rearmament or reunification. This fear dissipated partly because it became clear the Soviet Union would not relax its hold on East Germany for many years and, equally, that NATO forces would stay in West Germany. De Gaulle called for reunification precisely because he believed that it would not happen in the near future.

Konrad Adenauer (German chancellor from 1949 to 1963) had qualities that appealed to de Gaulle. The one-time mayor of Cologne was emphatically not a Prussian, he was a Catholic and he had treated the British occupying authorities of his city with such impu-dence that they had almost locked him up. Adenauer also had the advantage of being an old man with the air of a country solicitor – de Gaulle could be sure of overshadowing him, perhaps especially in Germany, where the general was well received during his visits. In the 1960s, no one but Charles de Gaulle could have got away with a speech in Germany, in German, lauding German military traditions. Adenauer was the only foreign leader to be received at de Gaulle's country house at Colombey-les-Deux-Églises – though at the same time de Gaulle was discreetly conducting more significant negotia-tions with the British and Americans.

Relations with Britain sometimes appeared to move in the oppo-site direction. During the war, de Gaulle had talked of France and Britain as being like warriors in the ancient world, chained together so that neither could abandon the other. It was not a metaphor that suggested much affection – though when he spoke with Churchill in November 1944, de Gaulle claimed to have hoped that the two coun-tries might cooperate to build a new kind of Europe.[16] In the 1940s, de Gaulle had also referred to the need for some kind of European unity and this partly accounted for his disappointment when he thought that Churchill had sided with the United States. By the 1960s, things had changed. Harold Macmillan's government applied to join the Common Market – or European Economic Community (EEC) – in 1963 and de Gaulle vetoed the application. He justified this in sweeping geopolitical terms:

> England is insular. She is maritime. She is linked by her trade, her markets, her supplies to countries that vary greatly and are often far away. She is essentially industrial and commercial and to a very small extent agricultural. In all her work, she has very marked and original habits and traditions.

There was a mundane reason for de Gaulle's position: he did not want the agricultural policy of the Common Market, from which France derived great benefit, to be disturbed. And he was generally suspicious of British associations with the United States and the Commonwealth. The veto offended not just the British but also other European countries. French diplomats were mystified. De Gaulle himself knew that the veto was a gesture rather than a definitive statement of policy and that his successors were certain to reverse his decision – one Gaullist assured the British: 'The General knew very well that Britain would sooner or later join the EEC.'[17]

British officials devoted much energy to studying de Gaulle's political strength, psychological stability and physical health and the impact that all these things might have on a future British application to join the Common Market. Philip de Zulueta, the prime minister's private secretary, wrote to Macmillan immediately after the generals' putsch of 1961: 'It will be very important to press on if we can with European unity before there is civil war in France … at least French political weakness might enable you to carry the country forward on the basis of Britain saving Europe by joining it. It is rather the argument which Sir Winston used in 1940.'[18] Pierson

Dixon, British ambassador in Paris from 1960 to 1964, recognised that de Gaulle was intelligent but 'almost unbelievably egocentric'. He thought that the general should be taken seriously in spite of the temptation to see him as 'a comic figure, an Emperor unaware that he is parading without clothes'.[19]

R. A. Butler, the British foreign secretary, circulated a report on de Gaulle with a note of his own:

> What it boils down to is that in dealing with President de Gaulle we have to weather a storm which should gradually subside after he disappears. We must go on treating him as a tricky kind of ally, but we can no longer think in terms of an Entente Cordiale.[20]

Harold Wilson, Labour prime minister of Britain from 1964 to 1970, was cooler in his enthusiasm for Europe than Macmillan and, perhaps for this reason, more patient as he negotiated for British entry. He wrote in 1966 that de Gaulle seemed to have absolute power but that he was not 'on the crest of a wave' as he had been in 1962: 'I am ... sure his subordinates are now thinking very deeply about the future of France without de Gaulle and that a great many of them realize how necessary to France in that period partnership with Britain must be.'[21]

Perhaps Wilson was also, like de Gaulle, privately amused by the discomfiture of Harold Macmillan, the British establishment and, especially, the Foreign Office. In 1967, Wilson asked diplomats to investigate whether it was true that de Gaulle had said, with regard to the negotiations over the Common Market, 'les Anglais je les aurai nus' (I will have the English naked). They concluded:

> There can be little doubt that de Gaulle did say something to this effect, and indeed may have used precisely these words; that he intended the remarks to be reported and circulated and also that he would not allow any authentic version of them to appear, so that he could deny that he ever said the words attributed to him, if he chose.[22]

There was a personal element in de Gaulle's view of British accession. Macmillan assumed that de Gaulle would be grateful for the help Macmillan had given him in Algeria in 1943. In fact, de Gaulle found it harder to be gracious to those who had done him favours than to those who had opposed him. Sometimes he treated Macmillan with a condescending indifference. He told the French ambassador in London that Macmillan was an old man (he was four years younger than de Gaulle) and that he had lost a son in the war (he had not, though his predecessor, Anthony Eden, had).[23] There were also ways in which de Gaulle's veto of British membership of the Common Market served more cold-blooded purposes. It made it clear to other Europeans that France was the dominant power in western Europe and made it clear to the French ruling class that de Gaulle could exercise personal control of French policy whenever he chose.

Reading the indignant reports from the British embassy in Paris brings home another point. Perhaps for the first time in his life, de Gaulle was enjoying himself: 'his face creasing with the malicious smile reserved for situations of particular discomfiture for an opponent or rival'.[24] When he told his ministers about Macmillan's reactions to the thwarting of his European policy, he cited the Edith Piaf lyrics 'Ne pleurez pas Milord' — a joke that did, one has to admit, puncture Macmillan's carefully contrived air of patrician self-confidence. He often had the uncomfortable suspicion that he was being laughed at. In 1959, Macmillan, Adenauer and Eisenhower met de Gaulle in Paris. De Gaulle, as Macmillan wrote in his diary, conducted business 'with great skill and grace, with periods of both high comedy and farce'. When it came to the location for the forthcoming summit between Western powers and the Soviet Union, everyone assumed that it would take place in Geneva. De Gaulle, who had decided that it would take place in Paris, intervened: 'Ce n'est pas très gai. Le lac. L'esprit de Monsieur Calvin. Non. Ce n'est pas très gai.'[25]

Oddly, de Gaulle was a shy man, so the formality that surrounded a French head of state suited him. His relations with people outside his immediate family were regulated by protocol now. Most of his conversations were brief and formulaic. The flashes of humour with which he occasionally enlivened his own role were all the more impressive because they contrasted with his official position. In May 1958, the American ambassador to Paris and the journalist Charles Sulzberger (who believed he had a special rapport with de Gaulle) came to see the general to express their concern about his foreign policy. Exasperated by their questions, de Gaulle said that 'he would of course take France out of NATO and do what he could to wreck the Common Market'. An officer at the Élysée had to explain to them that this was just an example of 'humeur noire.'[26]

As head of the Free French, de Gaulle had led a simple life,[27] and his private tastes remained modest. However, the Élysée Palace was a place to display the greatness of the French state. Furniture, wine and food were all selected with this in mind – Madame de Gaulle was outraged when the presidential chef was poached by the Rothschild family.[28] Ministers and ambassadors were summoned to Rambouillet for shooting parties in which twenty men killed 600 pheasants at a time. De Gaulle would stand behind a favoured guest and distract him with advice. He did not himself shoot but he treated game birds with the same brutal realpolitik as people. When a senator remarked that the dead pheasants laid out for inspection at the end of the day put him in mind of fallen soldiers, de Gaulle said: 'they served their purpose.'[29] Realpolitik even extended to fish. During an official visit to the Soviet Union, a sturgeon was caught and laid flapping at de Gaulle's feet. 'Il y a toujours des victimes,' he said.[30]

In the past, de Gaulle had often thrown tantrums when thwarted – tantrums that were undignified even when calculated as a means to get his own way. Now he could afford the luxury of calm and watch in amusement as his interlocutors were discomfited. Charles Bohlen, who became American ambassador to Paris in 1962, recalled that there was an 'almost liturgical' quality to the formality with which he was introduced into the general's presence.[31] Jean Chauvel, the French ambassador to London, noted that de Gaulle could be affable when standing up but that there was a frightening quality to him when he received visitors at his desk – like a 'morose examiner' watching the candidates dry up in front of him.[32] Encounters usually began with the chillingly unhelpful words: 'Je vous écoute.'

De Gaulle's personal contentment sprang largely from the state of France. The economy, which had grown slowly in the seventy years until 1945, grew rapidly from the late 1940s onwards. The economist Jean Fourastié talked of the three decades after the Second World War as the 'trente glorieuses'. Growth accelerated in the 1960s. This was partly because the end of the Algerian War reduced military spending and increased the labour supply as fewer young men were conscripted and as migrants, first European and then Muslim, came from Algeria. France began to feel different in the 1960s. An economy that had revolved around heavy industry and production in the previous decade became one associated with consumer goods. Roland Barthes celebrated the luxurious and beautiful Citroën DS (the model of car de Gaulle's driver had manoeuvred through a hail of bullets at Petit Clamart) as the symbol of a new civilisation. De Gaulle did not always approve of comfort but he liked France to be seen as a symbol of success and modernity.

The new image of France had a particular impact in Britain. Books about British economic decline and social sclerosis began to appear in the early 1960s just as de Gaulle's new France was becoming visible. In 1963, John Mander published *Great Britain or Little England?*[33] in which he reflected 'De Gaulle expects Britain to continue her slow, peevish, but untragic decline in the decade ahead.' The British middle classes often took their holidays in France and they became ever more obsessed, until the 1980s, with France's apparent economic superiority.

Individual British politicians felt the change too. Anthony Eden had been an important patron of de Gaulle – often defending him against Churchill. But Eden's brief tenure as prime minister had not been a success. For the whole period when de Gaulle was president, Eden, seven years his junior, was a retired politician in poor health and with a damaged reputation. De Gaulle received him on his visits to Paris but seems to have enjoyed the company of his young and vivacious second wife more than that of Eden himself – one imagines de Gaulle's amusement on being told that Eden was in Paris because his wife was judging an international flower show there.[34]

There was a painful contrast between de Gaulle and Churchill, and some felt that this reflected a wider contrast between Britain and France. De Gaulle once said 'old age is a shipwreck'. He was talking about Pétain but might just as well have been referring to Churchill – who was the same age in 1958 as Pétain had been in 1940. Churchill aged badly. Anyone could see that he was deaf and lame. Those around him knew that he was also incontinent and forgetful. Most of all, his admirers were troubled by the fact that Churchill had lost his extraordinary zest for life. A year after Churchill's death, his personal physician, Lord Moran, published a book in which he described his former patient's medical condition:

> After his retirement in April 1955, Winston made little effort to hide his distaste for what was left to him of life, and the historian might conclude that this reveals a certain weakness of moral fibre. Such strictures will, however, carry little weight unless due allowance is made for the way in which his will was sapped by old age and disease. It is therefore only proper and fair to him that the reader should be given the details of his mounting decrepitude.[35]

The Churchill family were outraged by the breach of medical confidentiality, but Moran had revealed little that would have been news to any member of parliament or political journalist.

Churchill's visit to Paris in 1958 left de Gaulle's entourage with a 'tragic impression'. Churchill inspected the guard of honour so slowly that those watching were unsure whether he would be capable of making the next step. There were long gaps between 'every word of a fantasy French'.[36]

De Gaulle and Churchill met when the former came to London on a state visit in April 1960. This visit illustrated how seriously de Gaulle took the fact that he was a head of state. The president, usually contemptuous of decorations, hoped to be made a Knight of the Garter, an honour accorded to foreigners only if they were of royal blood.[37] He had to make do with the Victorian Chain. He visited Windsor Castle, where he was shown the portraits in the Waterloo Chamber and commented on the fact that it had taken so many 'messieurs' to defeat Napoleon.[38] He refused Harold Macmillan's invitation to Chequers – rubbing in the fact that the prime minister was merely a head of government.[39] He addressed the members of both houses of parliament assembled in Westminster Hall. He praised the 'immortal glory' of Winston Churchill, alluded to small disagreements in June 1944 and expressed his admiration for the stability of the English political system. The British hoped that London would bring back happy memories of wartime comradeship, but when de Gaulle was asked who he might like to meet from among those with whom he had once worked, he replied vaguely that he had sent a list but could not remember who was on it.[40] On one point, de Gaulle was emphatic; he did not wish to see General Spears.

De Gaulle was reluctant to see Churchill but Chauvel, the French ambassador in London, persuaded him on the grounds that the former prime minister was a kind of monument 'like the Arc de Triomphe.' Chauvel remembered a parrot – probably Churchill's budgerigar – which sought to drink champagne from his glass.[41] Most writers assume this was the last encounter between the two men, but, six months later, Churchill was on holiday in Monte Carlo when he heard that de Gaulle was also in the South of France. They met in the prefecture at Nice – once the palace of the kings of Sardinia. Perhaps because neither man had to worry about appearances, the occasion seems to have been more relaxed and dignified than their meeting in London. De Gaulle asked Churchill whether he would have attended the United Nations General Assembly, as Harold Macmillan had just done despite the fact the president had specially urged him not to.[42] Obviously de Gaulle expected Churchill to condemn this concession to world opinion but Churchill considered it right that Khrushchev (who had addressed the assembly) and the 'anti-white' forces should not have things their own way. He said he approved of Macmillan's action. Apparently, de Gaulle was 'charming and affectionate'.[43]

Churchill's position in British public life after his retirement as prime minister was peculiar. He remained a member of the House of Commons until late 1964. Sitting on parliamentary benches – such a humiliation for de Gaulle – was according to Churchill, the greatest honour an Englishman could enjoy. Churchill's periodic arrivals in parliament were public ceremonies – though not a very dignified one. He was wheeled into the building and plugged into his hearing aid, after which he frequently fell asleep.

Anthony Montague Browne – the youngest of Churchill's private secretaries – was seconded to serve him in retirement, like a slave being buried with a pharaoh. Though Montague Browne would later be less publicly associated with the memory of Churchill than John Colville, he was closer to the old man in the last years of his life. He was the only person apart from members of the family, the doctor and nurses to be present when Churchill died and he walked behind the gun carriage at Churchill's funeral along with the adult men from the Churchill family. Churchill was allowed to see some government papers in retirement.[44] Montague Browne recalled:

WSC had one real power left. His approbation of his successor's policies was largely taken for granted, but if he had delivered a speech of severe criticism, even of disavowal, it would have been a thunderbolt. Like the use of the nuclear weapon, so extreme a step could not credibly have been taken, but WSC was well aware of its existence and it gave him some illusory comfort.[45]

Churchill's views on Egypt were particularly important to the government. While still prime minister, he had raged against the policy of the foreign secretary, Eden, of withdrawing troops from the Suez Canal – telling those around him that this was appeasement (a term calculated to offend Eden).[46] Some officials got the impression that Churchill relished the prospect of British troops being attacked because it would confound Eden's policy.[47] After his resignation, Churchill claimed he accepted withdrawal from Suez (partly because he thought that the hydrogen bomb had rendered all conventional military thinking obsolete) but not everyone believed him. Churchill helped create the political climate that pushed Eden, in alliance with France, into invading Egypt in 1956. In public, Churchill supported Eden during the Suez expedition; privately he suggested that he would have managed the operation better.

In the early 1960s, as Macmillan tried to take Britain into the Common Market, the views attributed to Churchill acquired significance in some circles. In August 1962, Field Marshal Montgomery visited him in hospital and claimed to have found him 'sitting up in bed, smoking a cigar, shouting for more brandy and protesting against Britain's proposed entry into the Common Market.' Montague Browne told his former colleagues in the Foreign Office that Churchill had no decided views on the Common Market but was receiving letters from admirers who assumed he shared their own opinions. He enclosed one example: 'Is Mr Macmillan out of his mind and has he no feelings for our country, sovereign rights and world prestige?' A letter was contrived in which Churchill said that he had no objection to Macmillan exploring terms on which Britain might enter the Common Market.[48]

Public figures were still mainly respectful of Churchill, but they did not necessarily express public opinion. Britain was an irreverent country in the early 1960s and irreverence was particularly marked with regard to war and to Britain's wartime leader. This was the time when the largest proportion of the British population had military experience. Many veterans of the two world wars were still alive;

the last peacetime National Service men were called up in December 1960 and sometimes literally saw the flags going down on the British empire. The notion that soldiers would be disrespectful to Churchill would have shocked some members of the officer class, but it would not have surprised anyone who had paid attention to the 1945 election result or anyone who had listened to what men said in barracks in the 1950s. Martin Gilbert, later Churchill's official biographer, recorded the comments of his own National Service comrades during basic training in 1955. One, a coach painter, decribed Churchill as 'the greatest man of the century' but added: 'I have not studied his career.' A former joiner said: 'I detest him. The ordinary man won the war.' A lumberjack called Churchill a 'warmonger who supplied the Germans with arms and equipment before 1939'.[49]

Some cruel jesters commented on this latter-day King Lear. When he was editor of *Punch*, Malcolm Muggeridge had published a cartoon that was seen as shockingly disrespectful while Churchill was still Prime Minister. A younger group of parodists (mainly post-war national servicemen) gathered around *Private Eye*, which was founded in 1961.Mockery of Churchill became a defining feature of the magazine. The *Eye* was served with the first of its many libel writs from Randolph Churchill who took exception to remarks it printed about his role in writing the biography of his father. Given that it was later sued by Robert Maxwell and Jonathan Aitken, this does not put him in distinguished company.Winston Churchill had himself been a litigious man – he had launched his first libel action as a young officer when someone implied that he engaged in 'Oscar Wilde activities' while a cadet at Sandhurst. Randolph breezily referred to Carter Ruck, lawyers specialising in actions for defamation, as 'the old firm'.[50]

Churchill took a long time to die. It had seemed possible that his stroke of 1953 would kill him, and many did not expect him to survive for long after he resigned as prime minister. In 1962, he fell and fractured his hip in Monte Carlo. He was quickly flown home to make sure that he would die in England, but he was still alive the next year for his ninetieth birthday. This was awkward for journalists. The foreign editor of the *Sunday Times* approached Eden to write a birthday tribute: 'Naturally, we have a mass of obituary material ready, but we cannot possibly unleash this. Yet the occasion will obviously call for something special, and I was wondering whether you felt you could help us.'[51]

Churchill finally died on 24 January 1965, the anniversary of his father's death. Montague Browne registered the death at Kensington Town Hall. The registrar asked him what he should record as Churchill's profession: '"Retired" didn't seem right. So I said "Statesman"'.[52] There was a state funeral. Queen Elizabeth broke with tradition to attend. Leaders from around the world came to London. There were eight pall bearers – of whom three (Attlee, Eden and Macmillan) were former prime minister and five (Alexander, Slim, Mountbatten, Ismay and Portal) had been important commanders in the war.* The conspicuous absence was the one person whose presence Churchill would most have valued – the president of the United States. Lyndon Johnson had been discouraged by his doctors from travelling. Churchill was buried in the churchyard near his birthplace at Blenheim Palace.

De Gaulle attended Churchill's funeral. He enjoyed such occasions and probably respected Churchill's memory enough to feel relieved that the old man was finally dead. De Gaulle commented on 'une famille dont le doyen vient de disparaître, et qui se serre autour de ses souvenirs', which the British translated 'as if a family were mourning its oldest and most honoured member'. No onehad any illusions about de Gaulle's sentimentality, though. Civil servants warned Harold Wilson: 'If de Gaulle raises the subject, the Prime

*Pall bearer in this context was a ceremonial function. The weight of the lead-lined coffin was taken by guardsmen.

Minister could emphasize his confidence in the future of the British economy. It would be best not to refer to French support for the pound, which was grudging and given on more stringent conditions than that of our main European creditors.'[53] Gladwyn Jebb (who had retired as ambassador to Paris) was delegated to attend to de Gaulle. After the funeral, de Gaulle teased Jebb, a passionate supporter of British entry into the Common Market:

> It seemed to him that the ceremony had been symbolic of the perennial greatness of *l'Angleterre*. Here was a national sentiment which should never be extinguished: something that was part of history and would in all probability, he thought, endure. I was a European, he knew that; but whatever solution I recommended he did hope that I would not support anything which tended to diminish or blur the Englishness of England, its integrity, its identity, so to speak. He naturally hoped that France would preserve her national identity also.[54]

Even some sceptical observers were moved by Churchill's funeral. The historian A.J.P. Taylor corrected the proofs of his *English History, 1914–1945* immediately after it. Next to the index entry for Churchill, he wrote: 'The Saviour of his Country'. But many recognised that there were contradictions and absurdities in public attitudes to the funeral. *New Society* (edited by the Conservative Timothy Raison) carried a piece by Ray Gosling that was part mocking, part hostile and part admiring. It began:

> When I was small I did believe John Bull was really Churchill. He has always been as dead as Pickwick or King Henry V. Yet I've often thought – what a day it's going to be when that man dies. What a funeral. *Our flags on Saturday won't be at half mast. No, sir. They'll be right out at the top of the pole. We'll have clubs open all night and dancing in the streets if we could, Because, I'll tell you, here [in the Nottinghamshire coal field] we are glad he's gone.*[55]

Richard Crossman was a minister in Harold Wilson's Labour government in 1965. He had recently been forced by the threat of libel action to withdraw allegations he had made in a newspaper about Churchill's role in a bombing raid. Crossman's diary for 25 January read:

> In the afternoon Parliament met for tributes to Sir Winston. By then I felt we had already had enough tributes, but here they came, Wilson, Douglas-Home, Jo Grimond. I sat on the front bench squeezed between Barbara Castle and Tony Crosland and fell into a quiet slumber while the lugubrious process went on.

He went three times to see Churchill's lying-in-state (members of parliament could jump the queue), taking with him first the doorman at his block of flats, then the economist Tommy Balogh and finally 'Mr Large who cuts my hair'. He did not want to attend the funeral but he did. After it, he wrote: 'oh, what a faded, declining establishment surrounded me. Aged marshals, grey, dreary ladies, decadent Marlboroughs and Churchills. It was a dying congregation ... It felt like the end of an epoch, possibly even the end of a nation.'[56]

Later that year de Gaulle had a revealing conversation with a journalist. Though he relished France's economic success, and particularly its superiority over Britain, he did not see prosperity as an end in itself. Rather it was a means to great-power status and he doubted whether either the French or the British had the resources, or above all the will, to sustain such status. This implied an awareness that his own definition of 'grandeur' was often a matter of image rather than reality. He also felt a certain pitying sympathy for Churchill: 'Even poor Churchill, coming back thirty years younger, would be able to do nothing with his Englishmen.'[57]

De Gaulle alone, 1965–70

'An edifice that depends for its solidity on
one man is of necessity fragile.'
Charles de Gaulle[1]

Solitude was in de Gaulle's nature; it was also a quality he considered necessary for a leader. From January 1959, his solitude was enshrined in the French constitution. He was now head of state – a person without equal in the French political system. In the Third and Fourth republics, the title 'président' had often been used to refer not just to the head of state but also to the numerous people who had held the office of prime minister (président du conseil) or even those who had presided over parliamentary commissions. After 1959, everyone understood that this title could refer only to one man. De Gaulle cultivated an air of inscrutability. The secretary general of the United Nations reported that he had been struck by de Gaulle's 'intellectual loneliness': 'Talking to him was at times rather like addressing the Buddha.'[2]

De Gaulle's special status was ever more marked as time went on. Constitutional change – especially the institution of direct election to the presidency – meant that the head of state was more elevated. As de Gaulle grew older, the political class got younger, a change that was especially pronounced in the case of the Gaullists: less than half of Gaullist deputies elected in 1962 were over fifty – the proportion for other parties was almost six in ten.[3] Fewer of those around de Gaulle had spent the war in London – not that he had been particularly intimate even with those old acquaintances.

The efficiency of the French administrative machine contributed to de Gaulle's solitude. Only on rare occasions, as when Alain Peyrefitte's daughter was gravely injured in a car accident, was de Gaulle required to acknowledge that his ministers and civil servants were human beings. He demanded loyalty of his associates but never gave it. Claude Guy, an aide who sacrificed much of his life to the general's service before being dismissed for a minor offence, recognised that men such as himself were 'interchangeable parts'. In the early 1960s, de Gaulle's last line of defence against assassins had been four 'gorillas' – Paul Comiti, Henri Djouder, Raymond Sasia and Roger Tessier – who would have thrown themselves on a grenade for him. But, as the threat of assassination receded, de Gaulle did not care to be surrounded by these rough, hard-drinking men. In 1965, he tried to dispense with their services.[4]

De Gaulle did not have many equals outside France. Churchill had ceased to be the man of 1940 before de Gaulle returned to power in 1958; Stalin and Roosevelt were dead. De Gaulle had had stormy relations with these men when they were in power, but he now relished his status as the last Gulliver in a time of Lilliputians. Harold Wilson, British prime minister from 1964 to 1970, was a small man with a plebeian manner, who had spent most of the war working as a civil servant in the Ministry of Fuel and Power. British Conservatives regarded him as the ultimate Lilliputian, especially when he sought to associate himself with Churchill's memory. De Gaulle appears to have treated Wilson no better or worse than any other British politician. Wilson wrote of 'this lonely old man obsessed by a sense of real impotence (a word he used twice with me)'.[5]

De Gaulle discerned an equal in someone whom he never met: Mao Tse Tung. By the 1960s, Mao was the only other major world leader who had risen to prominence during the Second World War. He too was the architect of a national myth and he too, from the mid 1960s, sought to present himself as subordinate to neither the United

States nor the Soviet Union. The murderous quality of Mao's regime was not as apparent in the 1960s as it has since become (not that de Gaulle ever gave much thought to the internal repression in countries he considered useful allies) and the fact that China was a closed society gave it an allure to which de Gaulle's minister of culture, André Malraux, was susceptible. A British diplomat reported de Gaulle's own views: 'The Chinese were a great people. He did not mean only geographically great, but a people who knew themselves to be great and considered themselves to be as great as any other nation on earth.'[6] At least as far as French people were concerned, de Gaulle and Mao had something in common. Some of those who espoused Maoism in Paris in the late 1960s would become enthusiastic admirers of de Gaulle a few years later. Henry Kissinger was later to say that Mao 'embodied more will than anyone he had ever met, except de Gaulle'.[7] In the last year of his life, de Gaulle was planning a visit to China.

American presidents perplexed de Gaulle. They seemed to lack every quality that he regarded as essential to a head of state, and they spent much of their time in the political activity he most disdained – running for election. De Gaulle believed in the nation state. He was troubled by states that were divided into nations – even the multiple national rugby teams in the British Isles struck him as odd. But America presented the even stranger spectacle of a nation that was divided into states which exercised considerable autonomy. He knew Eisenhower from the Second World War and treated him with ostensible respect – though Eisenhower's folksy style sat oddly with de Gaulle's notion of how a president ought to behave. At his last meeting with Churchill, in October 1960, de Gaulle discussed the American presidential election: he 'stated firmly that he supported Nixon ... but feared Kennedy was in the lead'.[8] He came to regard Kennedy with more favour – partly because of the cool nervehe displayed during the Cuban missile crisis and partly because of Kennedy's eloquence and sense of himself as an international statesman. It is hard to know how much of this admiration would have survived if Kennedy had lived to fight for a second term of office and then faced the problems of the Vietnam War.

Kennedy's assassination in November 1963 was an important moment for de Gaulle. This was partly because it removed the only leader of a democratic country who exercised as much fascination over other leaders as de Gaulle himself. It was also because Kennedy's funeral (the first funeral of a political leader to occasion a gathering of world leaders) was the kind of ceremony de Gaulle enjoyed. Lyndon Johnson, Kennedy's vice president and successor, had seen a report that de Gaulle had said that western Europe could not rely on US support in the event of a Soviet invasion and that 'America had been late for previous wars'.[9] In spite of this, Johnson agreed to meet de Gaulle and gave due recognition to the fact that he was a head of state. The two most impressive figures at the funeral were de Gaulle (tall and wearing no medals) and Haile Selassie (short and barely able to move under the weight of his).

Lyndon Johnson – a vulgar Texan with little formal education* – embodied everything de Gaulle disliked. He regarded Johnson as being 'a Radical politician of the Third Republic or Fourth Republic'[10] – preoccupied with deals in the legislature, clientelism and parochial considerations. De Gaulle did not begin to understand the most impressive of Johnson's achievements – pushing through legislation on civil rights. De Gaulle, like Churchill, expressed his racism in especially vehement terms with regard to the United States. When Jacques Foccart, his adviser on African affairs, said that racial problems in America were insoluble, de Gaulle replied:

You are right. And what's more [this is his real thought] one realizes that they are nothing. Because ... It is the characteristic of this race, which produces some elements who create an illusion,

*De Gaulle was particularly shocked when Johnson described Napoleon as an Italian – a remark that might actually suggest a good knowledge of history and a shrewd understanding of how to annoy de Gaulle.

that it is incapable of founding a great nation. The black American profits from the fact that the United States is a superior power; at least, he profits from it ... in a certain way; he sustains an illusion. But if black people were left to themselves in one of the states of the United States of America, they would achieve nothing, and very soon it would be chaos ... The last chance is to send them back to Africa.[11]

De Gaulle, in August 1967, believed that Johnson, discredited by Vietnam and civil rights, would be defeated in the next election 'by some general or other, who will promise to sort everything out'.[12] He was relieved when Johnson did not run for another term and was replaced by Nixon – a man who admired de Gaulle and whose most important adviser, Henry Kissinger, had written sympathetically about de Gaulle's world view.

De Gaulle's ministers came to appreciate Johnson more than their master did. Couve de Murville, the foreign minister, returned from Washington with an improved opinion of the American president. He was, said Couve, 'a man of authority ... suspicious and reserved'.[13] There must have been a few around the Cabinet table who recognized that this could equally well have been a description of de Gaulle. As for Johnson, he seems to have had the measure of de Gaulle. He regarded him as tiresome but did not waste time on arguing with him. He also knew that on the great issues de Gaulle was often right. Whilst the American government protested when de Gaulle recognised Communist China in 1964, privately Johnson admitted that the United States would have been wise to have recognised China several years previously.[14]

De Gaulle's solitude presented a problem for France. If he was a man without equal, then who would succeed him? Part of de Gaulle's strength in the early period of his presidency sprang from the fact that the French saw him as having no successor. Asked in an opinion poll who might be appointed president in place of de Gaulle, 5 per cent chose Guy Mollet, 4 per cent chose Pinay and 2 per cent chose Mendès France. No other candidate attracted more than 1 per cent of those surveyed; 58% of respondents said they did not know and 15 per cent said 'no one'.[15] The absence of successor meant that the threat of resignation was an effective weapon for de Gaulle. He claimed in 1962 that he wanted to institute direct elections for the presidency in order to make it easier for his successor but, in fact, only 19 per cent of voters supported this measure because they cared about it in itself; 62 per cent voted in favour because de Gaulle had threatened to resign if he was defeated in the referendum and they wanted him to stay as president.[16]

But de Gaulle understood that he was mortal. He knew he would die in the near future and did not want to retain office at an age when he would be unable to bear it with sufficient dignity or in circumstances where he could not be sure of getting his way on the matters about which he cared most. In an ideal world, the continuity of the French state would have been guaranteed by moving away from conventional politics entirely. De Gaulle had been brought up a monarchist. He admired the British royal family and believed they admired him – a rare example of self-delusion on his part.[17] He had met the pretender to the French throne in 1954 and subsequently corresponded with him.[18] The two men were drawn closer when the pretender's eldest son was killed fighting in Algeria. However, de Gaulle did not believe he lived in an ideal world and, though he talked about monarchical restoration, he took no steps to put it in train.

In the immediate future, de Gaulle's successor was going to be de Gaulle. This meant that he would run for the presidency at the end of his seven-year term in 1965. De Gaulle did not stoop to fight a conventional campaign. He announced his candidacy late. When he finally recorded a broadcast stating his intention to run, the recording technicians were locked in the Élysée for hours to make sure the news did not leak and spoil the dramatic effect.[19] De Gaulle did not want to hold meetings or appear on television asking for votes – in any case the state-run television service did not require encouragement to give de Gaulle favourable coverage so that news broadcasts might sometimes just as well have been Gaullist electoral propaganda.

Presidential elections in the Fifth Republic are fought in two rounds. The first involves multiple candidates; the second involves only the two who get most votes in the first round. If one candidate gets more than half the vote, there is no second round. Various people – including Antoine Pinay, the conservative who had been de Gaulle's minister of finance, and Gaston Defferre, the socialist mayor of Marseilles – suggested that they might run for the presidency. *L'Express* sought a 'Monsieur X' who might be an alternative to de Gaulle;though Françoise Giroud was an important figure at the magazine, no one considered that there might be a Madame X. The search owed much to the book *The Making of the President* by Theodore White about Kennedy's election campaign. This illustrated a sense that France needed leadership from someone younger (the ideal candidate was said to be approaching fifty years old) and more modern than de Gaulle.

In the end, neither Pinay nor Defferre ran and no one who quite fitted the profile of Monsieur X emerged either. Apart from de Gaulle there were five candidates, of whom three were serious enough to attract real attention. Jean-Louis Tixier-Vignancour was a lawyer who had held office under Vichy and who defended members of the OAS in court after the Algerian War. He represented an extreme right that was bitterly hostile to de Gaulle. He obtained 5 per cent of votes in the first round and his support was largely drawn from those southern areas in which Europeans from Algeria had settled after 1962. Jean Lecanuet was a worthy 45-year-old Christian Democrat; de Gaulle's advisers persuaded him not to say that Lecanuet's supporters looked like choir boys who had drunk the communion wine.

The most significant of de Gaulle's opponents was François Mitterrand. He was forty-nine years old (the same age as de Gaulle in June 1940) but had already seen a fair bit of political action. He had escaped from a German prisoner-of-war camp and joined a resistance movement while also serving Vichy. He had been a minister several times in the Fourth Republic and exemplified much of what de Gaulle despised about that period: he had been a member of a small party and often served in ephemeral governments. He was a skilful politician – good at negotiating deals, good at maintaining networks of power in the Nièvre, which he had represented as a deputy and then senator, and good at looking after the material interests of his supporters. He had built up a clientèle among veterans and former prisoners of war.

Mitterrand and de Gaulle had been hostile to each other ever since the war, when Mitterrand had manoeuvred de Gaulle's nephew out of the leadership of a resistance network. But they had more in common than either cared to admit. They both came from Catholic, conservative backgrounds, they had both shown courage in war and they both liked to think of themselves as writers. Mitterrand's most famous book, *Le Coup d'État Permanent* (1964), was, in fact, an attack on de Gaulle, or at least on the constitution of the Fifth Republic. Mitterrand received a third of the vote and it was he who went into the second round of the presidential election.

De Gaulle felt affronted by the results of the first round of the presidential election. At first, he told his ministers that he might not fight in the second round at all. He was persuaded to change his mind partly by the political scientist François Goguel, who explained the probability of a Gaullist victory. De Gaulle now campaigned more actively, though he gave three television interviews, broadcast on successive nights but recorded in a single session. He played a game that would already have been familiar to his entourage – ostensibly hesitating over whether he would appear on television at all and, if he did, whether he would be interviewed more than once. The format was new to de Gaulle. He had frequently addressed large, stage-managed press conferences, but it had been a long time since he was interviewed face-to-face by a single person. The journalist chosen to conduct the interviews, Michel Droit, was a loyal

Gaullist. His description of the occasion was interesting. While the technicians were setting up the equipment, de Gaulle and he spoke freely. The general – Droit addressed him as 'mon général' rather than 'monsieur le président' – recalled 1940, Reynaud and above all Churchill. He explained that he was running again partly because he despised his opponent – though he recognised that Mitterrand had an honourable resistance record.

The interviews themselves, based on questions that had been agreed in advance, did not touch on the Second World War at all and also barelytouched on Algeria. Instead, they focused on de Gaulle's personal reading of post-war France. He denounced the 'régime des parties' of the Fourth Republic. He implied that almost every benign change since 1944 had taken place when he was in power. He laid a heavy emphasis on economic change and technological progress. At times he produced torrents of statistics obviously prepared by civil servants. When it was suggested that he might record a new version of a passage in which he had made a factual mistake he replied that this was unimportant.

De Gaulle denied that his 'certain idea of France' meant a certain disdain for the French, though he insisted that France was eternal and did not belong to the 'present generation'. He also made much of France's position in the world and suggested that prosperity was mainly important as a means to sustain this position. There was an an extraordinary moment in the third interview when de Gaulle was asked to define Left and Right. He replied that the former meant progress and the latter meant order. He illustrated this with reference to a housewife. She wanted, he said, a fridge, a washing machine, a vacuum cleaner and even a car if possible. This was progress. But she did not want her husband to carouse ('bambocher') all over the place, her sons to put their feet on the table or her daughter to stay out all night. This was order.

Viewers must have been mystified that a man whose life had revolved around heroic causes should be talking about the politics of domestic appliances. Leaders of the French Left – who defined themselves with reference to republicanism, anti-clericalism and class struggle – would not have described progress in terms of consumer goods. In fact, the interview revealed something important. Gaullism had become banal – or at least become something different from the movement born in the great conflicts of the recent past.

The election of 1965 illuminated something else that had been true for some time. The greater part of de Gaulle's electorate, like that of most conservative politicians in France, was female. There were obvious reasons for this. Religious practice among French women was higher than s among French men, and the Left/Right division in France still owed something to the clerical/anti-clerical split. Women were less likely to work than men – especially large enterprises and heavy industries, in which the communist-domi-nated trade unions were most powerful. Finally, there were more older women, because so many men who would have been old in the 1960s had been killed in the First World War – and the old were more conservative than the young.

Some commentators thought that de Gaulle's appeal to women rested on their irrational nature and consequent susceptibility to 'mystical' appeals. Nancy Mitford, who had been the lover of the Gaullist Gaston Palewski for many years, claimed that her faithful maid in Versailles dreamt of de Gaulle during moments of national crisis.[20] The evidence suggests, though, that Gaullist voters were motivated more by hard-headed calculations than by the emotional appeal of de Gaulle's personality. Often they saw him as an alterna-tive to something worse. They looked to him to contain communism in 1945 or the army during the last stages of the Algerian War. By 1965, however, France was no longer threatened by crisis. The Communist Party was no longer likely to stage a revolution because its masters in Moscow did not want it to. Its energies were largely devoted to local government (particularly in the working-class red belt around Paris) and to trade unions. France had teetered on the edge of civil war during the generals' putsch of April 1961, but rebellious soldiers were now in prison or in exile.

By 1965, de Gaulle was a knight with no more dragons to slay. Surveys showed that he had been most popular during the Algerian war – approval ratings peaked at 74 per cent in February 1960, just after Barricades Week. The French had less confidence in his ability to deal with social and economic problems: during a miners' strike of March 1963, only 42 per cent of those polled were 'satisfied' with de Gaulle.[21] One Gaullist leader wrote, quoting Raymond Aron, that modern society had lots of problems but no single big problem. The absence of a big problem was de Gaulle's biggest problem. He was happy to claim credit for the rapid economic growth of the 1960s but actually this had its roots in policies that dated back to before 1958 – particularly the economic planning that had been instituted at the behest of Jean Monnet. No one supposed that de Gaulle's disappearance from the scene would have much effect on the French economy.

De Gaulle won the second round of the presidential election. Tixier-Vignancour told his supporters to vote for Mitterrand (by which he meant anyone but de Gaulle) and Lecanuet asked his to rally to de Gaulle. De Gaulle got the majority of the vote. In institutional terms this was his political apotheosis. He had been chosen as head of state by an electoral mechanism that he himself had instituted and he governed with a constitution that his supporters had written. The legal foundations of de Gaulle's position were now more secure than in 1958 or 1944 – let alone 1940. But the change was not an entirely positive one from de Gaulle's point of view. On previous occasions, his legitimacy had been founded, one way or another, on his own personality and on a sense, felt by himself and at least some of those around him, of his historical destiny. Speaking of 1958, he had said that his return to power was 'dans la force des choses.' After 1965, he was an elected politician like any other. Power conferred by an election could be taken away by an election. In this respect, Mitterrand was the real winner from 1965 – the mere fact that he had been shown to be a legitimate challenger to de Gaulle meant that, he would be an obvious candidate for the presidency from now on.

De Gaulle's physical and political mortality were always associated. The assassination attempts of the early 1960s had put him at the centre of the political stage. But, by 1965, a more mundane mortality was in people's mind. Many who voted for the 75-year-old candidate must have known there was a good chance that he would not live to see out his seven-year mandate. De Gaulle knew it himself. Towards the end of interview he gave between the two rounds of the presidential election, he said: 'if I am elected on Sunday, I will not stay long but whatever happens I will have fulfilled my destiny'. His advisers persuaded him that this might seem an unappealing conclusion and the tape was doctored so that the sentence became simply 'whatever happens I will have fulfilled my destiny'.[22]

The smooth running of the institutions de Gaulle had established – or had been established by those who wanted to serve his purposes – raised the possibility that there might be Gaullism without de Gaulle. The RPF had been his party and had effectively ceased to exist when he decreed it should do so. The UNR was an autonomous body which could – and as it turned out, did – outlive de Gaulle. The state administration had been renewed in 1944 by an influx of resistance veterans – men who sometimes derived some of their authority and much of their political direction from a relation with de Gaulle, even if they were also experienced civil servants. By 1965, the École Nationale d'Administration, founded by de Gaulle twenty years earlier, was turning out graduates, 'énarques' as they were known, who were confident that they could step into any position in the civil service or business or eventually politics. É narques often had a curiously detached view of de Gaulle. The class that graduated in 1958 had voted to name itself 'le 18 juin' but almost a quarter of its members joined the anti-Gaullist Jean Moulin Club.[23] Valéry Giscard d'Estaing had been eighteen at the liberation. He joined = the Inspectorate of Finances and then went into politics. De Gaulle was impressed, perhaps intimidated, by Giscard's technical virtuosity. Giscard succeeded his own patron Antoine Pinay as de Gaulle's minister of finances in 1962. He founded a political party that allied with the UNR, but he was never quite a Gaullist and eventually, when he was able to do so without risk to himself, he turned against de Gaulle. In 1974, Giscard became the first énarque president.

France in the mid 1960s was peaceful and prosperous. It was often seen by other countries as a model of successful modernisation that exported everything from the cinema of the *nouvelle vague* to the historical approach of the Annales school. De Gaulle accepted social change. It was his government that legalised birth control in 1967 – it had been illegal since 1920. The president himself – whose wife had had no further children after she gave birth to Anne at the age of twenty-eight – supported the change because he thought that choices in this matter should be 'rational'. He was not, though, entirely comfortable with French society in the mid 1960s, and perhaps this was because the idea of comfort was alien to him. Nothing epitomised his alienation better than the beach. Tourists had always come to France partly for its beaches (Churchill had floated around, surrounded by French policemen in bathing suits, during one of his visits in the late 1940s), but in the 1960s the beaches of the south of France, especially the village of St Tropez, acquired a new allure. Club Med, founded in 1950 but almost bankrupt in 1961, was revived and turned into a thriving business that purported to bring the innocent hedonism of Tahiti to the European middle classes. De Gaulle's son only once saw him in a bathing suit, and Harold Macmillan recalled a wartime visit to a beach in Algeria, when de Gaulle had sat in his full uniform while Macmillan plunged naked into the water.

On 15 March 1968, Pierre Viansson-Ponté published a famous article in *Le Monde*. It began thus: 'The French are bored. They are not involved directly or indirectly in the great convulsions that shake the world.' He added that de Gaulle was bored and reduced to the 'official bonhomie' of the agricultural show or the Lyon fair. De Gaulle, the article suggested, 'tried to dramatize daily life with loud statements about dangers the country faced' but despaired at the 'bovine' quality instilled in the French by the very political stability that de Gaulle had established.

Things changed fast because it turned out that the last great drama of de Gaulle's life was still to come. Almost immediately after Viansson-Ponté's article was published, a protest movement by students – partly about the conditions of their own universities and partly about wider political matters – erupted. It started at Nanterre (a campus of Paris university to the west of the city) and, when Nanterre was closed, moved to the Sorbonne in the Latin Quarter on the left bank of the Seine. In retrospect one can see that the protest had long-term roots. The number of students in France had expanded fast in the first ten years of the Fifth Republic and universities were overcrowded. The belief that the Parti Communiste Français had abandoned real hope of revolution made some young people turn to Maoist and Trotskyite groupuscules. The extreme-right had probably given up hope of overthrowing de Gaulle but some of its sympathisers threw their weight behind any protest directed against him. Despite all this, France had seemed an island of political calm when compared to the United States or even Italy at the beginning of 1968, and the scale of student protest, which peaked in May and June, surprised almost everyone.

If students alone had been involved, the protests of 1968 might have had a dramatic effect in Paris but would not have meant much in the rest of the country. The number of mainly student protesters who piled into the Odéon theatre in the Latin Quarter, where they were addressed by Sartre, among others , was greater than the total number of people who took their baccalauréat examination, giving access to universities, in the whole of the French Basque country in that year.[24] What made France different from every other western country except Italy was that workers joined the protests – a fact that surprised the students and perhaps the workers themselves. For a time, the Communist Party seemed to be an uncomprehending spectator at events it had not initiated but which shook the classes it claimed to represent. Some employers had moved their factories to the Catholic west of France (Brittany especially) in the hope that workers there would prove more docile. But workers in Nantes and Rennes now went on strike and helped transform a regionalist movement (traditionally identified with the anti-republican Right) into one that involved the new Left.

At first, de Gaulle and much of his entourage were mystified by the protests. Men who had faced down the paratroopers and legion-naires during the Algerian War could not take the idea of 'student revolution' seriously. They did not know how to respond to indus-trial strikes that were not primarily about pay and did not lend themselves to the usual union-led negotiations. Strikes became so common in May and June that the authorities could not even calcu-late the total number of working days lost. It was hard to distinguish those who had chosen to go on strike from those whose workplaces had been closed or those who were unable to get to work because transport had broken down and petrol become unavailable. In any case, the statisticians responsible for calculating these matters went on strike themselves.

It looked as though history was on the move again and de Gaulle had been left by the roadside. Just a few years earlier, his enemies had sought to kill him, but the students often seemed indifferent. There were few direct attacks on the general. It was not even clear that protesters disagreed with all his policies – he had, after all, criticised American involvement in the Vietnam War – rather than his style. Student leaders often romanticised the resistance. They belonged to the generation born during the war or soon after , and sometimes admired the de Gaulle of 1940, but they found it hard to believe that the 'historic de Gaulle' had much relation to the old man in the Élysée Palace in 1968. De Gaulle, so used to being hated, was now mocked. On 13 May 1968 (not an anniversary that de Gaulle much cared for since it suggested that his return in 1958 had been brought about by the army), demonstrators waved their handkerchiefs to bid the general 'goodbye'.

Television, which had so often provided de Gaulle with a means to reach the French, did not work this time. He broadcast he spoke in apocalyptic terms: 'a tidal wave of disorder, abandon and strikes' had brought France 'to the verge of paralysis'. However, the solution he proposed seemed absurd in its conventionality. He wanted a referendum to authorise an ill-defined process of 'reform'and declared that he would resign if the result of this referendum was against him – a dangerous threat at a time when the French people seemed, for the first time in a decade, to be indifferent to him. The sight of the president alone behind a desk underlined his remoteness from the dramatic events in the streets and factories. The good humour of his broadcasts of the mid 1960s was gone. A middle-aged Gaullist woman wrote to him after his broadcast: 'I can tell you are angry with us.'[25]

For a time ministers and officials understood what was happening better than de Gaulle. Particularly important was the prime minister Georges Pompidou. He had been on an official visit to Afghanistan when the students occupied the Sorbonne and consequently had not expressed any opinion that could be held against him. When he got back to France, he took matters in hand and ordered the police to leave the Sorbonne, of which they had taken control. Pompidou understood the culture of the 1960s – he admired the films of Jean-Luc Godard, a fact that the filmmaker found embarrassing. He was relaxed about sexual freedom for the young and moderately sympathetic to the idea that youth might express left-wing political ideas. His strategy was to appease the students – though it was less clear that he knew what to do about the workers' strike.

Maurice Grimaud, the prefect of the Paris police, was also important. He was keen to prevent violence against students and particularly emphasised that students (often middle-class) should not endure the savage treatment that the Paris police under his predecessor (Maurice Papon) had meted out to Algerian demonstrators a few years earlier.[26] Christian Fouchet, the minister of the interior, was brutally frank that students should be treated better than North Africans, 'for whom the Paris population did not have excessive affection.'[27]

Then, suddenly, de Gaulle himself was on the move again and briefly seemed to have caught up with history. On 29 May, he left the Élysée Palace – a place he did not like at the best of times and which must have seemed a gilded prison in the circumstances. His staff assured he was going to Colombey-les-Deux-Églises but he never arrived. For a time, his own ministers did not know where de Gaulle had gone and, oddly, absence brought him back to centre stage. For the first time since the protests began, people were talking about de Gaulle.

De Gaulle and his immediate family had flown by helicopter to Baden-Baden in Germany, where they went to the base commanded by general Massu – who had remained a Gaullist, in spite of de Gaulle having transferred him away from Algeria in 1960.[28] What was de Gaulle thinking? The British ambassador considered it possible that de Gaulle would go into exile – he imagined Italy or Switzerland to be the most likely refuges: 'I cannot see him returning to Britain if he has any choice in the matter.'[29] It is also possible that de Gaulle wanted to ascertain the mood of the army and particularly of Massu. Would soldiers obey him if he ordered them to crush the protests?

A central theme of de Gaulle's thought had been the need to subordinate the army to civilian control. During the war and again in 1958, many had feared that he might establish himself as a dictator, but he had not done so. Did he waver in late May 1968? Earlier in the month, the British ambassador had written 'prefects and politicians alike ruled out the use of the army'[30] and the British defence attaché had heard 'from the army authorities that no one wants to call on the army to use force and that they themselves would not be happy to order in troops against students or workers'.[31] Those around de Gaulle understood the dangers of recourse to the army – not least because their experience of Algeria had taught them how difficult it might be to contain the toughest units once they were taken off the leash. Pierre Messmer, the minister of the army, had said in early

May that legionnaires and paratroopers 'would not hesitate to shoot and then the worst could happen.'[32] However, for a brief moment, at the end of May, it looked as though troops might be deployed. The British reported that French units from West Germany had been posted back to Paris where they 'could intervene quickly'.[33] Officers at the staff college were sent back to their regiments.[34]

If soldiers had been let loose in 1968, then de Gaulle's career might have finished badly. He might be remembered as a man who had shed French blood. He might have survived in power for a time as a military dictator. Worst of all, he might have been pushed out of power by his own more moderate ministers.

Probably de Gaulle did not fully know what he intended to do when he left Paris. He sometimes acted on instinct as much as calculation and he often went through moments of apocalyptic gloom, in which he imagined the most terrible dénouements, before setting himself to relatively mundane and practical measures. He liked movement and taking the initiative. The mere act of flying may have put him in mind of 1940 and revived his spirits. He may also have been cheered by passing over eastern France (the part of the country least affected by the events of 1968). He may simply have responded to Massu's encouragement, or, possibly so annoyed by Massu's condescending tone that he resolved to seize control of events again.

Whatever the reason, de Gaulle returned to Paris almost immediately. His dramatic arrival drew attention to himself once again. He broadcast on the radio and thus evoked memories of 1940, or, at least, memories of what people thought they knew of 1940. On 30 May, de Gaulle's supporters organised a demonstration in western Paris. It was by far the largest such demonstration in France in 1968, but did not mark the end of the upheavals. Many workers stayed on strike in June, even after the leaders of the main trade union confederation had agreed concessions with regard to pay and other material conditions with the government.

De Gaulle dissolved parliament and legislative elections took place in late June. The Gaullists and their allies won almost half the votes, which meant that they took the great majority of seats in the National Assembly. The election results illlustrated something awkward for the president. Gaullism was increasingly independent of de Gaulle. For one thing, de Gaulle was a right-winger but one who had been most successful at times (as in 1940 or 1961) when he had been in conflict with much of the conventional right and when he attracted at least some support from people who regarded themselves as being on the left. The Gaullism of 1968, however, was emphatically right-wing. Jean-Louis Tixier-Vignancour – the veteran defender of Vichy and Algérie Française, who had opposed de Gaulle in 1965 – rallied to him in 1968. The newly elected deputies were conservatives.

De Gaulle tried to wrest control back into his own hands. He is said to have remarked of parliament: 'Here is an assembly of the PSF [i.e. of the extreme right] with which I will pursue the policy of the PSU [i.e. of the left]'. In fact, de Gaulle was not very successful at making left-wing policy with the new chamber. He dismissed Pompidou as prime minister – because, rather than in spite, of the fact that he had displayed such sangfroid when facing the student demonstrations. He replaced him with Maurice Couve de Murville – a more conventional figure and one with less of an independent political identity. No doubt de Gaulle hoped that Couve de Murville, who (Couve had begun his career as an *inspecteur des finances*, would simply do what he was told. The appointment illustrated the extent to which the administration and the Gaullist party had created a ruling class that was independent of de Gaulle.

De Gaulle's last political gesture was to call a referendum. He intended it to be about three things: the replacement of the Senate (the elected upper house of parliament) with a body that would represent economic groups; the devolution of power to regional councils and 'participation'. Participation was a vaguely defined concept – very characteristic of de Gaulle's search for policies that might provide the form, but rarely the substance, of progressivism. It meant, if it meant anything, that workers were to be given some power in their workplace. However, participation was dropped from the referendum proposals – perhaps because it suggested too much social radicalism or perhaps just because it would have been hard to formulate a precise proposal.

The referendum on reform of the Senate and regionalisation was scheduled for April 1969. It became clear, especially when Giscard turned against the proposals, that the country would vote against de Gaulle. Some of his advisers wanted him to cancel or delay the referendum. He did not do so. When the results came in, his response was instant. He announced he would resign as head of state and that his resignation would come into force from noon the next day. Within hours he was gone from the Élysée Palace. He had, in any case, never felt much affection for the official residence of the head of state – some said he regarded it as an officer might regard a provincial barracks. Most of his possessions had always been kept at Colombey-les-Deux-Églises, where he lived for the rest of his life. He only once returned to Paris – to attend the first communion of his granddaughter.

De Gaulle never returned to London after his resignation either. From then on, his foreign ensured that he was not in France on 18 June. In June 1969, he went to Ireland 'a beautiful, wild desolate country.[35] He was photographed walking along a windswept beach – the kind of place that evoked Chateaubriand more than Brigitte Bardot. He had an amicable exchange with the Irish president De Valera – who was now eighty-six years old and blind. De Gaulle seems to have found De Valera's political vision – nationalist, Catholic and traditional – appealing, as had many Pétainists. He attended a dinner in Dublin Castle – perhaps he knew that this had been Winston Churchill's childhood home for a few years while his grandfather was viceroy of Ireland. The official record of the dinner omitted the fact that de Gaulle had raised his glass to a 'unified Ireland'.[36] The next year, de Gaulle headed west again and was received by another right-wing Catholic ruler: General Franco in Spain.

This was the last time de Gaulle left France and close almost the last time he left his village. He devoted most of his days to preparing the final volumes of his memoirs. Sometimes he seemed trapped by this enterprise. He found writing painfully difficult and had lost the sureness of touch he had displayed when writing about 1940. He never used research assistants in the way that Churchill had done but he asked for help from a few former aides with regard to particular aspects of policy. He wanted to write three more volumes and anticipated that it would take him four years to do so. The second volume was never completed and the third – which would have been called *Le Terme* – was never started.

In the early afternoon of 9 November 1970, a couple of weeks before de Gaulle's eightieth birthday, René Piot, a neigbouring farmer, came to the Boisserie (de Gaulle's house) to discuss matters relating to their adjoining properties. De Gaulle received him in the library and offered him a Gitane. A few hours later, de Gaulle was playing patience while waiting for the regional news to come on television. Suddenly, he said: 'It hurts, there in my back' and then died. Yvonne de Gaulle was not the submissive woman that many observers assumed her to be, and she took control of matters in the hours after her husband's death. She had never been enthusiastic his post-war political career. She had been haunted by a fortune teller's prediction that he would die hanged. So perhaps she was relieved that his end was peaceful and relieved too that he had done nothing that might obviously put his soul in peril.

De Gaulle's death, unlike Churchill's, was private. There were no expectant crowds outside the house. The death was announced after the family had been told – until then, only the doctor, the priest and two elderly servants had known. However, de Gaulle was still central to French public life in 1970, in a way that Churchill had not been central to British public life at the moment of his death. Pompidou, who had succeeded de Gaulle as president, remarked that 'France was a widow'. She was, though, a merry widow – the early 1970s saw the fastest economic growth in French history. De Gaulle's death was his last service to his country. So much hostility had been concentrated on his person – particularly by those who were bitter about Vichy and the loss of Algeria – that his disappearance drew a good deal of political poison. Pompidou cultivated a deliberately undramatic style and distanced himself from the sharp conflicts of de Gaulle's career.

Though Pompidou had not been on good personal terms with de Gaulle at the time of his death, he was his executor because de Gaulle had entrusted him with instructions for his funeral in 1952, when he had been a private citizen, estranged from the French political class. De Gaulle had not changed his instructions in the intervening years: he wanted no official representatives at his funeral. The army was allowed to be present but there was to be no pomp. It appears that the instructions originated with Yvonne de Gaulle, who had said in April 1947 that de Gaulle should insist that no politicians be present at his funeral, which should take place 'between four candles at Colombey'.[37] On 12 November, a bitterly cold day, de Gaulle's coffin was carried by a dozen young men from the village. One was the son of the carpenter who had made the coffin, one was the brother of the farmer who had seen de Gaulle on the day of his death. Another, Gérard Natali, worked in the station restaurant at Chaumont and almost missed the service because his employer was reluctant to give him time off.

As always, there was an element of artifice behind the contrived simplicity. Thousands of people came to Colombey and the event was broadcast live on television. There were two ceremonies in Paris. In the morning, before the funeral, there was a service at Notre Dame Cathedral. Richard Nixon (president of the United States) and Henry Kissinger (the American national security advisor) attended. Prince Charles; the British prime minister, Edward Heath; and his three predecessors (Eden, Macmillan and Wilson) were there.* In the evening after the funeral, there was a march down the Champs Élysée and wreaths were laid at the Arc de Triomphe. The end of the funeral wasexactly as de Gaulle had anticipated in 1952: he was buried beside his daughter Anne.

---

*The British had difficulty in obtaining enough places at the funeral. Montgomery's request to send a representative was refused.

12

Afterlives

'For something like thirty years I have had dealings with history.
I have sometimes asked myself whether I should give her up'.
Charles de Gaulle, 1965

Churchill and de Gaulle gave a lot of thought to how they might be remembered after their death. They did so in different ways, though. For Churchill it had been a concern since his earliest years – he left a Lancer to ride behind the main body of troops he led into battle in the Sudan (in 1898, when he was twenty-three years old) so that there would be a survivor to recount his last action if he himself were killed.[1] But he seemed less interested in his long-term reputation towards the end of his life. From 1945 to 1955, he was concerned, perhaps more than ever before, to be a historical actor, rather than worrying about how his previous acts might be remembered. After 1955, Churchill entered a kind of purgatory – still alive but too old and infirm to take much interest even in the recounting of his own past. In the last years of his life, it was Churchill's associates – especially his private secretary John Colville – who fussed about his reputation. They arranged publishing contracts, raised money and threatened libel actions.

De Gaulle remained the author of his own myth until his last day alive. He retired from public life partly so that he could complete his memoirs. Alain de Boissieu, his son-in-law and aide, probably understood the general's last wishes correctly when he asked a loyal journalist to tell one last lie – that de Gaulle had been writing at the moment of his death.[2]

De Gaulle did not consider the reputation he had taken such care to construct as belonging to himself. Rather, he treated it as though he held it in trust for France. He understood that his image was something his country might find useful in future years. Whereas Churchill regarded his reputation as a private property. It was closely connected to his ideas of family inheritance. The fame of the Churchill name was one that he had inherited from illustrious ancestors, and it was one of the possessions he intended to leave to his own heirs. He must, by 1945, have abandoned the hope that his son Randolph would have a significant political career, but he did hope that Randolph would write his biography, as Winston had written the biography of his own father. He also hoped that his family would derive financial benefit from his literary legacy and more generally from his reputation. This in turn went with the fact that, even before his death, Winston Churchill had become an export brand – one that often found its most lucrative markets outside the British Isles, especially in the United States.

While de Gaulle was alive, he created sharp divisions. His opponents were sometimes the real Gaullists. Their feelings about the general were so intense that many came to believe that the whole political system revolved around his person. As far as right-wing anti-Gaullists in the aftermath of the Algerian War were concerned, de Gaulle mattered so much that only his death could save France. The mass of de his supporters felt less strongly. Many voted for him without wholly subscribing to his view of the world.

Anti-Gaullism was still strong at the moment of de Gaulle's death. The right-wing newspaper *Rivarol* greeted it with the head-line: 'It is for his victims that we weep.' Such feelings diminished after his death. Precisely because they had revolved so much around the person of de Gaulle, they were unlikely to survive him for long. It is significant that the two most important political innovations in France in the early 1970s were the foundation of the Parti Socialiste and the Front National. These new parties provided the political vehicles for François Mitterrand and Jean-Marie Le Pen, a veteran of the campaign to defend French Algeria and soon to become the most important figure on the extreme Right. Both men had been defined by their anti-Gaullism in the 1960s but were now free to develop a broader political position – one that in the case of the Front National came to take in some former Gaullists, including, eventually, one of de Gaulle's grandsons. De Gaulle became a more consensual figure after his death than he had ever been when alive – though there was not complete consensus about what kind of consensus he ought to represent. Eventually, the de Gaulle family forbade political demonstrations around his monument at Colombey-les-Deux Eglises because they wished to sustain the idea that the general belonged to all of France rather than to particular groups.

Churchill never drew the same animosity as de Gaulle. Attacks on Churchill in Britain would seem tame to anyone who had read what, say, André Figueras wrote about de Gaulle. There were no serious assassination attempts against Churchill. With a characteristically cavalier attitude to taxpayers' money, he often used his police guard as an extra member of his domestic staff. Even accounts of Churchill's life that look scathing at first glance express a degree of admiration. The Labour politician Michael Foot published a review of the first volume of Churchill's *History of the Second World War* under the title 'Churchill's Mein Kampf'. But he conceded that the book 'is written by one some of whose services to the British people are imperishable' and added: 'But because Churchill is a great man does not entitle him to write bad history for the benefit of the Churchill legend.'[3]

If no one was completely hostile to Churchill, few were unqualified in their admiration. Where debate about de Gaulle sometimes seemed to pitch two bitterly opposed camps against each other, debate about Churchill sometimes looked like a family quarrel among members of his own entourage. This was true when Lord Alanbrooke published his wartime diaries in the late 1950s. It was even more true when Lord Moran, Churchill's private physician, published his diary under the title *Churchill: The Struggle for Survival, 1940–1965* – which evoked much protest from other associates of Churchill. But even Moran was emphatic that he was not attacking Churchill and pointed out that Brendan Bracken and Jan Smuts (two of those closest to Churchill) had encouraged him to publish.[4] Furthermore, even those who defined themselves by loyalty to Churchill, sometimes expressed criticism in private – Isaiah Berlin was the author of a celebrated and admiring essay on Churchill but said in private that he regarded him as 'brutal.' Sometimes, there was a double edge to remarks about Churchill. His associates would profess admiration while letting slip remarks that were bound to arouse criticism on the part of others. John Colville dropped into a recorded interview the suggestion that Churchill might have had an extramarital affair in the 1930s.[5]

One feature of Churchill's reputation was the extent to which it was defended by what in the post-war years the British came to call the 'establishment': a group of powerful people – civil servants especially – whose influence was not directly connected to party politics. Norman Brook, Edward Bridges and Leslie Rowan had all been civil servants and all did much to promote Churchill's reputation.[6] Sometimes British officials acted as though Churchill was a kind of public monument that they were charged with protecting. When a lachrymose minister told Margaret Thatcher's last cabinet meeting that she had been the 'greatest Prime Minister this century',[7] which might have been taken to mean that she was greater than Churchill, the cabinet secretary merely recorded the minister as having said that Conservatives under Thatcher's leadership had been 'associated with greatness.'[8]

Both Churchill and de Gaulle were often recalled in published memoirs and diaries. In France such works were focused on the personality of de Gaulle with an intensity that sometimes seemed to obscure that of the author. Diaries by, say, Jacques Foccart or Alain Peyrefitte are largely devoted to recording de Gaulle's remarks. Memoirs and diaries that refer to Churchill do not have the same almost sacerdotal tone. Churchill is often a central – sometimes the central – figure but he is rarely presented to the exclusion of all other subjects, and he is rarely presented as a completely coherent or consistent personality. Sometimes, indeed, diaries capture the literally quotidian quality of Churchill's life – his changes of mood and inconsistencies.

De Gaulle was a remote figure even to those who saw him every day; Churchill's bonhomie sometimes made even those who encountered him briefly feel that they were his friends. Noel Annan – the archetypical member of, and commentator on, the establishment – recalled his service as a wartime officer in his mid twenties attached to the Joint Intelligence Staff and working in an underground bunker next to the cabinet war rooms. One night, as Annan and his comrades were restoring themselves with a stiff whisky, Churchill put his head round the door, grinned and said: 'Working hard, I see, gentlemen.'[9]

The Churchill cult in Britain was, at least for many years, partly constrained by the fact that Churchill, unlike de Gaulle, had worked within an existing constitution and party system. Churchill was never cast out of his country's ruling class in the way that de Gaulle was from 1940 to 1944 or, in a different sense, from 1947 to 1958. But Churchill was never as exalted in status as de Gaulle was from 1958 to 1970.

Churchill's cult was also always undercut by the simple fact that he lost the 1945 election and that to a large extent it was the Labour governments of Clement Attlee from 1945 to 1951 that defined post-war Britain – even Margaret Thatcher sometimes expressed her admiration for Attlee. Margaret Beckett – an understated Labour politician – acted briefly as leader of her party after the death of John Smith and before the election of Tony Blair to the leadership. She attended the fiftieth-anniversary commemorations of the D-Day landings and was, to her surprise, 'almost mobbed' by veterans. She realised that these old men with their campaign medals and regimental ties had voted Labour in 1945. At the opening of the London Olympics in 2012, an actor impersonated Churchill but there was also a celebration of the National Health Service, founded by the Attlee government.

Perhaps because of the constraints of British political institutions, Churchill sometimes seemed to attract a more effusive admiration outside the United Kingdom than in it. He was particularly admired in what he would have described as the 'English-speaking' world – by which he meant the white-settler dominions and the United States. Two of the most important institutional incarnations of interest in Churchill are in the United States at the Westminster College at Fulton, Missouri, where Churchill delivered his 'Iron Curtain' speech', and at Hillsdale College in Michigan, which houses the 'Churchill project'.

American admiration for Churchill was expressed by the grant of honorary citizenship in 1963. From the British point of view, the grant of citizenship was somewhat farcical. Churchill had turned the honour down in 1958. By 1963, he was in no position to make a lucid decision. The British prime minister was initially reluctant to recommend acceptance and the American president was relaxed about the matter.Kennedy, whose father had been ambassador in London and whose sister had married the son of the Duke of Devonshire, did not need to labour his associations with the English ruling class. The state of Nebraska granted Churchill honorary citizenship without asking his permission and British officials came to believe that congressmen who might be in a position to damage

British interests would be offended if Churchill refused citizenship of the United States. Members of the Foreign Office were taken aback when the Americans announced that the first anniversary of the award of citizenship would be 'Churchill Day'.[10] They did not appreciate that this anniversary would then be marked in every subsequent year. The British government decided against instituting a 'Churchill Day'after his death.

Canada, Australia and Rhodesia were also centres of admiration for Churchill – partly, one suspects, because they were also places in which those who disliked the socialism and racial heterogeneity of post-war Britain often sought refuge. Ian Smith, a former Spitfire pilot, was the prime minister of Rhodesia when Churchill died. Determined to avoid the imposition of democracy (which would have meant the white minority of the population being outvoted) he proclaimed a 'unilateral declaration of independence' on 11 November 1965. He also said that Churchill would have felt more at home in white-ruled Rhodesia than in the Britain of the late 1960s.

The word 'Gaullist' was used from 1940 and eventually became a central part of the French political vocabulary. 'Churchillian' was used by John Colville in 1981 to describe a group of people (including de Gaulle) who had been associated with Winston Churchill. It was used in a more systematic and interesting way by two writers at opposite ends of the political spectrum but reaching similar conclusions. In 1982, Anthony Barnett published *Iron Britannia*, in which he used the term to describe a consensus that he believed to had sprung from the Second World War.[11] This consensus derived part of its power from association with Churchill, though it did not necessarily reflect Churchill's personal views. In particular, Churchillianism entailed the alliance between governments and organised labour. In 1994, Andrew Roberts published *Eminent Churchillians*. Once again, he distinguished between 'Churchillianism' and the personal beliefs of Churchill. He ranged over a large number of Churchillians before and during the war but paid special attention to the government of 1951 to 1955. He saw this as a period during which Walter Monckton, the minister of labour, had 'appeased' the trade unions and also one in which Britain had begun to become a multi-racial society.[12] Both authors were writing under the shadow of the Thatcher government. Barnett's book was an attack on the government that took Britain into the Falklands War in 1982. Roberts saw the history of post-war Britain through the prism of an elegiac view of Thatcher's period in office.

Almost invariably, Thatcher and her ministers were deferential to Churchill's memory. Thatcher was the last British prime minister to have met him, though politicians who had more intimate associations with him did not always fare well under her government. Lord Soames, Churchill's son-in-law, was sacked from the cabinet in 1981. Thatcher was sometimes accused (without much justification) of seeking to strike Churchillian poses. Her historical vision placed a particular emphasis on 1940 – partly perhaps because she was keen to present a version of the Second World War that excluded the Soviet Union. She made much of the two countries which would arouse the most awkward memories for the USSR: Poland and Finland. Thatcher shared Churchill's bitter hostility to appeasement and his contempt for Stanley Baldwin – this was a matter that sometimes brought her into an unspoken alliance with the left-wing Labour leader Michael Foot – and Thatcherites sometimes extended the analogy to suggest that Baldwin might be used as a wider symbol of a willingness to compromise and abandon convictions.

Not all those close to Thatcher were uncritical admirers of everything that Churchill had done, or that had been done in his name. There were a few Conservatives who suggested that British entry into, or continuation of, the Second World War was a mistake that laid the way for the end of the British empire. Mainly this current of opinion was expressed or hinted at in universities or among journalists rather than by active politicians. Alan Clark – an eccentric right-wing junior minister in the Thatcher government – used a review of John Charmley's book *Churchill. The End of Glory* (1993) to present this case to a wider public. Clark argued that an early peace with Hitler would have left Britain with the resources to defend her far-eastern empire. But Clark was himself attacked by other Conservatives and his opinions of Churchill veered in odd directions anyway. His own diaries reflect an almost obsessive reading of diaries from the 1930s and 40s. On 10 May 1990, he noted that this was the anniversary of the day when Churchill became prime minister and added: 'I really don't know, I still can't judge, whether that was a good or bad thing for the Britain that I love and cherish, and whose friendly, stubborn, dignified and sensible people have so often been let down by their rulers.'[13] Two months later, reading the diaries of Alexander Cadogan, Clark noticed that it was the anniversary of Mers-el-Kébir and fired off a note to Thatcher about this subject – though he argued that the incident showed the need to take a robust line with the British Foreign Office rather than the desirability of sinking French ships.[14]

Most Conservatives divided Churchill's career, separatingthe wartime government, when they accepted that state management of the economy had been necessary, from what came after. Ministers talked of the second Churchill government with ostensible respect but in practice their attacks on the post-war drift of the Conservative Party implied something less than unqualified admiration for the ministers of 1951 to 1955. Andrew Roberts made explicit the link between revering Thatcher and condemning the post-war Churchillians when he wrote that it took 'the maiden rather than the knight' to slay the dragon of trade union power that Churchill's minister of labour had refrained from confronting in the 1950s.[15]

The figure who haunted some descriptions of Churchillianism was Charles de Gaulle. He was made to stand for different things. In 1982, Anthony Barnett believed that the Thatcher government was 'Gaullist' rather than Churchillian in that it sought a radical modernisation that would mark a sharp break with the past. There was an element of truth in this. The first Thatcher government took France as an economic model – it is no accident that Jean Fourastié's celebration of French post-war economic growth *Les Trente Glorieuses* was published in the same year that Thatcher came to power. Thatcherite ministers initially assumed that transforming the British economy would require technocratic and even dirigiste measures that would mirror policies in France.

By the time Andrew Roberts was writing in 1993, France had ceased to be an economic model. The deregulation of the City of London had created a prosperity that was based on services rather than industry and one that did not require state support. London became a destination for French people who sought to make their fortune. However, at the same time, a different view of de Gaulle began to influence British Conservatives. Some of this derived from Enoch Powell (1912–1998). Powell never held high office (he was a middle-ranking cabinet minister for just over three years) and broke with the Conservatives in 1974 over their support for entry into the European Economic Community, but he exercised an intellectual hegemony over generations of Conservatives. Powell and de Gaulle could have been creatures of each other's imaginations. De Gaulle's paranoid fantasies about the British would have been confirmed had he known that Powell, then a major in the British army, had written in January 1943 that Britain should seize French north Africa: 'we have defeated France. Hardly has a European nation been more mercilessly crushed. Her country occupied, her navy sunk, her colonies conquered or seized, her self-respect so humiliated that it is doubtful if she can ever look the world in the face again.'[16]

Powell, however, eventually became an admirer of de Gaulle. – Characteristically, his admiration grew as de Gaulle's measures to exclude Britain from the European Economic Community exasperated the British establishment. His feelings were expressed in a review of the last volume of de Gaulle's memoirs, a review that said as much about a certain idea of England as it did about France:

The intensity of de Gaulle's sense of French national identity, and of constitutional legitimacy in French terms, opens to him an emotional insight into the nature of British nationhood and legitimacy which contrasts with his instinctive antipathy for things British. To an Englishman some of the most arresting words in the book are his answer to the Queen's question, at the time of that memorable state visit in April 1960: 'When she asked me what I thought should be her role in such an uncertain world, I replied: "In the place where God has put you, be who you are, Madam. I mean, be the person in relation to whom, by virtue of your legitimacy, all things in your kingdom are ordered; the person in whom your people perceive their own nationhood; the person by whose existence and dignity the national unity is upheld."'[17]

Admiration for de Gaulle was widely felt among British Conservatives who were hostile to European integration, and Thatcher herself was increasingly prone to express such admiration as anti-Europeanism came to define the politics of her later years. When an Italian interviewer asked how her vision of Europe differed from the 'Europe des Patries' attributed to de Gaulle, she replied: 'I do not find the comparison in any way unflattering ... No more than de Gaulle do I want to see the suppression of the diverse political and cultural traditions that give Europe its strength.'[18] After her resignation as prime minister, she became more explicit in her admiration: 'There is only one 'ism' attached to a personal name for which I have much affection – Gaullism.'[19]

Sometimes the retrospective mystique of Churchill and de Gaulle was burnished by the fact that they felt so remote from the time in which they were recalled. Even before their deaths, there was an elegiac tone to much writing about Churchill and de Gaulle. In 1970, C. L. Sulzberger published a book – largely made up of articles about both men that had first been published in the 1950s and 60s – with the title *The Last of the Giants*. The Second World War often came to seem, at least as far as the democratic West was concerned, the last time when political choices had been truly momentous. On 22 June 1998, as Arthur Schlessinger listened to news broadcasts ('drab tales and drab times'), concerned with whether or not the president of the United States had spilled his semen on the dress of a young woman in the Oval Office, he found himself thinking back to the speech that he had heard Churchill make when the Soviet Union was invaded in 1941.[20]

Similarly, Frenchmen often came to admire de Gaulle precisely because he seemed to present such a contrast to the banality of the time that came after him. This was true of left-wingers – especially those who came to react against François Mitterrand (of whom more below). Even more strikingly, it was true of some on that part of the extreme-right that had once defined itself against de Gaulle. Born in 1935, Dominique Venner defended those who had collaborated during the occupation and fought for French Algeria. Mobilisation around the second of these causes induced violent anti-Gaullism and earned him a year in prison in the early 1960s. But in 2010 (three years before his last violent protest against the state of France, which ended with his public suicide in Notre Dame Xathedral), he published a book on de Gaulle, whom he compared with grudging admiration to the 'dwarves' who had come after him.[21]

In recent years there has been an important divergence between the reputations of Churchill and de Gaulle and rooted in the emphasis that some on the left place on race and the legacy of empire. Churchill's racism has been widely discussed – especially during and after the Black Lives Matter protests of 2020. There wasan interesting shift, though. The fact that Churchill had been, as Andrew

Roberts wrote in 1994, 'more profoundly racist than most' of his own contemporaries[22] had once been accepted as a distasteful but relatively unimportant part of his personality. More recently some have come to see racism and imperialism as central elements in Churchill's political identity. But the fact that there should be debate about this matter illustrates Churchill's curious status in British public life. Much of the establishment – not just the Conservative establishment – behaved as though denouncing Churchill as a racist would constitute an intolerable act of Lèse-majestéwhile parts of the left behaved as though referring to Churchill's racism would be a brave act of rebellion rather than a statement of the obvious. In 2020, there was a time when Churchill's statue in Parliament Square was boarded up to protect it from attack – that of his friend Jan Smuts (who invented the word 'apartheid') was left unprotected.

Black people in positions of public prominence often undertook complicated balancing acts. Perhaps this was because they understood how dangerous an attack on Churchill might be to their own reputations or to the causes that they espoused, but perhaps it was also because they had genuinely mixed feelings about a man who had been both a racist and a courageous opponent of Hitlerism. David Olusoga (the black television historian) criticised some things Churchill had done but named his television production company 'Uplands' after a line from a speech by Churchill. Barack Obama, visiting Britain in 2016, insisted that he 'loved' Churchill.

In contrast, de Gaulle's was oddly immune to effects of a new emphasis on race and empire. This was seen between 1997 and 2001 when France was wracked by the recollection of brutality during the Algerian War. Much was made of the massacre of Algerian demonstrators in Paris in 1961, when Maurice Papon was prefect of police, and of the confession of General Paul Aussaresses that he had tortured and murdered people suspected of belonging to the Front de Libération Nationale. There was an implicitly post-Gaullist tone to much of the discussion. De Gaulle's politics had always revolved around the state rather than the individual. His government had passed a law granting amnesty for those who had committed crimes during the Algerian War. It is true that some defenders of Algérie Française had either been, or become, anti-Gaullist but this was conspicuously not true of Papon (who had served as prefect of police while de Gaulle was head of state and who had later gone into politics, as a Gaullist, because he was so hostile to the demonstrations of 1968)* or of Aussaresses, who mischievously suggested he had published his book about his crimes in Algeria with Plon because it had been de Gaulle's publisher. De Gaulle was little referred to in the debates over French conduct in Algeria. His association with decolonisation (particularly the withdrawal from Algeria) seems to have erased association with all the crimes that might have been committed in Algeria and elsewhere under his rule. More generally, little has been made of the fact that de Gaulle so often defined his politics in racial or racist terms.

Discussions of race and empire illustrate something broader about the changing status of de Gaulle and Churchill. De Gaulle, so divisive during his life, has become a unifying force in France since his death – even, for example, campaigners for gay liberation sometimes evoke his memory. Churchill, on the other hand, having for several decades after the Second World War commanded ostensible respect among the political establishment (if not always the general population or among academic historians), is now a figure of controversy again. Once, historians who were critical of Churchill – from Robert Rhodes James in 1969 to Andrew Roberts in 1993 – were more likely to be drawn from the right than the left, though their criticism was always courteous and restrained. The mainstream left, on the other hand, usually talked of Churchill with reverence. As late as 2002, theLabour politician Mo Mowlam put the case, in

---

*Papon's loyalty to de Gaulle had a Talleyrandesque quality. In May 1961, the British ambassador reported a rumour that Papon had given a 'tacit promise' that the Paris police would not intervene if the army and OAS launched a further coup against de Gaulle.

a competition organised by the BBC, for Winston Churchill to be recognised as the greatest Briton of all time.

The left has become more dubious about Churchill since then, while the political right has become emphatic in its admiration. The two most recent biographies of Churchill to command wide attention are by Boris Johnson and Andrew Roberts. Both men are Conservatives and both present a picture of Churchill that is more admiring than that of most previous biographers – Roberts's great biography of 2018 was more admiring of Churchill than his own astringent essays of the early 1990s. Churchill, though, played a surprisingly small role in the case that Roberts and Johnson made for Britain leaving the European Union in 2016 – perhaps because both men were shrewd enough to know that Churchill had often contradicted himself with regard to European integration. Maybe it was also because some of the pro-European Conservatives (Macmillan, Soames and Sandys) had been close to Churchill or perhaps because Johnson published his biography of Churchill in 2014, before he himself had decided to support British withdrawal from the European Union.

The shift in Churchill's status in the United States is even more dramatic than that in the United Kingdom. For most of the late twentieth century, ritual obeisance to Churchill's memory was a part of mainstream American public life. His closest American political associate had been a Democrat – Roosevelt. Until recently, criticism of Churchill in the US mainly came from the extreme right. Anthony Montague Browne – Churchill's reactionary private secretary – was disconcertedto be heckled in the 1960s by members of the John Birch Society who regarded his views as dangerously liberal. The conservative Patrick Buchanan published a book in 2008 arguing that Churchill's war with Hitler had been 'unnecessary' and damaging to the interests of the West.[23] Buchanan's interpretation of Churchill's career was echoed in an interview of 2024 by the podcaster Darryl Cooper, but Cooper did not appear to reflect a significant strand of opinion on the American right, which was by that time generally more sympathetic to Churchill than ever before.

Churchill's status in America changed partly because race became, even more than in Britain, a central element in the politics of the left but also because part of the right radicalised around Donald Trump and began to brandish Churchill's reputation with increasing enthusiasm. Trump himself is said to model his scowl on Churchill's – or at least on the Karsh photograph of it – and sometimes referred to words or actions he attributed to Churchill. No one better exemplifies the changing political mobilisation of Churchill than Rudy Giuliani. In 2001, he was mayor of New York and said that he spent the night of 11 September of that year (after the attacks on the World Trade Center) reading a biography of Churchill. But the biography he read was that by Roy Jenkins – a one-time Labour cabinet minister fascinated by Asquithian Liberalism, who presented a view of Churchill that would be appealing to the centre left of British politics. By 2024, when he tweeted about 'Churchill day', Giuliani was closely associated with Donald Trump and denial of the result of the 2020 presidential election. Churchill is now an icon of the right in the United States in a way that would have seemed odd just a decade ago. It is not entirely flippant to suggest that the quickest way to determine the political complexion of an American president now is to find out whether or not the Epstein bust of Churchill is on display in the Oval Office.

The whole of modern France is a Gaullist monument. It is appropriate that the words Charles de Gaulle are now most frequently used with reference to the Paris airport that was named after him in 1974 – a structure that incarnates modernity and speed. The association of de Gaulle with the modernisation of France can, though, have curious consequences. He was the beneficiary of economic growth and technological modernisation rather than its architect. It is also odd that de Gaulle – who was uncomfortable with the 'bovine' quality that he believed prosperity had imparted to the French – is sometimes recalled with favour because he is associated with a consumerist golden age. In 1962, Françoise Hardy's song 'Tous les Garçons et les Filles' became a hit partly because she performed it on television while the votes in the referendum on direct elections to the presidency of the republic were being counted. Today de Gaulle is occasionally discussed as though he was mainly notable for being a figure in the France of Françoise Hardy.

Some of the paradoxes around the memory of de Gaulle in contemporary France were illustrated by the right-wing journalist-turned-politician É ric Zemmour. Zemmour was born during the interregnum of late 1958, after de Gaulle had returned to power but before he had established a new constitution and become head of state. He comes from a family of Algerian Jews who moved to the mainland in the early 1950s and therefore never experienced the bitter anti-Gaullism of many European settlers in 1962. Zemmour evokes de Gaulle's memory – his book of 2014 on *Le Suicide Français* dated the 'unmaking of France' from the death of de Gaulle and begins with a description of his funeral. However, Zemmour has also written with sympathy about Pétain (claiming in particular that he protected French Jews), reviving an argument (made by some right-wingers in the 1940s but rejected by de Gaulle himself) that Pétain and de Gaulle had worked in an unspoken alliance.

In the film with which he launched his 2022 presidential bid, Zemmour spoke into an archaic, outsized microphone, evoking an image of a BBC studio in June 1940, and talked of saving France. However, his nostalgia for de Gaulle went hand-in-hand with a nostalgia for the 1960s – a time when most of the extreme right hated de Gaulle. Like many people, Zemmour seems to associate de Gaulle with the general prosperity of France in the 1960s and his film celebrates figures such as Brigitte Bardot and Alain Delon – not, one assumes, people who played a large role in de Gaulle's thought.*

---

*Though Delon was an admirer of de Gaulle and played the Gaullist Chaban Delmas in the film *Is Paris Burning?*

Zemmour's references to de Gaulle draw attention to something else. It is hard for anyone to make a bid for the presidency of the Fifth Republic, and hard for a President (of any political affiliation) to govern, unless they adopt elements of a Gaullist style. The most unsuccessful president since 1958 (the only one who did not seek a second term) was François Hollande (in office from 2012 to 2017) and one suspects that his failure derived largely from his insistence on presenting himself in modest terms as a 'normal president'. Hollande's successor, Emmanuel Macron, never pretended to be normal. Macron is young (at the end of his second five-year presidential term he will be the same age as de Gaulle in 1940) and cosmopolitan – in 2024 he addressed those attending the commemorations to mark the anniversary of D-Day in English. He is the first president in French history to have no military experience, and is also very short. This might seem unpromising material with which to construct a Gaullist image. But Macron has a taste for theatrical politics, which lends itself to Gaullist gestures. In his official portrait photograph, there's a pile of books on his desk – one of them is the *Mémoires de Guerre*.

No one better incarnates the peculiar relation of Fifth Republic presidents with the Gaullist legacy more than François Mitterrand. In some ways, Mitterrand was the antithesis of de Gaulle. The two men had bad relations from their first encounter in 1943. De Gaulle despised him so much that he refused to pronounce his name in public. De Gaulle's son-in-law, Alain de Boissieu, resigned as chancellor of the Legion of Honour in 1981 to avoid having to bestow the grand cross on Mitterrand after his election as president.

Nevertheless, there were things that Mitterrand and de Gaulle had in common. Both had a strong sense of history and of their own place in it. Both plotted their political careers over a long time and both survived periods during which they were excluded from power. As president, Mitterrand did not sweep away the constitution he had once denounced. On the contrary, he was sometimes more Gaullist than de Gaulle. He was the only Fifth Republic president who served two full seven-year terms. He was rigorous in his insistence that due reverence be paid to the powers of the president and the convention that the president controls a *domaine réservé* of foreign and defence policy, while leaving more trivial matters to their prime minister, owes more to Mitterrand's practice than to theoretical statements about the constitution during the presidency of de Gaulle.

Mitterrand was president in the supercharged anniversary year of 1990 – a hundred years after de Gaulle's birth, fifty years after his call to honour and twenty years after his death. By this time, though, some, especially on the left, had turned against Mitterrand andsometimes turned back to de Gaulle, or at least to an image of de Gaulle partly constructed as a photonegative of Mitterrand's. Mitterrand, by that time, was often seen as corrupt. He had abandoned the economic radicalism and Communist alliance that had marked his government between 1981 and 1984, and was known to regard the memory of Pétain with some reverence and to maintain cordial relations with some former Pétainists.

The denunciations of Mitterrand were not entirely fair – he had never really hidden his distaste for communism or his complicated relations with Vichy. However, in the eyes of some, Mitterrand's serpentine subtlety made what they took to be the austere simplicity of de Gaulle more attractive. The new view was incarnated by R é gis Debray – a radical from the late 1960s and an aide to Mitterrand in the early 1980s. In 1989, Debray published À *Demain de Gaulle* – an ostensible *autocritique* of his own youthful illusions, though really directed against almost everyone other than himself, that presented failure to appreciate the true value of de Gaulle as the most important fault of his generation. André Glucksmann, another *soixante-huitard*, also wrote an admiring book on de Gaulle that made the comparison with Mitterrand explicit: 'greatness is only clear when contrasted to mediocrities more flagrant than itself ... François Mitterrand was necessary for the rediscovery of Charles de Gaulle'.[24]

Churchill was never memorialised in British institutions as much as de Gaulle was in French ones – the places most frequently named after

him are pubs. Civil servants headed off an attempt to name the branch
of the Hilton Hotel overlooking Hyde Park 'The Churchill', but failed
to prevent the spread of night clubs called 'Winston's'. There were
statues (notably the one in Parliament Square), but even stone or steel
memorials to Churchill sometimes seemed playful rather than solemn.
The quarters that were built for the *Financial Times* in the late 1950s
(Churchill's protégé Brendan Bracken was chairman of the company)
feature an astrological clock above the entrance. The face of the sun
and the moon are both modelled on Churchill. Journalists were curious to see what would happen to the images when the building was
owned for a time by the Industrial Bank of Japan.*

The most important memorial to Churchill was the authorised
biography entrusted first to Randolph Churchill and then to Martin
Gilbert. Indeed, Gilbert himself became a kind of *lieu de mémoire*,
enjoying a special status in British public life because of the link that
he seemed to provide with Churchill. Harold Wilson, prime minister
when Churchill died, was particularly interested in his predecessor, and accorded Gilbert long interviews. Thereafter, revealingly,
Gilbert had relatively little to do with the most long-serving and
electorally successful post-war prime ministers (Thatcher and Blair)
but was close to John Major and Gordon Brown. Major admired
Baldwin, and Brown's thinking was deeply rooted in the history
of the Labour Party, but both men also valued an association with
Churchill – perhaps because it reassured them that being prime
minister was a job that mattered. Major sometimes took Gilbert
with him on foreign trips as a kind of adviser or court historian and
Brown appointed him to the Privy Council so that he could sit on
the committee investigating the circumstances in which Britain had
entered the Gulf War of 2001.

The single most important physical monument to Churchill in
the British Isles is Churchill College Cambridge, created in 1960,

*The clock is still there.

largely as a result of the labours of John Colville, and intended to provide an English riposte to the Massachusetts Institute of Technology. It became a distinguished college, though informed observers knew that, towards the end of Churchill's life, no British institution could match the wealth and power of American universities. Churchill College, however, is anything but a centre of piety. The Churchill archives were eventually placed in the care of the college's archive centre. Since this meant removing them from the control of Martin Gilbert, the authorised biographer, it also meant that research by those who wished to write about Churchill in a critical spirit became easier. Stephen Roskill – who published an acerbic study of Churchill's interventions in naval matters[25] – was one of the first people to be elected to a fellowship of the college. Successive heads of the archive centre – Correlli Barnett, Piers Brendon and Allen Packwood[26] – have not sought to control writing about Churchill and have sometimes published critical work of their own. In 2020, Paul Boateng, a former Labour MP of Ghanaian descent, became chair of the Winston Churchill Archive Trust. He began his tenure with what he claimed to be an African proverb: 'Until the lion writes, we will only have history from the point of view of the hunter.' It is an intriguingly double-edged remark – which might be taken to imply that Churchill was the hunter rather than the lion.

The most arresting historical artefact on show in Churchill College is the tapestry that Charles de Gaulle presented on its foundation and that is hung in the library. Attentive students will note that, sewn into its fabric, are words, first spoken by Charles de Gaulle on 25 August 1944, that would have exasperated Winston Churchill: 'Paris libéré par lui-même'.

Conclusion

De Gaulle was the last great French tragedian. His performance was solemn and marked by a classical restraint. Though he had a sharp sense of humour, he hated the idea that he might be a comic character and was more offended by the mockery of student demonstrators in 1968 than by the violent attacks of the defenders of French Algeria a few years earlier.

Churchill was also an intensely theatrical politician. Isaiah Berlin wrote of him:

> Like a great actor – perhaps the last of his kind – upon the stage of history, he speaks his memorable lines with a large, unhurried and stately utterance in a blaze of light, as is appropriate to a man who knows that his work and his person will remain the object of scrutiny and judgement to many generations.[1]

Churchill's notion of performance was not rooted in tragedy; one of his most endearing characteristics was a capacity for self-mockery. His first speech was delivered during a riot at a music hall and a dark moment of the war he improvised a slapstick routine to amuse his private secretary.[2] Churchill was a warmer, more optimistic person than de Gaulle. He liked people and particularly the British. He loved France, but he loved it as an abstraction separate from the French people. He revealed much about himself when he commented that a part of the French royalist right was composed of 'exiles in their own country who resented France for being France'.[3] It is hard to imagine de Gaulle intervening, as Churchill did on the day of Allied victory in Europe, to ensure that beer supplies in the capital city would be adequate for the celebrations.

The key to classical tragedy is inevitability and Churchill railed against the idea that any event was unavoidable – insistingthat it ought to have been possible to prevent the Second World War. De Gaulle's thinking, by contrast, was permeated by a sense of the inevitable and by a melancholy, sometimes apocalyptic, belief that all human enterprises will fail sooner rather than later. In his darker moments he was not sure sure that even France would endure.

De Gaulle was not a complete determinist – he would hardly have broken with military discipline, flown to an alien country and risked a death sentence in 1940 if he had thought that his own actions would make no difference. He did, however, have a strong sense that history was governed by forces that went beyond the individual. His speech on 18 June 1940 made much of impersonal forces – the might of the French empire and the industrial power of the United States. Compare this to Churchill's 'Finest Hour' speech of the same day, calling on the British people to summon up their courage and imply-ing a real choice between absolute defeat (which might submerge even the United States) and victory.

Different views of history fitted with different circumstances in 1940. Churchill's determination that Britain should fight on probably had an influence on the course of the war – though an interpretation that revolves around him alone would underplay the more mundane advantages Britain enjoyed in 1940. One result of this was that Churchill's reputation, and a part of Britain's identity, came to balance precariously on this one year. George Orwell wrote that it might have been better for Churchill's reputation if he had, like Kitchener, gone down at sea before the war's end. For de Gaulle too, Churchill was the man of 1940 – 'magnificent', as he later put it, 'until Pearl Harbor', but thereafter a creature of the United States.

No one could claim that de Gaulle's reputation would stand higher if his career had ended in 1941. If he had been killed in one of the dangerous wartime journeys that he (like Churchill) so often undertook, then de Gaulle would be a curiosity of the Second World War – perhaps no more important to historians than the Polish general Władysław Sikorski, who died in a plane crash in July 1943. De Gaulle was most important after 1945 (and especially after 1958). A man who had not even been recognised as head of a government in exile before 1944 was, from 1959 to 1970, a head of state – and, as he might have added, a *real* head in command of a *real* state. He ruled a country that was more prosperous than ever before, more politically stable that it had been since 1870 and enjoying a greater degree of international prestige than at any time since 1815.

In spite of the fact that his name is so often associated with 18 June 1940, de Gaulle's reputation did not depend on what he did on that day or in that year. His decision to raise his standard in London had little military impact. Without it, the Allies would still have won the war, French North Africa would still have been invaded by the British and Americans in 1942 and mainland France would still have been liberated in June 1944. The difference de Gaulle made was a political one, and only became apparent after the event, when France was recognized as one of the victor powers with, among other things, a seat on the United Nations Security Council. De Gaulle and a small number of his associates may have had reason to look back on 18 June 1940 with a melancholy pride, but no French person, least of all those most associated with resistance to the Germans, had reason to remember the date with pleasure. Gilberte Brossolette set out to drink herself unconscious on 18 June 1945.[4] Her husband, the resistance leader Pierre Brossolette, had committed suicide while in Gestapo captivity in March 1944 to prevent himself from betraying his comrades under torture.

The British often misunderstood de Gaulle because they saw him, and themselves, through the prism of 1940 and never reconciled themselves to the change in de Gaulle's status and in the balance of power between France and Britain that happened after the war. The

British ambassador in Paris, Sir Pierson Dixon, wrote in 1963 with some disbelief that de Gaulle was 'now head of a great nation, different from the often exasperating leader of the Free French whom we knew (and created) in the war'.[5] successor later ambassador, Lord Soames (Churchill's son-in-law), wrote immediately after de Gaulle's death:

> it was his decision to snatch the Tricolor from the hands of a dying Republic and hold it aloft as the rallying point for that tiny band of French men and women who refused to accept their country's capitulation, that assured de Gaulle his decisive place in the story of France.

Soames went on:

> Perhaps de Gaulle's tragedy, as well as his strength, was that he too confounded myth with reality. The 'certaine idée' which he held of his country was surely – and sadly – a splendid but unattainable ideal. A country is, after all, largely what its people make it. De Gaulle realised that the French people ('the most fickle and unmanageable people on earth', as he called them) did not meet the rigorous standards which he set: yet he somehow believed that he, de Gaulle, could hold France to those standards. This was an impossible task and in his heart of hearts he knew it: which is why, in addition to all his other greatness, he was also a truly great pessimist, the last Cassandra of our times.[6]

De Gaulle understood, in the 1960s as much as in 1940, that his power to change history was limited. It had been limited in 1940 because he had so few resources at his disposal; it was limited after 1945 because France's fate, and that of all European countries, now depended on the alignments of the Cold War and on economic growth – both things that were largely beyond the control of any individual and perhaps of any single state. Churchill's restless belief that he personally would be able to change the course of history by, for example, talking to Stalin, was an embarrassing delusion , by this stage.

For English observers, de Gaulle was often an absurdly grandiose figure. But in private he recognised that measure and balance were the key to politics. For this reason, more than because of any moral belief in democracy, he was suspicious of authoritarian rule: 'In the short term dictatorships sometimes achieve great things. But they always finish badly, because, to make the weight of constraint and moral oppression bearable, they are soon forced to drag the country into exaggerated enterprises.'[7]

The difference between Churchill and de Gaulle was illustrated by one apparently small incident on 18 June 1940. Churchill was presented with two memoranda about a Frenchman – a temporary civil servant – who wished to return to France. It was unclear whether he hoped to rally his compatriots against an armistice or whether he proposed himself to join the Pétain government. Churchill was impatient and scribbled in red ink that 'We have shown ... [this man] too much consideration and attention. I recommend leaving him alone. We should certainly not facilitate his journey.'[8]

It was a dramatic display of power – as though a lion had swatted a mosquito. The temporary civil servant, however, was not swept from the face of history. His name was Jean Monnet, the architect of France's post-war economic planning and of the European Community. Everything about Monnet's style contrasted with those of Churchill and de Gaulle. Monnet avoided the limelight and worked behind the scenes. He thought that history rarely revolved around clear-cut choices and that the condemnation of the Pétain government was simplistic, though he did not, as it turned out, join that government. He saw that Britain did not have a choice in 1940 between America and Europe. He went to America to support the French cause during the war, and later believed that America would be most sympathetic to the countries of western Europe if they were united. With regard to Britain in 1940, Monnet believed that it needed a total mobilisation of its society and economy: 'far more revolutionary measures are necessary than have hitherto been taken'. He argued that the era of great powers was over or, at least, that no European country, including Britain and France, could hope to be a great power. He understood that the modern world was made by broad economic forces and that individuals, however brilliant or determined, could do little to resist those forces. Arthur Schlesinger, who had served with the American Office of Strategic Services in both Britain and France during the war, had lunch with Monnet in Washington in March 1962. After it, he wrote:

> A talk with Monnet enforces a fascinating change of perspective. Washington life inculcates a tremendous concern with the immediate and especially with the personal. Monnet could not care less about personalities. He has a lucid and profound sense of deep-running historical tendencies – tendencies which, he is confident, no personality can arrest and no politician can deflect. He could not care less about the attitude of Tory or Labour politicians in England towards the Common Market whatever its politicians may think. Similarly de Gaulle can confuse but not confound the inexorable movement towards economic integration in Europe. Monnet has seen inexorable tendencies effect so many revolutions in his lifetime that his confidence in the future may be easily understood. I must confess that his perspective has the effect of underlining the transience and triviality of so many things that concern me.[9]

De Gaulle and Churchill did not have easy relations with Monnet – though he regarded them both with an amused and wary respect. But de Gaulle grudgingly and quietly acknowledged that Monnet was right. It was largely de Gaulle who recognised that France needed a new style of economic policy after the liberation and, however reluctantly, he recognised that France needed to stay in the European Economic Community in the 1960s. De Gaulle knew that the United States overshadowed Europe and understood that his own anti-American gestures were means of sustaining French prestige but not of restoring French power.

De Gaulle made a difference to post-war France. It is, in particular, hard to see who else could have extracted the country from its involvement in Algeria in 1962. France would have been forced to decolonise eventually but without de Gaulle the decision would have come later and the withdrawal would have been more humiliating and probably occasioned an even greater amount of violence. However, there was also always some sleight of hand behind de Gaulle's politics. He understood that he could only rarely change the course of events and that his function was often to provide a dignified way of accepting the inevitable.

In private, de Gaulle occasionally expressed his exasperation at the artificiality of the role he played. In 1966, he told one of his aides:

> We are in a theatre where I have been contriving an illusion since 1940. Now, I give, or try to give, France the face of a nation which is solid, firm and resolved on expansion, when it is a bovine nation that only thinks of its comfort, which does not want to struggle, or to offend anyone, the Americans no more than the English.[10]

When he was director of the Bibliothèque Nationale in 1990, the great French historian Emmanuel Le Roy Ladurie was required to write an introduction to a book accompanying an exhibition to celebrate de Gaulle's centenary. It was a delicate operation because Le Roy Ladurie's father had been a Vichy minister. Le Roy Ladurie began by expressing his admiration for the 'intuition' that had inspired de Gaulle's stand on 18 June 1940 but then slyly pointed out that this 'bet' would have come to nothing if it had not been for Allied victory in the Second World War and that de Gaulle's later 'success' really owed much to the good fortune of French economic growth. He added that de Gaulle would not be considered great in the way the American founding fathers were because France would never again be a great power in the way the United States had become.*

*Text to Come.

De Gaulle would not have liked the essay, but one suspects that he would not have disagreed with it – and he might well have thought that Le Roy Ladurie, from a conservative Catholic background, understood him better than the former *soixante-huitards* who expressed such breathless admiration for him around 1990.

Adjusting to France's relatively modest position in the post-war world was made easier by three things. First, its defeat at the hands of the Germans encouraged a degree of realism. Unlike the British, the French did not look back to 1940 with nostalgia. Second, de Gaulle created a new sense of France's place in the international order that seemed to replace what the country had lost – France, unlike Britain, lost an empire but found a role. Third, spectacular economic growth between the late 1940s and the mid 1970s – growth that owed something to Jean Monnet and a good deal to circumstances not directly under the control of any individual or agency – made a decline in power and status easier to bear.

An awareness of relative decline hit Britain more painfully and hit her precisely in that period – the early 1960s – when de Gaulle looked to have conjured up a new France. The undignified end of Churchill's life sometimes felt like an awkward metaphor for the fate of the whole country. Theatre reflected this and playwrights in this period often took theatre itself as a metaphor for the falseness they detected in British life – hence the frequency of plays within plays and plays about plays. John Osborne's *The Entertainer* (produced as a play in 1957 and a film in 1960) revolved around ageing music-hall comedian Archie Rice. Tony Richardson, who produced the play later wrote that it was: 'the embodiment of a national mood ... Archie was the future, the decline, the sourness, the ashes of old glory, where Britain was heading.'

Churchill haunted post-war British theatre. The American playwright Arthur Miller recalled giving a lecture in London in 1950: 'the same basic question was asked by one after the other of the audience – why is English theatre so uninteresting?' Miller thought that the answer to this question lay in the English 'class or caste system' which Churchill epitomised. He described an episode in the House of Commons, itself like a scene from a play, when Churchill humiliated Willie Gallacher, the only Communist member, by muttering loudly: 'Take your hands out of your pockets, man!'[11] Around this time, English theatre was dominated by Noel Coward and Terrence Rattigan – both seen unfairly as staid writers and, more fairly, as associated with Churchill.

The revolution of the late 1950s and 60s, which was marked by plays such as *The Entertainer*, provoked a fighting retreat by the Conservative establishment because Lord Chandos (a friend of Churchill's and former minister in his government) was chairman of the newly founded National Theatre from 1962 to 1971. Churchill himself sometimes featured in the plays that offended men such as Chandos. He is the central figure in Howard Brenton's *Churchill Play* (first produced in 1974, the centenary of Churchill's birth, and set in a fictional England of 1984). He is an obscene prop in Joe Orton's *Entertaining Mr Sloane* (1969), which finishes with an object meant to be Churchill's penis being held aloft. Sometimes he is a disconcerting presence even when his name is never uttered – Alan Bennett's *Forty Years On* (1968) draws on writing by some of Churchill's associates (notably Harold Nicolson) and takes its title from the Harrow School song.

The actor Richard Burton, who was cast as Churchill on television and even provided an imitation of Churchill's voice for the *son et lumière* display at Blenheim Palace, once said: 'To play Churchill is to hate him.'* The remark was a reference to Burton's own upbringing in the Welsh working class but perhaps it also expressed

---

*Like many people, Burton did not have a consistent attitude to Churchill, whom he had known since the latter erupted into his dressing room during the interval in a performance of *Hamlet*. The playwright Stanley Price interviewed Burton and Elizabeth Taylor for an American magazine in 1965. The three of them watched Churchill's funeral in floods of tears and champagne. They turned off the sound and Burton himself provided commentary in Churchill's voice.

a feeling that Churchill made an uncomfortable theatrical character precisely because he was such a stagey personality that it was hard to impersonate him without being aware of falsity. British theatre often exposed – most explicitly in the case of Archie Rice – the way comedy could slide into tragedy. Churchill – whose energy and relish for life had once seemed to herald national salvation – was a sad figure in his last years. He was a target for satire but the cruellest of these satires – the cartoons that Malcolm Muggeridge published in *Punch* – were painful, not because they were funny, but because they drew attention to the tragedy of Churchill's old age.

De Gaulle was lucky. Lucky that France prospered under his rule for reasons that had little to do with anything he himself had done. He was lucky that he emerged from the Second World War young enough to have a second career as a peacetime politician. He was also lucky in his reputation. His association with the resistance in the war and then with decolonisation in 1962 meant that he was often portrayed as a defender of freedom – though his action was always guided more by the interests of France than the rights of individuals.

There is something odd about the fact that de Gaulle should have adapted to the modern world better than Churchill. Churchill had after all once been a progressive and always retained an affection for the Liberalism of his youth. On two occasions when he seemed most reactionary – when he denounced the Government of India Act in the early 1930s and when he attacked the Labour Party in his Gestapo speech of 1945 – he wasinspired partly by his admiration for liberal thinkers: John Morley and Friedrich Hayek. Curiously, it was this that made Churchill look backwards. He always felt that the reforming government in which he had served with Asquith and Lloyd George had once been the future and that the two world wars (which, in some ways, he so relished) had also been avoidable catastrophes that brought this *belle époque* to an end. Churchill was haunted by a past that felt close enough to be accessible. Eventually, the Second World War itself, and particularly that early heroic period of his first premiership, became part of the past that he sought to recapture. In contrast, de Gaulle was a reactionary. He sometimes suggested that every regime in France since 1789 had been illegitimate. This made him unsentimental. He looked back with regret but there was an almost playful self-consciousness about any suggestion that the past could be revived. When he said that the pretender to the French throne would be the only satisfactory successor to himself, he meant nothing except perhaps that there would be no satisfactory successor. In June 1960, as he prepared his country for the loss of Algeria, de Gaulle made a speech about his relation to the past:

> It is natural to feel nostalgic for what the Empire was, just as one might regret the gentle light of oil lamps, the splendour of the fleet at sail and the charm of the *temps des équipages*.* But so what!? There is no policy worth anything outside of realities.

It is fitting that a book about these two theatrical men should finish with the playwright they both admired: Shakespeare. In 1944, Laurence Olivier, the man who thirteen years later was to play Archie Rice, made a film of *Henry V*. It was wartime propaganda and dedicated to paratroopers and commandos. People often suggest that the film was 'Churchillian', and Churchill was in 'extasies' when he saw it.[12] But there must have been some who thought that the character of Churchill — old, sentimental, convinced that his past services would deserve gratitude — is Falstaff. Henry — the ruthless young prince who knows the past must die so n the future can be born — looks disconcertingly like de Gaulle.

---

*Literally 'the time of crews'. Perhaps it was an unconscious reference to the memoirs of Elizabeth de Gramont, *Au Temps des Equipages* (1928). This described the decadent world of the grand aristocracy and was just the kind of book that might have excited de Gaulle's prurient disapproval.

NOTES

Unless otherwise stated, place of publication for books in English is London and for books in French is Paris.

I have cited many of de Gaulle's pre-war publications from the collected edition of his work *Le Fil de l'Épée et Autres Écrits*, which encompasses several books as well as articles and unpublished documents. In the Bibliography I have not listed individual articles included in this collection but I have given details for each pre-war book (with its original date of publication) separately.

I have sought to keep notes to a minimum. Remarks made in the British parliament, except for wartime occasions when the House of Commons met in secret session, can be found in Hansard. Churchill's wartime speeches are easily located on the World Wide Web. The speeches, interviews and press conferences given by de Gaulle after 1959 are also easily available on the Web. Even those who do not understand French will gain something from watching these extraordinary performances. I particularly like the interview in which he mocked Christian Democrat enthusiasm for Europe saying 'one can jump in one's chair like a mountain goat' and then, for a moment, de Gaulle huge body does indeed seem to rise out of his chair. See https://www.ina.fr/ina-eclaire-actu/video/i12107935/charles-de-gaulle-comme-un-cabri-l-europe-l-europe-l-europe.

ABBREVIATIONS USED IN THE NOTES AND BIBLIOGRAPHY
CAC   Churchill Archive Centre at Churchill College Cambridge
CAD   Cadbury Research Library, University of Birmingham
LHCMA Liddell Hart Centre for Military Archives, King's College London
TNA   The National Archives at Kew

INTRODUCTION
1   In the first draft of his history of the Second World War, Churchill recalled having said 'l'homme de la destinée'. William Deakin, his research assistant, discreetly corrected his French in the published version.

David Reynolds, *In Command of History: Churchill Fighting and Writing the Second World War* (this edn, 2005), p. 167. As pointed out later in the Introduction, de Gaulle denied that these words had been spoken at all. Churchill himself seems to have appreciated that there might be doubt about what he had said. In the telegram that he sent to de Gaulle on 9 May 1945 (the day after the German surrender), he wrote: 'Although we had our ups and downs, I have never forgotten that day at Tours when I passed you amid the sorrowful crowd and said, in the hearing of several, "There is the man of destiny"', CAC CHAR 20/227/B.

2   François Kersaudy, *Churchill and de Gaulle* (1981).
3   Reynolds, *In Command of History*, p. 112.
4   John Colville, *The Fringes of Power: Downing Street Diaries, 1939–1955* (1985), 16 May 1940, p. 132.
5   Maurice Agulhon, *De Gaulle: Histoire, Symbole, Mythe* (2000). Thinking about de Gaulle also permeates Pierrre Nora (ed.), *Les Lieux de Mémoire* (three vol., this edn, 1997).
6   Alfred Fabre Luce, *L'Anniversaire* (1971), p. 1.
7   Winston Churchill, *Great Contemporaries* (this edn, 1947), p. 5.
8   TNA CAB 66/22/47, de Gaulle to Eden, 8 March 1942.
9   Robert Boothby, *Recollections of a Rebel* (1978), p. 45.
10 Edward Marsh and Christopher Hassall, *Ambrosia and Small Beer: The Record of a Correspondence of Edward Marsh and Christopher Hassall* (1964), p. 200.
11 Andrew Roberts, *Churchill: Walking with Destiny* (2018), p. 147.
12 Philippe de Gaulle, *De Gaulle Mon Père: Entretiens avec Michel Tauriac*, I (2003), p. 440.
13 Alain Peyrefitte, *C'Était de Gaulle* (this edn, 2002), 17 June 1965, p. 30.
14 Gaston Palewski, 'De Gaulle Avant de Gaulle', *Revue des Deux Mondes*, April 1988.
15 Richard Toye, *The Roar of the Lion: The Untold Story of Churchill's World War II Speeches* (Oxford, 2013), p. 12.
16 Harold Nicolson, *Diaries and Letters, 1939–1945*, edited by Nigel Nicolson (1967), 11 April 1940, p. 70.
17 https://history.state.gov/historicaldocuments/frus1940v01/d28, report by the under secretary of state (Welles) on his special mission to Europe. Account of meeting with Churchill, 12 March 1940.
18 Charles de Gaulle, *Mémoires d'Espoir: Le Renouveau, 1958–1962/ L'Effort, 1962–* (this edn, 1980), p. 26.
19 Charles de Gaulle, *Lettres, Notes et Carnets, 1919–Juin 1940* (1980), p. 255.

20 Nicolson, *Diaries and Letters, 1939–1945*, 16 February 1942, p. 212: 'I fear a slump in public opinion which will deprive Winston of his legend.'

21 Philippe Barrès, *Charles de Gaulle* (1941). See also Eric Jennings, *Free French Africa in World War II: The African Resistance* (2015) and Denis Saurat, 'Attention au Tchad', *La France Libre*, 20 June 1941.

22 Éric Roussel, later to be a journalist and biographer of de Gaulle, recalls hearing de Gaulle's name for the first time in 1958 (when he was seven); he vaguely assumed that there must be some association between this name and the ancient Gauls. Éric Roussel, *C'Était le Monde d'Avant: Carnets d'un Biographe* (2022), p. 39. Admiral Leahy, American ambassador to Vichy, insisted in his post-war memoirs that Gaullism referred to 'the ancient name of France' and did not imply loyalty to de Gaulle. W. D. Leahy, *I Was There* (1950), p. 56.

23 Kenneth Rose, *Who's In, Who's Out: The Journals of Kenneth Rose*, I: *1944–1979*, edited by D. R. Thorpe (2018), 18 February 1960, p. 153.

24 https://bdohp.chu.cam.ac.uk/wp-content/uploads/sites/8/2022/07/ Wood.pdf. Interview with Sir Andrew Wood; Alexander Werth, *Russia at War, 1939–1945* (1964), p. 832.

25 Maurice Ashley, *Churchill as Historian* (1968), p. 2.

26 Martin Gilbert, *In Search of Churchill: A Historian's Journey* (1994), p. 138.

27 Jean-Noël Jeanneney, *Le Rocher de Süsten: Mémoires*, I: *1942–1982* (2020), pp. 280 and 275.

28 John Stewart Collis, 'Homage to a Leader', *The Spectator*, 30 January 1982.

29 Toye, *The Roar of the Lion*, p. 63.

30 François Nourissier, *À Défaut de Génie* (2000), p. 111.

31 Julian Jackson, *A Certain Idea of France: The Life of Charles de Gaulle* (2018), p. 765.

32 Colville, *The Fringes of Power*, 13 December 1940, p. 311.

33 Jean Oberlé, *La Vie d'Artiste* (1956), pp. 213–14.

34 CAD Avon Papers, APM 23/19/12, Eden to Chauvel, 22 November 1959.

35 Claude Mauriac, *Un Autre de Gaulle: Journal, 1944–1954* (1970), 3 September 1944, p. 21.

36 Claude Guy, *En Écoutant de Gaulle: Journal, 1946–1949* (1996), 4 November 1947, p. 352. Guy commented with reference to the suicide of Winant, the former US ambassador to London, that de Gaulle never criticised suicides.

37 François Mauriac, *De Gaulle* (1964), p. 78.

38 David Lough, *No More Champagne: Churchill and His Money* (this edn, 2016), p. 318.

39 TNA PREM 11/201, Churchill to Jacob, 15 August 1952.

40 De Gaulle, *Mémoires d'Éspoir*, p. 37.

41 Henri Amouroux, *Le 18 Juin* (this edn, 1990), p. 364.

42 George Kennan, *Memoirs, 1925–1950* (this edn, 1967), pp. 454–5.

I. EARLY LIVES, 1874–1930

1   Randolph S. Churchill, *Winston S. Churchill, I: Youth, 1874–1900* (1966).

2   Diana Cooper, *Trumpets from the Steep* (1960), p. 189.

3   David Lough, *No More Champagne: Churchill and His Money* (this edn, 2016), p. 141.

4   TNA FO 371/28592, Morton to Mack, 3 October 1941.

5   TNA CAB 66/26/25, memorandum by Eden, 14 July 1942, recounting remarks made by de Gaulle on 3 July. De Gaulle referred to 'petite noblesse de campagne ... et j'en suis'.

6   Alain Peyrefitte, *C'Était de Gaulle* (this edn, 2002), 12 June 1963, p. 779.

7   John Colville, *The Fringes of Power: Downing Street Diaries, 1939–1955* (1985), 30 October 1940, p. 278.

8   CAC Papers of Duff Cooper, DUFC 4/8, memorandum by Macmillan, 5 January 1944.

9   Christine Clerc, *Les de Gaulle: Une Famille Française* (2000), p. 35.

10 Charles de Gaulle, *La France et Son Armée*, first published 1938, in Charles de Gaulle, *Le Fil de l'Épée et Autres Écrits* (this edn, 1994), pp. 327–500, p. 451.

11 Norman Rose, 'Churchill and Zionism', in Robert Blake and Wm. Roger Louis (eds.), *Churchill* (Oxford, 1993), pp. 147–66, p. 148.

12 Éric Roussel, 'De Gaulle et Barrès: Gaullisme et Gaullistes dans la France de l'Est sous la IVe République' [online]. Rennes: Presses Universitaires de Rennes, 2009 (generated 22 April 2024). Available on the Internet: <http://books.openedition.org/pur/122736>. ISBN: 978-2-7535-6668-2. DOI: https://doi.org/10.4000/books.pur.122736.

13 Lucien Rebatet, *Les Décombres* (1942).

14 Stéphane Rials, 'Pour un Anniversaire: La Conception du Pouvoir de Georges Pompidou', *La Revue Administrative*, 37, 218 (1984), pp. 126–32.

15 Jean-François Revel, *Le Style du Général* (1959), p. 171.

16 Winston Churchill, *The World Crisis: The Aftermath* (1929), p. 155.

17 Graham Farmelo, *Churchill's Bomb: A Hidden History of Science, War and Politics* (2013), pp. 37–8.

18 John Simon, *Retrospect: The Memoirs of the Rt. Hon. Viscount Simon* (1952), p. 37.

19   Martin Gilbert, *In Search of Churchill: A Historian's Journey* (1994), p. 82.

20   A. G. Gardiner, *Prophets, Priests and Kings* (this edn, 1917), p. 228.

21   Peter Clarke, *Mr Churchill's Profession: Statesman, Orator, Writer* (2012).

22   Violet Bonham Carter, *Winston Churchill as I Knew Him* (1965), p. 145.

23   David Lindsay, *The Crawford Papers: The Journals of David Lindsay, Twenty-Seventh Earl of Crawford and Tenth Earl of Balcarres, 1871–1940, during the Years 1892–1940*, edited by John Vincent (Manchester, 1984), 17 February 1906, p. 93.

24   Ibid., 18 April 1910, p. 151.

25   Philippe de Gaulle, *De Gaulle Mon Père: Entretiens avec Michel Tauriac*, I (2003), p. 51.

26   Ibid., p. 54.

27   Charles de Gaulle, 'La Condition des Cadres dans l'Armée', written in 1930 or 1931, in Charles de Gaulle, *Le Fil de l'Épée et Autres Écrits* (this edn, 1994), pp. 659–70, p. 669.

28   De Gaulle to Audet, 16 January 1928, in Charles de Gaulle, *Lettres, Notes et Carnets, 1919–Juin 1940* (1980), pp. 329–30.

29   Note to accompany publication of *La France et son Armée*, in ibid., pp. 474–5.

30   Daniel Halévy, 'Un Livre sur l'Armée de Métier', *Revue des Deux Mondes*, October 1934.

31   Gaston Palewski, cited in C. L. Sulzberger, *The Last of the Giants* (this edn, 1972), p. 9.

32   Claude Guy, *En Écoutant de Gaulle: Journal, 1946–1949* (1996), 14 October 1948, p. 442.

33   Ibid., 23 November 1946, p. 160.

34   Lindsay, *The Crawford Papers*, 5 May 1899, pp. 54–5.

35   Ibid., 12 August 1912, p. 279.

36   Ibid., 9 May 1910, p. 153.

37   Ibid., 3 May 1914, p. 333.

38   Ibid., 1 June 1911, p. 186.

39   Edward Grey of Fallodan, *Twenty-Five Years, 1892–1916*, II (this edn, 1928), pp. 59–60.

40   Roy Jenkins, *Churchill* (2001), p. 230.

41   Edward Marsh, *A Number of People: A Book of Reminiscences* (1939), p. 247.

42   Richard Toye, *Lloyd George and Churchill: Rivals for Greatness* (this edn, 2008), p. 146.

43   Grey, *Twenty-Five Years, 1892–1916*, II, p. 299.

44   Churchill, *The World Crisis: The Aftermath*, p. 276.

45   John Colville, *The Churchillians* (1981), p. 180.
46   Winston Churchill, *Great Contemporaries* (this edn, 1947), p. 229.
47   John Maynard Keynes, *The Economic Consequences of Mr Churchill* (1925), p. 10.
48   Churchill, *Great Contemporaries*, p. 230.
49   Victor Germains, *The Tragedy of Winston Churchill* (1931).

2. GATHERING STORMS, 1930–39
1   George Orwell, *The Complete Works of George Orwell: A Patriot After All, 1940–1941*, edited by Peter Davison (this edn, 2000), p. 182.
2   Charles de Gaulle, *Lettres, Notes et Carnets, 1919–Juin 1940* (1980), p. 401.
3   Martin Gilbert (ed.), *Winston Churchill and Emery Reves: Correspondence, 1937–1964* (Austin, TX, 1997), p. 11.
4   De Gaulle, *Lettres, Notes et Carnets, 1919–Juin 1940*, p. 494.
5   Charles de Gaulle, *Vers l'Armée de Métier*, first published 1934, in Charles de Gaulle, *Le Fil de l'Épée et Autres Écrits* (1994), pp. 226–326, p. 240.
6   David Reynolds, 'Churchill's Writing of History: Appeasement, Autobiography and "The Gathering Storm"', *Transactions of the Royal Historical Society*, 11 (2001), pp. 221–47. Churchill had used the phrase 'Gathering Storm' in an article of 30 October 1936. Winston Churchill, *Step by Step, 1936–1939* (1939), pp. 74–7.
7   Judith Brown, 'Imperial Facade: Some Constraints upon and Contradictions in the British Position in India, 1919–35', *Transactions of the Royal Historical Society*, 26 (1976), pp. 35–52.
8   John Gallagher and Anil Seal, 'Britain and India between the Wars', *Modern Asian Studies*, 15, 3 (1981), pp. 387–414.
9   Colin Thornton-Kemsley, *Through Winds and Tides* (1974), p. 48.
10   House of Commons, 5 June 1935.
11   John Colville, *The Fringes of Power: Downing Street Diaries, 1939–1955* (1985), 16 May 1940, p. 132.
12   David Lindsay, *The Crawford Papers: The Journals of David Lindsay, Twenty-Seventh Earl of Crawford and Tenth Earl of Balcarres, 1871–1940, during the Years 1892–1940*, edited by John Vincent (Manchester, 1984), 28 February 1935, p. 559.
13   Basil Liddell Hart, *The Liddell Hart Memoirs, I: 1895–1938* (1965), p. 205.
14   Martin Gilbert, *Winston S. Churchill, V: The Prophet of Truth, 1922–1939* (1976), pp. 480–1.

15 Victor Feske, *From Belloc to Churchill: Private Scholars, Public Culture and the Crisis of British Liberalism, 1900–1939* (Chapel Hill, NC, 1996).

16 Winston Churchill, *Great Contemporaries* (this edn, 1947), p. 72.

17 John Gallagher, 'Nationalisms and the Crisis of Empire, 1919–1922', *Modern Asian Studies*, 15, 3 (1981), pp. 355–68.

18 Edward Halifax, *Fullness of Days* (1957), p. 151.

19 Austen Chamberlain, *The Austen Chamberlain Diary Letters: The Correspondence of Sir Austen Chamberlain with his Sisters Hilda and Ida, 1916–1937*, edited by Robert Self (Cambridge, 1995), letter to Hilda, 28 November 1931, p. 395.

20 Duff Cooper, *Old Men Forget: The Autobiography of Duff Cooper* (1953), pp. 171–2.

21 LHCMA LH11/1945/8, 'Notes for History – May 1945', note of conversation Hankey, 23 May 1945.

22 Churchill, *Great Contemporaries*, p. 210.

23 House of Commons, 28 November 1934.

24 Keith Neilson, 'The Defence Requirements Sub-Committee, British Strategic Foreign Policy, Neville Chamberlain and the Path to Appeasement', *The English Historical Review*, 118, 477 (2003), pp. 651–84.

25 Winston Churchill, 'A Testing Time for France', first published 18 September 1936, in Winston Churchill, *Step by Step, 1936–1939* (1939), pp. 62–5.

26 Ivan Maisky, *The Maisky Diaries: The Wartime Revelations of Stalin's Ambassador in London*, edited by Gabriel Gorodetsky (this edn, 2016), 4 September 1938, p. 125.

27 Winston Churchill, 'Enemies to the Left', first published 4 September 1936, in Winston Churchill, *Step by Step*, pp. 59–61.

28 Winston Churchill, 'The Communist Schism', first published 16 October 1936, in ibid., pp. 70–3.

29 Editor's note in Noel Coward, *The Letters of Noel Coward*, edited by Barry Day (2007), p. 340.

30 Alexander Cadogan, *The Diaries of Sir Alexander Cadogan, 1938–1945*, edited by David Dilks (1971), 1 July 1938, p. 84.

31 Asked whether his father had friends, Philippe de Gaulle advanced the names of Nachin and Mayer, along with that of Gustave Ditte. Philippe de Gaulle, *De Gaulle Mon Père: Entretiens avec Michel Tauriac*, I (2003), pp. 223–4.

32 Gaston Palewski, 'De Gaulle Avant de Gaulle', *Revue des Deux Mondes* (April 1988), pp. 92–9.

33 Charles de Gaulle, 'Comment Faire une Armée de Métier', first published in *Revue Hebdomadaire*, 1 June 1935, in Charles de Gaulle, *Le Fil de l'Épée et Autres Écrits*, pp. 552–62, p. 555.

34 *Vers l'Armée de Métier*, in Charles de Gaulle, *Le Fil de l'Épée et Autres Écrits*, pp. 226–326, p. 267.

35 De Gaulle himself pointed out that Guderian had cited him in an article in a German military review. Charles de Gaulle, *Lettres, Notes et Carnets, 1919–Juin 1940*, de Gaulle to Reynaud, 14 February 1938, p. 465.

36 Albert Speer, *Inside the Third Reich* (1969), p. 170.

37 Alain de Boissieu, *Pour Combattre avec de Gaulle, 1940–1946* (1981), p. 316.

38 Jacques Binoche, ' L'Allemagne et le Lieutenant-Colonel Charles de Gaulle', *Revue Historique*, 248, 1 (1972), pp. 107–16.

39 David Reynolds, *In Command of History: Churchill Fighting and Writing the Second World War* (this edn, 2005), p. 99.

40 LHCMA LH11/1945/25, 'Mr Churchill's calculations.' And LH11/1945/26, 'Pronouncements of Mr Winston Churchill'. Both documents are lists of Churchill's public statements.

41 Cited in Alex Danchev, *Alchemist of War: The Life of Liddell Hart* (this edn, 1999), p. 121.

42 Handwritten notes in edition of *Vers l'Armée de Métier* (1934) in Liddell Hart Centre for Military Archives.

43 Churchill, preface, *Step by Step*, p. 9.

44 The book was published in 1940, though written earlier.

45 Alistair Horne, *Harold Macmillan, I, 1894–1945* (this edn, New York, 1989), p. 116.

46 Lindsay, *The Crawford Papers*, 18 February 1940, p. 614.

47 https://www.iwm.org.uk/collections/item/object/80016926. Interview with John Glassbrook.

3. THE FALL OF FRANCE

1 Winston Churchill, 'The New French Government', first published 14 April 1938, in Winston Churchill, *Step by Step* (1939), pp. 231–4.

2 Claude Guy, *En Écoutant de Gaulle: Journal, 1946–1949* (1996), mid-December 1946, p. 173.

3 R. A. Butler, *The Art of the Possible: The Memoirs of Lord Butler* (1971), p. 82. The original note can be found in Trinity College Cambridge, Papers of Lord Butler of Saffron Walden, RAB G 11/12, note to Halifax and Cadogan, 11 January 1940.

4 Clarissa Eden, *A Memoir: From Churchill to Eden*, edited by Cate Haste (this edn, 2008), p. 51.

5 Winston Churchill, *The Second World War, I: The Gathering Storm* (1948), p. 519.

6 https://history.state.gov/historicaldocuments/frus1940v01/d28. Report by the under secretary of state (Welles) on his special mission to Europe. Account of meetings with Reynaud on 9 and 14 March 1940.

7 Claude Mauriac, *Un Autre de Gaulle: Journal, 1944–1954* (1970), 7 March 1947, p. 267.

8 Peter Fleming, *Invasion 1940: An Account of the German Preparations and the British Counter-Measures* (1957), p. 23.

9 Alexander Cadogan, *The Diaries of Sir Alexander Cadogan, 1938–1945*, edited by David Dilks (1971), pp. 283, 284, 285, 286, 287, 288, 289, 292.

10 Alan Brooke, *War Diaries, 1939–1945: Field Marshal Lord Alanbrooke*, edited by Alex Danchev and Daniel Todman (this edn, 2002), p. 74.

11 Ibid., p. 82.

12 Paul de Villelume, *Journal d'une Défaite: Août 1939–Juin 1940* (1976), 13 March 1940, p. 233. This is the same meeting that Reynaud described to Sumner Welles (see above). Churchill himself wrote that he went to Paris to persuade the French to accept the mining of the Rhine and his official biographer accepts this interpretation. Neither mentions the meeting with Reynaud. Martin Gilbert, *Winston S. Churchill, VI: Finest Hour, 1939–1941* (1983), p. 187.

13 Emmanuel Berl, *La Fin de la IIIe République: 10 Juillet 1940* (1968), p. 57.

14 Cadogan, *The Diaries of Sir Alexander Cadogan*, 28 May 1940, p. 291.

15 Butler, *The Art of the Possible*, p. 84.

16 De Villelume, *Journal d'une Défaite*, 6 June 1940, p. 393.

17 Ibid.

18 TNA CAB 65/7/54, War Cabinet, 9 June 1940.

19 Roland de Margerie, *Journal, 1939–1940* (2010), pp. 297–300. Written retrospectively in September 1940.

20 De Villelume, *Journal d'une Défaite*, 10 to 14 June, pp. 402–22.

21 De Margerie, *Journal*, 11 June, p. 311.

22 TNA CAB 66/26/25, memorandum by Eden, 14 July 1942, recounting remarks made by de Gaulle on 3 July.

23 Gladwyn Jebb, *The Memoirs of Lord Gladwyn* (1972), p. 310.

24 De Villelume, *Journal d'une Défaite*, 11 June 1940, p. 404.

25 TNA CAB 65/7/63, War Cabinet, 16 June 1940. Meeting of 10.15 a.m.

26 De Villelume, *Journal d'une Défaite*, 16 June 1940, pp. 427–9.

27 Monnet had suggested to Churchill on 4 June that Britain should raise 'an

army of pioneers' to build fortifications while the Expeditionary
Force was sent back to France. Jean Monnet, *Mémoires* (1976), p. 166.
On Monnet's desire to see more aggressive mobilisation in Britain
see also TNA PREM 7/6, Morton to Churchill, 18 June 1940.

28 TNA CAB 65/7/64, War Cabinet, 16 June 1940, meeting of 3 p.m.

29 Ibid.

30 Charles de Gaulle, *Mémoires de Guerre, I: L'Appel, 1940–1942* (this edn,
1980), p. 86.

4. LONDON CALLING, 1940

1 Charles de Gaulle, *Mémoire d'Espoir: Le Renouveau, 1958–1962/L'Éffort,
1962–* (this edn, 1980), p. 25.

2 Aurélie Luneau, *L'Appel du 18 Juin* (2020), p. 224.

3 TNA FCO 33/85, note by Palliser, 18 June 1968.

4 TNA CAB 65/7/38, War Cabinet, 27 May 1940. Attached record of
telephone conversation between Churchill and Spears. The call to turn
against the Belgian king was notable because it was widely believed that
Weygand himself (who had been raised by an adoptive father in France)
was an illegitimate child of the Belgian royal family.

5 Nicolas Baverez, *Raymond Aron* (this edn, 2005), p. 202; Jules Moch,
Rencontres avec de Gaulle (1971); René Cassin, *Les Hommes Partis de Rien:
Le Réveil de la France Abattue, 1940–1941* (1975), p. 56.

6 Claude Hettier de Boislambert, 'Juin–Juillet 40: À Londres avec de
Gaulle', *Revue des Deux Mondes*, April 1978.

7 Philippe de Gaulle, *De Gaulle Mon Père: Entretiens avec Michel Tauriac*,
I (2003), p. 138.

8 Caroline Glorion, *Geneviève de Gaulle Anthonioz: Résistances* (this edn,
2015), p. 24.

9 Maurice Garçon, *Journal, 1939–1945*, edited Pascal Fouché and Pascale
Froment (this edn, 2017), 29 June 1940, pp. 198–9.

10 Emmanuel Berl, *La Fin de la Troisième Ille: 10 Juillet 1940* (1968),
pp. 148–9.

11 George Orwell, 'Propaganda and Demotic Speech', *Persuasion* (Summer,
1944).

12 John Ramsden, *Man of the Century: Winston Churchill and his Legend since
1945* (2002), pp. 62–5.

13 Richard Toye, *The Roar of the Lion: The Untold Story of Churchill's World
War II Speeches* (Oxford, 2013), p. 31.

14 John Colville, The *Fringes of Power: Downing Street Diaries, 1939–1955* (1985), 1 August 1940, p. 207.

15 David Fraser, *War and Shadows: Memoirs of General Sir David Fraser* (2002), pp. 136–7.

16 Trevor Harvey, *An Army of Brigadiers: Brigade Commanders at the Battle of Arras of 1917* (Solihull, 2017).

17 TNA WO 193/222, 'Points for Consideration', 24 June 1940, unsigned. See also TNA PREM 7/8, on 23 June, the Committee on French Resistance expressed the hope that Charbonneau, Béthouart and de Gaulle might make a joint appeal to Noguès.

18 Jean Charbonneau *Contribution à l'Histoire de la Ile Guerre Mondiale: L'Envers du 18 Juin* (1969).

19 TNA FO 892/15, 'Future Movements of General de Gaulle', unsigned and undated.

20 TNA PREM 7/2, Morton to Churchill, 26 July 1940.

21 Alan Lascelles, *King's Counsellor. Abdication and War: The Diaries of Sir Alan Lascelles*, edited by Duff Hart-Davis (2006), 28 July 1942, p. 43.

22 Edward Spears, *Fulfilment of a Mission: The Spears Mission to Syria and Lebanon, 1941–1944* (1977), p. 214.

23 Charles de Gaulle, *Mémoires de Guerre, I: L'Appel, 1940–1942* (this edn, 1980), p. 143.

24 Moch, *Rencontres avec de Gaulle*, p. 32.

25 Philippe de Gaulle, *De Gaulle Mon Père*, I, p. 205.

26 Alan Brooke, *War Diaries, 1939–1945: Field Marshal Lord Alanbrooke*, edited by Alex Danchev and Daniel Todman (this edn, 2002), p. 101.

27 TNA FO 371/28545, 2 September 1941, 'Points to be Made to General de Gaulle'.

28 TNA PREM 3/186A/7, note for circulation in Cabinet, 8 July 1942.

29 TNA FO 954/4B/421, telegram from High Commission in South African to Dominions Office, 24 March 1942: 'Hope it is realised that continued retention here of Vichy Minister and Consuls at specific desire and request of United Kingdom Government is bound to become increasingly embarrassing for Smuts.' The British did eventually encourage Canada to break with Vichy in April 1942. See TNA FO 954/8A/225, telegram from Dominions Office to Canadian government, 24 April 1942. See also CAC CHAR 20/45 High Commisioner in Canada to Dominions Office 24 November 1941.

30 Colville, *The Fringes of Power*, 8 July 1940, p. 187.

31 After his capture, General Frère, correctly sensing that he would not survive, asked a fellow prisoner to transmit a message to de Gaulle that

he, Frère, had voted against the death sentence. De Gaulle received this information without interest. Georges Pompidou, *Pour Rétablir une Vérite* (1982), p. 81.

32   TNA PREM 3/186A/5, Churchill to Halifax, 25 July 1940.

33   TNA CAB 66/9/5, 'Visit to Morocco', report by Cooper, 27 June 1940.

34   TNA CAB 66/9/6, 'Situation in Algeria and French Morocco', memorandum by Cooper, 28 June 1940.

35   TNA PREM 3/184/9, note to Churchill, 21 July 1942.

36   TNA PREM 3/186A/5, note by de Margerie, 27 July 1940.

37   TNA CO 968/31/7, telegram for de Gaulle from de Margerie, 8 April 1941.

38   Guillaume Piketty, *Français Libre: Pierre de Chevigné* (2022).

39   Jean-François Muracciole, *Les Français Libres: l'Autre Résistance* (2010).

40   https://www.iwm.org.uk/collections/item/object/80019913. Interview with Rolf Weinberg.

41   TNA CAB 65/8/1, War Cabinet, 1 July 1940.

42   TNA CAB 65/8/3, War Cabinet, 2 July 1940.

43   Luneau, *L'Appel du 18 Juin*, p. 99.

44   Harold Nicolson, *Diaries and Letters, 1939–1945*, edited by Nigel Nicolson (1967), 28 March 1943, p. 286.

45   Lucien Neuwirth, *Que la Vie Soit!* (1979), p. 30.

46   TNA FO 371/169108, note by J. Shakespeare, 1 February 1963.

47   Jean Oberlé, *La Vie d'Artiste* (1956), p. 215.

48   TNA CAB 67/8/11, memorandum by Churchill, 9 August 1940.

49   Winston Churchill, *Secret Session Speeches*, compiled by Charles Eade (1946), p. 5.

50   TNA CAB 66/9/44, Churchill to CIGS and others, 15 July 1940, memorandum by Churchill, 10 July and memorandum from the First Lord of the Admiralty, 12 July.

51   Brooke, *War Diaries, 1939–1945*, pp. 112–13.

52   Ibid., 16 October, p. 116; 24 October, p. 119.

53   Ibid., 10 January 1941, p. 134.

54   TNA PREM 7/6, Morton to Churchill, 3 June 1940. Churchill had enquired into the means by which radio communication between British units would be maintained after invasion.

55   Clarissa Eden, *A Memoir: From Churchill to Eden*, edited by Cate Haste (this edn, 2008), p. 55.

56   Oliver Harvey, *The War Diaries of Oliver Harvey, 1941–1945*, edited by John Harvey (1978), 8 July 1941, p. 17.

57   Paul de Villelume, *Journal d'une Défaite, 23 Août–16 Juin 1940* (1976), 11 June 1940, p. 412.

58 Fred E. Pollock, 'Roosevelt, the Ogdensburg Agreement, and the British Fleet: All Done with Mirrors', *Diplomatic History*, 5, 3 (1981), pp. 203–19.

59 De Gaulle, *Mémoire de Guerre*, I, p. 109.

60 Ibid.

61 TNA CAB 65/7/63, War Cabinet, 16 June 1940.

62 Anthony Montague Browne, *Long Sunset: The Memoirs of Churchill's Last Private Secretary* (1995), p. 160. 'His great heroine, or indeed hero for that matter, was Joan of Arc.' Churchill had written to his wife that Joan was 'the winner in the whole of French history', Andrew Roberts, *Churchill: Walking with Destiny* (2018), p. 444.

63 https://www.iwm.org.uk/collections/item/object/80018424. Interview with Elaine Barr.

64 Robert Mengin, *No Laurels for de Gaulle* (1966).

65 De Gaulle, *Mémoires de Guerre*, I, p. 166.

66 Robert Bruce Lockhart, *The Diaries of Sir Robert Bruce Lockhart, II: 1939–1965*, edited by Kenneth Young (1980), pp. 31–2.

67 TNA FO 660/16, report by Mack, 28 September 1943.

68 TNA PREM 3/120/4, note to Strang from Somerville Smith, 24 September 1941.

69 Luneau, *L'Appel du 18 Juin*, p. 150.

70 Jacques Duchesne, *Deux Jours avec Churchill: Londres, 21 Octobre 1940 – Paris, 11 Novembre 1944* (2008).

71 TNA FO 954/8A/136, Vansittart to Eden, 31 December 1940.

72 TNA FO 954/8B/369, Eden to Peake, 28 January 1943.

73 Philippe de Gaulle, *De Gaulle Mon Père*, I, p. 52.

5. MODUS VIVDENDI, JULY 1940–DECEMBER 1941

1 TNA CAB 66/13/1, Churchill to Chiefs of Staff Commitee, 15 October 1940.

2 Claude Guy, *En Écoutant de Gaulle: Journal, 1946–1949* (1996), 14 March 1947, p. 280.

3 TNA CAB 65/8/6, War Cabinet, 5 July 1940.

4 Anthony Montague Browne, *Long Sunset: Memoirs of Winston Churchill's Last Private Secretary* (1995), p. 160.

5 Robert Mengin, *No Laurels for de Gaulle* (1966), p. 98.

6 John Colville, *The Fringes of Power: Downing Street Diaries, 1939–1955* (1985), 13 December 1940, p. 311.

7 TNA CAB 79/6/12, Chiefs of Staff Committee, 13 August 1940.

8   CAC, papers of Edward Spears, SPRS 5/36, Spears to Churchill,
     17 September 1940.

9   TNA PREM 7/6, Military Mission Douala to War Office, 2 November
     1940. See also attached telegram from Colonel Williams contradicting
     Spears, 27 November 1940.

10   TNA FO 954/8A/165, Parr to Foreign Office, 14 May 1941.

11   TNA CAB 65/15/11, War Cabinet, confidential annex, 26 September
     1940.

12   TNA CAB 66/12/26, 'Policy Towards the Vichy Government',
     memorandum by the Admiralty, 30 September 1940.

13   TNA CAB 66/12/27, draft telegram from Foreign Office to Madrid
     embassy, attached to memorandum by Halifax, 1 October 1940.

14   TNA CAB 65/16/16, War Cabinet, confidential annex, 30 December
     1940.

15   TNA FO 954/31A/259, Keyes to Eden, 30 December 1941.

16   TNA FO 954/8A/191, Amery to Eden, 14 November 1941.

17   TNA PREM 7/3, Morton to Churchill, 14 November 1940: 'He
     [Weygand] is not pro-British but he has loathed Germans ever since
     1870. He has a morbid sense of duty. If he heard de Gaulle's broadcast
     on 11 November he would be outwardly furious but inwardly afraid. He
     worshipped Foch and worships an imaginary France of his own creation.'

18   Winston Churchill, *The World Crisis: The Aftermath* (1929), p. 271.

19   TNA CAB 65/10/5, War Cabinet, 8 November 1940.

20   TNA CAC SPRS 5/37, de Gaulle to Ismay for Churchill, 25 October
     1940.

21   TNA FO 371/28240, telegram de Gaulle to Weygand, 2 March 1941.

22   Charles de Gaulle, *Mémoires de Guerre, I: L'Appel, 1940–1942* (this edn,
     1980), p. 187.

23   CAC SPRS 5/37, Williams to Spears, 25 October 1940.

24   Colville, *The Fringes of Power*, 2 October 1940, pp. 255–6.

25   CAC SPRS 5/36, Foreign Office to Spears Mission, 22 October 1940. A
     summary of the Vichy reply to the last communication from the British
     was enclosed for de Gaulle.

26   TNA CAB 65/10/6, Churchill to War Cabinet, 11 November 1940.

27   TNA CAB 66/13/28, memorandum by Churchill, 14 November 1940.

28   TNA PREM 3/186A/7, Churchill to Sargent, 20 December 1941.

29   TNA CO 323/1791/38, meeting at the Foreign Office, chaired by Strang,
     6 September 1940.

30   TNA CAB 65/9/40, Halifax to War Cabinet, 28 October 1940.

31   De Gaulle, *Mémoires de Guerre*, I, p. 153.

32 TNA FO 954/8A/173, record of meeting between Churchill and de Gaulle, 12 September 1941, attached to note from Morton to Harvey, 15 September 1941.

33 Colville, *The Fringes of Power*, 9 January 1941, p. 330.

34 TNA CO 323/1791/38, meeting at the Foreign Office, chaired by Strang, 6 September 1940.

35 De Gaulle, *Mémoires de Guerre*, I, p. 186.

36 Peter Coats, *Of Generals and Gardens: The Autobiography of Peter Coats* (1976), p. 94.

37 William Maitland Wilson, *Eight Years Overseas, 1939–1947* (1948), p. 110.

36 Ibid., p. 118.

39 A. B. Gaunson, 'Churchill, de Gaulle, Spears and the Levant Affair, 1941', *The Historical Journal*, 27, 3 (1984), pp. 697–713.

40 Coats, *Of Generals and Gardens*, p. 113.

41 CAC DUFC 4/8, memorandum by Macmillan, 5 January 1944.

42 TNA FO 954/8A/165, Parr to Foreign Office, 14 May 1941.

43 TNA FO 371/28545, Churchill to Eden, 1 September 1941.

44 TNA FO 954/8A/173, record of meeting between Churchill and de Gaulle, 12 September 1941, attached to note from Morton to Harvey, 15 September 1941.

45 TNA CAB 65/19/29, War Cabinet, 15 September 1941.

46 TNA FO 954/8A/173, record of meeting between Churchill and de Gaulle, 12 September 1941, attached to note from Morton to Harvey, 15 September 1941.

47 TNA PREM 3/120/4, Somerville-Smith to Strang, 24 September 1941.

48 TNA PREM 3/120/4, note by Churchill, 23 September 1941.

49 TNA PREM 3/120/4, Eden to Churchill, 26 September 1941.

50 TNA FO 371/28545, Eden to Churchill, 31 August 1941.

51 TNA FO 371/28545, Morton to Cadogan, 3 September 1941.

6. '*LES JEUX SONT FAITS*': WORLD WAR

1 Charles de Gaulle, *Mémoires de Guerre, II: L'Unité, 1942–1944* (this edn, 1980), p. 7.

2 Ibid., p. 177.

3 TNA FO 660/330, note from Foreign Office, 20 November 1944.

4 De Gaulle, *Mémoires de Guerre*, II, p. 9.

5 LHCMA Brooke-Popham papers, LHH, 61/1, undated note from Brooke-Popham to Commander-in-Chief.

6 Eve Curie, *Journey Among Warriors* (1943), p. 73.

7 Winston Churchill, *The Second World War, III: The Grand Allliance* (1950), p. 551.

8 John Colville, *The Fringes of Power: Downing Street Diaries, 1939–1955* (1985), 22 May 1941, p. 389.

9 https://www.iwm.org.uk/collections/item/object/80011929. Interview with Ian Stonor.

10 Christopher Bayly and Tim Harper, *Forgotten Armies: Britain's Asian Empire and the War with Japan* (this edn, 2005), p. 132.

11 Oliver Harvey, *The War Diaries of Oliver Harvey, 1941–1945*, edited by John Harvey (1978), 16 April 1942, p. 117. 'More and more evidence comes in of the deplorable behaviour of all responsible in Singapore. No preparations, troops (British and Australian) refusing to fight, looting by troops, petty squabbling between officials, officials leaving their posts – 60,000 British troops beaten by 5,000 Japs! It must be pretty hard to beat as a national disgrace. Many disturbing resemblances with the fall of France.'

12 TNA FO 954/6C/560, extract from Cabinet conclusions, 6 April 1942.

13 Peter Coats, *Of Generals and Gardens: The Autobiography of Peter Coats* (1976), p. 154.

14 Harold Nicolson, *Diaries and Letters, 1939–1945*, edited by Nigel Nicolson (1967), 27 February 1942, p. 214.

15 Colville, *The Fringes of Power*, 2 May 1948, p. 624.

16 Arthur Schlesinger, *Journals, 1952–2000*, edited by Andrew Schlesinger and Stephen Schlesinger (this edn, 2008), 11 July 1984, p. 575.

17 TNA FO 892/78, Parr to Eden, 26 July 1941.

18 TNA FO 954/8A/335, Eden to Peake, 28 December 1942.

19 TNA CO 968/31/7, contains communications between de Gaulle and his representatives in the Far East.

20 Trinity College Cambridge, Papers of Lord Butler of Saffron Walden, RAB G 12/152, note by Butler, 19 March 1941.

21 TNA FO 954/8A/229, Eden to Peake, 11 May 1942.

22 TNA FO 892/78, Parr to Eden, 26 July 1941.

23 TNA FO 371/32082, Rapport Giraud, 26 July 1940.

24 Ibid., substance of telegram from American Embassy at Vichy, 7 May 1943, attached to note from Matthews to Mack, 11 May 1942.

25 Ibid., British Representative to the Free French National Committee to Foreign Office, 30 April 1942.

26 TNA CAB 66/26/15, memorandum by Eden, 8 July 1942.

27 Ibid.

28 TNA FO 954/16A/175, Eden to Mack, 12 November 1942.
29 TNA FO 954/8A/333, copy of telegram from de Gaulle to Giraud, relayed from Churchill to Roosevelt, 27 December 1942.
30 TNA CAB 65/33/37, War Cabinet, 3 March 1943.
31 TNA PREM 3/186A/7, Churchill to Eden, 14 June 1942.
32 TNA FO 371/36047, telegram from Churchill, 21 May 1943.
33 TNA FO 954/9A/159, 'Notes of Conversation between the Prime Minister and General de Gaulle', 4 June 1944. Churchill said that he had identified de Gaulle as a mystic when the two men met at Casablanca in early 1943.
34 Cited in François Kersaudy, *De Gaulle et Roosevelt: Le Duel au Sommet* (this edn, 2006), p. 481.
35 TNA HS 8/897/34, note to Churchill, 24 June 1943.
36 TNA CAB 65/34/36, War Cabinet, 7 June 1943. In response to a complaint by Roosevelt, Eden said that Gaullist correspondents in the USA were more active than those who supported Giraud.
37 TNA HS 6/316, report by 'Sea Horse', 7 May 1943.
38 TNA FO 954/9A/37, Cooper to Eden, 14 February 1944.
39 Diana Cooper, *Trumpets from the Steep* (1960), p. 175.
40 Ibid., pp. 185–6.
41 Jim House and Neil MacMaster, *Paris 1961: Algerians, State Terror, and Memory* (Oxford, this edn, 2009), p. 37.
42 Leo Amery, *The Empire at Bay: The Leo Amery Diaries, 1929–1945*, edited by John Barnes and David Nicholson (1988), 19 July 1943, p. 899.
43 CAC, papers of Duff Cooper, DUFC 4/8, memorandum by Harold Macmillan, 5 January 1944: 'Perhaps if the French critics had read the Field Marshal's speech more carefully they would have seen that in his view England also must accept a position of relatively reduced power.'
44 John Martin, *Downing Street: The War Years* (1991), p. 18. The list of visitors to Chequers in 1940 (in TNA PREM 14/7) does not feature Freyburg. Perhaps Martin was thinking of a visit to Ditchley Park.
45 TNA FO 954/9B/458, Churchill to Eden, 19 January 1945.
46 TNA CAB 66/53/9, Cooper to Eden, 30 May 1944, attached to memorandum from Eden, 25 July 1944.
47 Harold Nicolson, *Diaries and Letters, 1930–1939*, edited by Nigel Nicolson (1966), 14 June 1939, p. 403.
48 TNA CAB 67/5/14, memorandum by Churchill, 24 February 1940.
49 TNA CAB 66/10/25, Churchill telegram to Viceroy, 28 July 1940, circulated to War Cabinet, 30 July 1940.
50 Bayly and Harper, *Forgotten Armies*, p. 167.

51 George MacDonald Fraser, *Quartered Safe Out Here: A Recollection of the War in Burma* (this edn, 2000), p. xii.

52 Yasmin Khan, *The Raj at War: A People's History of India's Second World War* (2015), p. 53.

53 TNA CAB 195/2/17, secretary's notes on meeting of War Cabinet, 12 January 1943.

54 https://history.state.gov/historicaldocuments/frus1944v05/d281. Churchill to Roosevelt, 29 April 1944.

55 Khan, *The Raj at War*, pp. 170–1.

56 Archibald Wavell, *The Viceroy's Journal*, edited by Penderel Moon (1973), 24 June 1943, p. 3.

57 Quoted in Khan, *The Raj at War*, p. 68.

58 Judith Brown, *Modern India: The Origins of an Asian Democracy* (this edn, Oxford, 1994), p. 319.

59 Amery, *The Empire at Bay*, 27 July 1942, p. 822.

60 CAC, papers of Duff Cooper, DUFC 4/14, Anglo-French Conversations in Paris, 11 and 12 November 1944.

61 Coats, *Of Generals and Gardens*, p. 185.

7. A WAR OF PEOPLES AND OF CAUSES

1 TNA HW 1/1886, intercepted despatch Alba to Madrid, 27 July 1943.

2 Charles Rist, *Une Saison Gâtée: Journal de la Guerre et de l'Occupation, 1939–1945*, edited by Jean-Noël Jeanneney (1983), 31 August 1940, p. 91.

3 CAC, papers of Lord Vansittart of Denham, VNST II, 1/9, 25 February 1941.

4 John Colville, *The Fringes of Power: Downing Street Diaries, 1939–1955* (1985), 19 July 1940, p. 198.

5 TNA PREM 7/3, Morton to Churchill, 29 November 1940.

6 TNA PREM 7/3, Churchill to Morton, 30 November 1940.

7 TNA FO 371/28240, de Gaulle to Catroux, 27 December 1940: '[W]hat is called by one party the real France is entirely with us.' In a broadcast of 13 July 1940, de Gaulle said that on this day all French thought was for 'La France seule'. The same term was used on the masthead of the newspaper *Action Française* from the following month.

8 TNA CAB 66/26/25, memorandum by Eden, 14 July 1942, recounting remarks made by de Gaulle on 3 July.

9 Trinity College, Cambridge, papers of Lord Butler of Saffron Walden, RAB G 12/127, 4 March 1941.

10 TNA FO 892/69, Morton to Cassin, 14 July 1941.

11 CAC, papers of Duff Cooper, DUFC 4/8, memorandum by Harold Macmillan, 5 January 1944.

12 Charles de Gaulle, *Discours et Messages, I: Pendant la Guerre, 1940–1946* (1970), pp. 132–8.

13 Claude Mauriac, *Un Autre de Gaulle: Journal, 1944–1954* (1970), 25 June 1946, p. 207.

14 Colville, *The Fringes of Power*, 13 December 1940, pp. 311–12.

15 TNA CAB 66/26/25, memorandum by Eden, 14 July 1942, recounting remarks made by de Gaulle on 3 July.

16 Charles de Gaulle, 'La Bataille de la Vistule (1920)', first published as 'Carnet de Campagne d'un Officier Français' in *Revue de Paris*, 1 November 1920, in Charles de Gaulle, *Le Fil de l'Épée et Autres Écrits* (this edn, 1994), pp. 566–83, p. 581.

17 Charles de Gaulle, *Mémoires de Guerre, II: L'Unité, 1942–1944* (this edn, 1980), p. 65.

18 Charles de Gaulle, *Mémoires de Guerre, III: Le Salut, 1944–1946* (this edn, 1980), pp. 208–10.

19 Georges Pompidou, *Pour Rétablir une Verité* (1982), p. 56.

20 Remarks to Roger Stéphane cited in Herni Lerner, 'Le Nazisme et l'Idéologie de Vichy dans la Pensée du Général de Gaulle', *Guerres Mondiales et Conflits Contemporains*, 180 (1995), pp. 65–90.

21 TNA CAB 85/94, note signed by MIR, 23 May 1940.

22 TNA CAB 85/94, Monnet to Baudouin, 25 May 1940.

23 Colville, *The Fringes of Power*, 12 July 1940, p. 193.

24 Winston Churchill, *The Second World War, III: The Grand Alliance* (1950), p. 494.

25 Colville, *The Fringes of Power*, 3 November 1940, p. 286.

26 Roland de Margerie, *Journal, 1939–1940* (2010), 11 June 1940, p. 311.

27 Ibid., July 1940, p. 390.

28 Charles de Gaulle, *Mémoires de Guerre, I: L'Appel, 1940–1942* (this edn, 1980), p. 162.

29 Mauriac, *Un Autre de Gaulle*, 16 February 1946, p. 167.

30 Colonel Passy, *Mémoires du Chef des Services Secrets de la France Libre* (this edn, 2000).

31 https://www.iwm.org.uk/collections/item/object/80009239. Interview with Maurice Buckmaster.

32 TNA PREM 3/184/9, Churchill to Minister of Information, 23 October 1941.

33 Robert Bruce Lockhart, *The Diaries of Sir Robert Bruce Lockhart, II, 1939–1945*, edited by Kenneth Young (1980), 25 October 1941, p. 127.

34 TNA PREM 3/184/9, note by Bruce Lochkart, 24 October 1941.

35 Alain Peyrefitte, *C'Était de Gaulle* (this edn, 2002), 1 July 1964, p. 806.

36 Ibid., 31 July 1962, p. 305.

37 TNA PREM 7/6, Morton to Churchill, 28 August 1942.

38 TNA CAB 66/29/6, Desmond Morton, report circulated on 23 September 1942.

39 TNA CAB 65/38/9, Eden to Churchill, 23 May 1943.

40 Pierre Brossolette, *Résistance, 1927–1943*, edited by Guillaume Piketty (this edn, 2015), letter to de Gaulle, 2 November 1942, pp. 143–7 and 'Hommage au Général de Gaulle', 2 March 1943, pp. 165–71.

41 Robert Belot, 'L'Identité de la Résistance et la Nature du Gaullisme: l'Aveu de "l'Affaire Suisse"', *Commentaire*, 132 (2010), pp. 957–76.

42 TNA PREM 3/184/9, Morton to Churchill, 8 November 1943.

43 Ibid., interview with a Frenchman just arrived from France, 1 July 1943.

44 Ibid., note from Mack, 15 July 1943.

45 Ibid., interview with Jean Mousset, 17 May 1943.

46 Ibid., interview with Commandant Debré, 2 July 1943.

47 TNA FO 954/26B/525, Stalin to Churchill, 3 December 1944.

48 CAC CHAR 20/113, Stalin to Churchill, 26 June 1943.

49 TNA PREM 3/184/9, Morton to Churchill, 8 November 1943.

50 TNA FO 660/16, note of conversation by Macmillan, 2 November 1943.

51 TNA PREM 3/184/9, Morton to Churchill, 30 October 1941.

52 Philippe de Gaulle, *De Gaulle Mon Père: Entretiens avec Michel Tauriac*, I (2003), p. 304.

53 TNA HS 9/1044/4, note, 21 January 1944.

54 Charles de Gaulle, *Lettres, Notes et Carnets, Juillet 1941–Mai 1943* (1982), de Gaulle to Churchill, 10 March 1943, pp. 534–6.

55 TNA CAB 79/26/20, Chiefs of Staff Committee, 19 March 1943, draft letter Churchill to de Gaulle. See also TNA CAB 79/59/45, Chiefs of Staff Committee, 15 March and attached letter by 'CD' to Ismay, 14 March 1943.

56 Philippe de Gaulle, *De Gaulle Mon Père*, I, p. 296.

57 Jean Dutourd, *Conversation avec le Général* (1985).

58 Philippe de Gaulle, *De Gaulle Mon Père*, I, p. 298.

59 Arthur L. Funk, 'Churchill, Eisenhower, and the French Resistance', *Military Affairs*, 45, 1 (1981), pp. 29–34.

60 Cited in E. H. Cookridge, *They Came from the Sky* (this edn, 1976), p. 296. See also HS 6/316, 'Political Report by Capt Harcourt of

Jedburgh Cinnamon', attached to note from Buckmaster, 29 January 1945. Harcourt suggested that Landes had merely been required to leave the area.

61   TNA FO 146/4628, note by Tickell, 23 April 1965.

62   Christopher J. Murphy, 'The Origins of SOE in France', *The Historical Journal*, 46, 4 (2003), pp. 935–52.

63   Claire Andrieu, *Pour l'Amour de la République: Le Club Jean Moulin, 1958–1970* (2002).

8. SHADOWS OF VICTORY, 1944–55

1   Charles de Gaulle, *Mémoires de Guerre, III: Le Salut, 1944–1946* (this edn, 1980), p. 57.

2   Martin Gilbert, *Winston S. Churchil, VIII: 'Never Despair', 1945–1965* (1988), p. 545.

3   TNA PREM 3/339/6, WH confidential annex, 5 June 1944.

4   TNA FO 954/9A/161, 'Record of Conversation between the Prime Minister and General de Gaulle', 4 June 1944.

5   Ibid.

6   TNA PREM 3/339/6, Churchill to de Gaulle, 5 June 1944.

7   Diana Cooper, *Trumpets from the Steep* (1960), p. 201.

8   TNA FO 660/128, Churchill to de Gaulle, 16 June 1944.

9   Leo Amery, *The Empire at Bay: The Leo Amery Diaries, 1929–1945*, edited by John Barnes and David Nicholson (1988), 16 June, p. 988.

10   Philippe de Gaulle, *Mémoires Accessoires, I: 1921–1946* (1997), p. 296.

11   Alain Peyrefitte, *C'Était de Gaulle* (this edn, 2002), 30 October 1963, p. 675.

12   François Coulet, cited in Guillaume Piketty, *Français, Libre: Pierre de Chevigné* (2022), p. 176.

13   Claude Hettier de Boislambert, cited in ibid., p. 174.

14   Martin Gilbert and Larry P. Arnn (eds.), *The Churchill Documents, XX, Normandy and Beyond, May–December 1944* (Hillsdale, MI, 2018), Eden, 'Review of Foreign Affairs', 4 May 1944, pp. 56–63, p. 62.

15   Charles de Gaulle, *Mémoires de Guerre, II: L'Unité, 1942–1944* (this edn, 1980), p. 369.

16   Alan Lascelles, *King's Counsellor. Abdication and War: The Diaries of Sir Alan Lascelles*, edited by Duff Hart-Davis (2006), 27 August 1944, note added 15 September, p. 253.

17   https://www.charles-de-gaulle.org/wpcontent/uploads/2017/10/Leretablissement-de-lEtat.pdf

18 Élisabeth Verry, 'Au Nom de la France: Michel Debré, Commissaire de la République pour la Région d'Angers (10 août 1944–8 avril 1945)', in Jean-Luc Marais (ed.) *Les Préfets de Maine-et-Loire* (Rennes, 2000), <http://books.openedition.org/pur/16475>. ISBN: 978-2-7535-2556-6. DOI: https://doi.org/10.4000/books.pur.16475.

19 TNA FO 371/28240, telegram de Gaulle to Catroux, 14 February 1941: 'All information from France confirms the growing favour with which Free France movement is viewed not only by the people but also in administrative circles in proximity to the government.'

20 TNA PREM 7/4, report by Dupuy to Mackenzie King, 25 September 1941.

21 CAC CHAR 20/175, Churchill to Roosevelt, 15 November 1944.

22 TNA FO 954/9B/458, Churchill to Eden, 19 January 1945.

23 J. C. C. Davidson, *Memoirs of a Conservative: J. C. C. Davidson's Memoirs and Papers, 1910–37*, edited by Robert Rhodes James (1969), p. 171.

24 Edward Marsh, *A Number of People: A Book of Reminiscences* (1939), p. 150.

25 Andrew Roberts, *Churchill: Walking with Destiny* (2018), p. 671.

26 John Colville, The *Fringes of Power: Downing Street Diaries, 1939–1955* (1985), 30 October 1940, p. 278.

27 Michael Howard, *Captain Professor: A Life in War and Peace* (2006), p. 58.

28 Ibid., p. 117.

29 CAC CHAR 2/560, Maudy Wellington to Churchill, 27 July 1945.

30 TNA HW 1/1886, intercepted despatch, Alba to Madrid, 27 July 1943.

31 Winston Churchill, *Great Contemporaries* (this edn, 1947), p. 298.

32 Charles de Gaulle, 'Mobilisation Économique à l'Étranger', first published in *Revue Militaire Française*, January 1934, in Charles de Gaulle, *Le Fil de l'Épée et Autres Écrits* (this edn, 1994), pp. 527–49, p. 535.

33 TNA HS 6/316, report by 'Sea Horse', 7 May 1943.

34 Quoted in Claude Juin and Henri Leclerc, *Daniel Mayer: L'Homme qui Aurait Pu Tout Changer* (1998), p. 171.

35 TNA PREM 7/5, Morton to Churchill, 25 September 1944.

36 Duff Cooper, *Old Men Forget: The Autobiography of Duff Cooper* (1953), p. 365.

37 Claude Mauriac, *Un Autre de Gaulle: Journal, 1944–1954* (1970), entry 15 January 1948, p. 305.

38 House of Commons, 25 February 1954.

39 Harold Macmillan, *The Macmillan Diaries, I: The Cabinet Years, 1950–1957*, edited by Peter Catterall (this edn, 2004), 9 August 1950, p. 6.

40 Ibid., 1 February 1951, p. 51.

41   Claude Guy, *En Écoutant de Gaulle: Journal, 1946–1949* (1996), 26 June 1946, p. 85.

42   Letter to Gide, 31 December 1944, in Claude Mauriac, *Le Temps Immobile, V: Aimer de Gaulle* (1978), p. 105.

43   Evelyn Shuckburgh, *Descent to Suez: Diaries, 1951–56*, edited by John Charmley (1986), 4 March 1954, p. 141.

44   Richard Toye, *The Roar of the Lion: The Untold Story of Churchill's World War II Speeches* (Oxford, 2013), p. 30.

45   C. L. Sulzberger, *The Last of the Giants* (this edn, 1972), pp. 302–3.

46   Macmillan, *The Macmillan Diaries*, I, 20 January 1955, p. 382.

47   R. A. Butler, *The Art of the Possible: The Memoirs of Lord Butler* (1971), p. 141.

48   Anthony Montague Browne, *Long Sunset: Memoirs of Winston Churchill's Last Private Secretary* (1995), p. 131.

49   Harold Macmillan, *The Macmillan Diaries, II: Prime Minister and After, 1957–1966*, edited by Peter Catterall (2011), 15 March 1957, p. 18.

50   Macmillan, *The Macmillan Diaries*, I, 20 December 1950, p. 37.

51   House of Commons, 25 February 1954.

52   J. W. Young, 'Churchill, the Russians and the Western Alliance: The Three-Power Conference at Bermuda, December 1953', *The English Historical Review*, 101, 401 (1986), pp. 889–912.

53   Macmillan, *The Macmillan Diaries*, I, 14 December 1950, p. 37.

54   Richard Toye, 'Winston Churchill's "Crazy Broadcast": Party, Nation, and the 1945 Gestapo Speech', *Journal of British Studies*, 49, 3 (2010), pp. 655–80.

55   Anthony Seldon, *Churchill's Indian Summer: The Conservative Government, 1951–55* (1981), p. 71.

56   Malcolm Muggeridge, 'What Price Glory?', *New York Review of Books*, 25 February 1965.

57   Macmillan, *The Macmillan Diaries*, I, 28 October 1951, p. 113.

58   Montague Browne, *Long Sunset*, p. 220.

59   Colville, *The Fringes of Power*, 29 March 1955, p. 705.

60   Shuckburgh, *Descent to Suez*, 24 July 1953, p. 91.

61   Macmillan, *The Macmillan Diaries*, I, 6 July 1953, p. 325.

62   Montague Browne, *Long Sunset*, p. 133.

63   David Reynolds, 'Churchill's Writing of History: Appeasement, Autobiography and "The Gathering Storm"', *Transactions of the Royal Historical Society*, 11 (2001), pp. 221–47.

64   Winston Churchill, *The Second World War, III: The Grand Alliance* (1950) pp. 44–8.

65 Sulzberger, *The Last of the Giants*, p. 12.
66 The text of the letter de Gaulle sent to Churchill is published in Georges Pompidou, *Pour Rétablir une Verité* (1982), p. 144.
67 Guy, *En Écoutant de Gaulle*, p. 484.
68 Charles de Gaulle, *Mémoires d'Espoir: Le Renouveau, 1958–1962/L'Effort, 1962–* (this edn, 1980), p. 13.
69 Shuckburgh, *Descent to Suez*, 6 April 1955, p. 255.

9. RESURRECTION, 1955–62

1 Charles de Gaulle, *Lettres, Notes et Carnets, 1919–Juin 1940* (1980), p. 11. De Gaulle wrote in a private diary: 'J'ai passé l'âge où l'on souhaite voir couler les jours …même s'ils sont vides, ce sont des jours tout de même!'
2 Charles de Gaulle, *Mémoires d'Espoir: Le Renouveau, 1958–1962/L'Effort, 1962–* (this edn, 1980), p. 22.
3 Jean Dutourd, *Conversation avec le Général* (1985); Malcolm Muggeridge, 'What Price Glory?', *New York Review of Books*, 25 February 1965.
4 Lawrence Wylie, *Village in the Vaucluse* (Cambridge, MA, 1957).
5 Éric Roussel, *Pierre Mendès France* (2007), p. 469.
6 https://history.state.gov/historicaldocuments/frus1947v03/d507. Ambassador to Secretary of State, 26 October 1947.
7 Guillaume Piketty, *Français, Libre: Pierre de Chevigné* (2022), pp. 370–79.
8 Pierre Viansson-Ponté, 'L'Opération "Resurrection" et la "Libération" de la Corse', *Le Monde*, 15 May 1963.
9 https://history.state.gov/historicaldocuments/frus1958-60v07p2/d9. Embassy to Department of State, 21 May 1958.
10 De Gaulle, *Mémoires d'Espoir*, p. 33.
11 Georgette Elgey, *De Gaulle à Matignon: La République des Tourmentes* (this edn, 2012), p. 25.
12 https://history.state.gov/historicaldocuments/frus1958-60v07p2/d14. Embassy to Department of State, 31 May 1958.
13 Bernard Tricot, *Les Sentiers de la Paix: Algérie, 1958–1962* (1972).
14 De Gaulle, *Mémoires d'Espoir*, p. 113.
15 Philip Gordon, *A Certain Idea of France: French Security Policy and the Gaullist Legacy* (Princeton, N. J., 1993), p. 27.
16 https://history.state.gov/historicaldocuments/frus1958-60v07p2/d16. Embassy to Department of State, 1 June 1958.
17 TNA FO 371/147332, Jebb to Foreign Office, 2 March 1960.

18 Arthur Asseraf, '"A New Israel": Colonial Comparisons and the Algerian Partition That Never Happened', *French Historical Studies*, 41, 1 (2018), pp. 95–120.

19 Alain Peyrefitte, *Faut-il Partager l'Algérie?* (1962).

20 De Gaulle, *Mémoires d'Espoir*, p. 21.

21 Raphaëlle Branche and Sylvie Thénault, 'Le Secret sur la Torture Pendant la Guerre d'Algérie', *Matériaux pour l'Histoire de Notre Temps*, 58 (2000), pp. 57–63.

22 TNA FO 371/147341, Consul General in Algiers to Foreign Secretary, 22 December 1960.

23 Julian Jackson, *A Certain Idea of France: The Life of Charles de Gaulle* (2018), p. 344.

24 Robert Buron, *Carnets Politiques de la Guerre d'Algérie, 1954–1962* (this edn, 2002).

10. SURVIVAL AND DEATH, 1962–5

1 Harold Macmillan, *The Macmillan Diaries, II: Prime Minister and After, 1957–1966*, edited by Peter Catterall (2011), 25 November 1961, p. 429.

2 TNA FO 371/145600, minute from Robinson, 16 April 1959.

3 TNA FO 371/145668, Roland to Watson, 11 July 1959.

4 Alain Peyrefitte, *C'Était de Gaulle* (this edn, 2002), 2 August 1962, p. 222.

5 Roger Tessier with Jean-Paul Ollivier, *J'Étais le Gorille du Général, 1947–1970* (2002), p. 97.

6 Peyrefitte, *C'Était de Gaulle*, 22 August 1962, p. 221.

7 Agnès Bastien-Thiry, *Mon Père: Le Dernier des Fusillés* (2005), p. 74.

8 Peyrefitte, *C'Était de Gaulle*, 13 March 1963, p. 727.

9 Ibid., 3 March 1964, p. 759.

10 Jerôme Bourdon, *Histoire de la Télévision sous de Gaulle* (1990).

11 Emmanuel Le Roy Ladurie, *Paris-Montpellier: PC-PSU, 1945–1963* (1982), p. 238.

12 Max Egremont, *Under Two Flags: The Life of Major General Sir Edward Spears* (this edn, 1998), p. 196.

13 TNA FO 371/172070, Dixon to Home, 23 September 1963. The British ambassador in Paris was discussing a recent book on de Gaulle's foreign policy. He said that the Russians had asked the French embassy in Moscow what de Gaulle's phrase meant and received no answer.

14 Charles de Gaulle, *Mémoires de Guerre, III: Le Salut, 1944–1946* (this edn, 1980), pp. 211–12.

15 Michel Droit, *Les Clartés du Jour: Journal, 1963–1965* (1978),
11 December 1965, p. 261.

16 The British record of the meeting suggests that de Gaulle was, in fact,
sceptical about projects for West European Unity. CAC, papers of Duff
Cooper, DUFC 4/14, Anglo-French Conversation in Paris, 11 and
12 November 1944.

17 TNA PREM 13/1519, Tickell to Palliser, 15 September 1967, reporting
the words of Leo Hamon.

18 TNA PREM 11/3339, de Zulueta to Macmillan, 19 May 1961.

19 TNA FO 371/172070, Dixon to Foreign Office, 7 October 1963.

20 TNA CAB 129/118/2, memorandum by Butler, 12 May 1964.

21 Simon Smith (ed.), *The Wilson–Johnson Correspondence, 1964–1969*
(2015), Wilson to Johnson, 11 November 1966, p. 184.

22 TNA PREM 13/920, Bridges to Wright, 17 March 1966.

23 Jean Chauvel, *Commentaire, III: De Berne à Paris, 1952–1962* (1973),
p. 252.

24 TNA FO 371/172079, Dixon to Foreign Office, 18 September 1963.

25 Macmillan, *The Macmillan Diaries*, II, 19 December 1959, pp. 262–3.

26 TNA PREM 11/2339, Jebb to Foreign Office, 28 May 1958.

27 Harold Nicolson, *Diaries and Letters, 1939–45*, edited by Nigel Nicolson
(1967), 21 April 1944, p. 361. Simplicity was not always the same as
austerity. After dining with de Gaulle, Nicolson wrote: 'Caviar-eggs, and
sole and meringues. A good white wine. Very simple.'

28 Jacques Foccart, *Journal de l'Élysée, I: Tous les Soirs avec de Gaulle,
1965–1967* (1997), 1 September 1965, p. 205.

29 Peyrefitte, *C'Était de Gaulle*, 8 December 1964, p. 655.

30 https://archivesearch.lib.cam.ac.uk/repositories/9/archival_objects/
431503. Interview with Sir Andrew Wood.

31 Charles Bohlen, *Witness to History, 1929–1969* (New York, 1973), p. 510.

32 Chauvel, *Commentaire*, III, p. 251.

33 John Mander, *Great Britain or Little England?* (1963), p. 42.

34 CAD Avon Papers, AP 23/19/4, Eden to Chauvel, 24 March 1959.

35 Charles Moran, *Churchill: The Struggle for Survival, 1940–1965* (this edn,
Boston, MA, 1966), p. xi.

36 Pierre Lefranc, *Avec Qui Vous Savez: Vingt-Cinq An aux Côtés de de Gaulle*
(1979), p. 301.

37 Chauvel, *Commentaire*, III, p. 300.

38 Kenneth Rose, *Who's In; Who's Out: the Journals of Kenneth Rose, I,
1944–1979*, edited by D. R. Thorpe (2018), 30 June 1973, p. 479.

39 TNA PREM 11/3001, 'Notes on State Visit', 30 March 1960.

40 TNA FO 371/153910, Philip to Michael Wilford, 16 March 1960.
41 Chauvel, *Commentaire*, III, pp. 298–304.
42 TNA FO 371/153631, note by Gladwyn Jebb, 15 September 1960.
43 TNA FO 371/153894, Montague Browne to Samuel, 26 October 1960.
44 Martin Gilbert, *In Search of Churchill: A Historian's Journey* (1994), p. 260. Eden stopped the sending of ministerial red boxes to Churchill in 1955 but Macmillan resumed it in 1957.
45 Anthony Montague Browne, *Long Sunset: Memoirs of Winston Churchill's Last Private Secretary* (1995), p. 187.
46 Evelyn Shuckburgh, *Descent to Suez: Diaries, 1951–56*, edited by John Charmley (1986), 29 January 1954, p. 75.
47 Ibid., 25 February 1953, p. 136.
48 TNA PREM 11/3785, Montague Browne to de Zulueta, 3 August 1961.
49 Gilbert, *In Search of Churchill*, p. 4.
50 Winston S. Churchill, *His Father's Son: Randolph Churchill* (1996), p. 492.
51 CAD Avon Papers, AP 7/22/162, Frank Giles to Eden, 3 June 1964.
52 Montague Browne, *Long Sunset*, p. 326.
53 TNA PREM 13/317, 'Talking Points for PM's Talk with General de Gaulle', 29 January 1965.
54 Gladwyn Jebb, *The Memoirs of Lord Gladwyn* (1972), p. 330.
55 Ray Gosling, 'Winston's Wake', *New Society*, 4 February 1965.
56 Richard Crossman, *The Crossman Diaries: Selections from the Diaries of a Cabinet Minister, 1964–1970*, edited by Anthony Howard (this edn, 1991), for 25 January and 30 January 1965, pp. 69–71.
57 Droit, *Les Clartés du Jour*, 11 December 1965, p. 261.

11. DE GAULLE ALONE, 1965–70

1 [citation?]
2 TNA FO 371/145600, Harold Beeley to Anthony Rumbold, 6 August 1959.
3 Mattei Dogan, 'Note sur le Nouveau Personnel Parlementaire', in François Goguel (ed.), *Le Référendum d'Octobre et les Élections de Novembre 1962* (1965), pp. 429–32.
4 Jacques Foccart, *Journal de l'Élysée, I: Tous les Soirs avec de Gaulle, 1965–1967* (1997), 20 April 1965, p. 392. The gorillas were reprieved at Foccart's request.
5 Simon Smith (ed.) *The Wilson–Johnson Correspondence, 1964–69* (2015), Wilson to Johnson, 22 June 1967, p. 232.

6   TNA FO 371/172070, Dixon to Foreign Office, 18 September 1963.

7   Arthur Schlesinger, *Journals, 1952–2000*, edited by Andrew Schlesinger and Stephen Schlesinger (this edn, 2008), 27 July 1976, p. 418.

8   TNA FO 371/153894, Montague Browne to Samuel, 26 October 1960.

9   Robert Caro, *The Years of Lyndon Johnson, IV: The Passage of Power* (2012), p. 417.

10 Alain Peyrefitte, *C'Était de Gaulle* (this edn, 2002), 27 November 1963, p. 637.

11 Foccart, *Journal de l'Élysée*, I, August 1967, p. 693.

12 Ibid.

13 Peyrefitte, *C'Était de Gaulle*, 24 February 1965, p. 659.

14 Michael R. Beschloss (ed.), *Taking Charge: The Johnson White House Tapes, 1963–1964* (New York, 1997), conversation with Richard Russell, 15 January 1964, p. 162.

15 Jean Touchard and Jean-Luc Parodi, 'L'Enjeu du Référendum du 28 Octobre 1962', in François Goguel, *Le Référendum d'Octobre et les Élections de Novembre 1962* (1965), pp. 37–50, p. 45.

16 Guy Michelat, 'Attitudes et Comportements Politiques à l'Automne 1962', in ibid., pp. 193–288, p. 195.

17 Kenneth Rose, *Who's In, Who's Out: The Journals of Kenneth Rose, I: 1944–1979*, edited by D. R. Thorpe (2018), 26 June 1978, p. 561. The Queen Mother said in 1978: 'When he [de Gaulle] went back to France at the end of the war, he said that the King and I were the only two people in England who had been nice to him.' Tommy Lascelles, George VI's private secretary, despised de Gaulle. Alexander Cadogan reported in September 1940 that he had talked to the king about de Gaulle 'who didn't impress him much'. Alexander Cadogan, *The Diaries of Sir Alexander Cadogan, 1938–1945*, edited by David Dilks (1971), 4 September 1940, p. 324.

18 Charles de Gaulle and Henri d'Orléans, *Dialogue sur la France: Correspondance et Entretiens, 1953–1970* (1994).

19 Foccart, *Journal de l'Élysée*, I, 4 November 1965, p. 265.

20 Nancy Mitford, 'Diary of a Revolution', *The Spectator*, 31 May 1968.

21 Jean Charlot, *The Gaullist Phenomenon* (1971), p. 45.

22 Michel Droit, *Les Clartés du Jour: Journal, 1963–65* (1978), 13 December 1965, p. 275.

23 Claire Andrieu, *Pour l'Amour de la République: Le Club Jean Moulin, 1958–1970* (2002), p. 186.

24 Gisèle Lougarot, *Pays Basque Nord: Mai 68 en Mémoires* (Bayonne, 2008), pp. 116 and 95.

25 Jacques Foccart, *Journal de l'Élysée, II: Le Général en Mai, 1968–1969* (1998), p. 178.

26 Maurice Grimaud, *En Mai Fais Ce Qu'il te Plaît: Le Préfet de Police de Mai 68 Parle* (1977).

27 Christian Fouchet, *Mémoires d'Hier et de Demain, I: Au Service du Général de Gaulle: Londres 1940, Varsovie 1945, Alger 1962, Mai 68* (1971), p. 227.

28 Jacques Massu, *Baden 68: Souvenirs d'une Fidélité Gaulliste* (1983).

29 TNA PREM 13/2653, Reilly to Foreign Office, 29 May 1968.

30 Ibid., 22 May 1968.

31 Ibid., 20 May 1968.

32 Peyrefitte, *C'Était de Gaulle*, 11 May 1968, p. 1711.

33 TNA PREM 13/2653, report from British Army of the Rhine to Ministry of Defence, 29 May 1968.

34 TNA PREM 13/2653, Reilly to Foreign Office, 30 May 1968.

35 Jean-Noël Jeanneney, *Le Rocher de Süsten: Mémoires, I: 1942–1982* (2020), p. 278.

36 Jean Mauriac, *Mort du Général de Gaulle* (1972), p. 69.

37 Claude Guy, *En Écoutant de Gaulle: Journal, 1946–1949* (1996), 14 April 1947, p. 307.

12. AFTERLIVES

1 Winston Churchill, *My Early Life: A Roving Commission* (this edn, 1990), p. 197.

2 Jean Mauriac, *Le Général et le Journaliste: Conversations avec Jean-Luc Barré* (2008), p. 253.

3 Michael Foot, 'Churchill's "Mein Kampf"', *Tribune*, 8 October 1948.

4 Charles Moran, *Churchill: The Struggle for Survival, 1940–1965* (1966), p. x.

5 W. Dockter and R. Toye, 'Who Commanded History? Sir John Colville, Churchillian Networks, and the "Castlerosse Affair"', *Journal of Contemporary History*, 54, 2 (2019), pp. 401–19.

6 John Wheeler-Bennett (ed.), *Action This Day: Working with Churchill* (1968). Brook, Bridges and Rowan contributed essays for this collection.

7 Caroline Slocock, *People Like Us: Margaret Thatcher and Me* (2018), p. 308.

8 TNA CAB 128/97/17, Cabinet, 22 November 1990.

9 Noel Annan, *Changing Enemies: The Defeat and Regeneration of Germany* (1995), p. 64.

10 Exchanges among British officials on this matter can be found in TNA FO 371/168490 and TNA FO 371/174345.

11 Anthony Barnett, *Iron Britannia: Why Parliament Waged its Falkands War* (1982).

12 Andrew Roberts, *Eminent Churchillians* (this edn, 1995).

13 Alan Clark, *Diaries* (1993), 10 May 1990, p. 298.

14 Ibid., 4 July 1990, p. 309.

15 Roberts, *Eminent Churchillians*, p. 285.

16 Simon Heffer, *Like the Roman: The Life of Enoch Powell* (1998), p. 72.

17 Enoch Powell, 'Liberator of France', *The Spectator*, 7 November 1970.

18 Interview for *La Repubblica*, 27 April 1989. https://www.margaretthatcher.org/document/107471.

19 Speech in Korea, 'The Principles of Thatcherism', 3 September 1992. https://www.margaretthatcher.org/document/108302.

20 Arthur Schlesinger, *Journals, 1952–2000*, edited by Andrew Schlesinger and Stephen Schlesinger (this edn, 2008), 22 June 1998, p. 831.

21 Dominique Venner, *De Gaulle: La Grandeur et le Néant* (2010).

22 Roberts, *Eminent Churchillians*, p. 211.

23 Patrick Buchanan, *Churchill, Hitler and the Unnecessary War: How Britain Lost its Empire and the West Lost the World* (2008).

24 André Glucksmann, *De Gaulle où es-tu* (1995), p. 203.

25 Stephen Roskill, *Churchill and the Admirals* (1977).

26 Allen Packwood (ed.), *The Cambridge Companion to Winston Churchill* (Cambridge, 2023).

CONCLUSION

1 Isaiah Berlin, 'Winston Churchill in 1940' in Isaiah Berlin, *Personal Impressions* (Oxford, 1982), pp. 1–22.

2 John Colville, *The Fringes of Power: Downing Street Diaries, 1939–1955* (1985), 15 December 1940, p. 319.

3 Claude Guy, *En Écoutant de Gaulle: Journal, 1946–1949* (1996), 15 October 1947, p. 325.

4 I am grateful to Guillaume Piketty, the biographer of Pierre Brossolette, for this information.

5 TNA FO 371/172070, Paris Embassy to Foreign Office, 7 October 1963.

6 TNA FCO 33/1007, Soames to Douglas-Home, 4 December 1970.

7 Guy, *En Écoutant de Gaulle*, 4 June 1946, p. 80. De Gaulle's sentiments sound remarkably like those expressed by Raymond Aron in 'L'Ombre

des Bonaparte', *La France Libre*, 16 August 1943. Aron's article had been interpreted at the time as a veiled attack on de Gaulle.

8 TNA PREM 7/6, note by Churchill on minute from Morton, 18 June 1940.

9 Arthur Schlesinger, *Journals, 1952–2000*, edited by Andrew Schlesinger and Stephen Schlesinger (this edn, 2008), 31 March 1962, p. 152.

10 Bibliothèque Nationale de France, *Charles de Gaulle: La Conquête de l'Histoire* (1990).

11 Arthur Miller, *Timebends: A Life* (this edn, 2012), p. 432.

12 Colville, *The Fringes of Power*, 25 November 1944, p. 529.

BIBLIOGRAPHY

Agulhon, Maurice, *De Gaulle: Histoire, Symbole, Mythe* (2000)

Amery, Leo, *The Empire at Bay: The Leo Amery Diaries, 1929–1945*, edited by John Barnes and David Nicholson (1988)

Amouroux, Henri, *Le 18 Juin* (this edn, 1990)

Andrieu, Claire, *Pour l'Amour de la République: Le Club Jean Moulin, 1958–1970* (2002)

Annan, Noel, *Changing Enemies: The Defeat and Regeneration of Germany* (1995)

Aron, Raymond, 'L'Ombre des Bonaparte', *La France Libre*, 16 August 1943

Ashley, Maurice, *Churchill as Historian* (1968)

Asseraf, Arthur, '"A New Israel": Colonial Comparisons and the Algerian Partition That Never Happened', *French Historical Studies*, 41, 1 (2018), pp. 95–120

Barnett, Anthony, *Iron Britannia: Why Parliament Waged its Falklands War* (1982)

Barré, Jean-Luc, *Devenir de Gaulle, 1939–1943* (2003)

—, *De Gaulle, Une Vie, I: L'Homme de Personne* (2023)

Barrès, Philippe, *Charles de Gaulle* (1941)

Bastien-Thiry, Agnès, *Mon Père: Le Dernier des Fusillés* (2005)

Baverez, Nicolas, *Raymond Aron* (this edn, 2005)

Bayly, Christopher and Harper, Tim, *Forgotten Armies: Britain's Asian Empire and the War with Japan* (this edn, 2005)

Belot, Robert, 'L'Identité de la Résistance et la Nature du Gaullisme: L'Aveu de "l'Affaire Suisse"', *Commentaire*, 132 (2010), pp. 957–76

Berl, Emmanuel, *La Fin de la IIIe République: 10 Juillet 1940* (1968)

Berlin, Isaiah 'Winston Churchill in 1940' in Isaiah Berlin, *Personal Impressions* (Oxford, 1982), pp. 1–22

Beschloss, Michael R. (ed.), *Taking Charge: The Johnson White House Tapes, 1963–1964* (New York, 1997)

Bibliothèque Nationale de France, *Charles de Gaulle: La Conquête de l'Histoire* (1990)

Binoche, Jacques, ' L'Allemagne et le Lieutenant-Colonel Charles de Gaulle', *Revue Historique*, 248, 1 (1972), pp. 107–16

Blake, Robert, and Louis, William Roger (eds.), *Churchill* (Oxford, 1993)

Bohlen, Charles, *Witness to History, 1929–1969* (New York, 1973)

Bonham Carter, Violet, *Winston Churchill as I Knew Him* (1965)

Boothby, Robert, *Recollections of a Rebel* (1978)

Bourdon, Jerôme, *Histoire de la Télévision sous de Gaulle* (1990)

Branche, Raphaëlle and Thénault, Sylvie, 'Le Secret sur la Torture Pendant la Guerre d'Algérie', *Matériaux pour l'Histoire de Notre Temps*, 58 (2000), pp. 57–63

Brooke, Alan, *War Diaries, 1939–1945: Field Marshal Lord Alanbrooke*, edited by Alex Danchev and Daniel Todman (this edn, 2002)

Brossolette, Pierre, *Résistance, 1927–1943*, edited by Guillaume Piketty (this edn, 2015)

Brown, Judith, *Modern India: The Origins of an Asian Democracy* (this edn, Oxford, 1994)

—, 'Imperial Facade: Some Constraints upon and Contradictions in the British Position in India, 1919–35', *Transactions of the Royal Historical Society*, 26 (1976), pp. 35–52

Bruce Lockhart, Robert, *The Diaries of Sir Robert Bruce Lockhart, II: 1939–1965*, edited by Kenneth Young (1980)

Buchanan, Patrick, *Churchill, Hitler and the Unnecessary War: How Britain Lost its Empire and the West Lost the World* (2008)

Buron, Robert, *Carnets Politiques de la Guerre d'Algérie, 1954–1962* (this edn, 2002)

Butler, R. A., *The Art of the Possible: The Memoirs of Lord Butler* (1971)

Cadogan, Alexander, *The Diaries of Sir Alexander Cadogan, 1938–1945*, edited by David Dilks (1971)

Caro, Robert, *The Years of Lyndon Johnson, IV: The Passage of Power* (2012)

Cassin, René, *Les Hommes Partis de Rien: Le Réveil de la France Abattue, 1940–1941* (1975)

Chamberlain, Austen, *The Austen Chamberlain Diary Letters: The Correspondence of Sir Austen Chamberlain with his Sisters Hilda and Ida, 1916–1937*, edited by Robert Self (Cambridge, 1995)

Charbonneau, Jean, *Contribution à l'Histoire de la Ile Guerre Mondiale: L'Envers du 18 Juin* (1969)

Charlot, Jean, *The Gaullist Phenomenon* (1971)

Charmley, John, *Churchill. The End of Glory: A Political Biography* (1993)

Chauvel, Jean, *Commentaire, III: De Berne à Paris, 1952–1962* (1973)

Churchill, Randolph S., *Winston S. Churchill, I: Youth, 1874–1900* (1966)

Churchill, Winston S., *His Father's Son: Randolph Churchill* (1996)

—, *Great Contemporaries* (this edn, 1947)

—, *My Early Life: A Roving Commission* (this edn, 1990)

—, 'Why not the United States of Europe?', *News of the World*, 9 May 1938

—, *Step by Step, 1936–1939* (1939)

—, *The Second World War, I: The Gathering Storm* (1948)

—, *The Second World War, III: The Grand Alliance* (1950)

—, *The World Crisis: The Aftermath* (1929)

—, *Secret Session Speeches*, compiled by Charles Eade (1946)

Clark, Alan, *Diaries* (1993)

Clarke, Peter, *Mr Churchill's Profession: Statesman, Orator, Writer* (2012)

—, 'Churchill as Orator and Writer' in Allen Packwood (ed.), *The Cambridge Companion to Winston Churchill* (Cambridge, 2023), pp. 73–92

Clerc, Christine, *Les de Gaulle: Une Famille Française* (2000)

Coats, Peter, *Of Generals and Gardens: The Autobiography of Peter Coats* (1976)

Collis, John Stewart, 'Homage to a Leader', *The Spectator*, 30 January 1982

Colville, John, *The Churchillians* (1981)

—, *The Fringes of Power: Downing Street Diaries, 1939–1955* (1985)

Cookridge, E. H., *They Came from the Sky* (this edn, 1976)

Cooper, Diana *Trumpets from the Steep* (1960)

Cooper, Duff, *Old Men Forget: The Autobiography of Duff Cooper* (1953)

Coward, Noel, *The Letters of Noel Coward*, edited by Barry Day (2007)

Crossman, Richard, *The Crossman Diaries: Selections from the Diaries of a Cabinet Minister, 1964–1970*, edited by Anthony Howard (this edn, 1991)

Curie, Eve, *Journey Among Warriors* (1943)

Danchev, Alex, *Alchemist of War: The Life of Liddell Hart* (this edn, 1999)

Davidson, J. C. C., *Memoirs of a Conservative: J. C. C. Davidson's Memoirs and Papers, 1910–37*, edited by Robert Rhodes James (1969)

De Boislambert, Claude Hettier, 'Juin–Juillet 40: À Londres avec de Gaulle, *Revue des Deux Mondes*, April 1978

De Boissieu, Alain, *Pour Combattre avec de Gaulle, 1940–1946* (1981)

De Gaulle, Charles, *La Discorde chez l'Ennemi* (1924)

—, *Le Fil de l'Épée* (1932)

—, *Vers l'Armée de Métier* (1934)

—, *La France et son Armée* (1938)

— *La France et son Armée* (1938)

—, *Discours et Messages, I: Pendant la Guerre, 1940–1946* (1970)

—, *Mémoires d'Espoir: Le Renouveau, 1958–1962/L'Effort, 1962–* (this edn, 1980)

—, *Mémoires de Guerre, I: L'Appel, 1940–1942* (this edn, 1980)

—, *Mémoires de Guerre, II: L'Unité, 1942–1944* (this edn, 1980)

—, *Mémoires de Guerre, III: Le Salut, 1944–1946* (this edn, 1980)

—, *Lettres, Notes et Carnets, 1919–Juin 1940* (1980)

—, *Lettres, Notes et Carnets, Juillet 1941–Mai 1943* (1982)

—, *Le Fil de l'Épée et Autres Écrits* (this edn, 1994)

— and Henri d'Orléans, *Dialogue sur la France: Correspondance et Entretiens, 1953–1970* (1994)

De Gaulle, Philippe, *Mémoires Accessoires, I: 1921–1946* (1997)

—, *De Gaulle Mon Père: Entretiens avec Michel Tauriac*, I (2003)

De Gaulle, Philippe, *Mémoires Accessoires, I: 1921–1946* (1997)

De La Gorce, Paul-Marie, *De Gaulle* (this edn, 1999)

De Margerie, Roland, *Journal, 1939–1940* (2010)

De Villelume, Paul, *Journal d'une Défaite: Août 1939–Juin 1940* (1976)

Debray, Régis, *À Demain de Gaulle* (1989)

Dockter, W., and Toye, R., 'Who Commanded History? Sir John Colville, Churchillian Networks, and the "Castlerosse Affair"', *Journal of Contemporary History*, 54, 2 (2019), pp. 401–19

Dogan, Mattei, 'Notes sur le Nouveau Personnel Parlementaire', in François Goguel (ed.), *Le Référendum d'Octobre et les Élections de Novembre 1962* (1965), pp. 429–32

Droit, Michel, *Les Clartés du Jour: Journal, 1963–1965* (1978)

Duchesne, Jacques, *Deux Jours avec Churchill: Londres, 21 Octobre 1940 – Paris, 11 Novembre 1944* (2008)

Dutourd, Jean, *Conversation avec le Général* (1985)

Eden, Clarissa, *A Memoir: From Churchill to Eden*, edited by Cate Haste (this edn, 2008)

Egremont, Max, *Under Two Flags: The Life of Major General Sir Edward Spears* (this edn, 1998)

Elgey, Georgette, *La Fenêtre Ouverte* (1973)

—, *De Gaulle à Matignon: La République des Tourmenes* (this edn, 2012)

Fabre Luce, Alfred, *Gaulle Deux* (1958)

—, *Le Plus Illustre des Français* (1960)

—, *Le Couronnement du Prince* (1964)

—, *L'Anniversaire* (1971)

Farmelo, Graham, *Churchill's Bomb: A Hidden History of Science, War and Politics* (2013)

Feske, Victor, *From Belloc to Churchill: Private Scholars, Public Culture and the Crisis of British Liberalism, 1900–1939* (Chapel Hill NC, 1996)

Fleming, Peter, *Invasion 1940: An Account of the German Preparations and the British Counter-Measures* (1957)

Foccart, Jacques, *Journal de l'Elysée, I: Tous les Soirs avec de Gaulle, 1965–1967* (1997)

—, *Journal de l'Élysée, II: Le Général en Mai, 1968–1969* (1998)

Foot, Michael, 'Churchill's "Mein Kampf"', *Tribune*, 8 October 1948

Fouchet, Christian, *Mémoires d'Hier et de Demain, I: Au Service du Général de Gaulle: Londres 1940, Varsovie 1945, Alger 1962, Mai 68* (1971)

Fraser, David, *War and Shadows: Memoirs of General Sir David Fraser* (2002)

Funk, Arthur L., 'Churchill, Eisenhower, and the French Resistance', *Military Affairs*, 45, 1 (1981), pp. 29–34

Gallagher, John, 'Nationalisms and the Crisis of Empire, 1919–1922', *Modern Asian Studies*, 15, 3 (1981), pp. 355–68

—, and Seal, Anil, 'Britain and India between the Wars', *Modern Asian Studies*, 15, 3 (1981), pp. 387–414

Garçon, Maurice, *Journal, 1939–1945*, edited by Pascal Fouché and Pascale Froment (this edn, 2017)

Gardiner, A.G. *Prophets, Priests and Kings* (this edn, 1917)

Gaunson, A. B., 'Churchill, de Gaulle, Spears and the Levant Affair, 1941', *The Historical Journal*, 27, 3 (1984), pp. 697–713

Germains, Victor, *The Tragedy of Winston Churchill* (1931)

Gilbert, Martin, *Winston S. Churchill, V: The Prophet of Truth, 1922–1939* (1977)

—, *Winston S. Churchill, VI: Finest Hour, 1939–1941* (1983)

—, *Winston S. Churchil, VIII: 'Never Despair', 1945–1965* (1988)

—, *In Search of Churchill: A Historian's Journey* (1994)

— (ed.), *Winston Churchill and Emery Reves: Correspondence, 1937–1964* (Austin TX, 1997)

— and Arnn, Larry P. (eds.), *The Churchill Documents, XX: Normandy and Beyond, May–December 1944* (Hillsdale MI, 2018)

Glorion, Caroline, *Geneviève de Gaulle Anthonioz: Résistances* (this edn, 2015)

Glucksmann, André, *De Gaulle où es-tu* (1995)

Goguel, François (ed.), *Le Référendum d'Octobre et les Élections de Novembre 1962* (1965)

Gordon, Philip, *A Certain Idea of France: French Security Policy and the Gaullist Legacy* (Princeton NJ, 1993)

Gosling, Ray, 'Winston's Wake', *New Society*, 4 February 1965

Grey of Fallodan, Edward, *Twenty-Five Years, 1892–1916, II:* (this edn, 1928)

Grimaud, Maurice, *En Mai Fais ce Qu'il Te Plaît: Le Préfet de Police de Mai 68 Parle* (1977)

Guy, Claude, *En Écoutant de Gaulle: Journal, 1946–1949* (1996)

Halévy, Daniel, 'Un Livre sur l'Armée de Métier', *Revue des Deux Mondes*, October 1934

Halifax, Edward, *Fulness of Days* (1957)

Harvey, Oliver, *The War Diaries of Oliver Harvey, 1941–1945*, edited by John Harvey (1978)

Harvey, Trevor, *An Army of Brigadiers: Brigade Commanders at the Battle of Arras of 1917* (Solihull, 2017)

Heffer, Simon, *Like the Roman: The Life of Enoch Powell* (1998)

Horne Alistair, *Harold Macmillan, I: 1894–1945* (this edn, New York, 1989)

House, Jim and MacMaster, Neil, *Paris 1961: Algerians, State Terror, and Memory* (Oxford, this edn, 2009)

Howard, Michael, *Captain Professor: A Life in War and Peace* (2006)

Jackson, Julian, *A Certain Idea of France: The Life of Charles de Gaulle* (2018)

Jeanneney, Jean-Noël, *Le Rocher de Süsten: Mémoires, I: 1942–1982* (2020)

Jebb, Gladwyn, *The Memoirs of Lord Gladwyn* (1972)

Jenkins, Roy, *Churchill* (2001)

Jennings, Eric, *Free French Africa in World War II: The African Resistance* (2015)

Juin, Claude and Leclerc, Henri, *Daniel Mayer: L'Homme qui Aurait Pu Tout Changer* (1998)

Julliard, G., *Le Procès de 'Haute-Cour'* (1964)

Kennan, George, *Memoirs, 1925–1950* (this edn, 1967)

Kersaudy, François, *Churchill and de Gaulle* (1981)

—, *De Gaulle et Roosevelt: Le Duel au Sommet* (this edn, 2006)

Keynes, John Maynard, *The Economic Consequences of Mr Churchill* (1925)

Khan, Yasmin, *The Raj at War: A People's History of India's Second World War* (2015)

Lacouture, Jean, *De Gaulle, I: Le Rebelle, 1890–1944* (1984)

—, *De Gaulle, II: Le Politique, 1944–1959* (1985)

—, *De Gaulle, III: Le Souverain, 1959–1970* (1986)

Lascelles, Alan, *King's Counsellor: Abdication and War: The Diaries of Sir Alan Lascelles*, edited by Duff Hart-Davis (2006)

Le Roy Ladurie, Emmanuel, *Paris–Montpellier: PC–PSU, 1945–1963* (1982)

Leahy, W. D., *I Was There* (1950)

Lefranc, Pierre, *Avec Qui Vous Savez: Vingt-Cinq Ans aux Côtés de de Gaulle* (1979)

Lerner, Henri, 'Le Nazisme et l'Idéologie de Vichy dans la Pensée du Général de Gaulle', *Guerres Mondiales et Conflits Contemporains*, 180 (1995), pp. 65–90

Liddell Hart, Basil, *The Liddell Hart Memoirs, I: 1895–1938* (1965)

Lindsay, David, *The Crawford Papers: The Journals of David Lindsay, Twenty-Seventh Earl of Crawford and Tenth Earl of Balcarres, 1871–1940, during the Years 1892–1940*, edited by John Vincent (Manchester, 1984)

Lougarot, Gisèle, *Pays Basque Nord: Mai 68 en Mémoires* (Bayonne, 2008)

Lough, David, *No More Champagne: Churchill and His Money* (this edn, 2016)

—, 'The inheritance of Winston Churchill', in Allen Packwood (ed.), *The Cambridge Companion to Winston Churchill* (Cambridge, 2023), pp. 28–48

Luneau, Aurélie, *L'Appel du 18 Juin* (2020)

Lyttelton, Oliver, *The Memoirs of Lord Chandos* (1962)

MacDonald Fraser, George, *Quartered Safe Out Here: A Recollection of the War in Burma* (this edn, 2000)

Macmillan, Harold, *The Macmillan Diaries, I: The Cabinet Years, 1950–1957*, edited by Peter Catterall (this edn, 2004)

—, *The Macmillan Diaries, II: Prime Minister and After, 1957–1966*, edited by Peter Catterall (2011)

Maisky, Ivan, *The Maisky Diaries: The Wartime Revelations of Stalin's Ambassador in London*, edited by Gabriel Gorodetsky (this edn, 2016)

Malraux, André, *Les Chênes qu'on Abat* (1971)

Mander, John, *Great Britain or Little England?* (1963)

Marsh, Edward, *A Number of People: A Book of Reminiscences* (1939)

Marsh, Edward, and Hassall, Christopher, *Ambrosia and Small Beer: The Record of a Correspondence of Edward Marsh and Christopher Hassall* (1964)

Martin, John, *Downing Street: The War Years* (1991)

Massu, Jacques, *Baden 68: Souvenirs d'une Fidélité Gaulliste* (1983)

Mauriac, Claude, *Un Autre de Gaulle: Journal, 1944–1954* (1970)

—, *Le Temps Immobile, V: Aimer de Gaulle* (1978)

Mauriac, François, *De Gaulle* (1964)

Mauriac, Jean, *Le Général et le Journaliste: Conversations avec Jean-Luc Barré* (2008)

Mauriac, Jean, *Mort du Général de Gaulle* (1972)

McGilvray, Evan, *Churchill and de Gaulle: The Foundations of a Perplexing Franco-British Relationship, 1940–1946* (2024)

Mengin, Robert, *No Laurels for de Gaulle* (1966)

Michelat, Guy, 'Attitudes et Comportements Politiques à l'Automne 1962', in François Goguel (ed.), *Le Référendum d'Octobre et les Élections de Novembre 1962* (1965), pp. 193–288

Miller, Arthur, *Timebends: A Life* (this edn, 2012)

Mitford, Nancy, 'Diary of a Revolution', *The Spectator*, 31 May 1968

Mitterrand, François, *Le Coup d'État Permanent* (1964)

Moch, Jules, *Rencontres avec de Gaulle* (1971)

Monnet, Jean, *Mémoires* (1976)

Montague Browne, Anthony, *Long Sunset: Memoirs of Churchill's Last Private Secretary* (1995)

Moran, Charles, *Churchill: The Struggle for Survival, 1940–1965* (this edn, Boston MA, 1966)

Muggeridge, Malcolm, 'What Price Glory?', *New York Review of Books*, 25 February 1965

Muracciole, Jean François, *Les Français Libres: L'Autre Résistance* (2010)

Murphy, Christopher J., 'The Origins of SOE in France', *The Historical Journal*, 46, 4 (2003), pp. 935–52

Neilson, Keith, 'The Defence Requirements Sub-Committee, British Strategic Foreign Policy, Neville Chamberlain and the Path to Appeasement', *The English Historical Review*, 118, 477 (2003), pp. 651–84

Neuwirth, Lucien, *Que la Vie Soit!* (1979)

Nicolson, Harold, *Diaries and Letters, 1930–1939*, edited by Nigel Nicolson (1966)

—, *Diaries and Letters, 1939–45*, edited by Nigel Nicolson (1967)

Nora , Pierre (ed.), *Les Lieux de Mémoire* (three volumes, this edn, 1997)

Nourissier, François, *À Défaut de Génie* (2000)

Oberlé, Jean, *La Vie d'Artiste* (1956)

Orwell, George, 'Propaganda and Demotic Speech', *Persuasion* (Summer, 1944)

—, *The Complete Works of George Orwell: A Patriot After All, 1940–1941*, edited by Peter Davison (this edn, 2000)

Packwood, Allen (ed.), *The Cambridge Companion to Winston Churchill* (Cambridge, 2023)

Palewski, Gaston, 'De Gaulle avant de Gaulle', *Revue des Deux Mondes*, April 1988

Passy, Colonel, *Mémoires du Chef des Services Secrets de la France Libre*, (this edn, 2000)

Peyrefitte, Alain, *Faut-il Partager l'Algérie?* (1962)

—, *C'Était de Gaulle* (this edn, 2002)

Piketty, Guillaume, *Pierre Brossolette: Un Héros de la Résistance* (1998)

—, *Français, Libre: Pierre de Chevigné* (2022)

Pollock, Fred E., 'Roosevelt, the Ogdensburg Agreement, and the British Fleet: All Done with Mirrors', *Diplomatic History*, 5, 3 (1981), pp. 203–19

Pompidou, Georges, *Pour Rétablir une Vérité* (1982)

Pope-Hennessy, James, *London Fabric* (1940)

Powell, Enoch, 'Liberator of France', *The Spectator*, 7 November 1970

Ramsden, John, *Man of the Century: Winston Churchill and his Legend since 1945* (2002)

Rebatet, Lucien, *Les Décombres* (1942)

Revel, Jean-François, *Le Style du Général* (1959)

Reynolds, David, *In Command of History: Churchill Fighting and Writing the Second World War* (this edn, 2005)

—, 'Churchill's Writing of History: Appeasement, Autobiography and "The Gathering Storm"', *Transactions of the Royal Historical Society*, 11 (2001), pp. 221–47

Rials, Stéphane, 'Pour un Anniversaire: La Conception du Pouvoir de Georges Pompidou', *La Revue Administrative*, 37, 218 (1984), pp. 126–32

Rist, Charles, *Une Saison Gâtée: Journal de la Guerre et de l'Occupation, 1939–1945*, edited by Jean-Noël Jeanneney (1983)

Roberts, Andrew, *Eminent Churchillians* (this edn, 1995)

—, *Churchill: Walking with Destiny* (2018)

Rose, Jonathan, *The Literary Churchill: Author, Reader, Actor* (2014)

Rose, Kenneth, *Who's In, Who's Out: The Journals of Kenneth Rose, I: 1944–1979*, edited by D. R. Thorpe (2018)

Rose, Norman, 'Churchill and Zionism', in Robert Blake and William Roger Louis (eds.), *Churchill* (Oxford, 1993), pp. 147–66

Roskill, Stephen, *Churchill and the Admirals* (1977)

Roussel, Éric, *Charles de Gaulle* (2002)

—, *Pierre Mendès France* (2007)

—, *C'Était le Monde d'Avant: Carnets d'un Biographe* (2022)

—, 'De Gaulle et Barrès: Gaullisme et Gaullistes: dans la France de l'Est sous la IVe République' [online]. Rennes: Presses Universitaires de Rennes, 2009 (generated 22 April 2024). Available on the Internet, <http://books.openedition.org/pur/122736>. ISBN: 978-2-7535-6668-2. DOI: https://doi.org/10.4000/books.pur.122736

Saurat, Denis, 'Attention au Tchad', *La France Libre*, 20 June 1941

Schlesinger, Arthur, *Journals, 1952–2000*, edited by Andrew Schlesinger and Stephen Schlesinger (this edn, 2008)

Seldon, Anthony, *Churchill's Indian Summer: The Conservative Government, 1951–55* (1981)

Shuckburgh, Evelyn, *Descent to Suez: Diaries, 1951–56*, edited by John Charmley (1986)

Simon, John, *Retrospect: The Memoirs of the Rt. Hon. Viscount Simon* (1952)

Slocock, Caroline, *People Like Us: Margaret Thatcher and Me* (2018)

Smith, Simon (ed.), *The Wilson–Johnson Correspondence, 1964–69* (2015)

Spears, Edward, *Fulfilment of a Mission: The Spears Mission to Syria and Lebanon, 1941–1944* (1977)

Speer, Albert, *Inside the Third Reich* (1969)

Sulzberger, C. L., *The Last of the Giants* (this edn, 1972)

Tessier, Roger, with Jean-Paul Ollivier, *J'Étais le Gorille du Général, 1947–1970* (2002)

Thornton-Kemsley, Colin, *Through Winds and Tides* (1974)

Touchard, Jean and Parodi, Jean-Luc, 'L'Enjeu du Référendum du 28 Octobre 1962', in François Goguel, *Le Référendum d'Octobre et les Élections de Novembre 1962* (1965), pp. 37–50

Toye, Richard, *Lloyd George and Churchill: Rivals for Greatness* (this edn, 2008)

—, *The Roar of the Lion: The Untold Story of Churchill's World War II Speeches* (Oxford, 2013)

—, 'Winston Churchill's "Crazy Broadcast": Party, Nation, and the 1945 Gestapo Speech', *Journal of British Studies*, 49, 3 (2010), pp. 655–80

Tricot, Bernard, *Les Sentiers de la Paix: Algérie, 1958–1962* (1972)

Venner, Dominique, *De Gaulle: La Grandeur et le Néant* (2010)

Verry, Élisabeth, 'Au Nom de la France: Michel Debré, Commissaire de la République pour la Région d'Angers (10 août 1944 – 8 avril 1945)', in Jean-Luc Marais (ed.) *Les Préfets de Maine-et-Loire* (Rennes, 2000) <http://books.openedition.org/pur/16475>. ISBN: 978-2-7535-2556-6. DOI: https://doi.org/10.4000/books.pur.16475

Viansson-Ponté, Pierre, ' l'Opération "Resurrection" et la "Libération" de la Corse', *Le Monde*, 15 May 1963

—, 'Quand la France s'Ennuie', *Le Monde*, 15 March 1968

Wavell, Archibald, *The Viceroy's Journal*, edited by Penderel Moon (1973)

Werth, Alexander, *Russia at War, 1939–1945* (1964)

Weygand, Maxime, *En Lisant les Mémoires du Général de Gaulle* (1955)

Wheeler-Bennett, John (ed.), *Action This Day: Working with Churchill* (1968)

Wilson, William Maitland, *Eight Years Overseas, 1939–1947* (1948)

Wylie, Lawrence, *Village in the Vaucluse* (Cambridge, MA, 1957)

Young, J. W., 'Churchill, the Russians and the Western Alliance: The Three-Power Conference at Bermuda, December 1953', *The English Historical Review*, 101, 401 (1986), pp. 889–912

Archival Sources
The National Archives, Kew

CABINET OFFICE

CAB 128/97/17	CAB 65/7/63	CAB 66/29/6
CAB 129/118/2	CAB 65/7/64	CAB 66/53/9
CAB 195/2/17	CAB 65/8/1	CAB 66/9/44
CAB 65/10/5	CAB 65/8/3	CAB 66/9/5
CAB 65/10/6	CAB 65/8/6	CAB 66/9/6
CAB 65/15/11	CAB 65/9/40	CAB 67/5/14
CAB 65/16/16	CAB 66/10/25	CAB 67/8/11
CAB 65/19/29	CAB 66/12/26	CAB 79/26/20
CAB 65/33/37	CAB 66/12/27	CAB 79/59/45
CAB 65/34/36	CAB 66/13/1	CAB 79/6/12
CAB 65/7/38	CAB 66/13/28	CAB 85/94
CAB 65/7/38	CAB 66/22/47	
CAB 65/7/54	CAB 66/26/25	

COLONIAL OFFICE

CO 323/1791/38	CO 968/31/7

FOREIGN OFFICE (AFTER 1968 FOREIGN AND COMMONWEALTH OFFICE)

FCO 33/1007	FO 371/172070	FO 954/26B/525
FCO 33/85	FO 371/172079	FO 954/31A/259
FO 146/4618	FO 371/174345	FO 954/4B/421
FO 146/4628	FO 371/28240	FO 954/6C/560
FO 371/28545	FO 371/28545	FO 954/8A/136
FO 371/145600	FO 371/28592	FO 954/8A/165
FO 371/145668	FO 371/32082	FO 954/8A/173
FO 371/145668	FO 371/36047	FO 954/8A/191
FO 371/147332	FO 660/128	FO 954/8A/229
FO 371/147341	FO 660/16	FO 954/8A/333
FO 371/153631	FO 660/330	FO 954/8A/335
FO 371/153894	FO 892/15	FO 954/8B/369
FO 371/153910	FO 892/69	FO 954/9A/159
FO 371/168490	FO 892/78	FO 954/9A/161
FO 371/169108	FO 954/16A/175	FO 954/9A/37

SPECIAL OPERATIONS EXECUTIVE
HS 6/316   HS 8/897/34   HS 9/1044/4

GOVERNMENT CYPHER SCHOOL
HW 1/1886

PRIME MINISTER'S OFFICE

PREM 3/186A/5	PREM 7/4	PREM 11/3339
PREM 3/186A/7	PREM 7/5	PREM 11/3785
PREM 3/120/4	PREM 7/6	PREM 13/1519
PREM 3/184/9	PREM 7/8	PREM 13/2653
PREM 3/339/6	PREM 11/201	PREM 13/317
PREM 7/2	PREM 11/2339	PREM 13/920
PREM 7/3	PREM 11/3001	PREM 14/7

WAR OFFICE
WO 193/222

King's College London, Liddell Hart Centre for Military Archives
PAPERS OF OF BASIL LIDDELL HART
LH11/1945/8   LH11/1945/25

PAPERS OF BROOKE-POPHAM
LHH 61/1

Cadbury Research Library, University of Birmingham
AVON PAPERS
AP 2/22/156   AP 23/19/4

Churchill Archives Centre, Churchill College Cambridge
PAPERS OF SIR WINSTON CHURCHILL

CHAR 20/45	CHAR 2/560
CHAR 20/113	CHAR 20/175
CHAR 20/227/B	

PAPERS OF ALFRED DUFF COOPER

DUFC 4/8   DUFC 4/14

PAPERS OF MAJOR GENERAL SIR EDWARD SPEARS

SPRS 5/36   SPRS 5/37

PAPERS OF LORD ROBERT VANSITTART OF DENHAM

VNST II 1/9

Trinity College Cambridge

PAPERS OF LORD BUTLER OF SAFFRON WALDEN

RAB G 11/12   RAB G 12/152   RAB G 12/127

Sources Available on the World Wide Web

BRITISH DIPLOMATIC HISTORY ORAL PROGRAMME

https://archivesearch.lib.cam.ac.uk/repositories/9/archival_objects/
    431503. Interview with Sir Andrew Wood

FOREIGN RELATIONS OF THE UNITED STATES

https://history.state.gov/historicaldocuments/frus1940v01/d28. Report by the
    Under Secretary of State (Welles) on his Special Mission to Europe

https://history.state.gov/historicaldocuments/frus1944v05/d281. Churchill
    to Roosevelt, 29 April 1944

https://history.state.gov/historicaldocuments/frus1947v03/d507.
    Ambassador to Secretary of State, 26 October 1947

https://history.state.gov/historicaldocuments/frus1958-60v07p2/d14.
    Embassy to Department of State, 31 May 1958

https://history.state.gov/historicaldocuments/frus1958-60v07p2/d16.
    Embassy to Department of State, 1 June 1958

https://history.state.gov/historicaldocuments/frus1958-60v07p2/d9.
    Embassy to Department of State, 21 May 1958

FONDATION CHARLES DE GAULLE

https://www.charles-de-gaulle.org/wp-content/uploads/2017/10/
    Le-retablissement-de-lEtat.pdf

IMPERIAL WAR MUSEUM SOUND ARCHIVE

https://www.iwm.org.uk/collections/item/object/80009239. Interview with Maurice Buckmaster

https://www.iwm.org.uk/collections/item/object/80011929. Interview with Ian Stonor

https://www.iwm.org.uk/collections/item/object/80016926. Interview with John Glassbrook

https://www.iwm.org.uk/collections/item/object/80018424. Interview with Elaine Barr

https://www.iwm.org.uk/collections/item/object/80019913. Interview with Rolf Weinberg

THATCHER FOUNDATION WEBSITE

https://www.margaretthatcher.org/document/107471. Interview for *La Repubblica*, 27 April 1989

https://www.margaretthatcher.org/document/108302. Speech in Korea, 'The Principles of Thatcherism', 3 September 1992

ACKNOWLEDGEMENTS

I am grateful to James Pullen of the Wylie agency for having encouraged me to write this book and to my editors – Jonathan Jao at Simon and Schuster in the US and Ian Marshall at Bloomsbury in the UK – for having taken the project up with such enthusiasm.

The master and fellows of Churchill College Cambridge kindly elected me to an archive by-fellowship for 2024. I am grateful to them, to the archives fellowship committee and to all the staff at the Churchill Archive Centre. I have derived particular benefit from the erudition and helpfulness of Allen Packwood, the director of the Archive Centre. Andrew Riley is not really on the Churchill side of the Churchill Archive Centre but his company made my visits to Churchill all the more enjoyable. I am also much indebted to the staffs of the Cadbury Research Centre of Birmingham University, of the National Archives at Kew, of the Liddell Hart Centre for Military Archives at King's College London and the Wren Library at Trinity College Cambridge. Curtis Brown granted me permission to quote from Churchill's published works and I owe a special debt to Rachel Thorne for the speed and efficiency with which she handled my request for this permission.

The London Library in St James Square is a wonderful institution. I have particular reason to be thankful to the librarians there because they remained open when the British Library was closed by a cyber-attack, and they continued to send out books during the darkest days of the Covid lockdown. The London Library must also be the only institution in the world that lets its readers borrow bound volumes of *La France Libre*.

Julian Jackson interrupted a busy schedule to read a draft of this book and to provide much helpful advice. I am grateful to François Kersaudy for having answered a specific question of mine but also, more generally, for his inspiring example. For reading all or part of the draft of this book, I owe great debts to David Edgerton, Alison Henwood, Helen Parr, Sarah Howard, Kit Kowol and Allen Packwood. I have learned much from talking to two great experts on de Gaulle and Churchill: Guillaume Piketty in Paris and to Seth Thevoz in London.

The first person to read the manuscripts of my books is Munro Price. I have come, over the years, to trust his consistently shrewd judgements. The last person to read the manuscript of this book was Bela Cunha. Bela has copy-edited my last four books and I am enormously grateful to her for having taken up her pencil one last time on my behalf. There can be few people who combine such an attention to detail with an ability to see the big picture. I have benefited greatly from her sharp eyes and kindness.

I have learned much from my students at King's College London – particularly from those who, over more than thirty years, have taken my course on modern French history. My interest in Churchill and de Gaulle dates back to 1984, when I took Christopher Andrew's course on the political career of Charles de Gaulle. This is my belated answer to the some of the penetrating questions that Chris and my fellow students on that course posed.

My great debt is to Alison Henwood – for everything and especially for our children: Emma and Alexander.

INDEX

RICHARD VINEN

383

A NOTE ON THE AUTHOR

RICHARD VINEN is an author, historian and professor of history at Kings College London. Previously he was a Fellow at Trinity College, Cambridge and lecturer at Queen Mary College. He has written for the *TLS, London Review of Books, Independent, Boston Globe, Financial Times, New York Times* and *Nation* magazine. He has appeared on radio and television, on the subject of contemporary British politics.

A NOTE ON THE TYPE

The text of this book is set in Fournier. Fournier is derived from the *romain du roi*, which was created towards the end of the seventeenth century from designs made by a committee of the Académie of Sciences for the exclusive use of the Imprimerie Royale. The original Fournier types were cut by the famous Paris founder Pierre Simon Fournier in about 1742. These types were some of the most influential designs of the eight and are counted among the earliest examples of the 'transitional' style of typeface. This Monotype version dates from 1924. Fournier is a light, clear face whose distinctive features are capital letters that are quite tall and bold in relation to the lower-case letters, and *decorative italics, which show the influence of the calligraphy of Fournier's time.*